KU-533-590

₤20·00

British unemployment, 1919–1939

BRITISH UNEMPLOYMENT 1919–1939

A study in public policy

W. R. GARSIDE
University of Birmingham

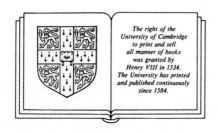

The right of the
University of Cambridge
to print and sell
all manner of books
was granted by
Henry VIII in 1534.
The University has printed
and published continuously
since 1584.

CAMBRIDGE UNIVERSITY PRESS
Cambridge
New York   Port Chester
Melbourne   Sydney

Published by the Press Syndicate of the University of Cambridge
The Pitt Building, Trumpington Street, Cambridge CB2 1RP
40 West 20th Street, New York, NY 10011 USA
10 Stamford Road, Oakleigh, Melbourne 3166, Australia

First published 1990

Printed in Great Britain at the University Press, Cambridge

British Library cataloguing in publication data

Garside, W. R. (William Redvers), 1944–
British unemployment, 1919–1939: a study in public policy.
1. Great Britain. Unemployment. Policies of
government, history
I. Title
331.13'7941

Library of Congress cataloguing in publication data

Garside, W. R.
British unemployment, 1919–1939: a study in public policy / W. R. Garside.
        p.   cm.
Bibliography.
Includes index.
ISBN 0-521-36443-4
1. Unemployment–Great Britain–History–20th century.   2. Great Britain–Full
employment policies–History–20th century.   3. Great Britain–Economic policy–
1918–1945.   4. Depressions – 1929 – Great Britain.   I. Title.
HD5765.A6G367   1990
331.13'7941 – dc20   89-33212 CIP

ISBN 0 521 36443 4

*For my wife Glen
and our children
David and Amy
who brighten
every day*

Contents

x   *Contents*

Tables

Preface

Many years ago I became convinced of the need for a comprehensive study of interwar unemployment which discussed within a single volume those relevant themes of public policy which were otherwise scattered amongst a wide variety of related studies. The dominant place which the subject held and still holds in the historiography of British economic and social change since 1919 has, of course, already spawned a considerable volume of literature on unemployment policy, strictly defined. In addition, detailed accounts of interwar industry, money and banking, fiscal policy, collective bargaining, trade and imperialism have provided constant reminders of the symbiotic links between their subject matter and unemployment, however incidental to their principal theme.

This wealth of material, however, poses its own difficulties. None of the general surveys of unemployment policy, apart from text books, covers the interwar period as a whole. Where the chronological treatment is reasonably satisfactory, the focus of attention tends to be on particular aspects of the problem, such as national insurance or the depressed areas. Moreover, to appreciate fully the substance and range of contemporary industrial, financial and academic opinion bearing upon interwar unemployment or its connection with macro- and microeconomic development in general, it is still necessary to refer to an increasingly large number of specialized monographs. Those which focus upon economic activity in general frequently detail the impact of policy upon unemployment, but only rarely on the extent to which persistent unemployment in itself influenced the nature and outcome of decision making in related areas of public policy.

This is not to deny the enormous debt we owe to particular authors in the field. Skidelsky's engrossing study of the second Labour administration and Gilbert's survey of interwar social policy, to mention but two influential works, have enriched our understanding of the origins and development of official concern over unemployment. Likewise, there has been an outpouring during the last decade or so of erudite studies on monetary and fiscal policy, the development of Keynes's thought and policy prescriptions, and on the role of the interwar Treasury and the Ministry of Labour which, together with a clutch of Ph.D. theses on government responses to the perceived failings of the labour market, have expanded the range and sophistication of debate surrounding the emergence and significance of mass unemployment after 1920. Interest in the nature and effectiveness of economic policy before 1939 has been sustained, moreover, by the availability of official records and by the supposed parallels between the slump of the 1930s and the British economic crisis of the early 1980s.

At the very least, this strengthens the need for a wide-ranging discussion of how governments reacted to one of the most politically troublesome issues of the interwar years. Any such undertaking requires not merely a detailed survey of ameliorative action, but an investigation of more broadly based economic strategies for economic recovery and development where they impinged on the formulation and impact of unemployment policy. It is necessary, in addition, to contrast official policy with the alternative economic advice pressed upon Ministers at the time, from within govern-ment and from outside critics. This book represents the results of such an endeavour.

I remain conscious of the dangers of attempting such a task and can only crave the indulgence of those historians and economists who have concentrated their research to such notable effect on themes which receive only passing treatment in this volume, or which retain a degree of complexity and significance in the continuing debate over Britain's interwar economic experience that are only palely reflected in my own compressed narrative. My search of the official record, moreover, has focussed largely upon the principal series of departmental papers held at the Public Record Office in London. Despite its bulk, this material goes only a short way towards revealing the real reasons for particular policy decisions. It cannot, therefore, be relied upon as a 'true' record, but it remains invaluable nonetheless as an indication of government thinking (or lack of it) during the search for a politically acceptable response to persistent unemployment between the wars. My decision to refer to as much near-primary and secondary material as the subject matter of the book and the deficiencies of the official record required was made in the knowledge that the final result would still be incomplete. Although I have attempted to strike a reasonable balance between official thinking and the rich variety of contemporary opinion and reaction, I have not drawn directly upon those collections of private papers, be they of individuals or organizations, which might usefully have supplemented the sources detailed in the text. Nor as I wrote did I have the opportunity of reading Peter Clarke's new study, *The Keynesian Revolution in the Making, 1924–1936*; that doubtless is my loss. If, however, the thematic coverage detailed here informs the reader of how and why governments responded in the way they did to the emergence of large-scale unemployment after 1920 and to its persistence and long duration in particular industries and regions in the 1930s, despite vociferous demands for policy to take a different course, then it will have served its purpose. If it prompts others to engage in further research to substantiate or modify the inferences I have drawn, that will be a welcome bonus.

I wish to acknowledge the generous financial assistance I received during the early stages of my research from the Social Science Research Council, the Nuffield Foundation, the Houblon-Norman Fund, the British Academy and the University of Birmingham. Professor Jim Ford and Professor Nicholas Deakin at Birmingham offered valuable advice and criticism on particular chapters, as did Professor Carol Heim (University of Massachusetts) and Professor Barry Eichengreen (University of California). None is responsible for any remaining errors of fact or interpretation.

Special thanks are due to Sue Kennedy for preparing the final typescript with consummate skill, enthusiasm and unfailing good humour. She was ably assisted by Diane Martin whose help I also gratefully acknowledge.

Academic research, it is said, has its own rewards. It also exacts a price in its relentless call on 'free' time. My family know this only too well, but they have remained a constant source of encouragement. I dedicate this book to them.

Acknowledgements

I wish to thank the editors of *The Economic History Review, Archiv für Sozialgeschichte, The Journal of European Economic History* and the *International Review of Social History* for allowing me to reproduce material I previously published in article form. Other copyright material appears by kind permission of A. Booth and S. Glynn, the Economic and Social Research Council, the Controller of Her Majesty's Stationery Office (Public Record Office papers) and the Social Science Research Council of New York.

PART I

Introduction

1 ✳ The nature, causes and dimensions of interwar unemployment

Ministry of Labour statistics relating to the working of the unemployment insurance scheme provide the basic source of information about the volume and nature of interwar unemployment. The number of unemployment books issued each July to those persons within the scheme enabled the Ministry from 1911 to calculate the total number of insured persons and to classify them by industry, region and sex. In order to claim benefit, insured persons had to lodge their unemployment books at an Employment Exchange; it was from the number of such books lodged combined with the numbers insured and unemployed that a monthly and yearly unemployment rate was derived. Until 1926, an alternative unemployment percentage was available from the monthly returns of a select group of trade unions which paid out-of-work benefit to their members.

Although the scope and validity of these two sources of unemployment data have been exhaustively discussed elsewhere,[1] a number of cautionary remarks are in order if we are to gain a proper perspective on the interwar period. The trade union returns, available in continuous form since 1888, cannot be regarded as an adequate indicator of unemployment amongst either the total working population, industrial manual workers or even all trade unionists. They related predominantly to skilled men; they were weighted, moreover, on the basis of trade union membership and not in proportion to the actual number of workers within the different industries covered. Nonetheless, though the returns cannot be relied upon as a general measure of unemployment at any particular date, contemporaries regarded them as a sufficiently accurate index of the variations of employment, a barometer of the state of the labour market.

Although the unemployment insurance scheme introduced in 1911 was expanded marginally in 1916 and more generally in 1920, covering by

---

[1] W. R. Garside, *The Measurement of Unemployment. Methods and Sources in Great Britain, 1850–1979* (Oxford, 1980).

Table 1. *Unemployment percentages derived from trade union and unemployment insurance statistics*

	Trade union	Unemployment insurance[a]
1913	2.1	3.6
1914	3.3	4.2
1915	1.1	1.2
1916	0.4	0.6
1917	0.7	0.7
1918	0.8	0.8
1919	2.4	na[b]
1920	2.4	3.9
1921	14.8	16.9
1922	15.2	14.3
1923	11.3	11.7
1924	8.1	10.3
1925	10.5	11.3
1926	12.2	12.5

[a] On a UK basis. Although our textual discussion relates to Great Britain only, UK figures are used to enable comparisons to be made with statistical material reproduced elsewhere in the chapter.
[b] No figures were available between December 1918 and October 1919 when the Out-of-Work Donation Scheme was in force. For details see chapter 2.
Sources: W. H. Beveridge, *Unemployment. A Problem of Industry* (1930), 424; Department of Employment, *British Labour Statistics. Historical Abstract 1886–1968* HMSO (1971), table 160.

then the majority of manual workers over the age of 16 and non-manual people earning less than £250 per year,[2] it was not sufficiently comprehensive to provide a totally reliable count of the volume or rate of unemployment. Excluded from the scheme were those occupied in agriculture, forestry, horticulture and private domestic service, along with teachers, nurses, the police, established civil servants, certain excepted classes employed by local authorities, and those in railways and the military service. Insurance statistics never embraced the total number of those 'gainfully occupied'; at the 1931 Census there were nearly 19.5 million people within the insurance age limits that were counted as gainfully occupied, of whom only 12.5 million were insured against unemployment.

Since wage earners were more susceptible to unemployment than salary earners or the self-employed, Ministry of Labour sources tended to overstate unemployment rates among the occupied population as a whole. Recogniz-

[2] Details of these changes are provided below in chapter 2.

Table 2. *Employment and unemployment, 1921–38*

	Employees at Work	Unemployment		Percentage unemployed	
		Insured persons aged 16–64	Total workers[a]	Insured unemployed as a proportion of insured employees	Total unemployed as a proportion of total employees
	('000s)	('000s)	('000s)	%	%
1921	15,879	1,840	2,212	17.0	12.2
1922	15,847	1,588	1,909	14.3	10.8
1923	16,068	1,304	1,567	11.7	8.9
1924	16,332	1,168	1,404	10.3	7.9
1925	16,531	1,297	1,559	11.3	8.6
1926	16,529	1,463	1,759	12.5	9.6
1927	17,060	1,142	1,373	9.7	7.4
1928	17,123	1,278	1,536	10.8	8.2
1929	17,392	1,250	1,503	10.4	8.0
1930	17,016	1,979	2,379	16.1	12.3
1931	16,554	2,705	3,252	21.3	16.4
1932	16,644	2,828	3,400	22.1	17.0
1933	17,018	2,567	3,087	19.9	15.4
1934	17,550	2,170	2,609	16.7	12.9
1935	17,890	2,027	2,437	15.5	12.0
1936	18,513	1,749	2,100	13.1	10.2
1937	19,196	1,482	1,776	10.8	8.5
1938	19,243	1,800	2,164	12.9	10.1

Note: [a] Insured persons plus those under 16 and over 64 and agricultural workers, private indoor domestic servants, and non-manual workers earning more than £250 per year.
Source: Adapted from C. H. Feinstein, *Statistical Tables of National Income, Expenditure and Output of the U.K. 1855–1965* (Cambridge, 1972), table 58.

ing this deficiency, Feinstein adjusted the UK insurance figures for the period 1921–38 on the strength of estimates derived from the 1931 Census of unemployment amongst groups of people otherwise excluded from the insurance scheme. Table 1 compares the measures of unemployment derived from the trade union and unemployment insurance returns during the period when they overlapped; table 2, following Feinstein, details the movement of the aggregate unemployment rate on an insured and on a working population basis.

These differing measures of interwar unemployment have tempted some writers to suggest that interwar unemployment was a far less serious problem than is customarily believed. Booth and Glynn, for example, argue thus:

Bearing in mind the impact of the peaks in cyclical unemployment in 1921–22 and 1931–33, the highly regionalised nature of unemployment before and particularly after 1914, the better recording and regularisation of work, one could suggest that the national unemployment rates for *most* of the period while very different in pattern, were not very much worse than the national average rates which prevailed before 1914 with, of course, the major exception of the years 1921–22 and 1931–33.[3] [Italics in original]

This conclusion was based largely on Feinstein's downward adjustment of the insurance data which reduces the average unemployment rate for the period 1921 to 1938 from 14.2 to 10.8 per cent. If we exclude the two 'exceptional' periods of 1921–22 and 1931–33, the percentages fall from 12.6 on the insurance figures to 9.6 on Feinstein's calculations.

It is by no means certain, however, that Feinstein's extrapolation of unemployment amongst uninsured groups in the 1931 Census produces an entirely reliable result. It was based on a year of severe cyclical unemployment and upon an assumption, difficult to verify, that the relative difference between unemployment rates for certain groups excluded from the insurance scheme remained stable over a number of years. Feinstein's figures may underestimate the average level of unemployment because changes in regulations regarding the receipt of unemployment benefit in 1931 rendered the proportion of the insured unemployed relative to the uninsured to an abnormally high level for a brief period during the Census.

Nor is it entirely valid to compare post-war unemployment returns with pre-war trade union data. As we have noted already, the latter source is generally regarded as a fair barometer of variations in employment over time, but not as an absolute measure of total unemployment in a particular year. During the period 1913 to 1926 when the trade union and unemployment insurance returns overlapped, there were times when the trade union percentage was higher and times when it was lower than the insurance percentage. The differences were most noticeable during the 1920s, perhaps because of the influence of the insurance scheme upon the benefit paying procedures of the trade unions.[4] When the trade union percentages are adjusted according to the number of workers employed in the covered trades instead of in proportion to the actual membership of the

---

[3] A. Booth and S. Glynn, 'Unemployment in the Interwar Period: A Multiple Problem', *Journal of Contemporary History*, 10 (1975), 614.
[4] For further discussion see Garside, *Measurement of Unemployment*, chapter 1.

representative unions, the disparity between the two series is significantly reduced.[5]

This fact, claim Benjamin and Kochin, encouraged Beveridge in a second edition of *Unemployment. A Problem of Industry* (1930, pp. 328–37), to recant the scepticism he had earlier expressed in 1909 over the precision of pre-1914 unemployment data and their usefulness for determining the comparative volume of interwar unemployment. 'Thus', they write, 'the primary sources agree that the pre-war and interwar unemployment series are comparable.'[6] Unfortunately the authors quote the correct pages of the wrong book and arrive at precisely the opposite conclusion to that of Beveridge himself. The equivalent pages of *Full Employment in a Free Society* (1944) detail Beveridge's misgivings over the intrinsic comparability of the two unemployment series. The bases of the trade union and unemployment insurance returns were different from one another and changed over time. Strict comparisons of the two would have to take into account the changing industrial base of the trade union data, the extent to which they generally excluded unorganized workers, the degree of underemployment resulting from short-time working, the altogether more complete statistical coverage of the postwar series, and the complex interplay of legislative and administrative factors which influenced the internal consistency of the interwar returns. Beveridge's own re-evaluation of the statistics, taking on board such considerations, led him to conclude that 'between the wars unemployment was between two and three times as severe as before the First World War'.[7]

THE PATTERN AND INCIDENCE OF INTERWAR UNEMPLOYMENT

Even if all the necessary data were available, which they are not, it is highly unlikely that any reconstructed pre-war and post-war unemployment series would belie the fact that the rate of unemployment between the wars was substantially greater than before 1914. Although we must concede that official statistics of interwar unemployment were neither complete nor unambiguous, it remains true that economic conditions were serious enough to dominate the adjustments which contemporaries and others since have made to account for changes in coverage and eligibility. As such the data reveal a volume of unemployment that never fell below one million and which peaked in 1932 at around three million.

---

[5] J. Hilton, 'Statistics of Unemployment Derived from the Working of the Unemployment Insurance Acts', *Journal of the Royal Statistical Society*, 86 (1923), 154–93.
[6] D. K. Benjamin and L. A. Kochin, 'Unemployment and Unemployment Benefits in Twentieth-Century Britain: A Reply to Our Critics', *Journal of Political Economy*, 90 (1982), 423. [7] W. H. Beveridge, *Full Employment in a Free Society* (1944), 328–37.

Table 3. *Annual percentage change in selected indicators, 1918–21*

	Industrial production	Consumers' expenditure	Wholesale prices
1918–19	+ 10.2	+ 20.9	+ 10.6
1919–20	+ 11.1	− 0.8	+ 24.4
1920–21	− 18.6	− 5.4	− 35.8

Source: Adapted from D. H. Aldcroft, *The Inter-War Economy: Britain 1919–1939* (1970), 32.

At the end of the First World War the combination of pent-up consumer demand, high money incomes, a large volume of liquid or near-liquid assets and a backlog of investment fuelled a boom in economic activity which lasted roughly one year, from March 1919 to April 1920. Though real enough, the boom was highly inflationary and essentially unstable, marked by intense speculative buying in commodities and securities and extensions of bank credit for industrial and other purposes. By the beginning of 1920 consumers' expenditure began to fall in the face of higher prices; many firms were already heavily in debt whilst the banks, saddled with large credit commitments to industry, were steadily becoming illiquid. With business confidence on the wane, the boom was destined to collapse. The turning point came in spring 1920. Production reacted swiftly to the squeeze in consumption and the decline in exports which occurred in the latter half of the year. A sudden rise in Bank Rate to 7 per cent in April 1920, coupled with systematic cuts in public expenditure, aggravated the downturn and by the middle of 1921 Britain was in the midst of one of the worst depressions in its recent history.[8] The sudden reversal of economic conditions is detailed in table 3.

It was the slump of 1920–21 which inaugurated mass unemployment. Paucity of data makes it difficult to be very precise about the extent of the deterioration in employment conditions, but at no time during the demobilization period down to April 1920 did unemployment emerge on anything like the scale that was about to develop. Provision had to be made for the emergency payments of Out-of-Work Donation to those civilians and ex-servicemen unable for a variety of reasons to make a legitimate claim to insurance benefit whilst looking for work. Fluctuations in the numbers receiving such payments did not accurately reflect fluctuations in unemployment, however, partly because of exhaustions of the right to benefit and

[8] D. H. Aldcroft, *The Inter-War Economy: Britain 1919–1939* (1970), 31–7.

partly because of claims by married women who did not intend to resume paid work in industry. According to trade union returns, employment improved from the time Out-of-Work Donation ceased for civilian workers in October 1919 down to April 1920 (and to June 1920 on insurance statistics) but declined thereafter for at least a year, the decline gathering momentum.

The pattern of interwar unemployment indicated in table 2 above is well known. Chronic disequilibrium in the labour market during late 1920 and early 1921 was further intensified by the 1921 coal dispute. Although a gradual improvement in registered unemployment occurred during 1922, the unemployment rate by the end of the year was significantly greater than any pre-war standard and in excess of what could reasonably be accounted for merely by deficiencies in the statistical count. An historically high rate of unemployment continued throughout the rest of the decade, giving way to substantially worse conditions in the early thirties as a result of the international recession of 1929–32. The slump was followed by a period of steady recovery for the remainder of the decade, interrupted by a downturn in 1937–38 only to be accelerated under the impact of rearmament expenditure.

Revealing though these general trends are, they disguise the extent to which cyclical fluctuations were imposed upon structural rigidities within the economy and as such provide little indication of the decline in economic fortunes at sub-aggregate level. Since subsequent chapters assess the impact of unemployment within particular industries, regions and demographic groups it is only necessary at this stage to provide an overview of the principal issues so far as the incidence of unemployment is concerned. Marked disparities occurred between the wars in the industrial and regional dispersions of unemployment, the largest concentrations occurring in the basic staple export trades and within the areas in which such industries predominated. Beyond that, the incidence of unemployment varied across subpopulations both in terms of which people were most at risk of becoming unemployed and for how long they would remain so. The spatial distribution of interwar unemployment can be gauged from table 4.

What emerges clearly from table 4 is that from the early twenties London, the south east, the south west and the midlands experienced unemployment rates below the national average, whilst the remaining regions, situated in what contemporaries came to describe as 'Outer Britain', bore the heaviest burden of registered unemployment, and to considerably more than a marginal degree. In southern Britain (London, the south east and the south west) the percentage of insured unemployment stood at 6.4 in 1929 before the depression, rose to 14.9 in 1932, and fell to 7.9 in 1936. In the north east, north west and Wales, the aggregate

Table 4. *Insured unemployment rate by administrative division, 1923–38*

	London	South east	South west	Midlands	North east	North west	Scotland	Wales
1923	10.1	9.2	10.6	10.7	12.2	14.5	14.3	6.4
1924	9.0	7.5	9.1	9.0	10.9	12.9	12.4	8.6
1925	7.8	5.9	8.5	9.1	15.0	11.4	15.2	16.5
1926	6.9	5.4	8.4	11.0	17.2	14.7	16.4	18.0
1927	5.8	5.0	7.2	8.4	13.7	10.7	10.6	19.5
1928	5.6	5.4	8.1	9.9	15.1	12.4	11.7	23.0
1929	5.6	5.6	8.1	9.3	13.7	13.3	12.1	19.3
1930	8.1	8.0	10.4	14.7	20.2	23.8	18.5	25.9
1931	12.2	12.0	14.5	20.3	27.4	28.2	26.6	32.4
1932	13.5	14.3	17.1	20.1	28.5	25.8	27.7	36.5
1933	11.8	11.5	15.7	17.4	26.0	23.5	26.1	34.6
1934[a]	9.2	8.7	13.1	12.9	22.1	20.8	23.1	32.3
1935[a]	8.5	8.1	11.6	11.2	20.7	19.7	21.3	31.2
1936[a]	7.2	7.3	9.4	9.2	16.8	17.1	18.7	29.4
1937[a]	6.4	6.7	7.8	7.3	11.1	14.0(17.9)[b]	16.0	23.3
1938[a]	8.0	8.0	8.2	10.3	13.6	17.9(18.4)[b]	16.4	24.8

[a]The figures exclude juveniles under the age of 16 and persons insured under the Agricultural Scheme, who first became insurable in September 1934 and May 1936 respectively.
[b]Figures for the new Northern Division created on 1 August 1936. This consisted of Northumberland (except Berwick district), Durham and the Cleveland district of Yorkshire (previously part of the North-Eastern Division) and Cumberland and Westmorland (previously parts of the North-Western Division). Details of the areas contained in all Administrative Divisions can be found in Department of Employment, *British Labour Statistics. Historical Abstract*, HMSO (1971), Appendix E.
Source: Ministry of Labour Gazette.

rate started at 15.4 per cent in 1929, rose to 30.2 per cent in 1932 but had fallen to only 21.1 per cent by 1936. This widening gap between high unemployment in the north and relatively low unemployment in the south was the result of a complex combination of factors, amongst which were the risks and costs of long-distance migration from the depressed areas in search of work and, more importantly, secular decline in the staple export trades in the face of surplus capacity and intense foreign competition. Regional unemployment disparities were conventionally regarded simply as a reflection of the concentration of declining industries in the north, but this does not entirely account for the observed differences since spatial differentials remain even after the variable mix of industries is controlled for.[9] Industries which were otherwise generally prosperous, for example, tended to suffer heavier unemployment if they were located in regions already containing declining staple trades; such regions, moreover, suffered stagnation in their whole economies via a downward regional multiplier process.

Within the industrial sector, those basic trades upon which much of Britain's nineteenth-century progress had depended, namely coal, cotton, wool textiles, shipbuilding and iron and steel, suffered both a substantial loss of labour and unemployment rates above the general average, despite rising output and productivity. These five industries (together with mechanical engineering) accounted for around one-half of total insured unemployment in June 1929. By 1932 almost half the workers in iron and steel were registered as unemployed, as were nearly two-thirds in shipbuilding and a third in coalmining.

Some industries experienced relatively high levels of unemployment whilst still growing, their expansion creating extra employment but not at a rate fast enough to engage the high proportion of additional workers attracted to them (building is an example), whilst others saw output, employment or both decline but not at a rate which rendered them amongst the more depressed sectors of the economy (e.g. clothing, leather, precision instruments, pottery, tinplate manufacture and minor textile trades such as jute, linen and hemp). It was secular decline in the industries suffering both a collapse in markets and a stagnating or slow growing home demand that gave rise to so much contemporary concern, not least because of their marked geographical concentration. Although considerable doubts remain about the role of 'new' industries in the overall performance of the interwar economy, their lower dependence on the volatile world market and their exploitation of new techniques and methods of production produced an

[9] T. J. Hatton, 'Structural Aspects of Unemployment in Britain Between the Wars', in *Research in Economic History*, Vol. 10, ed. P. Uselding (Connecticut, 1986), 55–92.

expansion of output and a lower rate of unemployment that served only to emphasise the scale of decline in the less favoured sectors, as table 5 illustrates.

Recorded unemployment rates tell us something about the composition of interwar unemployment, though space does not permit a detailed analysis of the disaggregated data.[10] The incidence of unemployment throughout the interwar period was generally higher for men than for women and for older workers and youths between the ages of 21 and 25. Insurance statistics show that the male unemployment rate was typically 50 per cent higher than that for women and was particularly acute amongst male unskilled manual workers. The fact that the more comprehensive Census returns display a similar relationship between the unemployment rate for the two sexes indicates that the differential went beyond mere underreporting of unemployment amongst women.[11] Women generally had a lower rate of labour participation (retirement on marriage obviously playing a part) and when they worked they tended to be occupied in industries with traditionally low unemployment rates (cotton being a notable exception). After job separation women were more likely to leave the unemployment register than continue to search for work. Amongst adult males, those between the ages of 30 and 39 appeared to suffer the lowest risk of unemployment throughout the 1920s and 1930s, whilst the old remained especially vulnerable. Unemployment rates rose with age, not because older men faced a greater risk of losing their job so much as the fact that they found it more difficult to obtain fresh employment once out of work.[12] This higher risk of prolonged unemployment with age was common across all regions, though more intensified in the depressed areas.

Juvenile workers under the age of 18, and especially under the age of 16, suffered more temporary, short-period unemployment. The full extent of juvenile unemployment was difficult to discern before 1934 because of systematic undernumeration, but its national rate was low compared to that of adults. Nonetheless declining apprenticeship, the continued existence of 'blind alley' occupations offering little in the way of training or security, the preference of employers for cheap labour, and a periodic over-supply of juvenile labour reduced the chances of many youngsters ever obtaining regular or worthwhile employment. Direct comparisons of juvenile and adult unemployment rates, moreover, reveal only part of the

---

[10] For a contemporary survey of the data see W. H. Beveridge, 'An Analysis of Unemployment', *Economica*, 3 (1936), 357–86; 'An Analysis of Unemployment II', *Economica*, 4 (1937), 1–17; 'An Analysis of Unemployment III', *Economica*, 4 (1937), 168–83.

[11] B. Eichengreen and T. J. Hatton, 'Interwar Unemployment in International Perspective: An Overview', in *Interwar Unemployment in International Perspective*, ed. B. Eichengreen and T. J. Hatton (Dordrecht, 1988), 31.

[12] Beveridge, 'An Analysis of Unemployment II', 13–15.

Table 5. *Percentage of insured workers unemployed, selected industries 1923–38*[a]

	1923[b]	1924	1925	1926	1927	1928	1929	1930	1931	1932	1933	1934	1935	1936	1937	1938
Old staples																
Coalmining	3.0	5.8	11.5	9.5	19.0	23.6	19.0	20.6	28.4	34.5	33.5	29.7	27.2	22.8	16.1	16.7
Shipbuilding	43.6	30.3	33.5	39.5	29.7	24.5	25.3	27.6	51.9	62.0	61.7	51.2	44.4	33.3	24.4	21.4
Cotton	21.6	15.9	8.8	18.3	15.4	12.5	12.9	32.4	43.2	30.6	25.1	23.7	22.3	16.7	10.9	23.9
Wool textiles	9.5	8.4	16.9	17.4	11.0	12.0	15.5	23.3	33.8	22.4	17.0	17.8	15.5	10.3	8.8	21.3
Iron and steel	21.2	22.0	25.0	40.4	19.4	22.4	20.1	28.2	45.5	47.9	41.5	27.3	23.5	17.4	11.4	19.5
'New' industries																
Chemicals	11.8	9.9	9.1	10.9	7.2	6.1	6.5	10.0	17.6	17.3	15.2	11.3	11.0	9.2	6.8	7.4
Cars and aircraft	9.7	8.9	7.1	8.2	8.1	8.1	7.1	12.1	19.3	22.4	17.6	10.8	9.0	6.9	5.0	7.2
Gas, water and electricity	7.2	6.3	6.2	6.0	5.4	5.8	6.1	7.0	8.9	10.9	11.0	10.1	10.4	9.7	8.3	8.3
Electrical engineering	7.3	5.5	5.6	7.5	5.9	4.8	4.6	6.6	14.1	16.8	16.5	9.6	7.0	4.8	3.1	4.7

[a] Averages of the percentages in January and July each year, excluding workers under 16 and persons insured under the Agricultural Scheme who became insured in September 1934 and May 1936 respectively. All figures on a UK basis.
[b] Figures are for July only.
Source: Adapted from Department of Employment, *British Labour Statistics. Historical Abstract*, HMSO (1971), table 164.

story since there were substantial regional disparities in the number of younger people out of work. Nor is it too fanciful to suggest that the sequence of unskilled, short-duration positions experienced by many young workers during an impressionable stage in their life may have weakened their capacity to secure and retain employment during early adulthood.[13]

Unemployment was clearly related to a variety of factors including labour market conditions, individual characteristics, demographic changes and household status. There has been little multivariate analysis of the correlates of unemployment between the wars. Eichengreen's study of household data in London is a notable exception;[14] its results, albeit derived from an unrepresentative area, confirm the impression gained from the wider range of official statistics and sample survey data presently available,[15] namely that unemployment fell typically upon adult males 'with low wages and few sources of income beyond their own wages and unemployment benefits, who rented their homes and who had large families'.[16]

THE DYNAMICS OF THE LABOUR MARKET: TURNOVER AND UNEMPLOYMENT DURATION

It would be extremely misleading to characterize interwar unemployment as a stagnant pool of jobless individuals simply awaiting an improvement in macroeconomic conditions.[17] To do so would be to presume that over time there was a constant flow into unemployment of a group of people whose individual characteristics played little or no part in influencing their chances of leaving the unemployment register for work or retirement. But the official count of the unemployed was in essence a 'snapshot'; an annual unemployment rate of 10 per cent was compatible with a condition in which all workers were out of work for 10 per cent of the year, or where 10 per cent of the labour force was out of work for the entire year, or anything between these extremes. Such data tell us little about the *process* (as distinct from the state) of unemployment. The registered unemployed were not an homogeneous group. Neither the risks of becoming unemployed nor the chances of leaving the unemployment register were shared equally by

---

[13] These issues are taken up in greater detail in chapter 4.

[14] B. Eichengreen, 'Unemployment in Interwar Britain: New Evidence from London', *Journal of Interdisciplinary History*, 17 (1986), 335–58.

[15] For commentary upon interwar sample surveys of the unemployed see Garside, *Measurement of Unemployment*, chapter 4.

[16] Eichengreen and Hatton, 'Interwar Unemployment', 35. For contemporary analyses see E. Bakke, *The Unemployed Man* (New Haven, 1933) and Pilgrim Trust, *Men Without Work* (Cambridge, 1938).

[17] This section draws upon M. Thomas, 'Labour Market Structure and the Nature of Unemployment in Interwar Britain', in *Interwar Unemployment in International Perspective*, ed. Eichengreen and Hatton, 97–148.

everyone. Fluctuations in the total number of persons out of work between the wars reflected the net effect of a large number of separate changes as different people in different industries in different parts of the country flowed on to and off the unemployment register at varying rates. In addition, the extent of labour force participation by different demographic groups altered over the course of the trade cycle. Much more information than merely a count of the stock of the unemployed is required, in other words, to determine the character of unemployment.

Ministry of Labour data on the duration of unemployment (available only from 1930), together with statistics of the number of wholly unemployed workers placed in vacancies notified to the Employment Exchanges, show that the burden of rising unemployment was not shared equally by all in the labour force but was distributed in the form of longer periods of unemployment for those individuals most at risk. The number of vacancies notified and filled in the 1920s and 1930s grew at a more or less constant rate. In the twenties, Hatton suggests, turnover is best explained as a queuing process. 'Workers were simply queuing at the exchanges and a rise in the unemployment rate merely lengthened the queue – it did not cause vacancies to be taken up any more quickly.'[18] Thereafter it appears that adverse changes in macroeconomic conditions fell on the rate of outflow rather than inflow, producing a bifurcated labour market in which there was at once rapid turnover and a rise in the proportion of the long-term unemployed.

As depression deepened after 1929 there was a marked increase in the duration of registered unemployment. As Thomas puts it:

Some two-thirds of labour market adjustment during the first year of the slump fell on to increased job loss. In 1930–31, however, the burden was picked up by the unemployed experiencing longer spells. By 1933, the average length of the year spent out of work was over 50 per cent higher than in 1929. As the economy began to recover, it is noticeable that the decline in days out of work was slower than the rate of recovery as a whole. By 1936, indeed, the proportion of workers experiencing unemployment had fallen below the 1929 level, while the average number of days out of work had risen by over 30 per cent.[19]

It was the extent of long-term unemployment that proved the key characteristic of unemployment in the 1930s. Whereas in September 1929 78.5 per cent of applicants for unemployment relief had been out of work for less than three months and only 4.7 per cent for more than a year, by 1936 only 55 per cent had been unemployed for less than three months and a quarter for more than a year.

[18] T. J. Hatton, 'The British Labor Market in the 1920s: A Test of the Search–Turnover Approach', *Explorations in Economic History*, 22 (1985), 257–70.
[19] Thomas, 'Labour Market Structure' 107.

Table 6. *Duration of male unemployment, 1929–38*

	(1) Percentage of applicants unemployed 12 months or more	(2) As (1) but omitting casual and temporarily stopped	(3) Average interrupted spell of unemployment of applicants[a] (weeks)	(4) As (2) but omitting casual and temporarily stopped
Sept. 1929	10.7	na	22.3	na
Mar. 1932	12.7	16.1	na	na
Sept. 1932	18.6	28.2	33.2	47.0
Mar. 1933	22.0	31.1	37.0	49.7
Sept. 1933	25.6	35.2	39.0	51.1
Mar. 1934	25.5	33.9	39.6	50.5
Sept. 1934	24.9	32.0	38.5	47.6
Mar. 1935	23.9	30.1	41.4	50.5
Sept. 1935	25.9	32.9	40.4	49.7
Mar. 1936	26.1	32.4	42.8	51.6
Sept. 1936	27.0	33.9	40.2	48.8
Mar. 1937	24.2	29.3	37.8	44.4
Sept. 1937[b]	27.1	34.0	41.6	50.5
Mar. 1938	21.3	27.1	37.9	46.4
Sept. 1938	20.4	27.8	36.4	47.7
Mar. 1939	21.1	25.8	38.7	45.8

[a] That is, how long on average the unemployed had been out of work at the moment of observation.
[b] Changes in the method of counting the unemployed were slightly improved from April 1937; earlier figures somewhat underestimate the degree of long-term unemployment. See Garside, *The Measurement of Unemployment*, chapter 6.
Source: Adapted from N. F. R. Crafts, 'Long-term unemployment in Britain in the 1930s', *Economic History Review*, 2nd ser., 40 (1987), 420.

Any comparison of duration statistics before and after the world slump, however, should acknowledge the fact that many of the long-term unemployed who were not strictly counted as claimants in 1929 were counted as such after 1931 because of changes in the regulations governing the receipt of unemployment assistance.[20] Even when the figures are corrected for this fact, as they are above in table 6, it is clear that there was a significant rise in the 1930s both in the percentage of long-term unemployment and in length of time spent out of work. Equally obvious, as table 7 shows, is the fact that rising long-term unemployment affected

[20] The details of this change are outlined below in chapter 3.

Table 7. *Changes in duration of unemployment, June 1932 to February 1938*

	Percentage applicants unemployed 12 months or more		Average interrupted unemployment spell (weeks)	
	June 1932	Feb. 1938	June 1932	Feb. 1938
London	4.4	5.8	16.2	15.5
South east	3.8	6.6	15.3	17.0
South west	8.8	8.6	19.7	20.0
Midlands	14.6	15.9	25.4	30.3
Northern/north west/north east	19.6	25.0	31.0	49.3
Scotland	27.6	29.7	46.8	56.1
Wales	21.1	30.7	33.8	61.8

Source: Crafts, 'Long-term unemployment in Britain', 422. The figures include temporarily stopped and casual workers.

'Outer Britain' – Scotland, Wales and northern divisions – far more severely than it did London and the south, reflecting the impact of structural decline in the basic staple trades.

An additional worrying feature of the 1930s was that the probability of regaining employment fell sharply with increased duration. We have already referred to the particular difficulties which older workers faced once they became unemployed. The phenomenon of duration dependence – the process whereby workers suffering long spells of unemployment grew increasingly detached from the labour market by virtue of declining skill and motivation – is difficult to distinguish from the tendency of more employable individuals to snap up the few job opportunities available.[21] Nonetheless examination of duration statistics for the thirties reveals a substantially greater percentage of those unemployed from nine to twelve months who were still unemployed after a year than was the case amongst the unemployed experiencing shorter durations.

Contemporary investigators frequently stressed that psychological impairment and physical deterioration among the long-term unemployed rendered their condition almost self-sustaining, not least because employers

[21] Official enquiries into interwar unemployment rarely considered this issue. It was not until the 1960s that the problem was investigated in any rigorous fashion and then primarily in relation to contemporary labour market problems. See Garside, *The Measurement of Unemployment*, chapter 6. For a useful contemporary study see H. W. Singer, 'Regional Labour Markets and the Process of Unemployment', *Review of Economic Statistics*, 7 (1939), 42–58.

frequently discriminated against workers who had already been jobless for some time.[22] But the mere fact that unemployment continuation rates rose during the 1930s as the period of unemployment rose does not in itself explain why long-term unemployment had become a more dominant feature of the decade compared with the 1920s. Sample surveys of the Ministry of Labour show no dramatic change in the personal attributes of the unemployed; it seems, rather, that though duration dependency did occur, lowering some individuals' chances of getting back into employment and perhaps their incentive or ability to seek work elsewhere,[23] workers simply faced an overall shortage of jobs. Where duration dependency occurred in the depressed areas, 'its primary effect was to force people down the unemployment queue, a queue that was extremely long to begin with'.[24]

None of this explains why employment opportunities remained restricted for so long. Although there is general agreement about the origins and timing of the shift from boom to slump in 1919–20, debate still rages over the causes of persistently high unemployment during the remainder of the interwar period. It is to the substance of that debate that we now turn, if only because of its implications for the permissible range and likely effectiveness of government ameliorative policy.

DEBATING THE CAUSES OF INTERWAR UNEMPLOYMENT

Structural adjustment

The features of unemployment which we have discussed so far encouraged contemporaries in the interwar period to distinguish different types of labour market maladjustment: short-period unemployment due to the turnover of labour between jobs and to seasonal factors, long-period unemployment occasioned by structural change in industry, unemployment arising from personal infirmities or characteristics, and cyclical unemployment in trade depressions. Though this typology was gradually modified by Keynes's emphasis on demand-deficient unemployment, numerous economists have since argued that the greater part of persistent interwar unemployment can best be explained in terms of structural factors.

Edwardian growth and the effects of the First World War, the argument runs, delayed structural adjustment away from the traditional nineteenth-

---

[22] Unemployment Assistance Board, *Annual Reports*, 1936–39; Pilgrim Trust, *Men Out of Work*.

[23] N. F. R. Crafts, 'Long-Term Unemployment in Britain', *Economic History Review*, 2nd ser., 40 (1987), 418–32.   [24] Thomas, 'Labour market structure', 134–5.

century staple industries, leaving Britain 'overcommitted' to resources singularly inappropriate to the emerging pattern of demand and international competition. When this narrow industrial base stagnated in the face of interwar secular decline, labour was shed from declining sectors, particularly in staple export industries and within the northern regions in which they were predominantly located. Unemployment emerged on a significant scale, and was essentially regional in nature, because this labour, otherwise surplus to productive needs, could not easily be absorbed in the 'new' capital-intensive industries situated in the south and the south-east. Though this industrial rejuvenation benefited the economy as a whole, raising economic growth and productivity to levels higher than those obtained in Britain's recent past, it bore heavily upon those industries and workers whose geographic and skill specificity rendered them the unfortunate victims of a long delayed but necessary process of structural readjustment.[25]

The difficulty with this argument is that the extent of structural change in manufacturing production between the wars compared with the period 1900–13 and the post-1945 years appears to be less substantial than previously thought. Moreover, the 'new' industries do not seem to be as distinctly identifiable or as characteristically expansive and less labour intensive than we have been led to believe. In short, existing evidence does not point to structural change as being the key to explaining high and persistent interwar unemployment.[26]

The role of demand

To Keynesian sympathizers, the reduction in employment in the basic staple industries, occasioned by a severe decline of exports both in total and as a proportion of Gross National Product, transmitted a considerable reduction in aggregate demand which proved to be the more determinant influence

[25] H. W. Richardson, 'New Industries Between the Wars', *Oxford Economic Papers*, 13 (1961), 360–84; H. W. Richardson, 'Over-Commitment in Britain Before 1930', *Oxford Economic Papers*, 17 (1965), 237–62; D. H. Aldcroft, 'Economic Progress in Britain in the 1920s', *Scottish Journal of Political Economy*, 13 (1966), 297–316; D. H. Aldcroft, 'Economic Growth in the Inter-War Years: A Reassessment', *Economic History Review*, 2nd ser., 20 (1967), 311–26.
[26] J. R. Dowie, 'Growth in the Inter-War Period: Some More Arithmetic', *Economic History Review*, 2nd ser., 21 (1968), 93–112; N. K. Buxton, 'The Role of the New Industries in Britain during the 1930s: A Reinterpretation', *Business History Review*, 49 (1975), 205–22; G. N. Von Tunzelmann, 'Structural Change and Leading Sectors in British Manufacturing 1907–68', in *Economics in the Long View*, Vol. 3, ed. C. R. Kindleberger and G. di Tella (1982), 1–49; S. Broadberry, 'Unemployment in Interwar Britain: A Disequilibrium Approach', *Oxford Economic Papers*, 35 (1983), 463–85; N. F. R. Crafts, *British Economic Growth during the Industrial Revolution* (Oxford, 1985), 174–7.

on variations in unemployment. Structural decline may have reflected the failure of the economy to adjust, but the essential problem was:

The contraction of declining industries with nothing to replace them. Any relative price changes, signalling a transfer of resources from old to new industries were . . . swamped by quantitative signals in the form of reduced aggregate demand. The economy became locked in a position of chronic under-employment, with the depressed state of aggregate demand acting as a disincentive to invest in any industry, new or old.[27]

From this perspective, the connection between the incidence of unemployment and the manner in which changes in aggregate demand for labour were distributed across industries and locations, casts doubt upon the structuralists' view that unemployment was the price of an adjustment process. Continued long-term unemployment in depressed regions at business cycle peaks in the thirties points to the existence of severe obstacles in the way of the reabsorption of displaced labour beyond the constraints of skill and location specificity.

The fact that unemployment in the more depressed areas tended to fall only when demand and employment rose in the more prosperous areas (either because of cyclical upturn or because of a major exogenous boost such as rearmament expenditure) suggests further that structural unemployment was as much a consequence of the overall level of unemployment as a cause. Unemployed workers would have been willing to work if they could have found a vacancy; by the same token the involuntarily unemployed could not hope to improve their position alone, by agreeing to work for a lower wage for example, when the number of men wanting to work exceeded the number for whom there was an effective demand.[28] In the interwar period, writes Matthews, 'the long-run tendency towards increasingly full absorption of the labour force and increasing scarcity of labour relative to capital as development advances was entirely overborne and concealed . . . by Keynesian demand deficiency on a large scale'.[29]

Labour market rigidities and voluntary unemployment

Although observers after Keynes have traditionally attributed high interwar unemployment to fluctuations in aggregate demand, contemporary economists in the classical tradition put greater stress upon supply factors

[27] Broadberry, 'Unemployment in Interwar Britain', 469.
[28] Crafts, *British Economic Growth*, 167–72; T. J. Hatton, 'The Analysis of Unemployment in Interwar Britain: A Survey of Research', Centre for Economic Policy Research, Discussion Paper No. 66, June 1985.
[29] R. C. O. Matthews, 'Why has Britain had Full Employment since the War?', *Economic Journal*, 78 (1968), 566. Cf. R. C. O. Matthews, C. H. Feinstein and J. C. Odling-Smee, *British Economic Growth, 1856–1973* (Oxford, 1982), 85.

and labour market rigidities. They argued that inflexibility of money wages in a downward direction in the face of falling prices distorted the otherwise fluid market mechanism, preventing employers during the 1920s from recruiting labour in anything like the volume required to ensure full or near-full employment. When the wage determination process altered during the 1930s, on the other hand, the previous expansion in real wages was moderated to an extent that permitted the profitable employment of less productive workers and hence a fall in the rate of growth of unemployment.

Despite evidence of a divergent movement between real wages and productivity during the period 1919–20, consequent upon a reduction in working hours sufficient to have raised the equilibrium rate of unemployment,[30] there is still considerable doubt over how much of the volume of interwar unemployment can be ascribed to real wage movements. Neo-classical economists argue nonetheless that, amongst other things, the existence and increasing availability of unemployment benefit payments enabled the unemployed to avoid low-waged work, the effect of which was to prevent wages falling to a level which would 'clear' the labour market.[31]

This argument bears closely upon Benjamin and Kochin's now celebrated view that the interwar insurance scheme reduced the opportunity cost of idleness, inducing workers either to opt for leisure instead of work or, at the very least, to extend the search for a job, thereby increasing the duration of their unemployment. 'The persistently high rate of unemployment in interwar Britain', they write, 'was due in large part not to deficient aggregate demand but to high unemployment insurance benefits relative to wages.' Moreover, 'while the members of the army of the unemployed were chiefly conscripts in the two major depressions of the era, they seem to have been willing volunteers during the late 20s and late 30s'. The insurance system, they further maintain, raised the average unemployment rate by almost five to eight percentage points.[32]

These somewhat startling conclusions rest on two principal foundations: first the performance of a time series regression of unemployment on a benefit-to-wages ratio (the chosen replacement ratio being that of the weekly benefit paid to an adult male with one adult dependant and two dependent children divided by the average weekly earnings of full-time

[30] S. Broadberry, *The British Economy Between the Wars. A Macroeconomic Survey* (Oxford, 1986), chapter 8.
[31] The notion that state unemployment benefits helped to protect union rates of pay has been discounted by Noelle Whiteside, 'Social Welfare and Industrial Relations, 1914–1939', in *A History of British Industrial Relations*, Vol. II: *1914–1939*, ed. C. Wrigley (1987), 211–42.
[32] D. K. Benjamin and L. A. Kochin, 'Searching for an Explanation of Unemployment in Interwar Britain', *Journal of Political Economy*, 87 (1979), 452–68, 474.

employees),[33] and second the observed level of unemployment amongst juveniles and women. Juvenile unemployment rates between the wars were only a fraction of those of the adult labour force, the result, it is claimed, of the low or non-constant levels of benefit available to younger workers.[34] Recorded unemployment among women, on the other hand, fell sharply after 1931 when regulations governing their claim to benefit were tightened, demonstrating that unemployment levels had previously been biased upwards by claimants not genuinely seeking work.

Benjamin and Kochin's assertions have brought forth a barrage of criticism and refutation. In particular, the robustness of their statistical model has been severely criticized on grounds of the unrepresentativeness of the replacement ratio, the distortion brought about by undue aggregation, especially the neglect of varying unemployment rates across industry, and the inappropriateness of the chosen sample period. Beyond this there is clear evidence that many individuals did not receive the maximum benefits on offer, for a wide variety of reasons. The substance of these counter-arguments has been extensively discussed elsewhere and need not concern us here.[35]

Details of the complex and variable benefits regime upon which the cross-sectional evidence relating to women and juveniles is based are provided below in chapters 2 and 3. Nonetheless we can raise considerable doubts even at this stage about how far the observed levels of unemployment for each group reflect any significant tendency amongst them to remain voluntarily out of work. The view that unemployment amongst younger workers was lower than amongst adults because the former were insulated from the strictures of the insurance regulations ignores fundamental features of the juvenile labour market which work on the side of demand

---

[33] The single equation model of the determinants of unemployment was expressed as:

$$U = {}_0 + {}_1\, B/W + {}_2\, (\log Q - \log Q^*)$$

where U is the percentage of the insured population unemployed, B/W the benefit to wage ratio, Q a measure of output and Q* its logarithmic trend over the sample period 1920–38.

[34] Until 1935 workers aged 14–15 were exempt from the unemployment insurance system and received no benefits. Workers aged 16–17 were eligible but had to have made 20 to 30 weekly insurance contributions before qualifying for benefit. Benefit rates were correspondingly low for those under the age of 18; moreover, juveniles were not eligible to draw benefits under the supplementary insurance schemes designed for individuals who had exhausted their regular benefits.

[35] M. Irish, 'Unemployment in Interwar Britain. A Note', University of Bristol, Mimeo, February 1980; M. Collins, 'Unemployment in Interwar Britain: Still Searching for an Explanation' *Journal of Political Economy*, 90 (1982), 369–79; D. Metcalf, S. J. Nickell and N. Floros, 'Still Searching for an Explanation of Unemployment in Interwar Britain', *Journal of Political Economy*, 90 (1982), 386–99; P. A. Ormerod and G. D. N. Worswick, 'Unemployment in Interwar Britain', *Journal of Political Economy*, 90 (1982), 400–9.

rather than on supply. Employers between the wars are known to have dismissed juvenile workers when they became old enough to claim adult wages. In addition, opportunities for young workers tended to be specific to the age group rather than the industry; the lower unemployment rate for juveniles compared to prime age males frequently reflected the structure of labour demand (especially within light domestic industries) rather than the impact of the insurance system on labour supply.[36] Moreover, if the age distribution of unemployment was the result of the unemployment benefit, the effect should not be apparent before such payments were introduced on any significant scale. But unemployment amongst juveniles during 1906–7 and 1910–11, as far as can be adduced from the scanty evidence available, was lower relative to the average than during the interwar period.

Evidence of a reduction in measured unemployment amongst married women following the introduction in 1931 of more demanding contributory requirements for the receipt of benefit does not mean that the individuals involved had previously been receiving benefit to which they were not entitled, insofar as they were not genuinely seeking work. Benjamin and Kochin assume, incorrectly, that registered and actual unemployment rates were the same. The introduction of more stringent regulations may have resulted in considerable numbers of married women now ineligible for benefit ceasing to register without them either leaving the labour market or obtaining the jobs they had supposedly spurned in more lenient times. There is little positive evidence that the participation rate of married women was directly associated with the availability of benefits. A comparison of the percentage of married women either occupied or economically active between the Census years 1911 and 1931 suggests that had employment opportunities been more favourable in the latter year the participation rate may have been much higher. Indeed it is quite probable that a proportion of women stayed out of the labour force before 1931 despite the relatively more favourable benefits regime. The contrast between the pre- and post-1931 situation is only circumstantial evidence of benefit inducement, given the decline in jobs available to women.[37] In short, tighter benefit regulations may have resulted not in a lower incidence of unemployment among married women but, by reducing the incentive to register, only a lower recorded unemployment figure.

It should not be inferred that the unemployment benefit system had no effect upon labour supply. It may have persuaded some unemployed

---

[36] These issues are considered in more detail in chapter 4.

[37] T. J. Hatton, 'Unemployment in Britain Between the World Wars: A Role for the Dole?' Essex Discussion Paper, No. 139, 1980.

workers to remain in depressed areas suffering decline rather than move in search of work elsewhere. It is doubtful, however, whether the prevailing levels of benefit had as much an influence in this respect as the prospect many potential migrants faced of trading down to less skilled work or breaking with a community to which they were strongly attached.

Contemporaries were fully aware of the effect which the insurance regulations had in encouraging 'systematic short-time'. The rule whereby any three days of unemployment occuring within a period of six consecutive days could be considered as continuous and therefore irrelevant so far as eligibility for benefit was concerned encouraged employers in such diverse industries as textiles, coalmining and the shoe and hat trades to arrange lay offs to satisfy the waiting period requirement. One version of the arrangment (the 'OXO' system) enabled employees to work three days on (O) and three days off (X).[38] Such practices, however, were not as widespread as is generally believed; nor were they acts of benevolence since they allowed employers to maintain their 'full-employment' workforce when faced with an economic environment constrained principally by inadequate demand.

To gain a more balanced perspective on the interwar period it is necessary to contrast evidence of so-called 'abuse' of the insurance system, together with the inferences drawn from aggregated data and econometric modelling, with the available volume of qualitative material concerning involuntary unemployment. Detailed enquiries into the provisions and administration of the insurance scheme during the twenties convinced contemporary investigators that widespread rumours of malingering were unfounded.[39] Employers and trade unionists canvassed in eight industrial

---

[38] Registered dockers, who were not expected to search for work outside their industry, benefited particularly from the system of 'three days on the hook, three days in the book'. Over £22 million was drawn in benefit in the docks industry between 1920 and 1931 for a total insurance contribution of only £6 million. N. Whiteside, 'Welfare Insurance and Casual Labour: A Study of Administrative Intervention in Industrial Employment, 1906–26', *Economic History Review*, 2nd ser., 32 (1979), 507–22. The manipulation of short-time working in accordance with insurance regulations did not attract the punitive response one might have expected from Whitehall, not least because it enabled depressed areas, particularly Lancashire, to survive with less distress than might otherwise have been the case. Indeed the government itself urged employers as early as February 1921 to adopt work sharing, encouraging them to put men on short time rather than dismiss them altogether. See chapter 4.

[39] See for example, M. Gilson, *Unemployment Insurance in Great Britain* (1931); J. Astor *et al.*, *Unemployment Insurance in Great Britain. A Critical Examination* (1925); H. Llewellyn-Smith, *New Survey of London Life and Labour* (1932); R. S. Gibson, 'The Incentive to Work As Affected by Unemployment Insurance and the Poor Law Respectively', *Manchester School*, 1 (1930), 21–7; E. Bakke, *Insurance or Dole? The Adjustment of Unemployment Insurance to Economic and Social Facts in Great Britain* (Yale, 1935).

areas of the country in 1925 reported that in their experience most workers genuinely desired work and actively sought it when unemployed.[40] An official report on labour transference went to considerable lengths in 1928 to correct:

A misunderstanding, so obstinate in certain quarters as to appear deliberate . . . that the unemployed are unemployable, that they could easily find work if they wished, but that they prefer to live in idleness on money derived from the state. The misconception in this attitude was so obviously absurd to anyone who studies, however cursorily, the industrial history of the last few years that we should not have thought it necessary to refute them had we not been struck by their prevelence in some quarters . . . Every impartial body that has examined this [unemployment insurance] scheme . . . has found that the allegations of general abuse are without foundation. The body of unemployed is not a standing army of vagrants and loafers, but a number of genuine industrial workers whose composition is constantly changing.[41]

Investigative surveys by the Unemployment Assistance Board and the Pilgrim and Carnegie Trusts established during the 1930s that, though a small proportion of younger unskilled workers without families may have been tempted to reject job offers at the going wage, the majority of people out of work regarded unemployment as an inferior status, even though few of them were willing or able to seek alternative employment elsewhere.[42]

Apathy, depression and loss of morale amongst the long-term unemployed persuaded many of them to reject casual jobs, but such choices were often made under duress rather than to satisfy some cynical desire to manipulate the benefits system. The ease with which many such people were absorbed into employment immediately prior to the Second World War illustrated how much they were able to rejoin the active labour force when a real opportunity arose. Far from being a 'volunteer army', the majority of the unemployed appeared to contemporaries to be the

---

[40] *Unemployment Insurance in Great Britain: A Critical Examination by the Authors of 'The Third Winter of Unemployment'* (1925). The areas covered were Shoreditch, Glasgow, Tyneside, Bolton, Leeds, Birmingham, Cardiff and Reading. Some critics maintained that the insurance benefits system had adversely affected the unemployed's desire to migrate to work overseas. An official report of the Ministry of Labour in 1926 rejected such an accusation as 'part of the silly parrot cry about new national decadence that arises from our ingrained habit of ironic self-deprecation . . . To hint that we have become deaf to the call (i.e. of adventure) because of the elaborate provision in our code of social legislation . . . is mere nonsense'. Inter-Departmental Committee Appointed to Consider the Effect on Migration of Schemes of Social Insurance, Report, Cmd. 2608, 1926.

[41] Ministry of Labour, Industrial Transference Board, Report, Cmd. 3156, 1928, 36–7.

[42] Pilgrim Trust, *Men Without Work*; Carnegie UK Trust, *Disinherited Youth* (Edinburgh 1943); Unemployment Assistance Board, *Annual Reports*, 1935–38.

involuntary victims of a lack of jobs rather than a body of sophisticated malingerers exploiting an over-generous scheme of unemployment relief.[43]

It is worth recalling, too, that compared to an absolute poverty line such as that defined by B. S. Rowntree in his *Human Needs of Labour* (1937), the 1936 benefit rate for a family of four was only two-thirds of this level, but close to that previously defined by Rowntree in 1899 as the minimum income necessary to provide a diet necessary simply to maintain physical efficiency. Although interwar unemployment benefits may have been high enough on occasion to blunt incentives for the short-term unemployed, they were rarely high enough to provide adequate income maintenance for the long-term unemployed, least of all those with large families.[44] Moreover, even when unemployment benefits rose relative to wages, and insofar as any increases in benefit levels were not offset elsewhere in the public sector accounts, they may actually have helped to raise employment by increasing aggregate demand.[45]

Ideally an analysis of the alleged relationship between high interwar unemployment and the insurance scheme ought to discriminate between the unemployed who were drawing benefits to which their contributions had entitled them and those who were not; between those in the latter group who were able and willing to work but unable to find it and those who were not; and between those amongst the unemployed whose 'demoralization' was the consequence more of continued involuntary unemployment than of having been tainted by receipt of unemployment benefit. It has yet to be proven that the scale of 'voluntary' unemployment in the interwar period extended much beyond the boundaries of those particularly unfortunate groups whose general personal, industrial and family situation provided them with a sufficiently strong financial incentive

[43] Eichengreen's analysis of household data for London during the period 1928–31 indicates a generally positive but small association between unemployment incidence and the replacement rate for all adult males, but the effect appears to be virtually non-existent so far as adult household heads are concerned. Positive evidence of an association between the probability of unemployment and the level of benefit exists for other adult secondary workers such as women and young men whose families did not depend too heavily upon their income. They comprised only a small share of the adult male labour force. Eichengreen concludes that while the scale and duration of unemployment and other factors contributed to interwar unemployment, the influence of the latter predominated. B. Eichengreen, 'Unemployment in Interwar Britain: Dole or Doldrums?' *Oxford Economic Papers*, 39 (1987), 597–623; Eichengreen, 'Unemployment in Interwar Britain: New Evidence from London', *Journal of Interdisciplinary History*, 17 (1986), 335–58.

[44] Hatton, 'The Analysis of Unemployment in Interwar Britain', 5–6; B. Sadler, 'Unemployment and Unemployment Benefits in Twentieth Century Britain: A Lesson of the Thirties', in *Out of Work: Perspectives of Mass Unemployment*, Department of Economics, University of Warwick (1984), 25–9; C. Webster, 'Health, Welfare and Unemployment During the Depression', *Past and Present*, 109 (1985), 204–30.

[45] T. J. Hatton, 'Unemployment Benefits and the Macroeconomics of the Interwar Labour Market: A Further Analysis', *Oxford Economic Papers*, 35 (1983), 502.

neither to seek nor to accept available employment. Such people tended to be so disadvantaged in other respects that many of them would have found it difficult to compete successfully in the labour market even if they had been positively seeking work. Certainly comparative analyses of the impact of benefit levels in the pre- and post-1945 periods have provided powerful support for the proposition that when correctly specified (using benefits actually paid rather than those nominally available), the replacement ratio for males in general has had no significant role in determining changes in the rate of male unemployment in Britain in the last 50–60 years.[46] Beveridge, perhaps, offers the most appropriate remark:

The danger of an effective scheme of unemployment insurance is less that it may demoralize the man who gets benefits and cause him to give up the search for work, than that it may demoralize the Government of the day and cause them to give up the search for remedies.[47]

Disagreements over the proximate causes of persistently high unemployment between the wars clearly have important implications for the substance and direction of government ameliorative policy. Contemporary followers of Keynes and many since have argued that the interwar economy was subject largely to severe demand shocks and was therefore unable to return to full employment without a large measure of government intervention. Policies aimed at expanding aggregate demand via a substantial growth in central government expenditure could thus have significantly reduced not only the overall level of unemployment, but also, had they been allied to a deliberate policy of regional development, some though not all of the worst features of decline in the depressed areas.

The opposing view regards such an interventionist stance as unnecessary and even harmful; its adoption would have delayed necessary structural adjustment and with it the economy's automatic tendency towards self-stabilization at an equilibrium level of unemployment. Those on the other hand who emphasize supply factors focus, as we have seen, on the movement of wages and on the development of an insurance scheme which together raised unemployment to levels higher than they might otherwise have been. It is in the conduct of official relief policy, therefore, that a prime source of Britain's mounting financial and industrial crisis can be found as employers and taxpayers were forced to shoulder the unproductive burden of a social insurance system responsible in part for labour market rigidity and continued international uncompetitiveness.

---

[46] Metcalf, Nickell and Floros, 'Still Searching for an Explanation of Unemployment'.
[47] W. H. Beveridge, 'Unemployment Insurance in the War and After', in *War Insurance*, Sir N. Hill *et al.* (1927), 249–50.

Bereft of the politician's dream – a monocausal explanation of unemployment sufficiently clear cut to permit of a swift and effective solution – interwar governments wrestled with a wide and sometimes conflicting range of policy options with wavering enthusiasm and conviction. The force of circumstance and sea changes in national and international economic conditions forced a heady mix of 'remedies', many of which appeared to contemporaries to be little more than anxious gestures rather than thoughtful attacks on one of the most pressing economic and social problems of the time.

In truth, there were no easy solutions. The interwar unemployment problem was partly cyclical, partly structural and partly regional, each element acting on and aggravating the other. Little wonder that Ministers sought refuge in policies aimed, amongst other things, at boosting trade, sustaining confidence in sterling, encouraging industrial reorganization and efficiency, promoting labour transference, bolstering the Empire and associated colonial development, and sponsoring productive work, all in an effort to deal with the 'intractable million' and restore Britain's standing within the international economic community. The fact remains that interwar governments spent much of their time merely containing the unemployment problem rather than actively seeking to solve it. Unemployment relief was central to this activity and it is to the troubled history of insurance and assistance that we first turn in our survey of ameliorative policy.

PART II

The labour market under strain

2 ✳ Defensive action: unemployment relief and public assistance, 1919–1932

The dominant response of every interwar government to large-scale and persistent unemployment was to provide cash benefits to the out-of-work, pending a revival in the demand for labour. The scale and duration of such payments, the circumstances in which they were introduced, the conditions under which they could be obtained and the impact which such a response had upon national finances were but some of the issues which kept unemployment relief at the centre of the interwar policy debate. For much of that period the crisis of unemployment and the crisis of unemployment insurance seemed but mirror reflections of one another, each a damning indictment of the failure of successive administrations to respond with any firm political conviction to the serious industrial and economic difficulties that confronted them.

The legal and administrative apparatus deployed for the payment of unemployment benefit had its origins in the Edwardian period. Before 1911 there was no provision at national level for meeting the immediate needs of the unemployed. Out-of-work benefits were available to members of selected trade unions, predominantly covering skilled workers. Outside of private charity, the remainder of the unemployed, at least in England and Wales, were forced to rely on relief from Poor Law Guardians. The system was degrading; men were regarded as being out of work because they were undeserving and lacking in moral quality. Their treatment, therefore, was based on the principle of less eligibility, providing either minimum out-door assistance on the performance of a task of work or recourse to the workhouse, each of which was designed to hasten the worker's desire to re-enter the industrial workforce as quickly as possible.

Evidence had been mounting from the turn of the century, however, that unemployment and poverty were not determined primarily by individual failings. The economic forces influencing industrial development were of a national and even world-wide character, giving rise to labour market problems beyond the capacity of local agencies to handle. Rapid changes in production methods, rising levels of industrial efficiency, cyclical fluctuations in trade, increased specialization and a considerable growth in casual and intermittent occupations, were tending to increase the volume and incidence of unemployment. As such they called for new forms of organization and methods of treatment altogether more varied and flexible than were currently available.

The co-existence of an antiquated Poor Law procedure and a system of indiscriminate relief by voluntary agencies highlighted the need for a more systematic means of dealing with the involuntarily unemployed. The 1905 Unemployed Workmen Act was designed to meet this need. Local authorities with more than 50,000 inhabitants were obliged to establish Distress Committees to supervise the administration of relief works in aid of the unemployed, especially the respectable workman of good character who was out of work through no fault of his own. The Act was not a success. Its new arrangements were neither well organized nor adequately financed and many workmen shunned them. If anything the Act discredited the idea of providing relief work for the temporarily unemployed, especially at local authority level.

This merely emphasized the shortcomings of existing policy. The Reports of the Royal Commission on the Poor Laws and Relief of Distress published in 1909 carried further condemnation of the existing Poor Law system, stressing that unemployment was an increasingly industrial and economic problem. Although the Majority Report was in favour of unemployment insurance, the Minority Report argued only for state subsidies to be given to trade unions paying out-of-work benefit. Compulsory unemployment insurance, it was argued, threatened both trade union membership and employment. If public funds had to be utilized, they would best be directed toward promoting insurance amongst unskilled and unorganized labour through an appropriate trade organization.

Yet within two years the first British system of compulsory insurance against unemployment was on the statute book. The origins of and responsibility for this 'daring experiment' are complex. They encompass a host of pressure group activities, an appreciation of the energies and vision of men such as Churchill and Beveridge, and matters of political opportunism, not least the Liberal Party's response to the shifting weight and influence of the working-class vote after 1906. These issues have been authoritatively discussed elsewhere and need not detain us here.[1]

The crucial point is that the unemployment insurance scheme which finally evolved was conceived from the outset as a limited one, designed to provide cover against cyclical unemployment within a narrow range of

---

[1] The best survey is J. Harris, *Unemployment and Politics. A Study in English Social Policy 1886–1914* (Oxford, 1972). See also B. Gilbert, *The Evolution of National Insurance in Great Britain* (1966).

industries. The basic provisions of Part II of the 1911 National Insurance Act applied to seven trades, with a workforce of about 2.25 million men in a total male labour force of just over 10 million. Eighty per cent of those covered by the new arrangements had not previously been covered by any insurance scheme. The trades included were not representative of British industry as a whole, but were those regarded as subject only to reasonable and fairly predictable seasonal fluctuations – namely building, construction of works, shipbuilding, mechanical engineering, construction of vehicles, iron-founding and certain kinds of sawmilling. Industries where restricted time was customary, such as cotton and coal, were excluded since unemployment benefit was regarded as an alternative to short-time working and not a subsidy in aid of it.

Under the original scheme, benefits were limited to 7s per week. The joint contribution from employers and employed, shared in equal proportions, was 5d per week (4d for persons under 18), to which the state added a subsidy which brought the total contribution up to 6⅔d, of which a net 6d went into an insurance fund. Women were excluded and no provision was made for dependants. Insured workers had to make contributions for 26 weeks before they could claim benefit, and were obliged to wait six days for payment after a claim was lodged. The maximum benefit claimants could obtain was limited to one week for each five weeks of fully paid contributions, or to a maximum of 15 weeks in any one-year period.

The scheme was never intended to cover all periods of unemployment. It was designed as a remedy for fluctuations in employment, not as a cure for longer-term unemployment. Nor was it meant to afford an adequate substitute for wages; the idea instead was to provide a first line of defence against distress. Those who remained out of work after having exhausted their right to insurance had recourse to the Poor Law, but only on the basis of need rather than of contractual right.

The strict definitions of eligibility and the limited periods during which benefit could be drawn were meant to assuage the fear that widespread insurance would encourage abuse and malingering. Nonetheless, contemporaries worried that the availability of benefits would aggravate unemployment by reducing the willingness of workmen to adapt to new occupations or to seek work where it might be found. Employers too might be relieved of the responsibility for maintaining a regular flow of work, thereby promoting excessive wage rigidity. Yet the insurance scheme attracted very little criticism before 1914, principally because it was launched during a period of relatively stable employment, permitting the Unemployment Fund to accumulate a substantial surplus capable of meeting need when it arose. The Board of Trade reported in 1913 that insurance benefits had proved perfectly adequate with recipients making little use of the Poor Law or private charity.[2] But underlying the entire philosophy of the scheme was the notion, firmly supported within government, that unemployment was a transitory phenomenon. It was this premise that proved to be the most potent cause of future troubles.

POSTWAR PRESSURES

The actuarial calculations underlying the 1911 national insurance scheme and the experimental nature with which it was applied to a specially selected group of workers narrowed the perceived risks of the venture. No permanent insurance reserve was established; current premiums were to be depleted by current benefits, subject to an extensive range of regulations regarding contributions and entitlement to benefit. Contributions began to be paid in July 1912 and benefits in January 1913. Thanks to high wartime employment, the average annual payment of benefits during 1916, 1917 and 1918 fell to less than £70,000 and the balance of the Unemployment Fund increased from just over £3 million at the end of its second year to £15 million at the time of the Armistice.

Following the outbreak of war, unemployment in the insured trades rose rapidly, from 3.6 per cent at the end of July 1914 to 6.2 per cent at the beginning of September. Special grants were made to trade unions to help them cope with the unanticipated shock. But the drain of men into the army and the labour demands of the munitions factories soon dispelled fears of widespread dislocation, and for the remainder of the war unemployment was almost negligible. The possible emergence of widespread unemployment in peacetime posed an obvious threat to the entire insurance scheme. Ministers were especially quick to recognize the uncertain employment prospects of munitions workers, only about half of whom were already covered by insurance. Consequently compulsory insurance was extended under Part I of the 1916 Insurance Act to all those engaged in 'munitions work' within any industry or trade, unless exempted by departmental order, and, under Part II, to all workers in various other trades[3] whether employed in munitions or not.

---

[2] Board of Trade, First Report of the Proceedings of the Board of Trade under Part II of the National Insurance Act 1911, Cd. 6965, 1913.

[3] The list was to include those engaged in machine woodwork, the repair of metal goods, the manufacture of munitions, chemicals, rubber, leather, bricks, wooden cases, artificial stone and other artificial building materials. Unlike the trades covered by the 1911 Act, those included in the 1916 scheme employed relatively large numbers of women. Although women in munitions works were included in the 1916 extension of the Insurance Act, the Minister of Labour tried unsuccessfully in 1917 to have the insurance scheme extended to include women who had been drawn into non-munitions work as substitutes for men. The Treasury opposed the idea, arguing that there was no actuarial basis upon which to calculate the effects of such an extension.

The possibility of further strengthening the Unemployment Fund from the contributions of an expanded insured population was dimmed, however, by the opposition of certain trade unions. Workers employed in industries with a low risk of unemployment, together with those already in receipt of trade union unemployment benefits relatively higher and more readily available than under the state scheme, objected to subsidizing employees in less secure trades. Union hostility to the extension of unemployment insurance was strongest in the cotton, boot and shoe,[4] and food and tobacco industries, where there was growing resentment against state interference in the labour market. In the event only 200,000 of the original 1.5 million workers destined to be brought under the insurance scheme by Part I of the 1916 Act were covered by January 1918.[5]

So far as members of the fighting forces were concerned, plans had been prepared to provide ex-servicemen with a free policy of unemployment insurance. Once it became evident that the cessation of war work would necessitate some form of state assistance for the unemployed in general and not just demobilized men, there seemed little option but to extend the payment of 'free' benefits to civilian workers. Thus was born in November 1918 the infamous Out-of-Work Donation scheme (OWD) which provided unemployed adults with emergency benefit payments (including, for the first time, dependants' allowances) irrespective of their entitlement under the unemployment insurance scheme.[6] The 'dole' had arrived.

Because of the urgency with which the improvised civilian scheme was introduced it operated in the earliest months with fewer limitations and checks than would otherwise have been the case. Employers condemned the non-contributory nature of the donation as an inducement to malingering, but an official enquiry rejected accusations that there had been much fraudulent abuse.[7] Widespread abuse or not, the OWD scheme damaged the principle of contributory insurance. Adults unable to find work

[4] The boot and shoe trade, as part of the leather trades, could not strictly be excluded by departmental order. But the trade engaged in passive resistance and was finally excluded by the Minister of Labour under powers conferred by an amendment to the Act in 1918.

[5] N. Whiteside, 'Welfare Legislation and the Unions During the First World War', *Historical Journal*, 23 (1980), 857–74; Civil War Workers Committee, Second Interim Report, Cd. 9192, 1918; W. H. Beveridge, 'Unemployment Insurance in the War and After'; R. Lowe, 'Welfare Legislation and the Unions during and after the First World War', *Historical Journal*, 25 (1982), 437–41.

[6] The scheme came into operation on 25 November 1918. It originally provided weekly rates of benefit of 24s for men and 20s for women, up to a maximum of 26 weeks during the twelve months following demobilization for ex-service personnel, and up to 13 weeks during the six months from the inception of the scheme for civilians. The rates of benefit and duration of entitlement were altered on various occasions thereafter as the government grappled with the post-war emergency.

[7] Final Report of the Committee of Inquiry into the Scheme of Out-of-Work Donation, The Aberconway Inquiry, Cmd. 305, 1919, paras 12, 20.

came to believe that the state had a duty to provide some degree of unconditional maintenance for their entire family. The available payments, moreover, were so much more generous than the insurance benefit rates that the latter were virtually suspended since practically all workers in insured trades were entitled to the 'donation'. The Unemployment Fund was thus able to save money[8] while the government, undecided what to do about unemployment insurance in general and embarrassed by its inability to provide any alternative programme, bought social peace by systematic extensions of the non-contributory scheme. By May 1919 650,000 civilians and 360,000 ex-servicemen were drawing Out-of-Work Donation, the Cabinet having already sanctioned further payments to those about to exhaust their right to benefit.

The government genuinely feared civil disorder 'if something were not done to provide economic security for the British working man'.[9] Although after some soul-searching the Cabinet agreed in November 1919 to refuse any further payments to civilians, it was still mindful of widespread discontent among ex-servicemen. Already the National Federation of Discharged and Demobilized Sailors and Soldiers had actively campaigned in the spring and summer of 1919 for 'Work not doles'. The 'Reports on Revolutionary Organizations', delivered secretly to the government from correspondents in major industrial centres,[10] only added to the fear and uncertainty. Initially the Ministry of Labour was in favour of ending all benefits rather than discriminating between deserving groups,[11] but with the benefit rights of more than 2.5 million ex-servicemen due to expire between November 1919 and the end of March 1920, it was the latter group which was eventually catered for by extended payments lasting until March 1921.

Of particular concern were the meagre employment prospects facing unskilled young ex-servicemen living in large urban areas. The notion of throwing the unemployed soldier to the mercies of the Poor Law was daunting. Surveys in London, Bristol, Wales and Dundee confirmed that 50 per cent of disabled ex-servicemen had been unemployed for more than half

---

[8] Out-of-Work Donation gave 29s to men and 25s to women, with dependants' allowance. This put the 7s available under the 1911 insurance scheme in the shade. The accumulated balance of the Unemployment Fund rose from £15,200,000 to £22,200,000 between November 1918 and November 1920.

[9] B. Gilbert, *British Social Policy 1914–1939* (1970), 66.

[10] These activities were the responsibility of the Home Office between 1919 and the autumn of 1921 and were supervised by a 'Directorate of Intelligence' under the control of Sir Basil Home Thomson, an Assistant Commissioner with Scotland Yard.

[11] Cab 24/92, Out of Work Donation. Memorandum by the Minister of Labour, 30 October 1919.

of the number of weeks since their discharge.[12] In a circular to the Cabinet in December 1920 the Home Secretary warned:

The temper of the men is becoming increasingly bitter . . . There is much muttering about the ostentation and luxury of the 'idle rich' and agitators have seized upon the real discontent and distress to carry on a ceaseless propaganda of class war. Peace with Russia as a panacea for unemployment is their constant theme.[13]

To a government clearly disturbed by recent mutinies and unrest in Europe the political repercussions of allowing extremists to mobilize discontented groups of the unemployed were alarming.

Political pressure was mounting meanwhile to secure a revised peace-time contributory insurance scheme. Beveridge had devised a plan in 1917 to extend insurance to all those persons earning less than £200 per annum. But the Treasury stalled, suspicious that low-risk industries would quickly break away. Employers' organizations on the other hand welcomed an expansion of insurance, knowing that trade union co-operation over wages and working conditions would not be forthcoming without a measure of security against unemployment. By 1920 both the Treasury and the Ministry of Labour recognized the futility of relying on unorganized and improvised methods of relieving distress; what was required was a more permanent scheme of 'universal insurance'.

The result was the 1920 Unemployment Insurance Act. Contributory insurance was extended to all manual workers and to non-manual workers earning not more than £250 per year, except for those in agriculture, private domestic service and those permanent employees normally regarded as free from the risk of periodic unemployment, such as public servants and railwaymen.[14] The number of insured workers rose to 11.75 million. Unfortunately the changes brought about by the Act made the insurance scheme financially more vulnerable. Benefit rates were increased from the 7s limit established in 1911 to 15s for men, 12s for women and half these rates for insured contributors under the age of 18. The rise in contributions and hence income to the Fund, however, was nothing like on the same scale. In addition, a large number of persons unemployed for short periods became eligible for benefit because of the reduction from six to three days in

---

[12] Cab 24/114, CP 2077, Enquiry into Classes of Ex-Servicemen Receiving Out of Work Donation at 15 September 1920. Note by the Minister of Labour, 9 November 1920.
[13] Cab 24/116, CP 2273, Report on Revolutionary Organizations in the United Kingdom, 9 December 1920.
[14] The insurance and banking industries contracted out of the state scheme and established separate schemes of their own. The power to do so was suspended by Acts of 1921 and 1924 and was finally abolished in 1927 without prejudice to the schemes which had already been approved.

the waiting period between unemployment and the payment of benefit. With unemployment falling at the time the Act became operative in November 1920, few questioned the merit of limiting the maximum entitlement to benefit to 15 weeks within any insurance year (as in 1911) or of establishing within this limit a ratio of one week's benefit for six (rather than five) weeks' contributions. Unfortunately the assumptions implicit in the Act – that unemployment would not exceed 6.6 per cent, that the 'one in six' rule would impose an automatic safeguard against abuse, and that the Fund would be able to retain a viable surplus to meet future contingencies – were soon to be brutally tested in a harsher economic climate.

THE DECAY OF INSURANCE

Within a month of its inception the revised insurance scheme had to cope with one of the severest industrial recessions on recent record. Ex-servicemen and women, unable to amass sufficient contributions to meet the requirements of the 1920 Act, were granted further emergency payments as the OWD scheme was extended yet again to the end of March 1921. Some 6.9 million workers in trades previously excluded from the insurance scheme had already been granted eight weeks' benefit for every four contributions in recognition of the difficulties they would face in meeting the strict requirements of the new legislation. Even this concession was modified as the unemployment problem grew worse. From December 1920 any person who had worked for four weeks since 4 July 1920 in a job not then within the scheme was allowed to receive eight weeks' benefit during the first three months of 1921 as if four insurance contributions had actually been paid.

Despite such modifications it soon became apparent that thousands of workers would exhaust their 'right' to any form of unemployment payment should the recession prove prolonged. Early in February 1921, the Minister of Labour warned the Cabinet that:

If unemployment continues at anything like its present level to the end of March – and there is no reason to expect anything else – the position will be that 300,000 unemployed ex-servicemen will have run out of out-of-work donations and from 500,000 to 700,000 other unemployed persons will have run out of their eight weeks' unemployment insurance benefit. Those who have exhausted Benefit are numerous at the present moment; the exhaustion of Donation will begin in the third week in February, and the numbers will increase rapidly week by week. This means that round about a million workers (not counting their dependants) will be penniless by the end of March.[15]

---

[15] Cab 24/119, Unemployment. The Immediate Future. Memorandum by the Minister of Labour, 10 February 1921.

By March 1921 the rate of insured unemployment had risen to 11.3 per cent from only 3.7 per cent in the previous November. With thousands of individuals denied the opportunity of establishing by contribution a legitimate right to further payments of unemployment benefit, the pressure to increase the periods during which benefit could be drawn (and at a more generous rate) became politically unbearable. The rule of one week's benefit for every six weeks' contributions was clearly unworkable in practice. Within the Ministry of Labour there was stern resistance to withholding the payment of benefit to those on short time, not least because the Government had encouraged firms to adopt restricted working as an alternative to dismissing employees.[16] Large numbers of workers in the cotton trade especially were already exhausting the special payment of eight weeks' benefit.

Economic depression and political expediency combined to breach the actuarial principles upon which the insurance scheme had originally been based. From 3 March 1921 weekly benefit rates were raised from 15s to 20s for men and from 12s to 16s for women, payable for a maximum of 26 rather than for 15 weeks in any insurance year. In addition the Unemployment Fund was permitted to borrow up to £10 million to permit workers who could prove to a Local Employment Committee that they were 'genuinely seeking whole-time employment' but unable to obtain it to draw 'uncovenanted benefit' (i.e. benefit paid in advance of the required minimum number of contributions) for 16 weeks in each of two special periods, March to November 1921 and November 1921 to July 1922. This enabled the payment of Out-of-Work Donation to be terminated in March 1921, finally bringing the ex-service unemployed into the state insurance scheme.

Hopes that the level of unemployment would stabilize were wrecked by the 1921 coal dispute. Alarm grew within the Cabinet over the financial burden of unemployment payments. By May 1921 the Unemployment Fund was losing £1,200,000 a week. In an effort to curb the mounting insolvency, adult benefit rates were cut in July 1921 to their 1920 level of 15s for men and 12s for women (against the opposition of the Minister of Labour),[17] and the scale of employers' and workers' contributions raised.[18] In addition the 'waiting period' for the payment of benefit was extended

---

[16] See chapter 4.
[17] The Minister argued strongly for rates to be reduced from 20s to 18s for men and from 15s to 14s for women. For the exchanges between Ministers see Cab 27/135, CP 2993, 30 May 1921; Cab 27/135, CP 2987, May 1921.
[18] The contribution requirement was modified, however, to permit workers who could show that they were normally in insurable employment and were genuinely seeking full-time employment but were unable to obtain it to claim covenanted benefits, even if they failed to satisfy the contributory condition.

from three to six days and the normal contributory condition tightened, requiring the payment of 20 contributions during the preceding insurance year. But there were political constraints upon curtailing expenditure any further. Though economy was sought in the insurance scheme proper, Ministers shrank from penalizing the victims of longer-term unemployment. Not only were uncovenanted benefits protected, they were allowed to be claimed for an extra six weeks (to a total of 22 weeks) in each of the two specified periods previously provided for.

Such expedients were adopted because of the government's politically naive, financially dangerous and empirically unjustified assumption that the rise in unemployment was merely temporary and cyclical, able to be met by a series of *ad hoc* adjustments to existing regulations. Uncovenanted benefit, in other words, could placate the unemployed, pending a revival in trade. However, the situation was far worse than the authorities dared to admit. A significant proportion of the unemployed had already been forced to rely on trade union funds and private resources to supplement their meagre income; many more turned to the Poor Law Guardians for additional assistance, particularly when the emergency payments of uncovenanted benefit ended in August 1921.

During the nine months prior to November 1921, continuously unemployed workers were restricted to 22 weeks of benefit, after which they were obliged to seek outdoor relief. Unfortunately the Poor Law system was in a far more parlous state than Ministers wanted to believe. Few of the Guardians in areas of high unemployment and low rateable values could cope. There were wide variations, moreover, in the scale of Poor Law relief and in the manner in which it was administered, particularly the extent to which other income was disregarded in the assessment of an individual's means. In Scotland it was illegal until November 1921 for Parish Councils to provide outdoor relief to the able-bodied, but so grievous was the situation in particular localities, such as Dundee and Fife, that the Scottish Office urged local authorities to act illegally to meet the emergency needs of the unemployed.[19]

Some Boards openly defied regulations concerning the appropriate Poor Law payments to be made to the unemployed, most notably at Poplar. At first the Cabinet resolved to hold tight until benefit again became payable in November 1921. But the threat of disorder grew more urgent. By mid-September the Minister of Labour was in a fearful mood:

Things have eventuated precisely as I forecasted . . . The Communists have done their best to exploit the fact that numbers of persons – about 380,000 at present and it will be not less than 500,000 before the new benefit commences – have for the

[19] Cab 24/128, CP 3345, The Unemployment Situation, 28 September 1921.

time being nothing to subsist upon . . . We shall have to carry through the winter at least a million persons unemployed. The Unemployment Benefit will be 15/- for men; 12/- for women. It was that figure last winter. But there is this vital difference. Last winter that figure was substantially augmented from Trade Union Out-of-Work Funds; from Local Guardians Relief; and from other sources. The continued depression has made such demands upon those additional sources of assistance that whilst 15/- Unemployment Benefit was only a part of the means of subsistence for a good many people last winter, *it will be their only income this winter* . . . Hopelessly embarrassed though our finances may be, the situation is one which has got to be faced if grave civil disorder is to be avoided. The Communists have . . . failed this time . . . but the winter will give them an opportunity the like of which they have not yet had.[20]

The King, Lord Stamfordham informed the Cabinet, was 'very much troubled about the unemployment question', adding:

His Majesty does most earnestly hope that the Government will agree to some scheme by which work, and not doles, will be supplied to the unemployed, the great majority of whom, His Majesty understands, honestly want to work . . . It is impossible to expect people to subsist upon the unemployment benefit of 15/- for men and 12/- for women.[21]

Mindful of the prevailing unrest but less so of the conventional rules of contributory insurance, the Cabinet decided to establish an emergency distress fund from which the unemployed drawing insurance benefits could claim an additional allowance, the value of which would be determined by the number of their dependants. This marked a significant change in policy. Now, far from denying the TUC's demand for the 'right to work or maintenance', the government nurtured the belief that the insurance scheme was concerned less with 'tiding over' individuals temporarily out of work than with providing adequate living standards for the unemployed.

Subsequent policy only made matters worse. Dependants' allowances became a formal part of the main state scheme in April 1922. A month earlier, the second 'special period', established the previous July for the payment of uncovenanted benefit, was prematurely shortened and replaced by two new periods running from 6 April to 1 November 1922 (the third 'special period') and from 2 November 1922 to 1 July 1923 (the fourth 'special period'). It was originally intended that during the third special period the unemployed in receipt of five weeks' uncovenanted benefit would have to wait five weeks before any further payments could be claimed, but such was the pressure on local Boards of Guardians to provide immediate assistance to the out of work that the government was forced to reduce the

[20] Cab 27/128, CP 3317, The Unemployment Problem. Memorandum by the Minister of Labour, 17 September 1921.
[21] Cab 24/128, CP 3329, Copy of Letter from Lord Stamfordham to the Secretary, Cabinet, 21 September 1921.

'gap' of non-payment of uncovenanted benefit to only one week and, in addition, to lengthen the third 'special period'.[22]

Although by 1922 insurance contribution rates were more than double those of 1920 and the proportion paid by the state greater than in previous years, the burden of unemployment expenditure had risen alarmingly. At the beginning of 1923 the Unemployment Fund, which in November 1920 had had an unexpended balance of over £22,000,000, was in deficit to the extent of £16,500,000 and losing over £200,000 weekly; more than half of the unemployment benefits paid since the autumn of 1920 had been uncovenanted.[23] By March 1923 Treasury advances to the Fund amounted to more than £17 million.

But exhaustions of benefit were already destined to increase rapidly from the beginning of April 1923 under the terms of the fourth 'special period'[24] threatening to create serious unrest and to intensify further the burden on Poor Law authorities. Existing legislation, moreover, provided for a reversion to the normal basis of benefit from July 1923, namely a maximum of 26 weeks in any insurance year (July to July), subject to a rate of one week's benefit for every six contributions paid. This requirement made it almost certain that if unemployment continued to increase after July 1923 many of those out of work would quickly be denied benefit.

With a logic born of dire necessity but nurtured by unbounding optimism and a keen sense of political survival, the Conservative administration extended the fourth 'special period' to 17 October 1923, during which time uncovenanted, or a combination of covenanted and uncovenanted, benefits were available for 44 weeks out of 50. A gap of two weeks without benefit was instituted if and when 22 weekly benefits had been drawn since November 1922. During the insurance year following the termination of the fourth 'special period', the maximum entitlement to uncovenanted benefit was fixed at 26 weeks with a gap of three weeks after 12 weeks' benefit had been received. Such concessions, the authorities argued, were aimed at protecting the principle of insurance by helping to reduce workers' reliance upon poor relief which merely eroded the incentive to pay contributions. In truth, they were the desperate response of an adminis-

[22] In December 1922 some 42 Poor Law representatives appealed unsuccessfully to the Prime Minister for grants to be made available to all Unions spending in excess of 1s in the £ on unemployment relief. Cab 27/124, CU 501, Committee on Unemployment. Necessitous Areas, 20 December 1922.

[23] Cab 27/210, Extended Grants of Unemployment Benefit. Memorandum by the Minister for Labour, 30 January 1923.

[24] During the fourth 'special period' (2 November 1922–1 July 1923) the maximum benefit available to applicants ranged from 12 to 22 weeks. Individuals eligible for 12 weeks' payment exhausted their right to further benefit on 24 January 1923; those eligible for 22 weeks on 4 April 1923.

tration to whom an abridged insurance scheme had become the principal means of allaying public disorder during a period of severe depression.

Inevitably the concessions made to the unemployed came to be viewed less as the price of social peace than as a portent of widespread demoralization and of impending financial disaster. Although organized employers at the beginning of 1923 conceded that uncovenanted benefit had prevented widespread disorder by allaying serious distress, they viewed the rising cost of insurance contributions as a burden on productive enterprise, hampering overseas competitiveness through its impact on industrial costs. Conscious of a growing divergence between the 'social' and the 'industrial' wage, the National Confederation of Employers' Organizations reported to the Minister of Labour in January 1924:

It is of the utmost importance that the framework of unemployment insurance should be re-established on its proper and permanent basis at the earliest possible moment, and on no consideration should further emergency measures be grafted on to the Insurance Fund or allowed to delay the date at which the 1920 Act provisions are re-established. If further emergency measures on a modified scale should prove to be, for a limited time, necessary, they should be in the form of an *ad hoc* State provision.[25]

This suggestion from the employers of transferring relief of the longer-term unemployed from insurance to some kind of state agency was in advance of official thinking, even within the Ministries of Labour and Health. It was destined, moreover, to re-emerge as an issue of major political contention but only after the course of unemployment relief policy had taken more tortuous twists.

THE RISE AND FALL OF THE 'SEEKING WORK' TEST

The average number of individuals signing on as unemployed at the Exchanges in 1924 was considerably lower than in any year since the extension of the insurance scheme four years earlier. By August 1924 the debt of the Unemployment Fund had fallen to below £4.5 million. It was against this background that the newly elected Labour administration began to remodel the benefits system. Under the terms of the Unemployment Insurance (No. 2 Act) 1924, covenanted (now renamed standard) benefit remained limited in proportion to contributions by the 'one in six' rule and in duration to 26 weeks in any insurance year. But the system of 'gaps' during which no benefit could be drawn was abolished. Ministerial

[25] National Confederation of Employers' Organizations, *Unemployment Insurance*, 31 January 1924, 16; T. Rodgers, 'Work and Welfare: The National Confederation of Employers' Organisations and the Unemployment Problem', Ph.D. Thesis, University of Edinburgh (1981), 134.

discretion to award or refuse uncovenanted (now renamed extended) benefit was withdrawn; applicants exhausting standard benefit were allowed to continue drawing extended benefit as a legal right for as long as they remained unemployed on condition that they, like standard benefit recipients, had paid 30 insurance contributions in the preceding two years. The 1924 Act further reduced the waiting period from six days to three days and raised benefit rates and dependants' allowances, permitting a married man with two children to receive 27s a week, a rise in real terms of 155 per cent over the rates paid in 1920.[26]

The Labour government recognized that parliamentary support for such significant changes in the insurance scheme would be forthcoming only if the available benefits were restricted to the 'deserving unemployed' who had demonstrated their eagerness to find work. Prevention of abuse was thus afforded the highest priority. The Insurance (No. 2) Act prescribed that from August 1924 applicants for standard benefit should, in addition to being 'capable of and available for work but unable to obtain suitable employment', as laid down in the 1920 Act, be also 'genuinely seeking work'. Applicants for extended benefit faced altogether tougher and more specific requirements. They had to prove that they were normally in insurable employment; that such employment as was suited to their capabilities was likely to be available to them in normal times; that in the previous two years they had been employed in insurable employment to a reasonable extent, having regard to local circumstances; and, finally, that they were making all 'reasonable' efforts to secure and would be prepared to accept employment suited to their individual capacities.

The 'genuinely seeking work' test was not new. It was first introduced in 1921 when applicants for uncovenanted benefit were required to prove to a Local Employment Committee that they were 'genuinely seeking whole-time employment but unable to obtain such employment'. But it proved at the time to be a haphazard and inadequate procedure given the absence of compulsory notification of vacancies and the practice of the Exchanges, anxious to retain some vestige of respectability, of submitting to employers only the most suitable candidates for work, leaving the remainder to lay claim to their maximum benefit entitlement.

The 'seeking work' test of 1924 introduced an entirely different situation. It put the onus of proof upon claimants to produce satisfactory documentary evidence of their search for work. Local Employment Committees could refuse benefit if they were dissatisfied with a claim, without having to prove

---

[26] The regulation introduced by the previous Conservative administration imposing a gap of three weeks after the receipt of 12 weeks' uncovenanted benefit had already been abolished by the Labour Government within a month of taking office.

that an applicant could have found a job had he made any greater effort to obtain one. The test now applied both to standard and extended benefit claimants and was clearly directed against potential abuse. Every person was deemed to be a malingerer unless he or she could produce evidence to the contrary.[27]

The Labour Party accepted the principle of the 'seeking work' test, despite the vigorous protests of a small group of Scottish MPs known as the 'Clydesiders'. To a considerable extent, the party's indifference rested upon ignorance of how the test operated, upon the erroneous assumption that it was directed primarily at married women, and upon the belief, shared by many of the unemployed themselves, that specific measures against malingering should exist in order to protect the rights of the 'genuinely' out of work. To the labour movement as a whole the administration of the insurance scheme was a far less crucial issue than was the level of benefit.

On the face of it the Unemployment Fund was prey to greater waste and abuse by late 1924 than it had been in previous years. The Labour Party may not have entirely fulfilled its long-standing political commitment to 'work or maintenance', but it had given the insured unemployed the right to receive benefit while genuinely unable to find work. Furthermore, it had abolished 'gaps' in the payment of benefit, thus freeing the unemployed worker from any association with the Poor Law Guardians, and had abolished means test regulations.[28]

The most obvious way of safeguarding the insurance scheme was to strengthen the administration of the 'seeking work' regulation. Already by the end of 1924 one in twenty of all claimants to extended benefit was being judged to have failed the test, principally because the Ministry of Labour ensured as far as it could that Local Employment Committees were composed of individuals guaranteed to exercise the tightest scrutiny of claims. It proved relatively easy, therefore, for the Conservatives to exercise even more discretionary control over the benefits system in future years when one of the available means of doing so had been already strengthened

---

[27] A. Deacon, 'Genuinely Seeking Work? A Study of Unemployment Insurance in Britain, 1920–1931', Ph.D. Thesis, University of London (1979), 100.

[28] The means test, initially introduced as an economy measure in February 1922, allowed certain individuals to be refused benefit (save in cases of severe hardship) namely, single persons living with relatives, married persons whose partners were working, short-time workers and aliens. Such 'discretionary rules', as they came to be called, had been bitterly opposed by the Labour Party which viewed with contempt the application of inquisitorial Poor Law concepts to workers previously compelled to pay insurance contributions, but whose benefit rights were now being determined solely on grounds of private income. Ministers at first denied that there was any scale of incomes above which benefit would not be granted in individual cases. But instructions to this effect were issued in May 1922 – although not publicly admitted until March 1926.

by a government believing itself to be the guardian of working-class interests.

The Conservative government elected at the end of 1924 found itself just as much torn between principle and political expediency as previous administrations had been. It was committed to stricter administration of relief expenditure, particularly on extended benefit, but was loath to thrust thousands of unemployed claimants to the mercy of the Poor Law by, for example, reintroducing 'gaps' in emergency benefit payments. Employers nevertheless were demanding the strict application of the 'one in six' rule to all claims for benefit. The new Minister of Labour, Steel-Maitland, compromised. The stringent statutory conditions built into the scheme by the previous government were preserved, but strengthened from June 1925 by permitting Ministerial discretion to be applied to claims for extended benefit. Few in government, however, denied the need for a more thorough examination of the unemployment payments system and in November 1925 a committee under the chairmanship of Lord Blanesburgh, a former Lord Justice of Appeal, was appointed to investigate what changes, if any, might be made to the insurance scheme in light of post-war experience.

This was no easy task. The TUC was campaigning for higher levels of non-contributory benefits, paid as of right, without a means test. Employers, on the other hand, wanted a return to the 1920 level of benefits, the establishment of a stricter ratio between contributions paid and benefits received and the abolition of any form of non-contributory relief. Repeating a demand it had made earlier in 1924,[29] the NCEO told the Blanesburgh enquiry that workers who had exhausted their contractual right to benefit should become the responsibility of public assistance authorities operating within a reformed Poor Law structure.[30]

In an attempt to steer a middle course between such opposing views, the Blanesburgh committee, reporting in January 1927, proposed a cut in the rate of insurance benefit for adult men, together with lower benefits for younger workers aged between 18 and 21, and the abolition of extended benefit. This would be replaced by standard benefit, subject to the prevailing statutory conditions of a 30 contribution rule and a genuinely seeking work clause. But there was to be no strict 'one in six' contributory ratio. Such an abrupt and arbitrary test threatened to transfer at least 500,000 unemployed workers to the Poor Law. Since the 30 contribution requirement posed a similar threat, the committee recommended that the requirement should be suspended for a period of up to 18 months, during which time anyone who had paid either eight contributions in the previous two years or 30 at any time could draw 'transitional' benefit for one year on the same

---

[29] See p. 43 above.   [30] Rodgers, 'Work and Welfare', 195–9.

terms as standard benefit, providing they satisfied a test of genuinely seeking work.[31]

The 1927 Unemployment Insurance Act reflected the influence of the Blanesburgh enquiry. Insurance benefit rates for adult men were reduced by 1s a week to 17s (though the allowance for an adult dependant was raised from 5s to 7s). Different rates of contribution and benefit were established for a new class of younger workers aged 18–21 years. Extended benefit continued until the Act came into force on 19 April 1928. Thereafter, insured workers unable to fulfil the normal requirements for standard benefit of 30 contributions in the preceding two years became entitled to 'transitional payments' at the same rate as standard benefit for twelve months until 18 April 1929, provided that they satisfied the modified contributory qualification of eight contributions in the preceding two years or 30 at any time.

Two features of the 1927 Act are particularly striking. First, it abolished the concepts of extended benefit and of 'gaps' during which no benefit was payable, granting to all insured workers who complied with the statutory conditions benefit as of right and for unlimited duration so long as they remained unemployed. Secondly, it removed the distinction between those judged to be making a 'genuine' search for work for the receipt of standard benefit and those making 'all reasonable efforts' to secure employment as a condition for extended benefit. All claimants were now required to prove that they were genuinely seeking work.

With the character and state of mind of the claimant to the fore, the operation of the 'seeking work' test became an increasingly subjective rather than objective exercise. The assessment of often inexperienced local Exchange officials and the information culled from neighbours and local tradesmen frequently became crucial in identifying those persons who were felt to prefer unemployment benefit to working. Since the appearance and demeanour of the claimant proved at times to be a greater influence than the social and industrial conditions prevailing in his locality, the nervous but honest applicant was often at a severe disadvantage. Whether the work claimants were expected to seek was actually or even potentially available was not the point at issue; for the unemployed to earn their benefit they had to 'prove' in ritual fashion their determination not to remain unemployed longer than was absolutely necessary. In practice, this led men and women to compile lists of employers to whom applications had supposedly been

[31] It was also proposed that insurance contributions should be divided equally among the three contributing parties, with the imposition of a temporary surcharge to help pay off the deficit on the Unemployment Fund. The Treasury successfully opposed the idea, intent as it was on reducing social services expenditure.

made and to allegations that fictitious lists were passed from one applicant to another for production to the statutory authorities.

More worrying still from the applicants' point of view was the limited room for manoeuvre left to the authorities. The Blanesburgh Report had based its assumptions on an estimated future rate of unemployment of 6 per cent. By the time the Report was published in January 1927 insured unemployment was double that figure, and the debt of the Unemployment Fund stood at over £21 million. Moreover, almost immediately after the 1927 Act was passed, the insurance scheme was burdened with over 100,000 unemployed workers who could not meet the 30 contribution rule, but who were granted transitional benefit.[32] With the abolition of the 'one in six' rule and the 26-week limitation on the duration of payments, the only legal means left to government to control the cost of relief was the requirement of 'genuinely seeking work'.

What followed was a systematic campaign to tighten up the existing administration of unemployment insurance. The 'seeking work' test, of course, had already made its mark. By 1927 one in ten of all claimants was being refused benefit because of an 'unsatisfactory attitude to work'. But thereafter the test was applied with particular severity. By June 1929 the proportion of benefit claims refused on 'seeking work' grounds had risen to nearly two-thirds of all disallowances, even though the total number of claims disallowed had fallen after 1927 as a result of the abolition of the means test.[33] Boards of Guardians in the depressed areas complained bitterly of being burdened with an excessive number of applications for relief following tighter administration of the test.[34] Ironically, it was Labour's preoccupation with the level and duration of benefits that had helped to deflect growing opposition to the 'seeking work' regulations among backbench MPs. Unfortunately, such opposition emerged only slowly down to 1928, except within the ranks of Clydeside MPs such as George Buchanan and James Maxton. Their vociferous condemnation of the test, however, was often couched in such vehement language that the Labour leadership was only too ready to dissociate itself from the protest.

---

[32] Rodgers, 'Work and Welfare', 248.

[33] The best summaries of this campaign are by A. Deacon, 'Concession and Coercion: The Politics of Unemployment Insurance in the Twenties', in *Essays in Labour History 1918–1939*, ed. A. Briggs and J. Saville (1977), 9–35 and Deacon, *In Search of the Scrounger: The Administration of Unemployment Insurance in Britain, 1920–31* (1976).

[34] For details of one area's complaints see Conference of Northern Poor Law Unions and Other Local Authorities, *Distress Due to Unemployment. Deputation to the Minister of Labour*, 27 October 1927. See also H. Witmer, 'Some Effects of the English Unemployment Insurance Acts on the Number of Unemployed Relieved Under the Poor Law', *Quarterly Journal of Economics*, 45 (1931), 262–88.

THE SEARCH FOR SOLVENCY

When the second Labour government took office in June 1929 the debt of the Unemployment Fund stood at £37,170,000. Margaret Bondfield, Minister of Labour, sought immediate action to stem the slide into indebtedness. Within a month Exchequer contributions were raised to a level equal to one-half of the sum of the joint contributions of employers and workers in an effort to improve revenue. But the prospects of financial betterment were bleak. The decision in September 1929 to appoint Local Boards of Assessors to review cases of doubtful entitlement to benefit purely on the basis of individual interview lessened the severity of the operation of the 'seeking work' test. During the six months the Boards were in operation the overall proportion of disallowances fell. At the same time, the government's own supporters stepped up their demand for even more generous maintenance; in the most depressed areas suffering hard-core unemployment the test was frequently ignored altogether. A systematic review by the Morris Committee[35] of the procedure for the determination of claims to benefit failed to resolve the conflict between employers, who insisted that the safeguards against potential abuse should, if anything, be strengthened, and the TUC which complained bitterly that it was fatuous to make payment of benefit dependent upon a search for non-existent work.[36]

The government finally relented to pressure from the Labour left and the trade unions and modified the Blanesburgh compromise in one crucial respect. Under the terms of the 1930 Unemployment Insurance Act the 'seeking work' test was abolished and replaced by a regulation whereby claimants would be disallowed benefit only if they refused an offer of suitable work or failed to carry out the written instructions of an Insurance Officer. The onus of proof, in other words, was transferred from the individual to the Exchanges, making unemployment benefit a right unless just cause could be shown why it should not be paid.

The 'seeking work' test may well have been 'a sledge hammer used to crack a relatively small – and often exaggerated – nut';[37] nonetheless, during the period of its operation it had resulted in nearly three million claims to benefit being disallowed. Now it seemed there was little or no effective control over the cost of unemployment relief. None of the

[35] Report of the Committee on Procedure and Evidence for the Determination of Claims for Unemployment Insurance Benefit, Cmd. 3415, 1929. The Chairman was Sir Harold Morris, President of the Industrial Court.
[36] The Morris Committee suggested that the Employment Exchanges should be made to prove that the work claimants were seeking was available and suited to their capabilities.
[37] Deacon, 'Genuinely Seeking Work?' 226.

provisions introduced in the 1930 Act could do much to ensure either that sufficient job offerings would be available to the unemployed (given the state of the labour market and the absence of compulsory notification of vacancies), or that the Exchanges would make what offers they could to those persons most in need of work. Applicants for transitional benefit, moreover, no longer had to prove that during the previous two years they had been in insured employment for a reasonable length of time. This at once threatened to bring within the scope of the insurance scheme people such as married women and seasonal workers who would not otherwise have regarded themselves as being legitimate candidates for benefit, plus a significant proportion of the long-term unemployed tempted to move back from public assistance to transitional benefit. Privately, the Ministry of Labour anticipated an addition of some 200,000 unemployed workers to the register.[38]

Nor were the liberal provisions of the new legislation the only cause for concern. The 1927 Insurance Act, it will be recalled, had permitted new claimants unable to fulfil the strict contributory requirements of the law to draw transitional payments for one year to April 1929 if they had paid eight insurance contributions during the previous two years or 30 at any time. Both the Conservative Minister of Labour, Steel-Maitland, and Labour's Margaret Bondfield tried unsuccessfully to remove from the insurance scheme the 'illegitimate burden' of those without the proper contribution record.[39] Steel-Maitland suggested to the Cabinet in march 1929 that at the very least men and women without dependants should be forced to meet the minimum contribution regulation at the end of the one-year period. But a pending general election and the pressure of mounting unemployment in the depressed areas persuaded Baldwin to extend entitlement to transitional payments for an additional year. Bondfield, supported by Arthur Greenwood, Labour's Minister of Health, also proposed in 1929 that the '30 contributions in two years' rule should be applied to all claimants, subjecting those unable to satisfy the condition to a means test. Instead the Labour Cabinet, loath to thrust the burden of the longer-term unemployed on to the Poor Law authorities, adopted the line of least resistance, agreeing in March 1930 to extend the preferential payment of transitional benefit for yet a further year to April 1931. More than that, the cost of transitional

[38] Rodgers, 'Work and Welfare', 258.
[39] Cab 24/202, CP63, Unemployment Insurance, Memorandum by the Minister of Labour, 2 March 1929; Cab 27/396, Unemployment Insurance: '30 Contributions' Rule. Departmental Memorandum by the Minister of Labour and Minister of Health, 29 July 1929. Steel-Maitland considered but rejected an alternative policy of subjecting all claimants after April 1930 to the '30 contributions rule' but in stages, making the qualifying number of contributions ten in the first year, 20 in the second and 30 in the third.

payments was henceforth to be transferred from the Unemployment Fund to the Exchequer, in effect entrenching a system of direct state dole.

For all this manoeuvring the government was still without any systematic policy towards the relief of the able-bodied unemployed. Increasingly, the interests of the majority of those contributing to the insurance scheme were being affected by a smaller but significant section of the workforce which had come to regard benefit without full contributions as a right and whose membership included from 1930 a number of persons who were not likely, even with improved industrial conditions, to obtain regular insurable employment. Moreover, the provision of maintenance outside the public assistance scheme, without any of the tests which normally accompanied either contributory insurance or Poor Law payments, made a mockery of denying benefit to those in agriculture and domestic service who were not covered by insurance at all.

The government was faced with three options. It could continue renewing the transitional period for particular groups of workers on an emergency basis; or it could initiate a more permanent dual system of contributory insurance for normal insured workers and Exchequer maintenance for all other able-bodied unemployed not entitled to ordinary benefit (in effect making the unemployed a national charge); or it could retain and develop the contributory insurance scheme, but transfer to the public assistance authorities, for relief according to need, those without a legitimate claim to insurance benefit.

CLEANSING THE SYSTEM

Neither the first nor the third option found any significant support within government. However, in July 1930 an all-party Advisory Committee on Unemployment Insurance proposed a scheme intermediate between insurance and the Poor Law.[40] Transitional benefit would be abolished but provision would be made 'for individual examination of the claimant's needs, both as regards maintenance and remedial treatment', with benefits financed by the Exchequer. Cabinet Ministers demurred yet again. Bereft of an agreed policy, the Labour government found refuge in the time-honoured fashion, announcing in October 1930 the appointment of a

---

[40] Bondfield, Greenwood and Vernon Hartshorn (Minister of Labour, Minister of Health and Lord Privy Seal respectively) represented the government, Sir Henry Betterton and Major W. Elliot the Conservatives, and Isaac Foot and Ernest Brown the Liberals. Its terms of reference were 'to receive from the Government a statement showing an analysis of the figures of unemployment and the financial payments from the Exchequer, and to consider if it is possible to come to some agreement on the questions they raise'. Cab 27/429, Advisory Committee on Unemployment Insurance, September 1930.

Royal Commission on Unemployment Insurance charged with the unenviable task of recommending the means by which the insurance scheme could be restored to solvency and the arrangements that ought to be made for assisting the unemployed falling outside its provisions.

Official concern to separate unemployment insurance from what in effect amounted to the payment of state relief to large numbers of the unemployed developed against a background of rising indebtedness and frequent allegations of abuse of the system. Already the borrowing powers of the Unemployment Fund had been increased to £50 million in March 1930, to £60 million in July and to £70 million in December, whilst Treasury advances in support of the unemployed amounted by the end of the year to nearly £60 million. 'Is it, or is it not, possible', asked *The Economist*, 'to make a clear division between two incompatible things which are merging in confusion – real actuarial insurance, and State relief pure and simple? . . . Charity and insurance cannot live together. Justice, as well as expediency, calls for their divorce'.[41] The Economic Advisory Council's Committee of Economists likewise complained that the insurance scheme was

now gravely abused. [It] impedes mobility from industry to industry. It encourages the adoption of methods for meeting fundamental industrial change, such as short-time . . . which tend to aggravate the disease it was intended to cure. It conduces to an artificial rigidity of wage rates and it constitutes a definite tax on employment.[42]

Contemporary allegations that the insurance scheme was being wilfully manipulated by the unemployed for personal gain were rarely substantiated. Such strictures nonetheless fed parliamentary critics with a wholesome diet of spurious innuendo and disingenuous 'fact' and they certainly played on Ramsay MacDonald's colourful imagination. But there was little evidence at the time and little has been produced since to suggest that abuse of the insurance scheme by 'work-shy' individuals or by a majority of employers intent on reducing working costs at the state's expense was a major source of justified concern.[43]

[41] *The Economist*, 23 August 1930.
[42] Cab 58/11, Economic Advisory Council, Committee of Economists, Report, 24 October 1930, para 41. MacDonald created the Economic Advisory Council in 1930 to keep him informed as to the state of the economy and as a forum for economists and other experts to suggest possible policy responses. A Committee of Civil Research had been appointed in 1925 for a similar purpose, and was itself the result of a proposal dating back at least to 1918 to have an established committee of economic enquiry. The Committee of Civil Research was absorbed into the Economic Advisory Council whose origins and activities are discussed fully in S. Howson and D. Winch, *The Economic Advisory Council, 1930–1939* (Cambridge, 1977).
[43] There were few allegations of fraudulent or illegal claims. The major complaint was that there were many claimants who, whilst acting within the letter of the law, had no moral

Labour Ministers realized, however, that it was only by offering some hope of a systematic reform of the insurance scheme, and particularly the correction of so-called 'abuses', that parliamentary approval would be forthcoming for the extra borrowing urgently required by the Unemployment Fund. They were urged by the Economic Advisory Council to restore a strict ratio of days of benefit to contributions, and to subject the payment of non-insurance relief to a means test accompanied either by work or by training.[44] Some way had to be found of stemming the mounting insolvency of the Unemployment Fund before the equilibrium of the budget was entirely wrecked. The cost to the Treasury of transitional benefit alone in 1931 was estimated to be of the order of £30 million; the burden of unemployment relief expenditure, warned the Chancellor of the Exchequer Philip Snowden, was threatening a Budget deficit the scale of which was likely to shatter confidence both at home and abroad.

Both the straightened circumstances of the Exchequer and the falling cost of living seemed to point to the need for a general reduction in the level of benefits. Sir Alfred Watson, Government Actuary, estimated in February 1931 that if benefits were reduced by one-fifth and adult male contributions increased by 5d per week (with proportionally smaller increases in the case of women and juveniles), the Fund's deficit would fall to only £10 million per annum on the basis of the prevailing level of registered unemployment.[45] In the same month the Minister of Labour herself raised the possibility of cutting benefit rates by 15 per cent and of introducing special restrictions on payments to married women and short-time workers. She even suggested abolishing transitional payments altogether.[46]

Such proposals were too immediately damaging to the unemployed to secure ready approval, but they illustrate the extent to which influential members of the government were moving slowly if uncertainly towards disentangling the principle of insurance from the morass of dole expenditure. Lansbury, Commissioner of Works, was one of the few who urged caution, arguing in Cabinet on 6 February:

The amount of benefit at present paid is, in most cases, miserably small . . . I am not convinced that retrenchment and reduction of expenditure on social services . . . is

claim to benefit. For discussion of the claim that unemployment benefits encouraged voluntary unemployment, see chapter 1.

[44] Cab 58/11, Economic Advisory Council, Committee on Unemployment Benefit. Report, 5 November 1930.

[45] *The Economist*, 21 February 1931.

[46] Deacon, 'Genuinely Seeking Work?' 210–13. MacDonald recognized the implications of such proposals and insisted that all copies of the relevant memorandum be handed in at the end of the Cabinet meeting.

money well saved . . . It is consumption that is needed, and every reduction in wages or reduction in unemployment pay, means a reduction in consumption.[47]

But however much economy was desirable, the urgent financial needs of the unemployed had to be met. The only practicable means then thought to be available was by increased borrowing. Thus from March 1931 the borrowing powers of the Unemployment Fund were further increased by £20 million to £90 million while transitional benefit payments were extended for six months after the date, 18 April 1931, on which they were due to expire.[48] *The Economist* voiced the exasperation of contemporary hard-line critics who felt that the growing demand for substantial reductions in unemployment expenditure was continually being deflected. It was, it argued:

The most mistaken kindness . . . to delude people into the belief that pensions for the able-bodied unemployed, at rates little below the economic wage in most trades, can indefinitely be maintained, regardless of individual need save at the risk of placing on our national finances a quite intolerable strain . . . The impossibility of continuing unemployment insurance as an undisguised dole, on the basis of a supposedly inexhaustible cash-box, wide open to every claimant, remains impossible.[49]

Meanwhile the Royal Commission on Unemployment Insurance was patiently gathering its evidence, receiving from the Ministry of Labour detailed analysis of alleged 'abuses' of the insurance scheme, from the Treasury repeated warnings of the intolerable strain which unemployment expenditure was imposing on the Exchequer, and from the TUC an impassioned plea for higher benefits financed by a graduated tax on incomes and payable for the entire duration of a person's unemployment. The Commission's Interim Report, issued in June 1931, was of cold comfort to the unemployed. It recommended a 2s reduction in adult standard benefit and a limit on the duration of payment to 26 weeks in any one year. 'There is no warrant for the assumption', the Report claimed, 'that unemployment benefit is or ever has been intended to provide full maintenance'. Although transitional benefit was to continue, it would be paid at the lower rate of standard benefit and would be means-tested in the case of single adults, married women and those in receipt of fixed incomes other than savings. Moreover, in an effort to rectify 'anomalies', married women and seasonal workers would be asked to prove that they had not abandoned insurable

---

[47] Cab 27/440, Panel of Ministers on Unemployment. Memorandum by the First Commissioner of Works, 6 February 1931. The spirit of Lansbury's proposals, however, was more Hobsonian than Keynesian. He urged that the attack on underconsumption should be linked to plans for a redistribution of wealth via an emergency tax on all incomes over £500 net, to be collected at source.   [48] See p. 50 above.
[49] *The Economist*, 21 February 1931.

employment and could 'reasonably expect' to obtain work in their locality. On the finance of insurance scheme, the Report recommended an immediate increase in the rate of contribution for the three parties involved. In all, such measures were expected on a live register of 2.5 million to reduce the annual deficit on the Unemployment Fund to £7.6 million and to cut by £30 million the total charge falling upon the Exchequer.[50]

In the main, employers welcomed the Interim Report even though the Commission had ducked the question of the future of transitional benefit claimants. Reaction within the labour movement was predictably hostile, not least because cuts in unemployment benefit were regarded as the precursor of a more general onslaught on wages.[51] Early in June the General Council of the TUC announced preparations for mass demonstrations against the Report and won the support of the miners, engineers and ship-builders.[52] But it soon became clear that the Government was unwilling to implement the Commission's principal recommendations. Though Ministers were willing to assuage public discontent by promising immediate action on anomalies, they refused to commit themselves to any systematic overhaul of the insurance system, least of all by reducing benefit levels or imposing a means test on transitional benefit claimants.[53]

The rapid introduction of an Anomalies Bill on 19 June 1931 reflected the government's calculated desire to be seen to be doing something about unemployment insurance without risking the vehement opposition that would result from altering the prevailing level of benefits and contributions. Representatives of the Independent Labour Party gave the Bill a stormy reception, pleading eloquently on behalf of the unemployed about to be dispossessed. But it was the argument that only by ridding the insurance scheme of 'sponging' could the rights of the genuinely employed be safeguarded that proved the more persuasive and the Bill passed into law on 31 July 1931. The Anomalies Regulations proved particularly successful in excluding married women from insurance. Such claimants were now to be disallowed benefit unless they had actually worked for a period since marriage and could prove that they were actively seeking work and likely to

[50] First Report of the Royal Commission on Unemployment Insurance, Cmd. 3872, 1930–31, paras 89, 96–7, 101, 119–25. Two Labour members of the Commission produced a Minority Report which rejected the suggested changes and called for the maintenance of the unemployed at a rate of subsistence no lower than the level then prevailing.
[51] Classical economists in the 1920s had stressed the effect which unemployment benefit had had in strengthening trade union resistance to wage cuts. Reductions in unemployment benefit were viewed, therefore, as an effective means of dismantling such resistance. For further discussion see chapter 10.
[52] R. Skidelsky, *Politicians and the Slump. The Labour Government of 1929–1931* (1970), 315.
[53] Cab 27/472, Unemployment Insurance. Report of Cabinet Committee, 9 June 1931.

obtain it in their local district.[54] By the end of March 1932 over 82 per cent of married women's claims had been disallowed. During the same period 75 per cent of seasonal workers' claims were rejected primarily because the claimants could not prove that in the 'off-season' of the preceding two years they had been in insurable employment to any substantial extent.

On the face of it, the decision to confine legislation to the narrow issue of anomalies pending the final report of the Royal Commission seemed but yet another reminder of the pusillanimity with which unemployment relief policy had developed. MacDonald's second administration had managed to defer taking the kind of action which would have had some direct effect upon the finances of the insurance scheme. It had resisted the efforts of Cabinet colleagues in June 1930 to have the long-term unemployed excluded from insurance, it had refused to impose a cut in benefits in February 1931 and it had rejected the Royal Commission's proposals for increasing contributions and reducing benefits.

In truth, the benefits system had by this time fallen into such disarray that it was almost impossible for Ministers to mount any effective defence of official policy. Although governments must be credited for having assumed direct responsibility throughout the 1920s for a nation-wide system of relief, providing the majority of the unemployed with some form of basic income support of rising real value, they had nevertheless brought the scheme into disrepute by recurring deficits, by the commitments and contradictions embodied in a barrage of insurance legislation, and by the apparently frequent need to tighten up on 'abuse'. Nor was there any easy escape from criticism since it was the central authorities rather than individual industries that had come to dominate the scene. Higher unemployment and proportionately lower wages among skilled workers in the staple trades had made it increasingly difficult for unions to raise the contributions required to fund their own comprehensive systems of support. Although the 1920 Insurance Act permitted industries to 'contract out' of the state scheme, it did so only on the most disadvantageous terms, thereby undermining the possibility, subsumed in the 1911 Act, of unemployment benefits and contributions being allowed to vary between different in-

---

[54] The Regulations were amended in 1933 following the growing opposition to one clause relating to the 'industrial circumstances of the district' that had led increasingly to disallowances of benefit simply because of general industrial depression, rather than because women had withdrawn from the labour market. The clause was subsequently changed to read: 'her expectation of obtaining insurable employment in that district is not less than it would otherwise be by reason of the fact that she is a married woman'. See J. Tomlinson, 'Women as "Anomalies": The Anomalies Regulations of 1931, Their Background and Implications', *Public Administration*, 62 (1984), 423–37.

dustrial sectors according to their level of risk. Even the facility to 'contract out' was abolished in the late 1920s.[55]

Once the actuarial basis of the insurance scheme was breached in 1921 to cater for those whose contributions record had collapsed, mass unemployment worked subsequently to transform the system into a publicly funded state service. This development was welcomed by a labour movement anxious to have social security established as an issue of public policy rather than one of private responsibility. But it was vehemently opposed by organized employers who viewed the financial burden of unemployment relief expenditure, imposed without proper regard for the variable risks faced by different types of industry or worker, as a prime cause of continued industrial depression. Treasury denunciation of the indebtedness of the Unemployment Fund, moreover, conveniently ignored certain realities, particularly the extent to which its own officials had fought hard in the twenties to minimize state contributions to the Fund, the manner in which insurance contributions had been hijacked for the relief of the non-insured, and the faintheartedness with which policies had been pursued to reduce the volume of unemployment which the Fund was expected to relieve.

At the heart of the problem was the political decision to render the insurance system a substitute for rather than a supplement to the Poor Law, forcing it to undertake the task of relieving long-term unemployment, for which it was clearly unsuited, instead of allowing it to meet the needs of the short-term cyclically unemployed. This compounded the problem which the system was designed to resolve, but no practical alternative strategy was ever proferred at the time. As a consequence the basis of the scheme was transformed from one in which the principle of insurance pre-dominated into a mixed system in which the insurance element became increasingly subordinated to the element of relief.[56] Little wonder critics were alarmed when the government's Chief Actuary, even in 1927, was

---

[55] Only two special schemes were established for insurance and banking before the provision was suspended in 1927. Space does not permit a full discussion of the debate surrounding 'insurance by industry'. Further details can be found in Ministry of Labour, Report on the Administration of Section 18 of the Unemployment Insurance Act, 1920. Special Schemes of Unemployment Insurance by Industries, Cmd. 1613, 1923; Rodgers, 'Work and Welfare', 137–64; R. Lowe, 'Welfare Legislation and the Unions During and After the First World War' and N. Whiteside, 'Industrial Labour and Welfare Legislation After the First World War: A Reply', *Historical Journal*, 25 (1982), 443–6.

[56] R. Lowe, *Adjusting to Democracy. The Role of the Ministry of Labour in British Politics, 1916–1939* (Oxford, 1986), chapter 5 and Whiteside, 'Social Welfare and Industrial Relations 1914–39', 211–42.

framing estimates for the finance of a permanent insurance scheme on the basis of an expected average rate of unemployment of only 6 per cent.

The fact remained that the easier qualifying conditions for the receipt of benefit laid down in the twenties, together with the increase in the proportion of total contributions borne by public funds, had shifted the financial burden of the unemployment relief scheme from its immediate beneficiaries to their employers and the general taxpayers. Governments had found it easier politically to relax the limitations and safeguards of the 1911 Act than attempt to expand employment opportunities on any realistic scale, but their later efforts to restrict claims on the public purse failed to contain mounting criticism of official policy. Ministers found themselves continually torn between two sets of pressures, one demanding economy, balanced budgets, reduced taxes and limited insurance, the other demanding publicly supported standards of living for the involuntarily unemployed. Once Britain's budgetary problems became caught up in the international financial crisis of the early thirties it was inevitable that the insurance scheme would come under further sustained attack.

UNEMPLOYMENT INSURANCE AND THE 1931 FINANCIAL CRISIS

From mid-1928 a steady rise occurred in the international demand for liquidity, particularly amongst primary producing countries anxious to regain their international investments in an effort to offset the drastic effects which the collapse of world commodity prices had had upon output and costs. The enforced bankruptcies and exchange depreciations which spread amongst them worsened during 1930. Capital outflows from creditor to debtor nations fell away as major financial centres such as France and the USA, facing their own bank crises, withdrew short-term capital from abroad. The European crisis came to a head in May 1931 with the collapse of the Credit Anstalt in Austria.

Foreign demand for liquidity increased enormously during June and July 1931 as continental banks sought desperately to preserve their own financial position. London's inability to retain short-term funds or to attract a substantial volume of additional foreign investment placed it in an unenviable position yet the Bank of England did little to check the sustained foreign disinvestment that was taking place. As interest rates fell, fears mounted over London's ability to maintain the gold standard. The sterling exchanges depreciated sharply on 15 July. Two days earlier the Final Report of the Macmillan Committee revealed the precarious position of London's short-term assets in relation to her foreign liabilities. The pressure put on sterling as a result of substantial gold losses to Paris and to other continental centres in the week after 15 July forced the Bank of England to consider ways of retaining confidence. Although gold losses eased by the end of the month, the Bank decided to strengthen its reserves and on 1 August obtained credits from New York and Paris totalling £50 million.

By this time politicians and bankers at home and abroad recognized that the efforts of the international financial community to protect sterling could be seriously undermined unless the British government took steps to improve the state of its own internal finances. Until the end of July 1931 the problems of external finance and growing unease about the Budget had co-existed without causing a major crisis of confidence. But during the early days of August the situation worsened noticeably as serious doubts arose over the stability of the British financial system. Borrowing for the Unemployment Fund had more than tripled between the financial years 1928/29 to 1931/32; the Fund's debt alone had increased from almost £25 million to £115 million. During the same period Exchequer liability for transitional benefit rose from nothing to £32.3 million.[57] Sir Richard Hopkins, Controller of Finance and Supply Services at the Treasury, issued his own warning to the Royal Commission on Unemployment Insurance in the winter of 1931. The enormity of Treasury loans, he maintained, 'are coming to represent, in effect, State obligations at the expense of the future, and this is the ordinary and well-recognised sign of an unbalanced Budget'.[58] The situation evoked such a campaign for economy that the government, under intense parliamentary pressure, accepted a Liberal demand in February 1931 that an independent enquiry be launched to investigate the means of balancing the Budget at a lower level.

But the resulting Committee on National Expenditure, chaired by Sir George May, merely exacerbated the already deep-seated anxiety over the cost of unemployment relief. Its final report, issued in July 1931, confidently (though mistakenly[59]) forecast that Britain's Budget deficit during 1931/32 would amount to £120 million. It was of paramount importance, it therefore claimed, that steps should be taken to stem the dangerous proclivity of politicians to increase social services expenditure, not least when it appeared to threaten national solvency. To meet the expected deficit, the Committee proposed increased taxation of £23.5 million and a £96.5 million reduction in national expenditure, £66.5 million of which was to come from cuts in unemployment insurance. It proposed a 20 per

---

[57] Final Report of the Royal Commission on Unemployment Insurance, Cmd. 4185, 1932, para. 668, cited in Lowe, *Adjusting to Democracy*, 138.

[58] Royal Commission on Unemployment Insurance. *Minutes of Evidence*, 29 January 1931, Vol. I, 381–91, 1932.

[59] This exaggerated figure was arrived at by including in current expenditure not only the borrowings of the unemployment insurance and road funds, but also annual provision for the redemption of the National Debt. This was taking the fetish for economy to the extreme.

cent cut in standard benefit, an increase in weekly insurance contributions, a limitation on the receipt of benefit to 26 weeks in any year, and the replacement of transitional benefit by means-tested assistance available only from Public Assistance Committees.[60]

International creditors viewed the gloomy predictions of the May Report with mounting alarm. Without investigating thoroughly whether British domestic indebtedness actually threatened her exchange standard or her ability to meet outstanding foreign obligations, they began almost immediately to make the availability of extended credit to Britain conditional upon the imposition of substantial economies aimed at balancing the Budget. Keynes, whose views on the May Report MacDonald had sought for 'guidance', warned of the 'futile and disastrous' consequences of accepting a deflationary policy to restore foreign confidence. 'The *first* effect of adopting the proposals of the Economy Committee', he wrote on 5 August:

would certainly be a further decline in business profits and a substantial increase of unemployment, because economies which are not balanced by reduced taxation must necessarily reduce demand relatively to supply, – the buying power of those immediately affected would be diminished, whilst no one else's buying power would be increased.[61]

In his view the only effective policy in a period of deep recession was to accept the inevitability of increased government borrowing – 'to suspend the Sinking Fund, to continue to borrow for the Unemployment Fund, and to impose a revenue tariff'.[62]

The May Report left no one in doubt that anticipated borrowing on behalf of the Unemployment Insurance Fund posed the greatest threat to sound budgetary practice. Immediately following its publication, MacDonald appointed a Cabinet Economy Committee[63] to consider over the parliamentary recess possible reductions in government expenditure. Its first meeting,

---

[60] Report of Committee on National Expenditure, Cmd. 3920, 1931. Apart from the reduction in unemployment expenditure, cuts were also proposed in education (£14 million), in the road programme (£8 million), and in the pay of teachers, police and the armed services.

[61] Letter to J. Ramsay MacDonald, 5 August 1931, cited in *The Collected Writings of John Maynard Keynes*, Volume 20, *Activities 1929–31. Rethinking Employment and Unemployment Policies*, ed. D. Moggridge (1981), 591. Volumes in this series are referred to hereafter as *JMK*.

[62] J. M. Keynes, 'Some Consequences of the Economy Report', *New Statesmen and Nation*, 15 August 1931. Months before the financial crisis came to a head, Keynes had joined other members of the Economic Advisory Council in recommending a balanced budget without increased direct taxes to help revive business confidence. This was to be accompanied by a revenue tariff and the stimulation of home investment, partly by public works and partly by reducing British overseas investment.

[63] Its members were the Prime Minister (MacDonald), the Chancellor of the Exchequer (Snowden), the Secretary for Foreign Affairs (Henderson), the Secretary of State for Dominion Affairs (Thomas) and the President of the Board of Trade (Graham).

scheduled for 25 August, was brought forward to 12 August as the financial crisis worsened. There was growing suspicion abroad that a socialist government would never carry through the necessary scale of economies for fear of political suicide. During the Committee's first meeting, Snowden informed his colleagues that the forthcoming budget deficit was likely, according to Treasury estimates, to be £170 million and not the £120 million forecast by the May Committee, primarily because of the burden of increased payments of unemployment insurance and transitional benefit. MacDonald and Snowden made it clear from the outset that they favoured ending the crisis, not by devaluation, but by eliminating the Budget deficit. The Chancellor was prepared to impose a 20 per cent reduction in the rate of standard benefit, raise insurance contributions and cut Exchequer support for transitional benefit.[64]

Members of the Economy Committee finally recommended cuts in national expenditure of £82 million (some £14.5 million less than the May Committee suggested) of which £45.5 million would be found from economies in unemployment relief payments. But they baulked at the idea of attacking standard benefit; savings would have to be found by alternative means. An increase in weekly insurance contributions to 10d, the Committee judged, could yield £10 million net of Exchequer contributions, the correction of 'anomalies' £3 million, a reduction in the maximum period for the receipt of standard benefit to 26 weeks £10 million, the imposition of a 1s a week deduction from all unemployment benefits, the so-called 'premium', £2.5 million, while an additional £20 million could be found by transferring the cost of transitional benefit from the Exchequer to the Poor Law authorities.

Although the government shared the Economy Committee's concern to restore confidence, it was not prepared to seek budgetary equilibrium at any cost. The suggested saving of £20 million from the transference of transitional benefit claimants to the Poor Law proved too much for the Labour administration to contemplate. A separate committee, chaired by the Minister of Labour, was hurriedly appointed to devise by noon the following day (20 August) a scheme which, in its financial results, would effect a similar £20 million saving without having to resort to the Economy Committee's proposal. Bondfield's response only added to the gloom. The savings necessary to cover transitional benefit expenditure, she reported, would have to be in the order of £28.5 million, and not £20 million as originally claimed. The idea of a 'premium' was condemned in principle; it was, after all, a small cut in benefit under another name. There was a

[64] W. H. Janeway, 'The Economic Policy of the Second Labour Government, 1929–31', Ph.D. Thesis, University of Cambridge (1971), 247–8.

possibility of raising £4 million by increasing workers' insurance contributions by an extra 2d to 1s a week, and an additional £5 million if the government was prepared to consider means-testing transitional benefit 'through such local machinery as may be devised'. But even if all the foregoing suggestions were adopted, there would still remain to be found, out of the revised figure of £28.5 million, a sum upwards of £19.5 million.[65] Yet if the government were to reject the 'premium' proposal and refuse to transfer the cost of transitional payments to the Poor Law authorities, offering only to raise an additional £4 million from increased insurance contributions, the scale of the adjustment borne by unemployment expenditure would amount to £27 million compared with the recommended £45.5 million.[66]

This was hardly a recipe for success. The Opposition parties were demanding substantial cuts in benefit payments; at the same time the TUC was urging equality of sacrifice, calling for new taxation on fixed-interest securities, a reduction in the burden of war debt through the suspension of the Sinking Fund, and the imposition of a graduated levy on the entire community in aid of the jobless.[67] The Cabinet was being pushed inexorably towards the agonizing choice of either abandoning its search for outside credits to defend the pound, or seeking to defend sterling by agreeing to much larger cuts in benefit expenditure.

Whereas pressure from the Bank of England and the Federal Reserve Bank of New York during the second week in August focussed on the need for a general reduction in government expenditure rather than upon specified cuts, the Deputy Governor of the Bank of England was telling MacDonald on 21 August that it was 'essential, particularly from the point of view of the foreign interests concerned, that very substantial economies should be effected on Unemployment Insurance. In no other way could foreign confidence be restored.'[68] But the bankers' scare and the sterling crisis merely reinforced what government ministers already knew – that substantial economies needed to be found to balance the Budget and to forestall such tax increases as might further damage industry and employment.

---

[65] Cab 27/458, CP 204. Cabinet Committee on Unemployment Insurance Finance. Report, 20 August 1931.
[66] That is, £3 million from the correction of 'anomalies', £14 million from increased insurance contributions and £10 million from the limit on the duration of standard benefit.
[67] D. Marquand, *Ramsay MacDonald* (1977), 620. Both Keynes and the TUC shared a desire to protect unemployment payments and were agreed upon the need to suspend the Sinking Fund. But whereas the TUC linked this with a demand for increased progressive taxation to finance benefits, Keynes feared that such a policy would deprive producers of profit. He argued instead that the Unemployment Fund should be sustained by further borrowing.   [68] Cab 23/67, Cabinet Minutes 43 (31), 21 August 1931.

The Cabinet immediately reviewed its previous economy programme in a desperate effort to save the situation. An 11.5 per cent reduction in standard benefit (in line with the fall in the cost of living from the 1929 average to the beginning of 1931) would yield £15 million; a 10 per cent cut on the other hand would save £12.5 million. No one in Cabinet believed that an alternative suggestion, of a 5 per cent reduction, would be of much practical consequence in the prevailing climate. Opinion remained divided over whether to impose a 10 per cent cut or none at all. Although the government was prepared to accept Bondfield's suggestion of subjecting transitional payments to a means test to save £5 million and to increase workers' insurance contributions by a further 2d to raise £4 million, this could only produce a saving of £22 million on unemployment expenditure.[69] The opposition parties, seeking greater economy in total national expenditure than the government was then suggesting (£56.4 million), were never likely to accept such proposals.

MacDonald pressed the Cabinet on 22 August to agree to an additional £20 million cut in national expenditure, £12.5 million of which would come from a 10 per cent reduction in standard benefit and £7.5 million 'in other ways'. They refused. When late on 23 August it appeared that bankers in New York and England were prepared to discuss the availability of credits on the basis of such an economy programme, the Prime Minister made a last minute attempt to win the Cabinet's unambiguous approval for a cut in unemployment benefit. He conceded that his proposal 'represented the negation of everything the Labour Party stood for', but he urged the Cabinet to accept it for the sake of national stability. After all, he warned, 'a scheme which inflicted reductions and burdens in almost every other direction, but made no appreciable cut in Unemployment Insurance benefit, would alienate much support and lose the Party their moral prestige which was one of their greatest assets'.[70] Eleven members of the Cabinet voted in favour of a 10 per cent cut in benefit, nine against, some of whom threatened to resign rather than accept the proposals. Since the foreign loan necessary to stem the financial crisis was dependent upon the Cabinet accepting MacDonald's economy programme as a whole, it was unthink-

---

[69] That is, this £9 million added to £3 million from the correction of 'anomalies' and the £10 million originally expected from an increase in insurance contributions to 10d. The Cabinet minutes record that there was some discussion about including the 'premium' in the list of revised economies to produce a saving of £2.5 million. A note to that effect was drafted but then crossed out. The Cabinet's Deputy Secretary subsequently reported that the Cabinet had proved hostile to the idea and had no intention of adopting the proposal. The Secretary of State for Foreign Affairs is recorded, however, as having 'vigorously asserted the opinion that the Cabinet had definitely accepted the proposal on August 21st'. Cab 23/67, Cabinet Minutes 43 (31), Note by the Deputy Secretary, 26 August 1931.

[70] Cab 23/67, Cabinet Minutes 43 (31), 23 August 1931.

able that the government could remain in office. On 24 August the Labour government fell, having refused to allow either circumstance or party pressure to force it to accept a policy essentially at variance with its basic political and humanitarian instincts.

The formation of a National Government on 24 August under Baldwin, MacDonald and Samuel revealed the strength of the conviction, long held by financiers abroad, that the restoration of confidence depended primarily upon a declared parliamentary consensus within Britain. Indeed within three days of its establishment, loans totalling £40 million were secured from New York and Paris to assist sterling, before any decisions had been made about specific reductions in national expenditure. The report of a new Cabinet Economy Committee issued on 28 August recommended a £70.3 million reduction in national expenditure, some £36.8 million of which would be borne by unemployment insurance, a proposed 11 per cent reduction in standard benefit adding £14.8 million to Labour's previous economy package. The idea of transferring the cost of transitional benefits to the local authorities was dropped in favour of making the Ministry of Labour ultimately responsible for such payments, leaving the determination of the actual amounts to be paid to the discretion of the Public Assistance authorities.[71]

When the time finally came to act on benefit levels the National Government proved less vindictive than might have been anticipated, suggesting that previous Conservative threats to cut deep into the insurance system had merely been part of a determined political strategy to expose Labour at its weakest point. Just over half of the target savings in national expenditure (£70 million) was to be borne by unemployment payments – £13 million from a 10 per cent cut in standard benefit (half the reduction recommended by the May Committee and less than the National Government's own Economy Committee had suggested), £3 million from the correction of 'anomalies', £10 million from increased weekly insurance contributions, and a further £10 million from the introduction of means-tested transitional payments. The duration of the now reduced standard benefit was fixed at 26 weeks and restricted to those claimants who had paid 30 contributions in the previous two years.[72]

Thus the dilemma of the twenties – what to do with the 'industrial'

---

[71] Cab 24/233, CP 208, Economy Committee Report, 28 August 1931.
[72] Persons who drew 26 weeks' benefit in one year were allowed to claim benefit in the following year if, in addition to satisfying the standard requirement of 30 contributions in the past two years, they had paid 10 additional contributions since the last benefit was drawn. Nevertheless the immediate effect of the new contributory rule was to disallow some 800,000 of the 2,800,000 people then drawing benefit.

unemployed who had exhausted their right to benefit – was met by dividing those out of work into two distinct groups and imposing upon the long-term unemployed a means test as a qualification for state assistance, a decision which ultimately forced a major reconstruction of the unemployment benefits system.

3 * Means to an end: insurance, assistance and the categorization of the unemployed, 1932–1939

TRANSITIONAL PAYMENTS AND THE COMING OF THE
UNEMPLOYMENT ASSISTANCE BOARD

The economy measures announced in mid-September 1931 succeeded temporarily in stemming the drain on gold reserves, enabling new foreign loans to be raised. But Britain was unable to shield herself sufficiently from the continuing crisis in international finance and further panic flights of foreign capital from London forced the authorities to abandon the gold standard on 21 September.[1] Anyone who expected that a release from the discipline of gold would usher in a more expansionist budgetary stance was soon to be disillusioned. The sudden departure in November 1931 from the principle of indefinite extensions of relief payments was an instinctive reaction to the mounting insolvency of the Unemployment Fund and a reflection of the government's determination to remove any lingering doubt as to the less eligible status of those unable to qualify for insurance benefit.

Henceforth the maximum amount payable to those persons already drawing transitional benefit and to those about to do so, including those who had reached the 26 weeks' limit of insurance benefit, was to be equal to the amount of standard benefit (now reduced) to which applicants would have been entitled if they could have satisfied the contributory requirements. Applicants were required to meet the same conditions as insurance claimants regarding availability for work and willingness to accept suitable employment. But there was to be no agreed schedule of payments; they were to be determined according to need, with the local authorities acting in each case as if they were assessing a claim for public assistance. The use of a means test outside of the Poor Law was, of course, not new. Payment of uncovenanted and, later, extended benefit had in theory been made conditional upon a means test between 1922 and 1928, with a break in 1924–25. Nonetheless the introduction of means-tested benefits caused

---

[1] See chapter 5.

immediate alarm among the unemployed, one of whom wrote to the Prime Minister in September 1931 asking whether or not it would be necessary to sell one's home in order to claim transitional benefit. He was assured it would not.[2] But neither setting the maximum amount of transitional payments at the level of standard benefit nor the decision to have the determination of eligibility conducted at the Employment Exchanges by Public Assistance Committees (PACs) proved sufficient to free the transitional scheme from the stigma of the Poor Law. 'Applicants for transitional benefit', the TUC complained bitterly, 'are . . . treated as if they were liars and malingerers (who) . . . cannot be trusted with a few shillings.'[3]

Although in essence the transitional payments scheme was a pragmatic device for alleviating the indebtedness of the Unemployment Fund by denying benefit to those whose insurance rights had expired and who could not prove need, its ultimate significance lay in the way in which it forced the authorities to seek a more permanent solution to the problem of able-bodied relief. There is no denying that it effected some saving to the Treasury, though it is difficult to determine the precise amount since the levels of benefit and unemployment prevailing before and after November 1931 are not comparable. In the country as a whole, about 50 per cent of applicants were granted transitional payments at the full rate between November 1931 and January 1935, while 31 to 35 per cent were granted payments which averaged 73 per cent of the full rate. Further savings were made when applicants whose cases were reviewed after eight weeks found their payments renewed at a lower rate. The Ministry of Labour estimated that the system saved the national Exchequer approximately £44.5 million between 1932 and 1934, a sum equal to about one-third of the actual expenditure on transitional payments in the period.[4]

To a considerable extent the potential for saving money depended upon active co-operation between central and local government and difficulties arose almost from the outset. The Ministers of Health and Labour reported as early as the second week in January 1932 that a number of local authorities were reluctant even to start the scheme, some threatening to strike.[5] At the heart of the problem was the decision to apply to the unemployed the same standards of assessment of need as those used for determining Poor Law assistance. The level of insurance benefits set the maximum amount which any family could hope to receive, whereas the prevailing scale of local relief determined what proportion of the tran-

[2] Cab 27/463, Emergency Business Committee, 16 October 1931.
[3] W. Hannington, *Ten Lean Years: An Investigation of the Record of the National Government in the Field of Unemployment* (1940), 47.
[4] E. Burns, *British Unemployment Programs, 1920–1938* (Washington, 1941), 140–1.
[5] Cab 24/227, CP 8, Transitional Benefits, 11 January 1932.

sitional rate was necessary to bring the household up to the local standard of maintenance.

This inevitably gave rise to unwelcome anomalies. Widespread variations arose in the severity with which the means test was administered, primarily because, with the Exchequer financing transitional payments, there was less incentive for the local committees to administer the scheme economically. Authorities were free to define the household resources and level of income that might be set against the needs of a family, but had to apply their chosen standards to workers of differing industrial backgrounds. Those authorities who sought to apply deterrent standards invoked bitter resentment among able-bodied workers whose rights to insurance benefit had been lost only because of continued unemployment and the operation of the 26 weeks' rule; other authorities who wished to grant applicants more favourable treatment were obliged to operate two different scales of relief at a time when the dividing line between the unemployed who could or could not qualify for transitional payments was becoming increasingly blurred.

In practice the rules 'tended to follow election returns . . . There was no discernible relation of relief to need, only a relation to the extent to which a party was firmly entrenched in a given area.'[6] Some authorities regarded transitional payments as an extension of insurance and therefore a matter of contractual right. Others adopted very different standards as to what constituted an individual's available resources, especially with regard to such items as capital assets, workmen's compensation, disability pensions and savings. In Leicester and Manchester, applicants had to have spent all but £5 of their savings before benefit was allowed; in Edinburgh they were permitted to keep as much as £500.[7] There were equally glaring discrepancies between the proportion of income, especially earnings from dependent adults, regarded as available to an applicant for the purpose of determining need – variations which existed even between assessment committees within the same local authority.

The National Government, aware that the problem of permanent

[6] F. Miller, 'National Assistance or Unemployment Assistance? The British Cabinet and Relief Policy, 1932–33', *Journal of Contemporary History*, 9 (1974), 163–84.
[7] E. Briggs and A. Deacon, 'The Creation of the Unemployment Assistance Board', *Policy and Politics*, 2 (1973). The Minister of Labour, Henry Betterton, made his views on savings clear to the Prime Minister. 'The solution of the problem', he wrote on 7 June 1932, 'is not necessarily that the man with the savings should not use them. Many taxpayers have had to raid their small savings in recent months in order to meet taxes, required among other things to assist the unemployed. To pay transitional payments regularly to applicants known to possess two or three hundred pounds would quickly arouse bitter resentment, especially in Lancashire where many small shopkeepers, who are not insured, would be glad to get what the insured cotton operatives are complaining about'. Lab 2, 30/69/442, 1932.

provision for those falling outside the insurance scheme was still before the Royal Commission, was initially reluctant to press wayward authorities to comply with the established regulations. In any case the Minister of Labour had no power to regulate, only to supersede local PACs. Yet within three months of the inauguration of the scheme it became clear that several committees had little or no intention of co-operating with the government. Betterton, Minister of Labour, reported to the Cabinet in February 1932 that in parts of South Wales and Durham there was 'a definite disregard of the requirements . . . not in technical matters of detail, but violating flagrantly and deliberately the principle that assistance should be given only according to need'.[8] Whereas during the first seven months of 1932 the proportion of applicants receiving transitional payments at the full rate was 50.8 per cent for the country as a whole, it stood at 98.7 per cent in Rotherham, 98.8 per cent in Merthyr but at only 11.2 per cent in Aberdeen.[9] Commissioners were eventually appointed to administer the means test in Durham where the County Council refused to obey the law, and in Rotherham where it was reported that 'the determinations that have been given are not such that any Public Assistance Authority in the country would publicly defend them . . . Transitional payments at the full rate or a little less are being given to applicants who are members of a household with quite substantial incomes coming in.'[10] Even by mid-1934 it was reported that the Barnsley PAC was 'issuing determinations . . . at the full unemployment benefit rates in all cases, irrespective of the resources of the applicants', an act which Betterton construed as 'political' and 'a direct and deliberate defiance of the law'.[11]

Such notorious cases apart, it appears that the majority of PACs did not deliberately discriminate in favour of the unemployed; indeed, some operated relief scales below the reduced benefit rates even for applicants with no other resources. The impact of the means test lessened somewhat after 1932 as the government and the local authorities reached a tacit understanding, the former accepting the need for a certain degree of leniency and the latter, including many Labour authorities, agreeing to operate some form of modified test without openly flouting the principles of official policy. The Transitional Payments (Determination of Need) Act of

[8] Cab 24/228, CP 84, Administration of Transitional Payments. Memorandum by the Minister of Labour, 26 February, 1932.
[9] Burns, *British Unemployment Programs*, 130.
[10] Cab 24/230. CP 186, Administration of Transitional Payments, 10 June 1932. For details of the situation in Durham see Report to the Minister of Labour by the Commissioners appointed to Administer Transitional Payments in the County of Durham, Cmd. 4339, 1933.
[11] Cab 24/250. CP 192, Administration of Transitional Payments at Barnsley. Memorandum by the Minister of Labour, 16 July 1934.

November 1932 permitted the authorities to take a more generous view of income and savings in their determination of allowances.[12] In practice, however, only a fraction of the authorities adopted noticeably more lenient rules. The generosity of the Act, moreover, stopped short of any fundamental change in the household income rule. Government Inspectors informed the Prime Minister in November 1932 that allegations of families splitting up because of the reluctance of a dependent wage earner to have his income counted as part of household resources had 'very little substance'. To relax the regulations further, the Minister of Labour contended, would run 'the danger of destroying the whole basis of the Needs Test and seriously prejudice the ultimate solution of the problem'.[13]

The frustrations arising from the operation of the transitional payments scheme only masked a more fundamental problem, namely the continued absence of any permanent relief scheme able to deal effectively with an unemployment problem of varying characteristics and duration. Local authorities continually appealed for more precise definition of the conditions under which relief should be paid whilst the Treasury complained of the arrangement whereby local officials assessed the needs of the longer-term unemployed but the Exchequer found the money. Elsewhere in government support grew for a greater measure of central control over the payment of unemployment relief.

First indications of what kind of permanent provision might be made for the longer-term unemployed came with the publication in November 1932 of the final reports of the Royal Commission on Unemployment Insurance. The Majority Report, signed by five of the seven members, recommended the continuation of a dual scheme of unemployment insurance and relief, incorporating a system of discretionary means-tested payments administered by a new committee of the local authorities – the Unemployment Assistance Committee. Individual relief payments would continue to vary locally and be assessed according to household income. Although the

---

[12] The Act allowed 50 per cent of any disability pension or workmen's compensation to be disregarded for payment purposes. No regard was taken of the value of residential property. Capital in the form of money or investments was ignored up to the value of £25. Thereafter it was treated as equivalent to a weekly income of 1s for every £25 up to £300; capital over £300 was defined as being available to meet current living expenses.

[13] Cab 24/233, CP 345, The Needs Test. Memorandum by the Minister of Labour, 17 October 1932. Too little is known about the fate of those who were disallowed unemployment benefit and who did not apply for outdoor relief. A sample enquiry conducted at the request of the Royal Commission on Unemployment Insurance in 1931 found that the largest proportion of such individuals in the eight sample areas were supported either by their wives and children or by distant relatives, friends and neighbours. See Appendices to the Minutes of Evidence taken before the Royal Commission on Unemployment Insurance. Part III: *Report of a Special Investigation in Eight Industrial Areas into the Subsequent History of Persons with Disallowed Claims to Unemployment Benefit* (1931).

Report recommended that the Minister of Labour should exercise a greater measure of supervisory power, laying down general rules for the guidance of the new committees, it insisted that locally elected bodies should retain a substantial degree of independence. The Minority Report, on the other hand, argued in favour of eligibility for assistance being decided by a system of statutory rules administered by the Minister of Labour. The benefit payable to those outside of insurance would be determined on a non-discretionary basis according to an individual's declaration of personal income.[14]

Ministers found little comfort in any of the Commission's recommendations. The Minority's proposal to abolish the distinction between insurance and relief and to substitute, in effect, the principle of unconditional 'compensation for loss of employment' was never destined to gain approval, not least because of its prohibitive cost. At the same time, the unsatisfactory experience since 1931 with locally administered means-tested payments virtually ensured the rejection of the Majority's viewpoint. Fresh proposals were required, and the government promptly established its own Unemployment Insurance Committee to conduct the necessary enquiries.

Chamberlain, Chancellor of the Exchequer, offered the Committee the first alternative scheme of unemployment relief, arguing vigorously in December 1932 in favour of greater uniformity, economy and central control. Conscious of the political and social pressures which many local authorities had faced during their administration of centrally financed transitional payments, he proposed removing the local agencies entirely from any scheme of assistance, substituting instead administration by a quasi-judicial Statutory Commission, independent of parliamentary control. Under his plan, a sharp distinction was to be made between those entitled to insurance benefit and those not so entitled. The duties of the Ministry of Labour with regard to transitional payments and those falling to the Public Assistance Committees in connection with domiciliary relief would be transferred entirely to the Statutory Commission. There would be no separation between the various classes of persons not entitled to benefit; the unemployed, industrial and otherwise, plus all the able bodied on outdoor relief would receive means-tested assistance at public expense subject to nationally uniform rules.[15]

[14] Cmd. 4185, paras. 142–55, 278–94, 401. Local authorities were, however, to be encouraged to shoulder some financial responsibility for the scheme, with a proportion of their expenditure above a certain minimum level met by an Exchequer grant.

[15] Cab 27/552, CP 10, Unemployment Insurance Committee, Memorandum by the Chancellor of the Exchequer, 23 January 1933. Chamberlain's plan was supported by the Minister of Health who argued that if the idea of a Statutory Commission was rejected then the entire administration of outdoor relief (including transitional payments) should be handed over to the Public Assistance Committees, subject to increased financial aid from the Exchequer.

Unfortunately this form of nationalized poor relief, designed to remove public assistance from the realm of party politics, threatened not only to establish a distinct 'pauper class' among the unemployed, the majority of whom were neither unemployable nor destitute, but also to undermine all previous efforts to safeguard otherwise regular workers from the taint of the Poor Law. As such it was bitterly attacked by the Minister of Labour. It was absurd. Betterton maintained, to claim that a Statutory Commission would take unemployment relief out of politics. The administration of relief payments was an issue of acute parliamentary concern and debate; to abandon direct ministerial responsibility for such a task would be irresponsible, dangerous and a major political blunder. The Cabinet, particularly sensitive to the issue of ministerial responsibility, agreed. Although it endorsed Chamberlain's plan in principle on 25 January 1933 it called for further discussion of ways of safeguarding some measure of parliamentary control.

A draft Bill introduced by the Minister of Labour in April 1933 offered an alternative scheme. An Unemployment Assistance Board would be established with jurisdiction over all the unemployed under 65 who normally worked for a living. The Board would be subject to the Minister of Labour so far as relief standards were concerned but would be free from interference in executive administration. But neither the Treasury nor the Ministry of Health was prepared to countenance the separation of the long-term unemployed into a distinct group. The Chancellor of the Exchequer offered a compromise, suggesting a division of responsibility for cash payments between the Ministry of Labour (dealing with all those in receipt of outside relief and transitional payments) and the Ministry of Health (dealing with 'the unemployables'). It was of paramount importance to the Minister of Labour, however, that any legislative programme should seek to reform the relief payments system as an essentially *industrial* problem rather than attempt to reconstruct the entire machinery of the Poor Law.[16]

Betterton's persistence was not in vain; it was his plea to limit discussion to the unemployed class only which formed the basis of policy making in the summer of 1933. Part II of the 1934 Unemployment Act established an Unemployment Assistance Board responsible for all the unemployed who had exhausted their benefit and for all other able-bodied unemployed between the ages of 16 and 65 receiving Poor Law relief.[17] The Board was

---

[16] Cab 27/552, Unemployment Insurance Policy Committee. Memorandum by the Minister of Labour, 30 May 1933.

[17] Provided in the latter case that their normal occupation was one in which contributions were payable under the Widows', Orphans' and Old Age Contributory Pensions Acts and provided that, for those unemployed reaching the age of 16, their normal occupation might reasonably have been expected to be one in which such contributions were payable.

empowered to draw up national regulations governing relief scales for approval by the Minister and by parliament. Payments were to be financed directly from tax revenue. This outcome was very much a personal triumph for Betterton; other Ministry officials were in favour of the long-term unemployed being supported by means-tested benefits administered by local authorities, assisted by Treasury grants, rather than by a centralized bureaucratic system.

Despite these changes the government's obligation still fell far short of the demand for 'work or maintenance'. On the contrary, the household means test was, for the first time, given statutory force and only the unemployed found to be in need were to be given help.[18] Since the underlying purpose of the scheme was to establish a clear division between those with and those without an entitlement to benefit based on contributions, it was critical to establish the point that insurance was a matter of rights and assistance a matter of needs. Although allowances were payable indefinitely, applicants had to show their availability and capacity for work to remain eligible and it was to be illegal for public assistance authorities to supplement assistance allowances. Whilst in theory it was possible to appeal against the determination of an allowance to an outside tribunal, the chairman of the Board was given discretion to refuse leave of appeal unless he was convinced that the regulations had been improperly applied.

The Minister of Labour found little difficulty in justifying the 'nationalization' of unemployment assistance. 'The local authorities are at present administering transitional payments on behalf of the central government, but without any financial responsibility at all', he told MPs. 'There is a complete divorce between the responsibility of the central authority which

Part I of the Act dealt with unemployment insurance. It extended the benefit period, restored benefits to their 1931 levels, introduced increased coverage for juveniles, and established an Unemployment Insurance Statutory Committee to safeguard the solvency of the Fund. The members of the UAB were Sir Henry Betterton, previously Minister of Labour, as chairman, Sir Ernest Strohmenger, a former Under Secretary of the Treasury, as vice-chairman, together with Miss Violet Markham, chairman of the Central Committee on Women's Training and Employment, H. M. Hallsworth, Professor of Economics at the University of Durham, T. Jones, former deputy Secretary to the Cabinet, and M. A. Reynard, director of Public Assistance for Glasgow. Miss Markham succeeded Strohmenger as vice-chairman in 1937.

[18] The retention in a supposedly comprehensive unemployment relief system of the principle that the individual should exhaust his own resources and those of his family before receiving government aid only heightened the unemployed's anger against the means test. The government, however, refused to consider the household as anything other than a distinct economic and social unity. Although there was evidence from 1935 that earnings belonging to family members other than assistance applicants formed a significant proportion of assessable resources and that the means test placed a disproportionate burden upon younger workers, the number of reported cases of the break-up of homes because of the effect of the means test was much smaller than commonly supposed. Burns, *British Unemployment Programs*, 247–8, 250; Pilgrim Trust, *Men Without Work*, 149.

is providing the money, and that of the local authority which disburses it . . . If the responsibility is to be a national obligation, the administration . . . must be national also.'[19]

The primary purpose of the 1934 Act was to fashion unemployment expenditure to meet the needs of the prevailing industrial climate, preserving by bureaucratization and centralization a clear distinction between the short-term and the long-term unemployed, whilst at the same time safeguarding economy and uniformity by the removal of what were regarded as the suspect and discretionary activities of locally elected bodies. From the government's point of view the establishment of the Board guaranteed a measure of central control over policy and standards hitherto absent without making the Minister of Labour responsible for individual cases. The transfer to the Board of the responsibility for unemployment assistance was, moreover, clearly designed to assuage growing Treasury hostility to the mounting cost of unemployment relief. By creating a buffer between itself and those demanding more generous benefits for the unemployed, the government was able 'to accomplish politically unpopular ends without suffering from the political consequences thereof.'[20] In like manner, the creation of unemployment assistance tribunals was a deliberate attempt to protect the Minister from the hostility expected to arise once UAB uniform scales were imposed in place of the varied practices of the Public Assistance Committees.[21]

But although the cleavage between unemployment insurance and unemployment assistance was given statutory recognition, critical issues of policy remained unresolved. Could resort to an 'independent' body take unemployment relief 'out of politics' and rid it of 'corruption'? Could a national relief standard be devised that would prove flexible, economic and popular with claimants?

FREE FROM POLITICS? THE UAB IN PRACTICE, 1935–38

The Unemployment Assistance Board was to assume responsibility for the unemployed in two distinct stages – on the First Appointed Day, subsequently set at 7 January 1935, it was to take over all those persons receiving transitional payments under the system begun in 1931, and on the Second Appointed Day, 1 March 1935, all the able-bodied unemployed then supported by local authorities. Prior to embarking upon its administrative duties, however, the Board was obliged to submit to the Minister of

---

[19] H. C. Debs, 5th ser., vol. 283, 30 November 1933, cols. 1091–2.
[20] J. D. Millet, *The Unemployment Assistance Board* (1940), 220.
[21] For further details see T. Lynes, 'Unemployment Assistance Tribunals in the 1930s', in *Justice, Discretion and Poverty*, ed. M. Adler and A. Bradley (1975), 5–31.

Labour draft regulations as to the proposed scale of assistance. It was anxious not to depart too radically from the levels of transitional payments previously determined by the PACs, though the imposition of reduced standards was inevitable in areas where local authorities had refused to apply the household means test. With large numbers of the unemployed destined to receive less in relief from the UAB than they had become accustomed to, it was all the more important for the Board to produce a uniform scale which would win general public approval.

Although the UAB had complete discretion in proposing scale rates it sought to protect itself from the most obvious sources of criticism. It was determined from the beginning to avoid undermining the credibility of the insurance scheme by ensuring that assistance scales were not set above prevailing benefit rates. To provide for adequate maintenance without abandoning the time-honoured principle of less eligibility, relief payments in general were to be less than the unskilled wage level and were to operate in such a manner as to restrict the total amount paid to above-average size households. There was to be no resort to 'scientific' assessments of minimum subsistence or dietary standards; the Board was to determine by practical means and in light of prevailing working-class living standards the level of income on which households and single individuals could 'reasonably' manage. To this end a complex set of rules had to be devised identifying the type and amount of household resources to be deducted from the basic scale.[22]

Guided by such general considerations the Board submitted draft regulations to the Minister of Labour, Oliver Stanley, as reproduced in table 8. Not unnaturally the government was unwilling to allow the UAB complete autonomy in determining the financial burden of unemployment relief. The Minister of Labour was empowered, if he so wished, to lay amended regulations before parliament provided an explanation was given for the changes and that they were accompanied by a statement of the Board's reactions to them. The Ministerial intervention subsequently employed, however, proved to be of an entirely different character. Oliver Stanley, who had succeeded Betterton as Minister of Labour in June 1934, feared that the Board's original proposals would result in unacceptable reductions in the incomes of the unemployed. He immediately sought for political reasons to persuade the Board to raise the schedule of allowances to ensure that the total payments due to a one-child family without other resources would at least equal the prevailing level of unemployment benefit. The Board's declared intention to protect the viability of the insurance scheme was thus

---

[22] T. Lynes, 'The Making of the Unemployment Assistance Scale', Supplementary Benefits Commission, SBA Paper No. 6, *Low Incomes* (HMSO 1977), Appendix I.

Table 8. *Scale of needs in draft regulations submitted to Minister of Labour, 26 October 1934*

	Male	Female
I. Application by member of household of two or more persons:		
(a) Householder and wife or husband	23s	
(b) Householder where (a) not applicable	16s	14s
(c) Other members of households, aged 21 or over: first	10s	8s
subsequent	8s	7s
18–20	8s	7s
14–17	6s	6s
11–13	4s 6d	4s 6d
8–10	4s	4s
5–7	3s 6d	3s 6d
Under 5	3s	3s

Where provision is made for needs of more than four persons, total to be reduced by 1s per person in excess of four.

	Male	Female
II. Application by a person not in a household of two or more persons:		
Aged 18 or over	15s	14s
Under 18	13s	12s

immediately threatened, but rather than invite the formal rejection of its draft regulations it reluctantly agreed to meet the Minister's wishes. It increased the suggested rate for a married couple by 1s and established a minimum payment of 4s for an only child, providing a potential weekly allowance for such a family of 28s, equivalent to the insurance benefit rate under Part I of the 1934 Act.

Political interference with the 'independence' of the Board did not end there. The Cabinet Committee established to examine the original draft regulations received instead the revised version on 12 November 1934. Even so the Committee remained concerned that the suggested rates would involve embarrassing reductions in cash payments to the unemployed, especially in areas where there had been little or no enforcement of the means test. The situation grew even more complicated when only three days later Stanley withdrew his support for the revised draft after sample enquiries had indicated that even on its own terms a far greater proportion of recipients stood to suffer reduced allowances than was originally anticipated.

With the date of the Board's takeover of transitional cases fast approaching, there was little opportunity of investigating fully the likely impact of the regulations upon different groups of people throughout the country. The only acceptable solution was for the Board to substitute fresh draft regulations for those originally submitted to the Minister. But political pressure did not abate. Stanley and the Cabinet Committee succeeded in forcing upon a reluctant and antagonized Board improved allowances for members of large households and the introduction of an element of discretion into the operation of the rent allowance rule which, in its original form, would almost certainly have resulted in severe reductions in payments in areas where rents were lower than the UAB had realized.[23] The amended regulations reproduced in table 9 were finally approved by the Cabinet on 20 November 1934, debated in Parliament on 17 December and put into operation as planned on 7 January 1935.

Political interference with the Board's activities may have offended the principles laid down in recent legislation, but the fact remained that the benefit rates originally submitted by the Minister of Labour to the Board were more generous than those which were finally imposed. The government subsequently declared that the agreed scale would increase payments to the majority of the unemployed to a total of about £3 million a year. But however laudable in intent, the final re-jigging of the scheme did not produce anything like the positive results officials originally hoped for. There was still a sufficiently large number of regulations specific to a whole range of personal and family circumstances that threatened to reduce the benefits of nearly half those transitional payments claimants about to be transferred to the UAB. The worrying aspect was that the majority of such persons were hardly distinguishable from those on insurance benefit, except for the duration of their unemployment, and were located predominantly in industrial regions of Wales, Scotland and Northern England still suffering substantial economic decline.

No one within or outside of government anticipated the wave of public protest and indignation that finally greeted the imposition of the new UAB scales. The weekly payments of almost half of the UAB's clients stood to be reduced. From the second week in January 1935, widespread and spontaneous demonstrations occurred almost daily within Scotland, Wales

---

[23] The changes in detail were as follows. The former rule whereby allowances were reduced by 1s per person in families of more than four people now applied only to families in excess of five. The normal rent rule provided for an adjustment between the 'basic' rent for a household – calculated on a sliding scale but averaging about one-quarter of the total allowance – and the rent actually paid. If the latter proved greater an additional allowance of up to one-third of the basic rent allowance was to be given. But where the actual rent proved less than the basic there was to be a corresponding reduction, unlimited in amount. The revision accepted by the Cabinet at the end of November 1934 relaxed the rule so that instead of any difference between the actual rent and the 'basic' rent of one-quarter of the scale rates resulting in an adjustment of the assessment, a fixed rent allowance was applied to all cases where the scale rates were determined at between 24s and 30s inclusive. Moreover, the first 1s 6d of any adjustment for low rent could now be waived in special circumstances. Lynes, *Low Incomes*, 55–6, 60.

Table 9. *Unemployment Assistance Board, weekly allowances to the unemployed*

	Unemployment insurance rate under Part I of the 1934 Act	Proposed UAB rate	Increase (+) or decrease (−)
	s d	s d	s d
Husband and wife	26 0	24 0	−2 0
Single householder, male over 21	17 0	16 0	−1 0
Single householder, female over 21	15 0	14 0	−1 0
Adult living with family, male	17 0	10 0	−7 0
Adult living with family, female	15 0	8 0	−7 0
Second and subsequent male adults living with family	17 0	8 0	−9 0
Second and subsequent female adults living with family	15 0	7 0	−8 0
Age 18–21 years, male	14 0	8 0	−6 0
Age 18–21 years, female	12 0	7 0	−5 0
Age 17 to 18 years, boys	9 0	6 0	−3 0
Age 17 to 18 years, girls	7 6	6 0	−1 6
Age 16 to 17 years, boys	6 0	6 0	nil
Age 16 to 17 years, girls	5 0	6 0	+1 0
Dependants' allowances:			
Between 14 and 16 years		6 0	+4 0
Between 11 and 14 years	fixed at	4 6	+2 6
Between 8 and 11 years	2s	4 0	+2 0
Between 5 and 8 years		3 6	+1 6
Under 5 years		3 0	+1 0

Source: Adapted from W. Hannington, *Ten Lean Years* (1940), 127.

and the north of England, denouncing the enforced cuts in working-class living standards. By the end of the month the agitation had spread to Sheffield, Oldham, Manchester, Stoke, Bolton and Blackburn, attracting the sympathetic support of church leaders and local public assistance officials.[24]

Although the amended scale rates were meant to ensure that unemployment assistance recipients were treated at least as favourably as they had

[24] For further details see F. Miller, 'The British Unemployment Assistance Crisis of 1935', *Journal of Contemporary History*, 14 (1979), 329–51.

been by the local authorities, the scheme proved relatively less generous than had been expected. Lax enforcement of the means test in previous years made it almost inevitable that fairly substantial reductions in allowances would occur in some areas, but the regulations themselves created difficulties and antagonisms. The administratively tidy code of instructions under which local officials operated had been expected to provide a simple and less arbitrary means of providing relief to the unemployed. But few of the personnel involved in the operation were equipped to determine realistically the amount of relief required to balance human need against declared resources and the temptation to work within the strict letter of the law, whatever the cost in human misery, was reinforced.

The Board itself did not encourage the widespread use of local discretion. It was of little comfort, either, to find that few in government had any clear idea as to what constituted an adequate or reasonable level of assistance. Ministers were woefully ignorant about the constituent items of working-class expenditure, especially with regard to rent payments. In the discussions prior to the establishment of the UAB scale the Board agreed, albeit reluctantly, to liberalize the rule whereby reduced allowances were imposed upon those paying noticeably less rent than the 'basic' level stipulated for their household.[25] Not only were these slightly more generous regulations purely discretionary, they only applied to certain applicants for benefit. The proportion of working-class families living in low rent areas had never been fully appreciated before 1935 and it was this group, together with larger families and those with pooled income, who suffered most under the UAB.

Although in theory appeals tribunals were empowered to examine cases where the strict application of the regulations produced unacceptably harsh results, the complexity of the procedural rules plus the pressure which the Ministry of Labour put on the tribunals' chairmen to conform to internal case law robbed the system of the flexibility and sensitivity required to make it an effective 'safety valve' through which popular dissatisfaction could be channelled.[26] That said, it would be going too far to suggest any conspiracy to enforce reductions in benefit. The National Government remained intent on raising the general level of unemployment benefit to counterbalance the reductions imposed on those who had previously been receiving illegally high payments. Administrative complexity, financial miscalculation and bureaucratic insensitivity produced instead an hiatus that undoubtedly damaged the reputation of the UAB.

The unemployed's growing sense of impotence and disappointment at being unable to secure relief payments at least equal to those ruling after

[25] See above p. 77.   [26] Lynes, 'Unemployment Assistance Tribunals'.

1931 finally roused parliament into action. After a two-day emergency debate at the end of January 1935, Stanley began to press the Board for concessions. The intervention was as unwelcome as it had always been; the Board was, after all, a supposedly non-political body. It offered to encourage greater discretion at local level, in cases involving low rent and married relatives for example, but no more. But protest and resistance were in vain. By early February the extent of the political crisis forced the abandonment of the principles of centralization, standardization and autonomy that had foreshadowed the introduction of the Unemployment Act. Far from taking relief 'out of politics', the early operation of the regulations had produced such a storm of individual protest that the government, fearing the political consequences in an election year, could no longer deny its responsibility for the scales. It therefore beat a hasty retreat. The uniform national standard for the determination of needs operated only during the first six weeks of the Board's administration. Henceforth there was to be a 'standstill' during which UAB clients would be subject to a complicated double standard of assessment.[27]

From 14 February 1935, applicants who would have received more by way of transitional payments than was payable under the new regulations were granted a supplementary allowance to make up the difference. Critical here was the fact that in over one-half of the public assistance areas the transitional scales were greater than those of the UAB. Since past reductions were to be restored there was thus an enforced continuation of transitional payments anomalies, the abolition of which had been one of the principal reasons for the creation of the Board in the first place. Moreover, the transfer of the uninsured unemployed from the PACs to the Board, scheduled for March, had to be indefinitely postponed.

The 'standstill' lasted until July 1936, allowing the government to remain true to its orthodox principles – able on the one hand to nurture the passivity of the unemployed through minor adjustments to a relief programme which still incorporated a means test and a strict division between assistance and insurance, and on the other to deflect any concerted pressure to introduce positive interventionist measures to create employment.[28] Having learned how to compromise in the face of obvious public grievances, all that remained was for government officials to administer the assessment and payment of allowances as efficiently as possible. Unemployment relief was now a considerably less controversial issue.

At first diversity rather than uniformity reigned. Persons in areas

[27] Under the terms of the Unemployment Assistance (Temporary Provisions) Act, more generally referred to as the Standstill Act.
[28] The payments crisis coincided with Lloyd George's renewed plea for a national programme of public works. See below chapter 13.

previously paying transitional payments below UAB standards were paid the new level set by the Board, while those in the more prosperous or administratively lenient areas were permitted to retain their privileged position. However, a liquidation of the 'standstill' began in November 1936; thereafter the right to claim either the Board's allowance or that which would have been payable under the transitional payments scheme was withdrawn, albeit gradually. Rather than repeat the mistakes of 1935, it was agreed to supplement over an 18 month period those assessments of need found to be less than the amount which would have been paid under the 'standstill'. During 1937 more than one-third of the applicants whose allowances were reassessed under the new regulations obtained payments in excess of what they were receiving under the 'standstill' arrangements.[29] These additional payments were themselves gradually phased out so that by May 1938 a uniform national standard was in operation. This was subject to modification only for the purpose of meeting special circumstances, such as the effects of price increases, or where there were wide variations in local rents or differing standards of living between rural and urban areas.[30]

The full impact of the 1934 Unemployment Act had yet to be realized. It came only when the UAB assumed responsibility for those unemployed workers unable to satisfy even the modest contributory requirements of the transitional payments scheme. Their inception into unemployment assistance, postponed from 1935, finally occurred on 1 April 1937. This ensured that thereafter the major part of the cost of unemployment relief would be shouldered by central government. The percentage of the unemployed aided by national schemes in March 1935 stood at 44.1 (insurance) and 32.5 (unemployment assistance) compared with 8.8 (local authority assistance). By March 1939 the proportions were 54.0, 30.1 and 1.5 respectively.[31]

THE NATIONAL GOVERNMENT AND THE INSURANCE FUND

The idea fostered in parliament that the 1934 Unemployment Act was to mark a 'new beginning' in financial aid to the unemployed was not entirely confined to its anticipated effects on those previously receiving transitional or Poor Law payments. Now that insurance contributions conferred a right to non-means-tested benefits, there occurred a gradual liberalization of benefit payments for insured claimants. Between 1935 and 1938 the rates prevailing before the emergency of 1931 were restored, additional days of benefit were granted to workers with a good record of past employment, and

[29] Unemployment Assistance Board, Report for the Year 1937, Cmd. 5752, 1938.
[30] For details see the *Annual Reports* of the Unemployment Assistance Board, 1936–39.
[31] Burns, *British Unemployment Programs*, 156–7.

the allowances for adult and child dependants were raised. In addition, the waiting period during which no benefit could be drawn was reduced from six to three days. From 1934 juveniles under the age of 16 were brought within the scope of the insurance scheme, whilst in 1936 an entirely new scheme incorporating lower rates of contribution was established for agricultural workers. These changes were facilitated by the recovery in the domestic economy which helped to swell contribution income. The rise in employment between 1933 and 1937 was the result not just of a general reduction in registered unemployment, but also of a sharp rise in the number of people entering or re-entering the labour market, many of whom would have dropped out of insurance had it not been for the improved economic climate.

Far more significant in the longer term, however, was the establishment of the Unemployment Insurance Statutory Committee, under the chairmanship of Sir William Beveridge, charged with overseeing the solvency of the Fund. The £105,780,000 debt on the insurance scheme was immediately removed, to be funded by an annual payment of £5 million over the next 37 years. Relieved of the financial burden of past mistakes, it was to be the Committee's duty to recommend such changes in the rate of insurance benefits and contributions as would render the scheme self-supporting. It performed its task remarkably well. The funded debt was reduced to a little over £81,530,00 by the end of 1938, while the balance of the Fund itself rose from £21,450,000 at the end of 1935 to almost £45,000,000 by the end of 1938, despite the liberalization of the insurance scheme referred to above. In discharging its responsbilities, the Committee soon displayed considerable forethought and expertise, deciding that reserve financing would take precedence over any desperate effort to finance the system on a year-to-year basis.[32]

But like the UAB, the Committee was not entirely free from political pressures. It was the Treasury, for example, which pressed for a reduction in the waiting period from six days to three on 1 April 1937, largely because the former requirement had the effect of driving the unemployed with an unquestioned right to standard benefit to claim tax-supported assistance relief whilst waiting for benefit payments to begin. Having supported an

---

[32] The Committee reported in 1934 that 'accumulation in advance of a balance sufficient to cover the losses of a normal trade depression is the first condition of saying that the Unemployment Fund is, and is likely to continue to be, sufficient to discharge its liabilities'. Unemployment Insurance Statutory Committee, *Financial Report*, 1934, 11. In order to determine an appropriate balancing period and to assess the probable future trends of unemployment upon which decisions about rates and contributions could be based, the Committee thereafter assumed for the eight year period 1936–43 a mean level of unemployment of 16.75 per cent, of which 48 per cent would rank for benefit. Howson and Winch, *Economic Advisory Council*, 134–5.

extended waiting time in the 1920s to effect savings on the Unemployment Fund, the Treasury was now anxious to cut the period in order to reduce the level of expenditure for which it was entirely responsible. And however hard it tried to confine itself to purely financial matters, the Committee found itself increasingly drawn into politically sensitive areas of social and economic policy. The choice between alternative ways of disposing of a declared surplus, for example, often involved fundamental decisions as to whether unemployment relief should be financed by insurance income or by general tax revenues. Similarly, proposals to raise benefit rates involved judgements as to the proper relationship between wages and benefits and the likely disincentive effects on the unemployed.[33] Moreover, the Committee's decision to adopt reserve financing reflected, albeit only palely, the contemporary clash between supporters of interventionist deficit-spending and those implacable defenders of Gladstonian financial orthodoxy. Thus, whilst the Committee took immense pride in striking a balance between the income and expenditure of the Unemployment Fund, its desire to build up future reserves hinted at the possibility of insurance benefit being used as a form of economic regulator. Beveridge certainly never suggested that benefit payments should be used as a counter-cyclical measure, but he did argue that reductions in benefit in periods of slack demand served only to reinforce depression.[34]

The earnest efforts made during the 1930s to rescue the unemployment payments system from the confusion and arbitrariness of the previous decade reflected the continued priority given to meeting the immediate cash needs of the involuntarily unemployed. In this the authorities were fortunate in the unfolding of events, particularly from 1933. Cyclical recovery aided the re-establishment of the insurance system proper. And although persistent long-term unemployment in the depressed areas marred any sense of general economic betterment, governments could at least convince themselves that those deserving individuals most in need of assistance were being catered for in a deliberate and systematic fashion.

[33] Burns, *British Unemployment Programs*, 304–6.
[34] J. Harris, *William Beveridge. A Biography* (Oxford, 1977), 358.

Appendix 3.1. Unemployment relief payments, 1921–1938

| | Insurance Scheme | | | | Supplementary scheme | | | | Poor Relief payments to the unemployed | |
| | Number of authorized claims[a] | Expenditure (£m) | | | Number of authorized claims[a] | Expenditure (£m) | | | Number of persons (excluding dependants) relieved on account of unemployment only[e] | Total expenditure (£m) |
		Benefits[b]	Administration	Total[c]		Payments[d]	Administration	Total		
1921	—	34.1	1.1	35.4	—				—	—
1922	954,000[f]	52.9	4.8	59.8	253,000[f]				239,000	12.1
1923	800,000[f]	41.9	4.5	51.6	261,000[f]				174,000	8.4
1924	544,000	36.0	4.0	50.4	491,000				113,000	5.4
1925	—	44.6	4.6	54.4	—				162,000	5.4
1926	—	43.7	4.9	51.4	—				264,000	7.0
1927	—	38.7	3.5	42.9[g]	—				154,000	13.7
1928	973,000	36.5	4.9	46.6	119,000				112,000	8.1
1929	—	46.8	5.1	54.4	—				94,000	5.9
1930	1,973,000	42.3	5.2	54.2	383,000	3.7	0.3	4.0	59,000	4.8
1931	1,345,000	73.0	5.3	81.0	762,000	19.2	1.0	20.2	101,000	2.6
1932	1,200,000	80.2	5.4	90.5	1,039,000	30.7	1.6	32.3	168,000	4.0
1933	854,000	54.2	4.2	64.0	936,000	50.4	3.4	53.8	192,000	6.5
1934	952,000	40.2	3.8	57.7	728,000	48.4	3.7	52.1	222,000	8.1
1935	822,000	43.8	4.1	54.1	688,000	42.2	4.0	46.2	173,000	9.7

1936	744,000	42.7	4.6	52.7	579,000	42.4	4.3	46.7	144,000	9.6
1937	896,000	35.3	4.9	45.8	556,000	37.4	4.4	41.8	30,000	7.8
1938	1,076,000	36.7	5.1	67.3	554,000	36.7	4.7	41.4	28,000	2.5

[a] The number of authorized claims is known for only ten dates between 1922 and 1929, as a result of special reports by the Ministry of Labour or estimates based on sample studies.

[b] Standard insurance and expanded insurance benefits.

[c] Includes expenditure on travelling expenses, approved courses of instruction and repayment of Treasury advances and interest.

[d] Includes transitional benefits, transitional payments and unemployment assistance allowances.

[e] December of each year.

[f] Figures of authorized claims refer to December each year except for 1922 and 1923 which refer to November and April respectively.

[g] 9 month period only.

Source: E. M. Burns, British Unemployment Programs, 1920–1938 (Washington, 1941), 347, 360–1, 367.

Appendix 3.2. *Benefit rates prevailing under the Unemployment Insurance Acts, 1913–1939*

Period[a]	Men	Women	Young men			Young women			Boys	Girls	Adult dependant	Each dependent child
	s d	s d	s d	s d	s d	s d	s d	s d	s d	s d	s	s
General system	Age 18 and over								Age 16–17	Age 16–17		
8 Jan. 1913–24 Dec. 1919	7 0	7 0	—	—	—	—	—	—	3 6	3 6	—	—
25 Dec. 1919–7 Nov. 1920	11 0	11 0	—	—	—	—	—	—	5 6	5 6	—	—
8 Nov. 1920–2 Mar. 1921	15 0	12 0	—	—	—	—	—	—	7 6	6 0	—	—
3 Mar. 1921–29 June 1921	20 0	16 0	—	—	—	—	—	—	10 0	8 0	—	—
30 June 1921–9 Nov. 1921	15 0	12 0	—	—	—	—	—	—	7 6	6 0	—	—
10 Nov. 1921–13 Aug. 1924	15 0	12 0	—	—	—	—	—	—	7 6	6 0	5	1
14 Aug. 1924–18 Apr. 1928	18 0 (Age 21–64)	15 0	Age 20	Age 19	Age 18	Age 20	Age 19	Age 18	7 6	6 0	5	2
19 Apr. 1928–4 July 1928[b]	17 0	15 0	17 0	17 0	15 0	15 0	15 0	15 0	6 0	5 0	7	2
5 July 1928–12 Mar. 1930	17 0	15 0	14 0	12 0	10 0	12 0	10 0	8 0	6 0 (Age 17 / Age 16)	5 0 (Age 17 / Age 16)	7	2

Period													
13 Mar. 1930– 7 Oct. 1931	17 0	15 0	14 0	14 0	12 0	12 0	12 0	9 0	6 0	7 6	5 0	9	2
8 Oct. 1931– 30 June 1934	15 3	13 6	12 6	12 6	10 9	10 9	10 9	8 0	5 6	6 9	4 6	8	2
1 July 1934– 30 Oct. 1935	17 0	15 0	14 0	14 0	12 0	12 0	12 0	9 0	6 0	7 6	5 0	9	2
31 Oct. 1935– 30 Mar. 1938	17 0	15 0	14 0	14 0	12 0	12 0	12 0	9 0	6 0	7 6	5 0	9	3
Agricultural system													
29 Oct. 1936– 30 Mar. 1938	14 0	12 6	10 6	10 6	9 6	9 6	9 6	6 0	4 0	5 0	3 6	7	3
31 Mar. 1938– 29 Mar. 1939	14 0	12 6	12 0	12 0	9 6	9 6	9 6	6 0	4 0	5 0	3 6	7	3

[a] The periods are those during which the rates indicated were in operation.

[b] The Unemployment Insurance Act, 1927, which became effective on 19 April 1928, for the first time distinguished young men and women from boys and girls. The special rates for young men and women, however, came into effect on 5 July 1928, and prior to that date they continued to receive benefit at the same rate as adults.

Source: E. M. Burns, *British Unemployment Programs, 1920–1938* (Washington, 1941), 368.

4 ✳ In and out of the labour market: hours of work, pensions and the school-leaving age

Although public disquiet and party politics convinced Ministers that they had to be seen to be 'doing something' on behalf of the involuntarily unemployed, the adoption of alternative strategies beyond insurance and relief was constrained for much of the 1920s by the lingering belief that in the restoration of pre-war normality lay the basis of future prosperity and stability. It was thus the acknowledged responsibility of officials to shape policy according to their assessment of prevailing conditions without undermining the 'natural' impulses to economic recovery.

Remedial policy did not always work in that direction; witness the challenge which the revamped insurance scheme posed to orthodox finance. But with the search for politically acceptable responses to unemployment to the fore, pressure groups within and outside of Whitehall were tempted to popularize policies seemingly blessed with the virtue of commonsense. With insufficient work for all it seemed obvious to consider sharing available jobs amongst the labour force by changes in working hours. Intense competition for vacancies, moreover, suggested the possibility of manipulating the supply of labour at each end of the age scale, either by extending the period of compulsory schooling or by revising the terms governing the availability of retirement pensions. It is with these related issues that this chapter is concerned.

SHORT-TIME WORKING

Following the collapse of the post-war boom, organized short-time working came to be viewed as a potentially effective anti-unemployment device, its purpose being to share out the available volume of work by occupying men for fewer hours per day or week at wages set at an appropriate proportion of the full-time rate. Ministers were aware that both sides of industry had already reported some support for the idea to the National Industrial Conference in 1919, principally as a means of stabilising employment.[1]

---

[1] R. Lowe, 'The Erosion of State Intervention in Britain, 1917–1924', *Economic History Review*, 2nd ser., 31 (1978), 274–5.

Short-time working was already the customary response to industrial depression in a number of industries, particularly cotton, coal, iron and steel, linen, woollen and worsted, boot and shoes and jute. For a brief period during August 1920 the government considered making the practice compulsory for most trades, but they met stern opposition from the Treasury, fearful that the government would be forced to subsidize full weekly wages.[2] As the industrial situation worsened towards the end of 1920 the National Alliance of Employers and Employed pressed the government to support publicly the 'scientific' distribution of work 'in order to relieve distress and unemployment'.[3] The government hesitated. Without Exchequer support to maintain wages, it risked aggravating unemployment further by encouraging restricted output and enforced price rises.[4] It would be preferable, Ministers argued, merely to publicize the desirability of short-time working, leaving private industry to grapple with any attendant problems that might arise. On 31 December 1920 the government circularized employers' organizations, trade unions, Trade Boards and Joint Industrial Councils claiming that 'much can be done to alleviate distress by distributing the existing opportunities for employment among as many employees as possible, so that the largest number may be enabled to earn a portion of their normal wages'.[5] To facilitate the process short-time was introduced in areas of direct government control. From January 1921 hours and earnings were reduced in dockyards, Royal Ordinance factories, and War Office establishments, the estimated effect of which was to absorb an additional 8,000 men within three weeks.[6]

The response within private industry was anything but encouraging. Among the trade unions that replied, many opposed short-time working as a subversive means of meeting recession by enforced reductions in working-class living standards. Labour leaders and employees, the Home Office's Directorate of Intelligence reported to the Cabinet in January 1921, 'not unnaturally fear that wages will be forced below subsistence level'. To allay

[2] Cab 24/110, CP 1747, Unemployment. Joint Memorandum by the Minister of Health and the Minister of Labour, 6 August 1920.

[3] Lab 2/1210/17624, Verbatim Report of Deputation from the National Alliance of Employers and Employed to Dr. Macnamara on Tuesday, 7 December 1920. The question of holidays with pay as a form of worksharing found advocates amongst the ranks of organized labour in the 1920s but its potential for creating extra jobs was never adequately discussed.

[4] Cab 27/115, CU 17, Cabinet Committee on Unemployment. Short Time as an Alternative to Employment. Memorandum by the Minister of Labour, 14 September 1920.

[5] Lab 2/867/ED/196, Ministry of Labour Circular Letter, 31 December 1920. The letter was not sent to agriculture, fishing, shipping, building and railways on the grounds that those industries did not lend themselves to short-time, nor to mining or docks where short-time or casual working had been well established before the war. A different letter was sent to the boot and shoe and cotton trades which already operated a recognized system of short-time working.   [6] *Ministry of Labour Gazette*, February 1921, 60.

such fears, the government announced that 'when, as a result of short time, wages touch a certain figure, a portion of the unemployment dole would be available'.[7] The labour movement remained sceptical. Both the Parliamentary Committee of the TUC and the Executive Committee of the Labour Party condemned short-time working as 'impracticable' and 'inequitable', particularly since it ignored 'the diminution of home demand' and 'the suffering of the entire wage-earning class' that would ensue. If the policy was to be adopted, they argued, it should be accompanied 'by an under-employment allowance on the same scale as that now proposed for unemployment benefit.'[8]

Despite further prompting by Ministers during 1923[9] the majority of workers already in jobs refused to consider any systematic reorganization of working hours for the benefit of the unemployed, fearful of reduced earnings. Short-time continued to be operated in those industries which had traditionally opposed enforced redundancies, but with dwindling enthusiasm. Its effect in the cotton industry was to increase unit costs of production above the competitive level and to aggravate the industry's parlous financial state. Many cotton firms became seriously overcapitalized during the boom of 1919–20 and subsequently found themselves incapable of repaying debts. Rather than enforce their liquidation the banks permitted industrial overdrafts to reach unprecedented heights. Short-time working as a guarantor of employment became an expensive luxury (see chapter 8 below). Unable because of restricted output to raise prices to a level high enough to meet their immediate financial needs, firms in the fine spinning sector ultimately resorted to full-time working in a desperate effort to salvage their position. In truth, there was never much hope of improving employment conditions by organized short-time in industries suffering secular decline. Reducing the number of days worked per week was a singularly inappropriate and ineffective response to the problem of long run excess capacity and by the mid-twenties it was fast being regarded as a policy likely to compound the very problems it sought to alleviate.[10]

EMPLOYMENT AND THE 'NORMAL WORKING WEEK'

The question of the length of the 'normal working week' added another dimension to the alleged relationship between the volume of unemploy-

[7] Cab 24/118, CP 2429, Directorate of Intelligence. Home Office. Report No. 87, 6 January 1921.
[8] *British Labour and Unemployment. Resolutions to be Discussed at the Special Conference of the Trades Union Congress and the Labour Party*, 27 January 1921.
[9] Lab 2/867/ED 196, 1 October 1923.
[10] For elaboration see J. H. Porter, 'Cotton and Wool textiles', in *British Industry Between the Wars*, ed. Buxton and Aldcroft, 25–47 and G. W. Daniels and J. Jewkes, 'The Post-War Depression in the Lancashire Cotton Industry'.

ment and the hours of work of those in jobs. Negotiations among trade unionists, employers and the government on the length of the working week continued throughout almost the entire interwar period. Understandably, the concern prior to 1920 was less with unemployment than with the establishment and enforcement of working practices aimed at improving social welfare in general. Although the industry-wide reduction of weekly working hours in 1919 from an average of 54 to 48 affected fewer workers in manufacturing industry than is generally supposed, it nevertheless signalled concern for an important subject of national industrial negotiation. Employers and trade unionists pledged themselves at the 1919 National Industrial Conference to the legal enforcement of a 48-hour week. The government, equally committed, endorsed the same principle at international level by signing the Washington Hours Convention in 1919. Neither major political party, however, proved able during the twenties to secure the implementation of practical legislation.[11]

Employers thereafter refused to accept that the unemployed would benefit very much from a cut in working hours. They complained that the workforce, having failed since 1919 to respond to lower hours with increased productivity, had forced up production costs, hampered international competitiveness and damaged employment.[12] This accusation angered the TUC, not so much because of the employers' carping attack on labour as much as their apparent ignorance of the effect reduced hours could have on demand. As it explained in 1933:

The possible increase in costs which might result from the reduction of hours of work would, by virtue of the dynamic nature of economic development, be offset (a) by the increase in purchasing power of the workers (which would not necessarily be accompanied by a decrease in the purchasing power of the other classes of society), (b) by the decrease in the overhead charges per unit of production since the number of units would be increased by the revival of economic activity, (c) by the decrease and perhaps the disappearance of social charges represented by unemployment benefit. As a consequence production could well bear an increase in wage costs.[13]

This emphasis upon manipulating working hours as a means of sustaining purchasing power and demand as a bulwark against unemployment emerged briefly during the early thirties. A 40-hour week, an Engineering delegate informed the 1932 Congress, would 'put into employment another 260,000 men in the metal trades, but that does not finish there. Every man is a consumer, every man is a market . . . The effect of employing more men

---

[11] For further discussion see R. Lowe, 'Hours of Labour: Negotiating Industrial Legislation in Britain, 1919–39', *Economic History Review*, 2nd ser., 35 (1982), 254–71.

[12] Lowe, 'Hours of Labour', 256. For a critical reappraisal of this view see J. A. Dowie, '1919–20 is in Need of Attention', *Economic History Review*, 2nd ser., 28 (1975), 429–50.

[13] International Labour Office, *Report for the Preparatory Conference, 1933*, cited in Lowe, 'Hours of Labour', 263.

is cumulative.'[14] Colin Clark, the Cambridge statistician, tentatively suggested in 1933 that such regularized hours could bring some 1,300,000 men into employment 'if we assume that output would remain unaffected' and if the measure 'was accompanied by a considerable degree of industrial organisation'.[15]

Employers rejected such reasoning. The effect of reduced working hours on prices would only further aggravate the already uncompetitive condition of the troubled export sector; counter-claims by the TUC that the ratification of a 40-hour week at international level would eventually standardize labour conditions in Europe to the benefit of British exporters were summarily dismissed. The opposition of the Engineering and Allied Employers' National Federation was not untypical:

> The advocates of the 40-hour week claim to increase employment by sharing out presently existing work, and suggest that the resulting high employment will increase purchasing power and thus bring about an increase in trade. The argument that by the handing out of more wages the purchasing power of the nation is increased is fallacious. It is increased production which is the true basis of increased purchasing power and giving more wages without such increase in production is merely transferring to a less productive source capital essential at the present time to industrial development.[16]

There were individual employers with a more positive outlook. The Chairman of Associated Portland Cement publicly declared that lower working hours would reduce unemployment. Oliver Lyle, a director of Tate and Lyle, called upon the Minister of Labour in 1932 to persuade the Prince of Wales to launch a national appeal to prosperous firms to lower the length of the working week without wage reductions 'as a means of increasing purchasing power'.[17]

The appeal fell on deaf ears. What was being overlooked, Ministers complained, was that:

> The new purchasing power of the additional employees does not represent an addition to the aggregate volume of purchasing power in the country. It coincides with a reduction in profits and therefore a reduction in the purchasing power of the owners of the concern. The result then would be not an aggregate increase in demand but the transfer of purchasing power from one set of persons to another set of persons, and on this basis, although the direction of trade might be changed a little, its volume would not necessarily be affected to any appreciable extent.

Such a proposal, moreover, assumed:

---

[14] Cited in A. Booth and M. Pack, *Employment, Capital and Economic Policy. Great Britain, 1919–1939* (Oxford, 1985), 110.
[15] E. Bevin, *My Plan for 2,000,000 Workless* (1933), appendix I.
[16] Engineering and Allied Employers' National Federation, *Unemployment. Its Realities and Problems* (1933), 56.   [17] Lowe, 'Hours of Labour', 263.

the existence of a considerable number of undertakings making profits sufficiently large to enable them to meet a considerable increase in the costs of production without losing business, and willing to sacrifice those profits . . . in order to promote employment. To say the least of it this is a very doubtful assumption.[18]

Although towards the end of 1934 Oliver Stanley, Minister of Labour, invited the National Confederation of Employers' Organizations and the TUC to tripartite talks on the question of unemployment and hours of work, it was already clear that the government was opposed to interfering on any universal scale with existing working practices. Committed to a policy of 'industrial self-help' the government preferred an industry-by-industry approach, convinced that the problem of unemployment was not 'simply a question of creating . . . vacancies regardless of the industry, the occupation or the locality in which they were made.'[19]

Negotiations on hours of work during the thirties put both the National Government and the employers on the defensive. They revealed the latter, in Lowe's words, 'at their most conservative . . . devoid of any positive, dynamic, macro-economic viewpoint'. But that was precisely because employers, like the government, earnestly believed, on grounds of practicability and economic logic, that a systematic reduction of hours with wages intact would merely worsen unemployment. Industrial profitability would be badly affected and workers would price themselves out of jobs without any guarantee that vacancies, if created at all, would occur in those occupations or regions most desperately in need of assistance. Neither the Treasury nor the National Confederation of Employers' Organizations was prepared to accept unreservedly the claims made for increased purchasing power. And once unemployment was able to be portrayed as a problem 'only' of those particular industries and localities unfortunate enough not to be sharing in a general domestic market recovery of the mid thirties, even the TUC gradually dropped its strident demand for a 40-hour week on economic grounds. The lacklustre campaign it launched later in the decade emphasized less that a reduced working week would establish 'the right to work' or be 'a cure for unemployment' than that it would provide some reward for those workers in staple industries prepared to co-operate with schemes of industrial rationalization.[20]

On the whole those supporters of a shorter working week who emphasized the potential expansion of employment by the creation of additional purchasing power had to battle constantly against orthodox economic thinking. Shorn at the time of an adequate reply 'the attacks of

[18] Lab 2/1007/IR/1246, December 1932.
[19] Absorption of the Unemployed Into Industry. Discussions between the Minister of Labour and Representatives of Certain Industries, Cmd. 5317, 1936, 2–3.
[20] Lowe, 'Hours of Labour', 263–4.

the heretics' resembled 'short, sharp forays followed by quick retreats back to the sheltering walls of orthodoxy or obscurity, rather than a sustained campaign'.[21]

Contemporary critics found it relatively easy to denounce the 'hours of work 'stratagem as a dangerous irrelevancy destined to damage industrial competitiveness and economic recovery rather than to remedy unemployment. As we have seen, this criticism held however much the policy was couched in terms of the stimulus it might provide to purchasing power and the eventual creation of additional jobs for the out-of-work. When parallel policies were pressed to eliminate surplus competition in the labour market by raising the school-leaving age and by altering pension provisions, in effect stemming the inflow of labour at both ends of the age span, they too made little headway. Not only did such proposals ruffle orthodox opinion by posing unacceptable threats to the status quo, they also failed to win unequivocal support from radical interventionists. The latter were concerned less with redistributing the volume of existing employment than with raising the trend level demand for labour. But there were pressure group activists who held that a 'young and old' policy offered a valuable if partial corrective to mass unemployment and it is to the substance of their arguments that we now turn.

JUVENILE LABOUR AND THE SCHOOL-LEAVING AGE[22]

Much of the official concern over school-leavers in the years before 1914 had been directed at easing the transition from school to work by providing advice on the choice of suitable employment. The drift of youngsters into blind-alley occupations which endangered their future prospects of useful employment, and the pressure to deprecate further education in favour of wage earning, had given rise to an acknowledged concern for juvenile welfare long before unemployment emerged as a serious threat. The outbreak of the First World War aggravated this already difficult problem of juvenile labour and at the same time created a potentially more serious situation. Munitions output achieved such priority that boys and girls, who in normal times would have been advised to accept low wages as apprentices in a skilled trade, were hurried into factories where they worked

[21] S. Pollard, 'Trade Union Reactions to the Economic Crisis', *Journal of Contemporary History*, 4 (1969), 110.

[22] This section draws upon W. R. Garside, 'Juvenile Unemployment and Public Policy Between the Wars', *Economic History Review*, 2nd ser., 30 (1977), 322–39 and Garside, 'Unemployment and the School-Leaving Age in Inter-War Britain', *International Review of Social History*, 26 (1981), 159–70.

for long hours at high wages in occupations which taught them little and which were almost certain to collapse in the coming peace.[23] Because so many juveniles would be forced to find jobs other than those in which they were engaged during the war, the process of adaptation to lower wages and more normal prospects was bound to be difficult, whatever the state of the economy.

In the event, the immediate post-war juvenile employment situation proved more serious than the mere temporary dislocation anticipated. The problem was not so much to ease the transition of youngsters from an abnormal market situation into less lucrative and more constructive occupations through improved and extended advisory facilities, as to accommodate those under 18 years of age whose services were no longer required. One estimate claims that more than half of the total number of juveniles thrown out of work at the cessation of war were unable to obtain other jobs.[24] The government's initial response to the problem was destined to become the hallmark of official policy towards unemployed youngsters for most of the interwar period and displayed most of the fundamental weaknesses and myopia that characterized the attack on adult unemployment. Shortly after the Armistice, and in default of any effective remedial action through the reorganization of industry or an alteration in the conditions of entry into the juvenile labour market, Juvenile Unemployment Centres were established to mitigate the risk of physical and moral deterioration resulting from the loss of work. The centres aimed predominantly at maintaining the employability of boys and girls through their involvement in various forms of non-vocational handcrafts, homecraft, physical training, and organized games. Attendance was compulsory for those over 15 in receipt of Out-of-Work Donation and after 1920 for those over 16 in receipt of unemployment benefit. With full financial support from the government the number of centres quickly spread, reaching a peak in May 1919, only to decline significantly thereafter following a 50 per cent reduction in the scale of grant aid. But a substantial rise in the numbers unemployed under 18 during 1922–23 led to a swift revival of this ameliorative policy on the basis of more generous assistance from the Exchequer.

However laudable in intent, there were a number of reasons why the Unemployment Centres were unable to fulfil satisfactorily even their most modest aims. They were sanctioned merely as temporary measures and as such discouraged long-term planning. In the absence of reliable estimates of

---

[23] Final Report of the Departmental Committee on Juvenile Education in Relation to Employment After The War, Cd. 8512, 1917, para. 4.
[24] J. B. Seymour, *The British Employment Exchange* (1928), 41.

the rate of juvenile unemployment[25] neither local nor national authorities could be confident that resources were being committed to areas of greatest need. Moreover, the teachers engaged had no security of tenure, worked in poor accommodation with inadequate equipment, and found it difficult to conduct any programme effectively when the number of juveniles in continuous attendance formed only a small proportion of the total involved. As long as juveniles under 16 were uninsured and ineligible for unemployment benefit they were free from any compulsion to attend. It proved almost impossible to secure satisfactory attendance on a purely voluntary basis and the serious gap in public supervision between the age juveniles normally left school and when they qualified for benefit left those 14–16 year olds in greatest need of care and direction without compulsory contact with the authorities most able to help retain their industrial efficiency. Furthermore, local authorities in the early twenties proved particularly reluctant to share the cost of running the centres owing to the burden of existing rate demands, and so restrained any significant expansion of the scheme.[26] By the end of 1923, 75 centres catered for only 6,500 youngsters out of an estimated total of 150,000 unemployed 14–18 year olds.[27]

Although Juvenile Unemployment Centres provided, within limits, a useful expedient for protecting the out-of-work from the worst consequences of their plight, ideally they ought to have complemented more pertinent remedial measures. Both Labour and Conservative administrations between the wars considered more fundamental policies with varying degrees of commitment and enthusiasm. One of the most obvious ways of easing the pressure on vacancies for juveniles was to raise the age of obligatory school attendance, but despite increasing pressure from within and outside of government this never figured prominently in either the Labour or Conservative party's industrial programme before 1929.

Although the 1918 Education Act had fixed obligatory school attendance to the end of the term in which children reached the age of 14, it empowered Local Education Authorities to make by-laws, subject to Board of Education approval, requiring attendance to 15. Before 1929, however, discussions regarding the school-leaving age featured more in the controversy over the nature and speed of educational reform than as an important element of industrial and economic strategy. The Conservatives

[25] It is not generally recognized that there are many gaps in our statistical knowledge of the dimensions of interwar juvenile unemployment. For further details see W. R. Garside, 'Juvenile Unemployment Statistics Between the Wars: A Commentary and Guide to Sources', *Bulletin of the Society for the Study of Labour History*, 33 (1976), 38–46. Some calculations can be found in Garside, 'Juvenile Unemployment and Public Policy', appendices I-III.

[26] Cab 24/160, Juvenile Unemployment Centres. Report of an Enquiry, May 1923.

[27] T161/518, Memorandum on Juvenile Unemployment, December 1923.

consistently pinned their faith on Juvenile Unemployment Centres as the most effective means of relief and, even in the educational field, proved extremely wary of any proposals to extend school life at national or local level which involved considerable financial outlay. Early in the decade a small number of local authorities sought approval to raise the school-leaving age by by-law specifically for the purpose of relieving juvenile unemployment, but were met with stern Conservative opposition. Apart from the financial consequences, noted a Cabinet Committee in 1923, such a concession, if made, would be a most embarrassing and undesirable precedent.[28]

The first Labour administration was more amenable to such local enterprise thanks largely to the persistent demands of Trevelyan, President of the Board of Education, to have the leaving age in particular localities determined in light of prevailing employment conditions for both juveniles and adults. Nevertheless, in 1924 Labour's Juvenile Unemployment Sub-Committee rejected the idea of any general manipulation of the school-leaving age for industrial purposes, repeating the Board of Education's view that the nature of the problem of the unemployed leavers was such that special arrangements organized apart from the main educational system, such as Juvenile Unemployment Centres, would offer better prospects. Though Trevelyan continued his campaign within government, the education authorities themselves proved unenthusiastic and often blatantly stubborn. Many were afraid of the financial commitment and believed that to keep children at school an extra year would merely deprive them of jobs which would be snapped up by 14 year olds in neighbouring areas.

The return to power of the Conservatives in November 1924 did not produce any major reversals of policy. They had available a report of the Juvenile Organization Committee of the Board of Education, initiated during the previous Labour administration, which scorned the notion of raising the school-leaving age as a means of easing the pressure on the juvenile labour market as a remedy disproportionate to the dimensions of the evil that it sought to combat. 'It would appear . . . a point for consideration', the report noted, 'whether questions of important and permanent educational developments can fairly be dealt with primarily from the point of view of measures designed to meet a special industrial problem. There may even be some danger lest, by hasty improvisation to bring such developments into operation at an early date as a remedy for unemployment difficulties, permanent educational advance may be prejudiced.'[29] Armed with such an

[28] Cab 27/228, Juvenile Unemployment Committee. Report, 15 December 1923.
[29] Cab 27/267, Report of the Juvenile Organizations Committee of the Board of Education on the Problem of the Unemployed Juvenile between 14 and 16 years of age, 20 November 1929.

indictment, the Conservatives continually refused to encourage local action by by-law on the grounds that even such a specific legal authority was never meant to meet temporary emergencies and, in any event, could not easily be restricted to those authorities in areas of severe juvenile unemployment. To cater for the unemployed juvenile even where unemployment was serious was, from their point of view, a far smaller proposition than to develop the facilities for a generally extended school life.

Guided thus, the Baldwin administration toyed with the idea of making it compulsory under law for all juveniles seeking employment to attend an Unemployment Centre,[30] though in itself this could do nothing to create jobs or stem the flow of thousands of school leavers on to the labour market. The only positive action taken was to strengthen the operation of the centres as a first line of defence for the unemployed by providing increased financial assistance in areas of abnormal unemployment – 100 per cent grants after 1927 in areas where juvenile unemployment exceeded 7 per cent.[31] But there was no clear evidence that the formidable practical problems of conducting the centres were being overcome or that the facilities were being provided in areas of greatest need. This is not altogether surprising since there was no comprehensive index of the rate of juvenile unemployment, even of those over 16, available at local or national level before 1929. Where information of local conditions was sufficiently accurate to indicate a juvenile unemployment problem of some seriousness it did not necessarily guarantee ameliorative action. There were many instances where the number of unemployed juveniles claiming benefit was insufficient or the length of their individual periods of unemployment too short to enable separate centres to be established according to rule, even if the total number of youngsters, many of whom might be ineligible for unemployment benefit, demanded some form of public intervention.[32] Attendance for those under 16 remained voluntary until 1934 and in areas such as Lancashire where there was a large amount of short-time working it was, until amending legislation was passed in 1930, manifestly more difficult to provide anything in the nature of systematic instruction. In addition, the 1927 Unemployment Insurance Act made juveniles ineligible for benefit until they had had insurable work for thirty weeks after reaching

---

[30] Cab 24/171, Juvenile Unemployment. Joint Cabinet Memorandum, 20 January, 1925.
[31] For details of variations in financial aid see Report of the Ministry of Labour for the Year 1929, Cmd. 3579, 1930. The Exchequer had met the full cost of all centres during the period 1 April 1924 to 31 March 1926.
[32] In November 1929 only 129 out of a total of 837 Employment Exchanges and Juvenile Employment Bureaux in England and Wales had more than 20 boys claiming unemployment benefit. National Advisory Council for Juvenile Employment (England and Wales), Third Report. Provision of Courses of Instruction for Unemployed Boys and Girls, Cmd. 3638, 1930, 4.

the age of 16 – in effect increasing the number of youngsters who had no incentive to attend centres. But, despite their weaknesses, the JUCs received increasing support in the late 1920s and early 1930s following national investigation of their activity, changing their name in 1930 to Junior Instruction Centres but little of their basic approach or activity.

The economic and social aspects of a higher school-leaving age were never entirely divorced from the continuing debate over the future of British elementary and secondary education which developed with such vigour after 1918. As Ministers and educationalists struggled with the vexed questions of resources and the relationship between elementary and secondary schooling, they found themselves obliged to consider related matters, almost inadvertently focussing on the condition of the juvenile labour market. The Board of Education's *Report on the Education of the Adolescent* (the Hadow Report), issued in 1927, recommended raising the minimum age of compulsory school attendance to 15 from the beginning of 1932 as part of a considered reorganization of the educational system. It emphasized its concern, however, over 'the tragic paradox of a situation in which year to year some 450,000 young lives are poured into industry at a time when industry cannot find employment for its adult workers'.[33]

Influential supporters of extended compulsory education, particularly R. H. Tawney, capitalized on the contemporary industrial malaise to strengthen their case. Raising the leaving age to 15, Tawney argued in 1927, would result in an annual reduction of expenditure on unemployment of between £9 million and £12 million, on the assumption that the enforced 14–15-year-old vacancies would be taken up by unemployed juveniles below 18, and then by unemployed adults in the ratio of one adult to two juveniles. He claimed, moreover, that the diminution in the supply of young juvenile labour would raise the wages of older juveniles, and thereby encourage employers to adopt cost-reducing production methods to compensate for the increased wage bill.[34]

Support for a higher school-leaving age as a specific weapon against unemployment increased noticeably in the late 1920s and drew much of its strength from arguments such as these. The Trades Union Congress, the Melchett–Turner Conference on Industrial Reorganisation and Industrial Relations, and both the Labour and Liberal parties embraced the idea, though there was little general agreement as to the expected impact of such

---

[33] Board of Education Consultative Committee. *Report on the Education of the Adolescent* (1927), 144.

[34] R. H. Tawney, *The Possible Cost of Raising the School-Leaving Age* (1927), 5. Cf. International Association for Social Progress (British Section), *Report on 'The Raising of the School Age and its Relation to Employment and Unemployment'* (1928), 5–10.

a policy.[35] The Melchett–Turner Report announced in 1929, albeit on the basis of an incorrect estimate of the total number of juveniles likely to be withdrawn from the labour market, that raising the school-leaving age to 15 would directly create 200,000 adult jobs.[36] According to the Ministry of Labour, an extension of compulsory schooling by one year would release 300,000 vacancies, 215,000 of which would be taken up directly by 15–18 year olds, and the remainder by unemployed adolescents or adults.[37] Oswald Mosley maintained that a leaving age of 15 would provide employment for 150,000 at a cost of £4.5 million a year.[38]

Estimates such as these were based on extremely precarious and often unjustifiable assumptions about the complementarity of adult and juvenile labour, and about the prevailing and expected responsiveness of industry to short-term fluctuations in the supply of labour. They rarely took into account the existing degree of prosperity within particular industries or regions, or the distribution therein of juveniles merely moving between jobs (and readily available to replace those who would ultimately be kept at school) or those with personal disabilities likely to make them difficult to place whatever the demand for labour. There were areas in the country in which the general employment position of both juveniles and adults was sufficiently buoyant for there to be but a small reservoir from which substitute labour could be drawn. In other regions the vacancies created by a higher leaving age were likely in total to be negligible compared with the existing pool of surplus unemployed labour. Furthermore, even if a higher leaving age had immediate beneficial effects on the employment of 16 and 17 year olds in the depressed areas, the effect of holding out hopes of employment in the future for young adults may well have been to anchor both them and their parents more firmly to areas of chronic industrial decline.

The wide variations throughout industry in the skill, habits of work, and the distribution required at a given wage level of workers of different

[35] Liberal Party, *Britain's Industrial Future. Being the Report of the Liberal Industrial Inquiry* (1928), 393–98; *We Can Conquer Unemployment. Mr. Lloyd George's Pledge* (1929), 50. M. Parkinson, *The Labour Party and the Organization of Secondary Education, 1918–65* (1970), 24. MacDonald's acceptance of a higher school-leaving age in the 1929 Election manifesto was due in part to 'the necessity to put something definite in the programme that might aid the solution of the unemployment problem'. D. W. Dean, 'Difficulties of a Labour Education Policy: The Failure of the Trevelyan Bill 1929–31', *British Journal of Educational Studies*, 17 (1969), 288.
[36] Lab 2/1361, Interim Report on the Melchett Turner Conference on Industrial Reorganisation and Industrial Relations, 1929.
[37] Lab 2/1328, Effects on Unemployment Problem of Raising the School Leaving Age to 15, 16 July 1929. Five years earlier it had been suggested that an extension of the leaving age to 16 would immediately prevent 700,000 boys from entering the labour market. J. Astor, W. Layton, A. L. Bowley and S. Rowntree, *Is Unemployment Inevitable?* (1924).
[38] HC Debs., 5th ser., vol. 239, 28 May 1930, col. 1360.

age and sex rendered the idea of a general substitution of one adult for two juniors either wholly inappropriate or virtually impossible to implement in practice. Substituting older workers for younger ones invariably involved increased labour costs, particularly damaging in unsheltered and uncompetitive trades. Nor was there any guarantee that with the loss of an entire age group of industrial recruits there would be sufficient elasticity in the wages paid to older groups or enough inducement among employers towards greater mechanized production either to prevent rising costs and disrupted production or to promote sufficient additional demand for an industry's product to provide adequate compensation. Protagonists of a higher leaving age were generally agreed that vacant 14–15-year-old jobs would be quickly filled by the next immediate age group, who in turn would be replaced by those from the next group above. But at each stage there were likely to be considerable leakages because of the prevailing (though unknown) volume of unemployment among 14 year olds, because of the loss of jobs which might not be filled if school-leavers were no longer readily available, and perhaps because of the more intensive use by employers of youngsters previously working part-time.

By the end of the 1920s a number of factors combined to influence official attitudes towards juvenile unemployment. The country was experiencing both a shortage and surplus of juvenile labour. The poor prospects facing youngsters in areas of exceptionally severe industrial depression occasioned a special juvenile labour transference scheme in 1928. The government met the cost of actually transferring most boys and girls to new employment. In the case of transferees from distressed mining areas additional assistance was available from employers and the Lord Mayor's Fund to supplement juvenile wages in the receiving areas.[39] Labour transference was a new experiment which presented obvious difficulties. There were the natural objections of parents to be overcome, plus the fact that many were unable, being unemployed themselves, to contribute to the support of their children, whose initial wages in many industrial occupations would not cover the cost of living away from home, whilst many of the girls were unaccustomed to seeking work outside their own home.[40]

As efforts proceeded to ease the situation in places of surplus juvenile labour, employers in the hosiery and boot and shoe trades were complaining of a shortage of boys and girls. Areas in which there had been heavy recruitment during the early years of the First World War and a notable fall

[39] Ministry of Labour, *Memorandum on the Transfer of Juveniles from Distressed Mining Areas to Employment in Other Districts*, 1928. In Scotland similar assistance was provided by a Coalfields Distress Fund. For further discussion see chapter 9.

[40] The transfer of girls was limited in the first instance to resident domestic employment though provision was made in 1929 for their transfer to industrial vacancies.

in the birth rate found themselves with fewer 14 and 15 year olds during 1927–30, though there was little widespread dislocation. Indeed, the general trend of employment improved for boys and girls during the second half of the decade. Whatever criticisms had been made of policy in the recent past there appeared now to be little reason to embark upon a more determined programme of preventative or ameliorative action if only because demographic trends were expected to ease significantly, if not obliterate entirely, the problem of juvenile unemployment. Local Juvenile Employ-ment Committees of the Ministry of Labour confidently reported that because of the wartime birth-rate the number of juveniles available for employment would fall naturally between 1927 and 1933. According to the Balfour Committee the number of males and females aged 14 to 17 years likely to be available for employment in the country would decline slowly from 2.2 million in 1927 to 2.1 million by 1930 and more rapidly to 1.7 million by 1933.[41] Moreover, because there were wide variations between industries in the use of juvenile labour there was no obvious connection between fluctuations in the supply of young industrial recruits and the availability of vacancies for those presently unemployed. The 1931 Census of Population showed that among the groups of industries most likely to be affected by a reduction in the supply of juveniles, because they employed considerably more than the average proportion of workers under 18, three were important sheltered industries – printing, distribution, and personal services – and only one, textiles, was particularly vulnerable to foreign competition.

In the circumstances, the Conservative government remained practically immune down to the late twenties to the economic arguments advanced in support of a higher school-leaving age. It did not believe that the expected shortfall in the supply of juvenile labour would cause industry more than 'temporary inconvenience'.[42] Opponents feared that the potential relief which demographic trends might afford to the competition for jobs would be used merely as an excuse to mark time. There was no guarantee, they argued, that population changes in particular areas would necessarily concur with national trends. Indeed in some districts where there had been disproportionately less military recruitment because of munitions produc-tion and where there had occurred a net influx of labour during the war, the birth rate had actually risen. Even where local reductions in the supply of juvenile labour were expected it was uncertain whether any future revival of trade would accommodate even the existing surplus labour.

---

[41] Balfour Committee, *Factors in Industrial and Commercial Efficiency* (1927), 150–1.
[42] Ministry of Labour, Memorandum on the Shortage, Surplus and Redistribution of Juvenile Labour during the years 1928 to 1933. Based on the views of Local Juvenile Employment Committees, Cmd. 3327, 1929.

It was the pressure of mounting adult unemployment in the later twenties, however, that widened support for an alteration in the length of compulsory schooling on economic grounds. Both the Liberal and Labour parties, supported in principle by the TUC and the Conference on Industrial Reorganisation and Industrial Relations, began to advocate a higher school-leaving age as an effective labour market strategy. For the majority of the Labour Party this was a complete reversal of policy. From 1927 many Labour MPs who had hitherto shown little or no interest in educational matters were suddenly drawn into discussions of advancing the leaving age as a weapon against unemployment.[43] This was not altogether surprising. The protracted discussions in the post-war period over the reorganization of elementary education had already led to firm proposals to seek an extension of compulsory schooling. Amid this contemporary enthusiasm for reform, it proved relatively easy to emphasize the industrial advantages of withdrawing 400,000–500,000 juveniles from the labour market by means already regarded as an acceptable part of future educational policy. Furthermore, the Labour Party (having been persuaded to accept the Hadow Report on the reorganization of elementary education as a compromise for the more far-reaching and contentious ideal of secondary education for all) found even the Board of Education more sympathetic to calls for extending the school age. Once in power the party developed its more positive policy with full vigour, emphasizing how a leaving age of 15 could reduce unemployment amongst 16 and 17 year olds to negligible proportions and create vacancies equivalent to 85,000 adult jobs, saving the Unemployment Fund almost £12 million.[44] However, the Bills introduced into the Commons during 1929–30 on the school-leaving age foundered over the difficulties with voluntary denomination schools and the growing reaction against the cost of expanding state services.

This proved particularly unfortunate in that contemporary expectations that the shortage of 14–18 year olds after 1929 would help reduce juvenile unemployment down to 1933 were not fulfilled. Earlier prognostications

[43] R. Barker, *Education and Politics, 1900–51* (Oxford, 1972), 58.

[44] Cab 27/391, The Raising of the School Leaving Age. Anticipated Effects on Unemployment, 18 July 1929. Previous independent estimates had put the saving to the Unemployment Fund at between £9 million and £12 million. International Association for Social Progress (British Section), *Report on 'The Raising of the School Age and its Relation to Employment and Unemployment'* (1928), 4–8; R. H. Tawney, *The Possible Cost of Raising the School-Leaving Age* (1927). The assumptions implicit in each of these calculations – that unemployed juveniles of 16 and 17 would be immediately absorbed following the withdrawal of 14-year-olds from the labour market and that the jobs subsequently available to adults would be filled in the ratio of one adult job for every two juvenile vacancies – were dismissed by the Conservatives as practically worthless. See Lab 2/1328. Note on Certain Statements in Mr. Tawney's Pamphlet 'The Possible Cost of Raising the School-Leaving Age', 27 October 1927.

had not anticipated the degree of industrial depression which subsequently occurred, independent of demographic movements. It was precisely in 1929 when the supply of young workers was falling off that juvenile unemployment began, like adult unemployment, to grow at an appreciable rate as industry's capacity to absorb even a reduced number of workers noticeably weakened. The rate of unemployment amongst insured boys in the country as a whole rose from just over 3 per cent in 1929 to 8.3 per cent in 1932, with even more marked increases in the north-eastern, Scottish and Welsh districts.[45] The Ministry of Labour estimated that the increase in the total number of juveniles (insured and uninsured) registered as unemployed, from an average of 61,318 in 1929 to 125,041 in 1931, represented in reality a total of over 166,700 unemployed youngsters under 18.[46]

Conditions improved substantially in 1933 because of fortuitous circumstances. The effects of the low wartime birth rate were felt for the first time throughout the whole of the 14–17 age group. By the end of the year the number of juveniles registered as unemployed in each of the administrative divisions of the Ministry of Labour taken together was the lowest total recorded in the previous four years. There were some 390,000 fewer boys and girls in the labour market than in 1929 and as the number available for employment reached its lowest point, trade revival simultaneously stimulated the demand for juvenile labour causing shortages in some industrial areas, especially London. As always, the degree of recovery varied considerably throughout the country. In December 1933 there were one-and-a-half times as many juveniles registered for employment in Glasgow as in the whole of the Midlands Division and no less than 20 per cent of the total number of juveniles recorded as unemployed was confined to the five towns of Liverpool, Glasgow, Bristol, Manchester and Newcastle.[47]

With the influence of demographic trends now so closely linked to prevailing economic conditions, new fears were expressed in the mid-thirties over the future of juvenile employment. If the low wartime birth-rate had eased pressure on the juvenile labour market in the recent past, its substantial rise in the immediate post-war years would certainly add to the total number of juveniles seeking work after 1933. Official investigations by

[45] See Garside 'Juvenile Unemployment and Public Policy', appendix 2.
[46] The Ministry considered that unemployment amongst the young uninsured was no greater than that amongst the insured and estimated that the total number of juveniles unemployed at any time was probably not in excess of the number recorded on the Live Register plus 40–50 per cent. The Register contained details of those boys and girls aged 14 and under 18 who had applied for employment and by renewed application had kept their names 'alive', but for whom jobs had not been found. Garside, *The Measurement of Unemployment*, chapter 2.
[47] Ministry of Labour, Report on Juvenile Employment for the Year 1933 (1934), 4, 11.

the Ministry of Labour suggested that in the absence of any remedial action there were clear expectations of large surpluses occurring in the juvenile labour market, especially during 1935–37.[48] This was a matter of particular concern, not only because the future demand for juvenile labour could not be guaranteed, but also because the Board of Trade had shown that many important industrial areas were already overstocked with labour. Even if trade was to recover to its 1929 level, the north east, south west, Scotland, south Wales, Merseyside and Lancashire were expected to carry a permanent labour surplus of insured persons which could only be reduced in the immediate term by a fall in the numbers entering industry or through labour transference.[49] But already there was evidence that juveniles persisted in seeking openings in the overmanned cotton industry[50] and that employers in areas which normally received transferred juveniles were beginning to rely for their labour on an expansion in the number of local youths available for work.

The most noticeable effect of these predictions of a reversal in juvenile employment prospects was to increase pressure-group activity in support of an extension of the school-leaving age. Most protagonists were seeking a greater measure of educational reform, a cause to which the stark reality of juvenile unemployment added a sense of poignancy and immediacy. The Labour Party and the TUC renewed their call for a higher leaving age as a direct means of improving juvenile and adult unemployment.[51] Given existing surpluses of labour in particular depressed industries and regions, and given the uncertainty surrounding the likely strength and direction of revival impulses in the economy, there was every likelihood, they argued, of the potential increase in the supply of cheap labour increasing the scramble for jobs to the detriment of the living standards of older juveniles and adults alike.[52] To these demands were added similar appeals from the National Union of Teachers, the Association of Education Committees, the International Labour Office, the Bishop of Durham, and the Archbishops of York

[48] Ministry of Labour, *Memorandum on the Shortage, Surplus and Redistribution of Juvenile Labour in England and Wales During the Years 1930–38* (1931); Ministry of Labour, National Advisory Council for Juvenile Employment (Scotland), *Fifth Report. Supply of, Demand for and Redistribution of Juvenile Labour in Scotland During the Years 1932–40* (1933).
[49] Board of Trade, *An Industrial Survey of the Lancashire Area (excluding Merseyside); An Industrial Survey of South Wales; An Industrial Survey of the North-East Coast Area; An Industrial Survey of South West Scotland* (1932). For details of these reports see below chapter 9, pp. 249–50.
[50] Board of Trade, *An Industrial Survey of the Lancashire Area (excluding Merseyside)*, 13.
[51] Labour Party, *Annual Conference Report*, 1933, 180; Trades Union Congress, *Annual Report*, 1934, 71.
[52] R. H. Tawney, *Juvenile Employment and Education* (Oxford, 1934), 11. See also Tawney, 'Unemployment and the School-Leaving Age', *New Statesman*, 18 November 1933.

and Canterbury.[53] If the raising of the leaving-age to 16 could be completed within two years, Ernest Bevin claimed in 1933, some 840,000 boys and girls would be withdrawn from the labour market, enabling total unemployment among men and women to fall by 560,000.[54]

The policy officially adopted towards juveniles after 1934 turned out to be more limited and pragmatic, largely because juvenile unemployment proved a less ominous problem than had earlier been anticipated. The earlier investigations by the Ministry of Labour into the prospective state of the juvenile labour market during the remainder of the thirties had presupposed that the employment demand for juveniles to 1938 would remain for England and Wales as it was in May 1930 and for Scotland as it was in May 1932. But with a marked upswing in industrial activity from 1934 employment conditions improved and the total number of juveniles registered as unemployed declined nationally between 1935 and 1937, irrespective of the overall increase in the numbers available for work[55] and the more accurate system of registration following the extension of unemployment insurance to 14 and 15 year olds. Furthermore, there is evidence that the proportion of boys and girls under 16 who had left school but had had no full-time employment fell during 1934–37. There was a corresponding increase also in the proportion of those juveniles unemployed who had been in full-time employment at some date since leaving school.[56]

In 1934 the minimum age of entry to unemployment insurance was reduced to 14. At the same time, Local Education Authorities were compelled in certain circumstances to provide courses of instruction for all unemployed insured juveniles which even non-benefit claimants would be made to attend. This at once enhanced the effectiveness of Junior Instruction Centres by extending official contact to the majority under 18. Industrial transference was extended to all areas in which there was an appreciable surplus of juvenile labour, thereby adding weight to a policy already hailed as a most effective solution to regional industrial de-

---

[53] *Times Educational Supplement*, 7 April, 26 May and 16 June 1934; *The Times*, 14 November 1934; *Unemployment Among Young Persons. Report Submitted to the Nineteenth Session of the International Labour Conference* (Geneva, 1935).

[54] Bevin, *My Plan for 2,000,000 Workless*, appendix I.

[55] It was estimated that the total number of juveniles under 18 available for employment in Great Britain by the end of 1934 exceeded the number available in 1933 by 80,000. By the end of 1936 there were altogether 150,000 more juveniles available than in 1935. Ministry of Labour, Report for the Year 1934, Cmd. 4861, 1935, 39; Report for the Year 1936, Cmd. 5431, 1937, 36.

[56] *Ministry of Labour Gazette*, 1934–37. There were still, of course, noticeable differences in the ability of industry to absorb juveniles in different parts of the country.

pression.[57] This move, combined with a policy of relief to the Special Areas, was expected to cater adequately for the needs of youngsters in areas of exceptional distress. When action was taken in 1936 towards raising the school-leaving age to 15 within three years, it proved to be more a calculated act of political expediency than a recognition of the need to stem the flow of young industrial recruits on to the labour market. Indeed, children could avoid the extra year at school if they were able to secure beneficial employment. 'Employment as cheap labour from the age of 14 (was) thereby contemplated with equanimity as a proper alternative for working-class children whose parents could do no better for them.'[58]

There were, in addition to the varying circumstances outlined above, more fundamental reasons why the issue of the school-leaving age failed to make a more significant impact on interwar discussions about the reduction of unemployment. Treating the school-age question as a branch of the unemployment problem involved a profound misconception of both. Once the raising of the leaving age became an acknowledged feature of the planned reorganization of post-primary education from the mid-twenties onwards, educationalists adamantly refused to have what they regarded as a significant item of public concern made dependent upon the state of the labour market at any given time. Even when argued on purely educational grounds, it was difficult enough to agree on the scale of the necessary resources and on the academic and organizational changes involved in the sudden imposition of another year of school life. Moreover, if the raising of the school age was to represent a genuine educational advance rather than merely an extension of the waiting time which had hitherto characterized the last year of elementary schooling, it could not take effect immediately. But from the point of view of unemployment, there was little merit in any proposal which only began to produce results – and doubtful results at that – some years ahead.

The dominant cry, especially from Conservative administrations, was that the country could not afford increased educational expenditure, especially if provision had to be made for paying maintenance allowances to those compulsorily kept at school. Parental pressure on children to forgo extra schooling in favour of immediate wage earning (especially keen if the male householder was unemployed) and the scepticism of employers as to the alleged benefits in efficiency and adaptability of an older and more educated workforce kept the issue of extended schooling further at bay.

Furthermore, official efforts to foster the widespread adoption of Juvenile

---

[57] Ministry of Labour. *Reports of Investigations into the Industrial Conditions in Certain Depressed Areas*, Cmd. 4728, 1934. Cf. chapter 9, pp. 242–6, 265–71.

[58] B. Simon, *The Politics of Educational Reform, 1920–1940* (1974), 303.

Unemployment (and, later, Instruction) Centres as a means of engaging unemployed youngsters in non-vocational activity appeared to offer a more immediate and practical form of relief than did reliance on future changes in educational policy. In addition, regional variations in the intensity of juvenile unemployment made the problem appear transitory and insufficiently serious to warrant any alteration in the period of compulsory education. Those in more prosperous regions viewed with alarm the prospect of imposing a higher leaving age on what were generally regarded as spurious economic grounds.

The inevitable delay involved in agreeing an increase in the minimum leaving age and actually implementing the change on a national scale further encouraged the belief that, in so far as juvenile unemployment was concerned, demographic change would, in the time available, effect a 'natural' cure of any existing shortages or surpluses in the labour market, obviating the need for corrective action from any other direction. Political commitment, moreover, was forever faltering and uncertain. Though the Conservative-dominated National Government readily embraced some of the arguments for extending compulsory schooling in a desperate effort to appear progressive and forward thinking in policy, it defended nevertheless the right of employers to cheap juvenile labour and opposed any fundamental educational reform which threatened the prevailing elitism of British society.

RETIREMENT PENSIONS

It was but a small step to extend the argument for reducing competition in the overcrowded labour market by increasing the length of compulsory schooling to achieving a similar effect by an enforced reduction in the retirement age. Contemporaries frequently regarded the two policies as inextricably linked. The joint TUC/Labour Party proposals on the prevention of unemployment published in 1926 called for action on retirement pensions on employment grounds[59] as did those trade union and employer representatives involved in the Mond–Turner talks during 1929. The latter acknowledged the 'enormous value' and the 'experience and steadiness' of older workers, but argued that:

if by some more liberal retiring allowance than the present Old Age Pension affords, a greater inducement could be given to those above the age of 65 to take a well-earned rest from their work to allow the younger men, who are waiting for a job, to

[59] See *On the Dole or Off? What to do with Britain's Workless Workers: Report on the Prevention of Unemployment by a Joint Committee representing the General Council of the Trades Union Congress, the National Executive of the Labour Party, and the Executive of the Parliamentary Labour Party* (1926).

come into their place, then a step forward would be taken both in industrial efficiency and in diminishing the number of those who to-day are on the unemployment register.[60]

It was preferable, the argument ran, for public funds to be used in pensioning older workers at a higher than customary rate than it was to pay benefits to young and vigorous workers who were unemployed. An added attraction would be that firms contemplating a reduction in their labour force as part of a planned scheme of industrial rationalization would be better able to deal with any remaining surplus by retiring their older employees rather than having to discharge younger workers. Thus the Transport and General Workers' Union, 'profoundly dissatisfied' with the Labour Government's 'long range' policy, wrote privately to Ramsay MacDonald in 1930 reminding him that:

a very large and influential body of Employers as well as Trade Unions, are absolutely unanimous in trying to meet the problems which rationalisation inevitably creates, by raising the school age at one end and by making provision for Pensions at 65 at the other end. Whilst this is by no means a complete solution it does grapple with more people affected by industry than any other single proposal.[61]

By the time it took office again in 1929 the Labour Party, on the insistence of the miners, had already embraced the idea of seeking higher pensions as a means of reducing unemployment. A Cabinet Committee chaired by George Lansbury, First Commissioner of Works, was established in June 1929 to produce a workable scheme. At first the Committee considered increasing old-age pensions from the existing 10s a week to insured persons aged 65 to 30s a week for married couples over 65, at a cost of £60 million. Fearful however of Exchequer opposition, the Committee eventually abandoned the proposal in favour of a plan devised by Oswald Mosley offering pensions at 60 to workers in coalmining, iron and steel and shipbuilding, subject to their retiring from work. Once it was realized that very few vacancies would be created on such a narrow industrial base, the Committee finally proposed that all insured workers (plus railwaymen) aged 60 on an appointed date should be offered a pension of £1 a week for a single man and 30s a week for a married couple, on condition that they retired from work within six months. With 677,000 persons eligible, 390,000 were expected to accept the pension, creating 278,000 vacancies at a gross average cost of £21.6 million per year (£10.9 million net of savings on unemployment benefit). It

---

[60] Conference on Industrial Reorganisation and Industrial Relations. *Interim Report on Unemployment* (1929), 9.
[61] Transport and General Workers' Union, Letter to the Prime Minister, 27 August 1930. Trades Union Congress Library.

was preferable, in the Committee's view, for the old 'to be maintained in idleness' rather than the young.

Civil servants, particularly at the Treasury, had their misgivings. The countervailing benefits in terms of the potential reabsorption of the unemployed and saving on unemployment insurance were judged to be too problematic and too long delayed in their effects to justify the immediate costs involved. Even if there were willing recruits amongst the pensionable class the retirement scheme would create resentment among those workers who had previously retired on a pension of 10s a week. And there were doubts within the Cabinet. Whatever measures of taxation were devised to finance the scheme, warned J. H. Thomas, 'the cost must tend . . . to hamper productive industry and . . . to contract the volume of employment'. The Cabinet finally rejected the proposed scheme in November 1929.

But the debate over retirement pensions was not yet dead. Among the 'short term schemes for the relief of unemployment' raised by Oswald Mosley in 1930 was an Emergency Retirement Pensions plan designed, in conjunction with a higher school-leaving age and loan-financed public works, to reduce unemployment by 700,000.[62] And it was George Lansbury who urged the Cabinet in 1930 not to think it 'stupid or uneconomic . . . to substitute able-bodied workers for aged workers'. Some 280,000 people could be found work as substitutes for those retired at higher rates of pension. No one, Lansbury warned, should believe that the policy would create 'new work for anybody'; it would, however, 'leave vacancies for able-bodied people to fill, and thus . . . would reduce the number . . . receiving money for nothing'.[63] But it was precisely because pension plans appeared incapable of creating additional jobs speedily or necessarily in the places where they were most needed that they failed to surmount the opposition of hardline civil servants, or even to gain the respect of otherwise committed radicals such as Keynes and Henderson.

Ernest Bevin breathed new life into the idea in the mid-thirties. An optional pension at 60, he maintained in 1933, paid at a weekly rate of £1 per week to a single person and 35s for a married couple, would encourage the unemployed between the ages of 60 and 65 to give up the unequal struggle for work. If it was combined with compulsory retirement at 65 and the provision of invalidity pensions, some 600,000 people could be removed from the unemployment register at an estimated cost of £47 million.[64] Government officials remained sceptical; Bevin's scheme was 'a counsel of despair' incapable of reducing unemployment to any appreciable degree.

[62] R. Skidlesky, *Oswald Mosley* (1981), 186.
[63] Cab 24/211, CP 143, Unemployment Policy (1930) Committee. Memorandum by the First Commissioner of Works, 6 May 1930.
[64] Bevin, *My Plan for 2,000,000 Workless*, 9–14, 23–4.

'The grant of optional pensions to unemployed persons aged 60 to 65', the Treasury complained, 'would merely involve the payment to them of unemployment benefit under another name at a higher rate than that payable under the Unemployment Insurance Acts'. Moreover, it was only likely to apply to some 150,000 people. Extra vacancies would only be forthcoming from the relatively few insured persons over 65 in industry (perhaps 100,000) tempted to accept a retirement pension. With projected savings of only £10 million from both schemes compared with an estimated outlay of £100 million (the excess of the annual cost of Bevin's proposals over the prevailing cost of pensions and disablement benefit under existing legislation) the country was being asked to incur a net expenditure of £90 million in the vague hope of reducing unemployment by upwards of 250,000.[65]

The arguments were well rehearsed. Both the retirement pensions and the school-leaving programme were vulnerable to veto on grounds of cost, particularly in comparison with their anticipated effects on total unemployment. And although each was projected as a potentially useful way of augmenting demand, whether by transfer payments or by boosting jobs, they were continually regarded as defeatist and diversionary, unworthy of serious attention by those committed to defending the status quo and the public purse.

[65] T172/1800, Comments on Bevin's Proposals for the Relief of Unemployment, 1933.

PART III

The international context

5 ✻ On and off gold: unemployment, monetary policy and the exchange rate

The defence of 'sound money' proved a powerful and dominant influence upon the official response to interwar unemployment. Government concern about confidence in the pound and the stability of the budget was of paramount significance in the debacle over unemployment insurance. Questions of cost, likewise, were never far from Ministers' minds whenever alternative schemes to relieve the plight of the unemployed were under consideration, as the previous chapter briefly indicated. The links between domestic and international finance and the unemployment problem were, however, more complex and endemic than have so far been demonstrated. Subsequent chapters will detail the conflict that emerged between fiscal probity and the debate over job creation. We turn first to the effects of monetary policy and the exchange rate upon official attitudes toward unemployment during the 1920s and beyond.

GOLDEN SACRIFICE? UNEMPLOYMENT AND THE STERLING PARITY, 1919–31

To Edwardian observers, the gold standard represented the bedrock of economic stability at home and abroad. It was customarily believed, more as an article of faith than as an established fact, that the free movement of gold occasioned self-adjusting balance of payments equilibria. In classical terms, any differences between foreign receipts and payments would induce changes in a country's stock of gold, forcing a shift in monetary circulation sufficient by its effects on incomes and prices to alter the demand for imports and exports in the requisite direction to correct the balance of trade. More significantly, the discipline of fixed exchange rates and the widespread use of the pound as a medium of international exchange strengthened the presumption that Britain's trading position and London's dominant standing in international finance were based almost entirely upon her successful defence of the gold standard regime. When, therefore, the dislocations of war and the pains of reconstruction appeared to threaten the

115

viability of both the national and international economic order by making it difficult to operate fixed exchange rates in the short term, it became a prime object of British financial policy to restore the 'normality' of the pre-war period as swiftly as conditions would allow.

In truth, the success of the gold standard before 1914 had depended upon a number of fortuitous circumstances unlikely to operate again as favourably as they had done in the past. These enabling factors included the absence of divergent movements in imports, exports or interest rates among major industrialized countries sufficient to prevent serious disequilibrium within the international payments system, and a marked degree of economic stability and price flexibility at home. The strength of the gold standard, in other words, depended upon the inherent strength of London as an international financial centre, not the reverse. But so long as the opposite belief prevailed, it was understandable that the monetary authorities should interpret external and internal stability as a natural concomitant of the successful operation of a fixed-exchange gold standard.

Although the pre-1914 gold order was effectively shattered by the First World War, the authorities remained determined to restore orthodox international monetary policy during the reconstruction period. The appointment in January 1918 of a Committee on Currency and Foreign Exchanges after the War (the Cunliffe Committee) reflected this concern. Its First Interim Report declared it essential, even in 1918, to impose a cut in government borrowing and to use Bank Rate to check a foreign drain of gold in order to create 'the conditions necessary to the maintenance of an effective gold standard'. The Cunliffe Committee was not unaware of the fact that high interest rates, apart from attracting foreign capital to help stabilize the reserve position, could also depress output and employment. But it remained convinced that the trade-off between internal and external balance in the short run was the essential price to be paid for stability and prosperity in the long term.[1]

Britain had been forced during the war to suspend gold exports and to develop a 'managed' paper standard. The official sterling/dollar exchange rate was pegged at $4.76 from 1916; deficits incurred by the purchase of foodstuffs, munitions and raw materials were financed by selling off assets and by borrowing. However, wartime inflationary finance, coupled with a vigorous post-war boom at a time of general scarcity, pushed up British internal prices to such a level that it proved politically embarrassing to attempt to restore parity by deflation, as the gold standard system dictated, if only because of the unemployment and social unrest that was likely to

[1] Committee on Currency and Foreign Exchanges after the War, First Interim Report, Cd. 9182, 1918.

ensue. In the circumstances, the cost of maintaining the sterling/dollar exchange became prohibitive and in March 1919 the gold standard was formally abandoned. Sterling was allowed to find its own level to protect the gold reserves; the unsupported dollar rate slid to a low point of $3.20 in February 1920 compared to its pre-war parity of $4.86.

Faced with excessive price rises, the authorities found it necessary to invoke a severe deflation. Bank Rate, which had already been raised from 5 to 6 per cent in November 1919, was increased further to 7 per cent in April 1920. This tightening of domestic credit threatened both trade and employment. At the time the imposition of 'dear money' seemed perfectly justified given the danger which inflation posed to the basis of contract and to social peace. It even found favour with Keynes, who was later to emerge as one of the most severe critics of orthodox monetary policy. Any induced financial crisis, he wrote, 'ought to prevent our staple industries from having twice as many orders as they can fulfil; but there is a very wide margin of safety before they would be reduced to working below their capacity'.[2]

The inflationary boom collapsed in the autumn of 1920 following a fall in home demand and exports. Hawtrey at the Treasury had supported the previous rises in Bank Rate, but argued subsequently that once expansion had ceased the Rate should be lowered again to prevent serious trade depression and unemployment. It was kept at a crisis level, however, for nearly a year and undoubtedly aggravated the slump. As wholesale prices tumbled unemployment rose, from an average recorded rate among trade union members of 2.4 per cent (1919–20) to 15.2 per cent during 1922,[3] and as a percentage of the civilian working population from 2.0 per cent in 1920 to 9.8 per cent in 1922.[4] Industrialists within the FBI, alarmed at the deflationary impact of official policy, called repeatedly during 1921 for a fresh enquiry into monetary policy. Employment, they complained, was being unduly jeopardized by the City's overriding determination to bring down prices to facilitate a return to pre-war parity.

Though severe deflation enacted a high domestic price in Britain, the greater decline of UK compared to US wholesale prices helped the sterling/dollar exchange rate recover from its previous low point of

[2] S. Howson, '"A Dear Money Man"? Keynes on Monetary Policy, 1920', *Economic journal*, 83 (1973), 459. Keynes did not at the time support 'dear money' as a means of restoring the gold standard. In 1920 he felt that the ultimate value of monetary policy was compromised by excessive price inflation, in much the same way as he considered the efficiency of monetary policy in the thirties to be compromised by businessmen's lack of confidence amidst chronic unemployment.
[3] D. E. Moggridge, *British Monetary Policy, 1924–1931. The Norman Conquest of $4.86* (Cambridge, 1972), 25.
[4] Feinstein, *National Income, Expenditure and Output*, table 58.

$3.20. By mid-1922 prices had stabilized and Bank Rate, held at 7 per cent until April 1921, fell to 3 per cent. By that time, however, the Bank of England became concerned about the emergence of an unfavourable differential in interest rates between London and New York and looked towards an appreciation of sterling as a step towards achieving a post-war parity of $4.86.

The authorities were in a dilemma. Sterling parity could not be restored without appreciating the pound and increasing unemployment, especially in the export industries. On the other hand, domestic expansion could not be undertaken without prejudicing the prospect of returning to gold. At the Genoa Conference in 1922, Britain attempted to ease her difficulties by seeking a means of strengthening London's traditional position as world banker without aggravating unemployment through the imposition of severe deflation. The idea – to have sterling or the dollar act as a reserve asset rather than gold, permitting European currencies to be stabilized on a gold exchange standard – was vetoed by the Americans.

At home, meanwhile, the perceived link between a restrictive monetary policy and rising unemployment attracted widespread condemnation and put the authorities on the defensive. Keynes, who had acquiesced in 'dear money' during 1919–20 for the sake of liquidating inflation, argued that prices had already been forced down too far relative to wage costs, and that the authorities were deliberately destroying jobs. At first it seemed that such criticisms had found their mark; for almost a year after mid-1922 domestic considerations took priority over the exchanges. But thereafter the desire to strengthen the pound against the dollar proved too overwhelming. Bank Rate, which had fallen to 3 per cent, was increased by 1 per cent in July 1923. The Treasury opposed the increase for fear of its anticipated effects on unemployment. Already, however, the Minister of Labour had warned the Cabinet of the inflationary threat posed by rising unemployment relief expenditure. If exports and jobs were to be protected it was necessary to stabilize the economy at a still lower level of prices.[5]

The authorities' attitude was not entirely perverse. Stabilizing the exchanges, they felt, would facilitate monetary stability on an international scale, thereby liberalizing trade and easing unemployment problems within the staple export sector. The difficulty was that in the short term someone would have to pay the price for enforcing parity via domestic deflation. 'You can only get back to a gold standard', judged the Chairman of the Midland Bank, Reginald McKenna, in 1924:

by a rise in prices in the United States relative to our price level. There is no other means of getting back. The notion that you can force down prices here until you get

[5] R. S. Sayers, *The Bank of England, 1891–1944* (Cambridge, 1976), 131.

to the level of the United States if they remain constant is a dream . . . The attempt to force prices down when you have a million unemployed is unthinkable . . . You cannot get on the gold standard by any action of the Chancellor of the Exchequer . . . He could cause infinite trouble, infinite unemployment, immense losses and ruin.[6]

He and Keynes, together with representatives of the Federation of British Industries, warned of the increase in unemployment that would follow upon any premature return to gold. Their acceptance at the time of the monetary theory of the trade cycle emphasized falling prices as a cause rather than a consequence of unemployment. The goal of monetary policy, they therefore argued, should be price stability for the sake of stable employment, not enforced credit restriction. Even the Governor of the Federal Reserve Bank in New York, Benjamin Strong, warned that it would be difficult:

practically and socially for the British government and the Bank of England to force a price liquidation . . . beyond what they have already experienced in the face of the fact that their trade is poor and they have over a million unemployed people receiving government aid.[7]

Such warnings did not go unheeded. They were embraced by the (Chamberlain–Bradbury) Committee on the Currency and Bank of England Note Issues[8] which warned in a draft report in September 1924 that to attempt to restore gold to parity by deflating domestic prices posed an 'undesirable' threat to employment and industry. It would be preferable to await events abroad; after all, a fortuitous inflation of American prices would enable the authorities to secure parity without domestic 'inconveniences'.

Any inflation abroad which breached the gap between British and foreign prices and costs would have made the authorities' task of restoring the gold standard more palatable in political and social terms. Neither the Bank of England nor the City disguised their belief that a degree of painful adjustment might ultimately prove necessary, though they entertained somewhat optimistic estimates of the economic cost likely to ensue. In their view it was necessary nonetheless to fulfil foreign expectations of British credit worthiness. They hoped that prices abroad would at least stabilize;

---

[6] Cited in Moggridge, *British Monetary Policy*, 44.
[7] Cited in Moggridge, *British Monetary Policy*, 52.
[8] Committee on the Currency and Bank of England Note Issues, Report, Cmd. 2392, 1925. The Committee first met in June 1924 'to consider whether the time has now come to amalgamate the Treasury Note Issue with the Bank of England Note Issue, and, if so, on what terms and conditions the amalgamation should be carried out'. The question before the Committee became inseparable from the larger question of the restoration of a free gold market.

or, failing that, that any enforced deflation at home would be accompanied by a degree of wage flexibility and an accommodating Bank Rate policy, such as had occurred during 1920–22, sufficient to temper any damaging effects. The more likely outcome was that the unemployed would be the victims of British internationalism. There was little point, however, in the out-of-work looking to the Labour Party to defend their interests. Socialist Ministers embraced the declared priorities of monetary policy with a clear conscience, welcoming a 'sound and healthy' deflation in 1924 as the necessary means by which trade, prosperity and employment could ultimately be restored.

The wartime measures modifying the gold standard had been replaced in 1920 by the Gold and Silver Export Embargo Act which was itself due to expire on 31 December 1925. By that time speculation had forced sterling towards its pre-war parity and the monetary authorities came under intense pressure to formalize their declared policy objective. But neither the underlying price and cost situation within the economy nor the prevailing level of insured unemployment (which had fallen only from 11.9 per cent in 1923 to 11.3 per cent in 1925) warranted stabilization of the pound at its pre-war level. None of this troubled the official mind. 'If it is agreed that we must have the gold standard', wrote Niemeyer, Controller of Finance at the Treasury:

is it not better to get over any discomforts at once and then proceed on an even keel rather than have the disolocation (if dislocation there be) still before us? No one believes that unemployment can be cured by the dole, and palliatives like road digging. Every party – not least Labour – has preached that unemployment can only be dealt with by radical measures directed to the economic restoration of trade . . . On a long view – and it is only such views that can produce fundamental cures – the gold standard is in direct succession to the main steps towards economic reconstruction . . . and is likely to do more for British trade than all the efforts of the Unemployment Committee.

Only by stabilizing currencies, reconstructing 'the broken parts of Europe', and encouraging thrift and capital accumulation could unemployment be remedied.[9] None of Niemeyer's confident assertions was buttressed by any analysis, sophisticated or otherwise. There was, it seemed, no need to argue the case for a return to parity; the moment had arrived to act in accordance with 'best opinion'. If the opportunity was missed it would be interpreted abroad as a dangerous reversal of policy, threatening further unwelcome speculation on the exchanges.

The Conservatives' electoral victory towards the end of 1924, combined with a rise in American prices in the winter of 1925, led to heavy

[9] T172/1499B, 'The Gold Export Prohibition. Commentary', 2 February 1925.

speculation in sterling; the exchange rate rose in the expectation of an early return to gold. Even the Chamberlain–Bradbury Committee, which had earlier counselled in favour of waiting upon events abroad for up to twelve months, argued that it would not require much more than 'inconveniences' to force the February 1925 exchange rate of $4.79 to parity at $4.86. Such 'inconveniences', stripped of their euphemism, were likely to involve an enforced control of credit in order to adjust the internal purchasing power of the pound to its exchange parity, with a consequent fall in wages and employment. But few in authority bothered to consider the real cost of pursuing monetary orthodoxy. There was an almost total disregard of the relationship between sterling and other European currencies and little or no thought given to the speed or effectiveness with which Bank Rate could effect any subsequent internal adjustments. Likewise, hardly any consideration was given to the resurgence of German and other foreign competition, whilst too much weight was accorded to the view that wages, having already displayed a marked degree of flexibility during the troubled years of 1920–22, would respond appropriately if called upon to do so. Devaluation was never considered.[10]

The consequences for unemployment if internal costs did not adjust and if inflation did not proceed abroad once Britain fixed its exchange rate at a higher level than then prevailing were obvious to a few informed critics. They even troubled Churchill as Chancellor. To his credit, he proved more cautious over the appropriate policy to pursue than did some of his closest advisers. Although ultimately he succumbed to the combined weight of Treasury and Bank of England orthodoxy, he was by no means a fumbling amateur at the mercy of 'a narrow clique of unscrupulous officials'.[11] He baulked at the idea that financial and currency issues alone should dominate the discussion of restoring gold. 'The Governor of the Bank of England', Churchill wrote to Niemeyer on 22 February 1925:

shows himself perfectly happy in the spectacle of Britain possessing the finest credit in the world simultaneously with a million and a quarter unemployed . . . The community lacks goods, and a million and a quarter people lack work. It is certainly one of the highest functions of national finance and credit to bridge the gulf between the two . . . At any rate while that unemployment exists, no one is entitled to plume himself on the financial or credit policy which we have pursued.

It may be of course that you will argue that the unemployment would have been much greater but for the financial policy pursued; that there is not sufficient demand for commodities either internally or externally to require the services of this million and a quarter people; that there is nothing for them but to hang on like a millstone round the neck of industry and on the public revenue until they became permanently demoralised. You may be right, but if so, it is one of the most sombre

---

[10] See W. Reddaway, 'Was $4.86 Inevitable in 1925?' *Lloyds Bank Review*, 96 (April 1970), 15–28.   [11] L. S. Pressnell, *The Times*, 23 February 1977.

conclusions ever reached. On the other hand I do not pretend to see even 'through a glass darkly' how the financial and credit policy of the country could be handled so as to bridge the gap between a dearth of goods and a surplus of labour; and well I realise the danger of experiment to that end. The seas of history are full of famous wrecks. Still if I could see a way, I would far rather follow it than any other. I would rather see Finance less proud and Industry more content.[12]

So too would others outside of government. Within the serried ranks of economists, industrialists and trade union leaders, there were a few lone voices warning of the dangerous and slavish presuppositions upon which official monetary policy was based. If, after the restoration of gold at pre-war par, foreign inflation proved insufficient or unavailable to accommodate prices and costs at the ruling exchange rate, critics argued, domestic economic activity, and particularly money wages, would have to be depressed on such a scale as to make widespread industrial disputes and intensified unemployment practically inevitable. Labour activists such as Bevin, Brailsford and Hobson, together with members of the FBI, urged Churchill to delay any decision on the gold standard.[13] G. D. H. Cole likened the emphasis on monetary policy to 'a Great God named Par who is worshipped daily at the Treasury . . . Par likes unemployment; it is his form of human sacrifice.'[14]

What the country really needed, preached McKenna at the Midland Bank, was not deliberate deflation but an 'expansion of credit'; it was absurd to enforce deflation for the sake of restoring the exchanges with over one million unemployed.[15] Even Hawtrey at the Treasury agreed that high interest rates threatened output and employment by inducing traders to cut back upon their holdings of stocks. With Bank Rate at 5 per cent in July 1925, he wrote:

The treatment of adverse exchanges by a high Bank Rate may accurately be described as inducing a depression of trade, with its accompaniments of a shrinkage of profits and employment. If this were not so, there would have been no reason against forcing the exchange back to parity at any time since 1921.[16]

The problem with much of the informed opposition to monetary policy, however, was that it emphasized the particular difficulties of restoring parity in the immediate term whilst accepting the inevitability of a return to gold at some more propitious time. In July 1924, for example, the FBI

[12] T172/1499B, Churchill to Niemeyer, 22 February 1925.
[13] G. McDonald, 'Insight Into Industrial Politics: The Federation of British Industries' Papers, 1925', *Business Archives*, (June 1973), 29–37.
[14] Cited in E. Durbin, *New Jerusalems. The Labour Party and the Economics of Democratic Socialism* (1985), 59–60.
[15] L. J. Hume, 'The Gold Standard and Deflation: Issues and Attitudes in the 1920s', *Economica*, 30 (1963), 235.
[16] Cited in R. Catterall, 'Attitudes to and the Impact of British Monetary Policy in the 1920s', *International Review of the History of Banking*, 12 (1976), 45.

warned that the pursuit of parity would be injurious to industry, but it was sanguine about the long-term implications of restoring gold. Keynes was the notable exception.[17] He refused to accept that sterling was entitled to any special consideration or that the country had no option but to deflate and cut costs in order to restore domestic prosperity and employment. His rejection of the underconsumptionist view (that the remedy for unemployment lay in reducing the amount of savings in order to redistribute wealth towards consumers) led him in the early twenties to advocate a less restrictive financial policy, in favour of one aimed at reducing interest rates in order to stimulate investment. This, he argued, should be accompanied by the 'management' of sterling through adjustable exchange rates, in order both to preserve price stability and to insulate the economy from inflationary or deflationary pressures originating abroad. In Keynes's view, it was worse 'in an impoverished world to provoke unemployment than to disappoint the rentier'.[18]

This view, in turn, was modified once matters came to a head in 1925. Moving away from the theoretical 'best' solution of adjustable exchange rates, he urged the authorities not to hasten stabilization at the pre-war rate, as if duty bound to do so. Any subsequent appreciation of sterling would only damage exports and encourage imports. It would necessitate, moreover, such a high level of interest rates to prevent losses of gold that, in the absence of inflation abroad, Britain would have to suffer even more deflation and intensified unemployment until prices and costs adjusted to the new situation.[19]

The monetary authorities never denied that returning to gold at par would involve some degree of deflation but they remained convinced that the consequent damage would be neither substantial nor long term in nature. To the Bank of England restoration of gold was synonymous with the restoration of its own pre-eminence. Whether the exchange rate was appropriate in terms of its likely effects on employment and the balance of payments was not an issue which troubled the Bank unduly. Stability of the exchanges was able to be presented as a meaningful alternative to full employment because it was associated with the restoration of London as an international financial centre.

In the event, the unanimity of opinion within business, financial and political circles, that the restored gold standard would prove the guarantor

---

[17] We have already referred to his preference for stable or even slightly rising prices to stable exchanges. See p. 19.

[18] J. M. Keynes, *A Tract for Monetary Reform* (1923), 36.

[19] H. D. Henderson shared this view, writing in 1925: 'A return to gold this year cannot be achieved without terrible risk of renewed trade depression and a serious aggravation of unemployment.' 'Will Unemployment Increase?', *The Nation*, 4 April 1925.

of employment if viewed in the context of Britain's improved standing in the field of international finance, enabled Norman at the Bank of England and Niemeyer at the Treasury to assuage Churchill's earlier misgivings as to the consequences of official monetary policy. On 28 April 1925 the Chancellor, deafened 'by the clamorous voices of conventional finance',[20] formally announced Britain's return to the gold standard at the pre-war parity of $4.86. The decision, in Moggridge's words, represented 'an act of faith in an incompletely understood adjustment mechanism undertaken largely for moral reasons'.[21] Oswald Mosley put it more bluntly, if somewhat unfairly:

> Faced with the alternative of saying goodbye to the gold standard, and therefore to his own employment, and goodbye to other people's employment, Mr. Churchill characteristically selected the latter course.[22]

A TARNISHED EXISTENCE: LIVING WITH GOLD, 1925-31

It is now widely accepted that the restoration of gold at the pre-war parity burdened the country with an overvalued exchange rate. Research on purchasing power parities has confirmed Keynes's contemporary view that sterling was overvalued in relation to the dollar by at least 10 per cent, and perhaps to the order of 11–14 per cent when judged against measures of domestic costs such as Gross National Product and consumers' expenditure. Compared to a basket of foreign currencies other than the dollar, moreover, the extent of the appreciation has been put at between 20 and 25 per cent in 1925 and between 15 and 20 per cent in 1929.[23] The effect of the appreciation was aggravated by external developments. Devaluations elsewhere, plus divergent wage–price–productivity movements abroad, particularly in Germany, rendered Britain less competitive after 1925 than she had been in previous years.

Following restoration, sterling came under continuous pressure as the international economy became subjected to major disequilibriating forces. The dominance of New York as a rival centre of international finance was paralleled by London's increasing difficulties as a short-term debtor to the rest of the world. Falling commodity prices in a period of excess supply impoverished British customers in primary producing countries, whilst her capacity as a foreign lender was weakened by the flight of 'hot money' in

---

[20] See J. M. Keynes, *The Economic Consequences of Mr. Churchill* (1925), in *JMK*, Vol. 9, 207–30.   [21] Moggridge, *British Monetary Policy*, 228.
[22] Cited in Skidelsky, *Oswald Mosley*, 143.
[23] N. Dimsdale, 'British Monetary Policy and the Exchange Rate 1920–38', in *The Money Supply and the Exchange Rate*, ed. W. A. Eltis and P. Sinclair (Oxford, 1981), 306–49; J. Redmond, 'The Sterling Overvaluation in 1925: A Multilateral Approach', *Economic History Review*, 2nd ser., 37 (1984), 520–32. For Keynes's views see *The Economic Consequences of Mr. Churchill*.

search of a better return. And despite the favourable impact on the balance of payments of falling prices and an improvement in the terms of trade, the volume of British imports continued to outstrip the rather limited expansion of exports gained from the improvement in world trade up to 1929; only an improvement in the net volume of invisible income enabled the balance of payments on current account to improve prior to the world slump.[24]

With sterling and the balance of payments under strain, the damaging effects of the overvalued exchange rate in aggravating the existing disparity between internal and external values became increasingly apparent. As Keynes and others had warned, internal stability of output and employment ran contrary to the need to maintain the external value of the pound. The re-establishment of a fixed exchange rate foreclosed other policy options. In particular, expansion of the domestic economy to reduce unemployment could not be considered if there was any likelihood of endangering gold convertibility. In the event, most of the authorities' gold standard expectations were disappointed; money wages proved inflexible down-wards, accommodating price inflation abroad failed to materialize, and though co-operation among international bankers was more apparent in the 1920s than it had been before the war, it was too underdeveloped to provide any effective solution to the prevailing malaise. Thus with British monetary policy geared to the short-term needs of the market, further deflation appeared inevitable. And since the recognized means of imposing such deflation, namely credit restriction and high interest rates, reduced the financial ability of employers to retain labour at the existing levels of prices and wages, the jobless seemed destined to be sacrificed yet further on a cross of gold.

Both the Chancellor of the Exchequer and the President of the Board of Trade strenuously denied that sterling's appreciation had much to do with rising unemployment or industrial strife. The gold standard was no more responsible for the 1925 coal dispute, Churchill declared, 'than was the Gulf Stream'. But a 12 per cent increase in the value of sterling between July 1924 and April 1925, in anticipation of a decision on gold and the subsequent fixing of sterling at par at a time when Belgian and French currencies were depreciating, made an already difficult situation in the coalfields much worse. 'The miners', wrote Keynes in one of his most blistering attacks on monetary policy:

are the victims of the economic juggernaut. They represent in the flesh the 'fundamental adjustments' engineered by the Treasury and the Bank of England to satisfy the impatience of the City fathers to bridge the 'moderate gap' between $4.40

---

[24] D. Moggridge, 'Bank of England Foreign Exchange Operations 1924–31', *International Review of the History of Banking*, 5 (1972), 1–2.

and \$4.86. *They* (and others to follow) are the 'moderate sacrifice' still necessary to ensure the stability of the gold standard. The plight of the coal miners is the first, but not – unless we are very lucky – the last, of the economic consequences of Mr. Churchill.[25]

The first fruits of the gold standard left him equally disillusioned. In the twelve months after restoration, he reflected ruefully in June 1926:

we have had a million unemployed and all the penury of a slump. The export industry, namely coal . . . least able to endure a further handicap, has been reduced to the verge of ruin. Our largest group of export industries, namely textiles . . . are, in spite of the comparative cheapness of wool and cotton, almost in despair at the losses. The output of iron and steel have been maintained with the assistance of subsidized coal; but no profits have been earned. The results have been what . . . I feared they would be, but worse than I dared or cared to prophesy.[26]

Finance may have been rendered proud but industry was far from content. In 1928 Sir Alfred Mond and Sir Peter Rylands of the FBI demanded that the Prime Minister launch an immediate enquiry into the working of monetary policy. Similar calls came from representatives of the cotton textile, electrical manufacturing and engineering industries. However, neither the Labour Party nor the organized labour movement canvassed strongly for the abandonment of gold; nor did they take sides with industrialists in calling for a fundamental reappraisal of the implications of sustaining a fixed gold parity. As a consequence Churchill as Chancellor, though increasingly aware of the effect of restoration in aggravating unemployment, found it relatively easy to portray the gold standard as the vehicle of stability and a bulwark against the subversion of the existing social order.[27]

It might be argued in retrospect that an exchange rate some 10 per cent lower could have moderated the growth of unemployment in critical industries, especially during the later twenties. H. G. Johnson put the case in the strongest terms, claiming that:

Had the exchange value of the pound been fixed realistically in the 1920s – a prescription fully in accord with orthodox economic theory – there would have been no need for mass unemployment.[28]

The less extreme view holds that a lower exchange rate, even on relatively generous assumptions, might not have solved the unemployment problem of the late 1920s, but could have substantially improved it. Moggridge, for example, calculates that an exchange rate 10 per cent lower could have

[25] Keynes, *The Economic Consequences of Mr. Churchill*, in *JMK*, Vol. 9, 223.
[26] J. M. Keynes, 'The First Fruits of the Gold Standard', *Nation and Athenaeum*, 26 June 1926.
[27] R. W. Boyce, *British Capitalism at the Crossroads, 1919–1932* (Cambridge, 1987), 95.
[28] H. G. Johnson, 'Keynes and British Economics', in *Essays on John Maynard Keynes*, ed. M. Keynes (Cambridge, 1979), 110.

improved the current balance of payments in 1928 by £70 million with unchanged income, assuming a foreign price elasticity of demand for British exports of −1.5 and a sterling price elasticity of demand for imports of −0.5. Assuming further a marginal propensity to import of 0.3, he argues that the authorities could have used the improved current balance to reduce unemployment from 8.2 per cent to 4.7 per cent, the imputed full employment level.[29] Hatton, taking a low (−1) and high (−2) alternative value of the price elasticity of demand for exports, estimates that a similar 10 per cent reduction in the exchange rate could have improved the 1928 balance of payments by £48 million and £93 million respectively. Allowing for income adjustments and assuming a Keynesian expenditure multiplier of 1.5, the subsequent rise in expenditure is estimated to have been sufficient to raise the demand for labour by between 200,000 and 400,000. Beyond that, Hatton maintains, the resulting balance of payments surplus, even when corrected for rising import demand, could have allowed for a less restrictive monetary policy with lower interest rates, stimulating domestic investment and employment. And with an increased yield of taxation from higher incomes and a reduction in unemployment benefit expenditure, he argues further, government spending could have been expanded, even within the confines of budgetary orthodoxy, to provide an extra fillip to output and jobs.[30] Dimsdale, using a low price elasticity of demand for British exports of −0.5 and a multiplier estimate of 1.4, has likewise suggested that an exchange rate 10 per cent lower could have raised employment by 450,000 in 1928 and reduced unemployment from 8.2 per cent to 5.8 per cent after four to five years.[31]

Such counterfactual reasoning has to be treated with caution. It rests on controversial assumptions about the elasticity of demand for imports and exports, the responsiveness of money wages to increased demand, the scale and direction of expenditure switching and the objectives of budgetary policy. Estimates of the improvement in employment that might have followed from a change in the exchange rate, moreover, rarely distinguish between the effects of the real (as distinct from the nominal) exchange rate.

In any event, it is highly unlikely that any small difference in the exchange rate would ever have been enough to eliminate depression in the basic export industries. Critics claim that the benefits allegedly accruing to the balance of payments from a more realistic rate ignore the fact that many British staple goods were not wanted at any price and that any consequent rise in aggregate demand could have done little to ease the structural

[29] Moggridge, *British Monetary Policy*, appendix I.
[30] T. J. Hatton, 'The Outlines of a Keynesian Solution', in *The Road to Full Employment*, ed. S. Glynn and A. Booth (1987), 82–94.
[31] Dimsdale, 'British Monetary Policy and the Exchange Rate'.

problems of the basic trades, at least to an extent sufficient to absorb the prevailing surplus of unemployed labour.

Structural changes, on the other hand, tend to be easier to effect at higher rather than lower levels of aggregate demand and it is tempting to follow Moggridge in arguing that a lower exchange rate might well have eased the transition to a more modern industrial framework. As we shall see below, maintaining gold at a par of $4.86 involved raising Bank Rate to a level which, by reducing credit and investment, aggravated an already serious problem of unemployment, accelerating the cumulative process of decline in the staple export regions. After all, the return to gold was a policy destined to have a differential impact upon particular industries and regions. Jones contends that a 10 per cent higher value of sterling in 1924 would have caused the three regions of the north east, Scotland and south Wales to suffer 23 per cent of the total number of job losses, although they had only 14 per cent of the industrial workforce.[32] There is little doubt, in other words, that the enforced overvaluation in 1925 worked to the relative disadvantage of such regions in the later twenties. That said, there are dangers in attaching too much weight to the monetary shock we call 'the return to gold'. Unemployment and declining competitiveness in the basic export trades preceded the restoration of gold by at least five years and continued thereafter. Though stabilization at the old parity undoubtedly maintained relative prices at an inappropriate level, Britain already faced intractable problems of competitive weakness, a prime source of which occurred in the immediate post-war period as industry was forced to shoulder a major reduction in working hours without accompanying reductions in labour costs.

It is when we examine the contemporary effects of sterling's overvaluation that the authorities' problems of economic management become clearer. Given their policy goals of pre-war levels of unemployment, free trade, unrestricted overseas lending and international economic stabilization, and given that devaluation was ruled out as a deliberate act of policy, the authorities could have looked to restore balance of payments equilibrium by reducing employment and incomes by an amount sufficient to reduce imports. The expectation would be that increased unemployment, engendered by deliberate deflation, would reduce sterling money wage costs per unit of output relative to costs abroad. In that way the rise in overseas costs relative to those in Britain would, through their effects on relative prices, increase exports and reduce imports.[33]

Herein lay the irony so far as the unemployed were concerned. Had the

[32] M. E. F. Jones, 'The Regional Impact of an Overvalued Pound in the 1920s', *Economic History Review*, 2nd ser., 38 (1985), 393–401.
[33] Moggridge, *British Monetary Policy*, chapter 4.

authorities pursued such a policy the intensification of unemployment resulting from high interest rates and enforced deflation would have proved greater than that which actually pertained. The urge to retain and to attract gold reserves certainly fostered a restrictive Bank Rate policy, particularly after 1928. At the same time the fear of aggravating domestic decline put both the Bank of England and the Chancellor under intense political pressure to moderate interest rates. Throughout the period from December 1925 to February 1929 the Treasury openly opposed every Bank Rate increase and attempted to influence the Bank to lower the Rate whenever possible, largely to ease unemployment. Though the Bank of England formally rejected the view that Bank Rate restored external balance by creating unemployment, it nevertheless broke the 'rules of the game'[34] of the classic gold standard by modifying its use of a higher Bank Rate to defend any loss of reserves. It went a long way during 1927–29 to insulate internal credit conditions from variations in its international reserves, primarily because of its concern over the anticipated impact of its discount rate on the domestic economy once Bank Rate exceeded a critical level. The pre-1925 presumption that Bank Rate movements could raise unemployment sufficient to bring down wage costs no longer held. 'When mass unemployment developed', writes Sayers, 'the Bank – especially from 1925 – became politically sensitive on the subject.' Churchill's personal letter to Norman in May 1927 on the seriousness of unemployment, he notes further, 'may have stiffened the Bank in its reluctance to touch Bank Rate during the next two years'.[35] We cannot be certain of the 'gain' to employment as a result of this modification of policy. Nonetheless there is evidence that the Bank of England reacted more sympathetically in the late twenties than it had done before to factors affecting the cost of credit to industry and trade. And it was the raised price of bank credit which Keynes maintained increased the cost to business of holding inventories, inducing them thereby to liquidate stocks, reduce final prices and cut production, to the detriment of jobs.[36]

Partly, therefore, as a result of the constraints imposed on monetary policy by domestic economic conditions, the tendencies towards adjustment under the gold standard were less powerful than contemporaries antici-

---

[34] Faith in the ability of the gold standard to effect balance of payments adjustments rested partly on a belief that central banks would intervene to reinforce the impact on domestic money and credit markets of anticipated gold flows, either by deliberate use of Bank Rate or by direct intervention in the securities market.

[35] Sayers, *Bank of England*, 222n, 633.

[36] There are grounds for believing that such was the Bank of England's asset position after 1925 that it would have found it difficult to engage in a significant measure of deflation even if there had been a willingness on the part of the authorities to see interest rates rise. Moggridge, *British Monetary Policy*, 3.

pated. With Bank Rate effectively immobilised as a short-term instrument of adjustment, the authorities found themselves obliged to adopt moral suasion and to engage in a succession of temporizing palliatives to meet the difficulties facing sterling. Active intervention in the gold and foreign exchange markets designed to set 'appropriate' rate levels, controls on the export of capital, and attempts to foster central bank co-operation at an international level reflected a determined effort to increase the pull over the exchanges exerted by a given level of Bank Rate, primarily to make living with an overvalued currency more tolerable.[37] Without such developments, the effect of the restored gold standard in aggravating an already serious unemployment problem would probably have been greater.

But the significance of this compensatory relief should not be exaggerated. Although the Bank of England strove to reduce the domestic impact of the overvaluation of sterling, it never accepted any direct responsibility for sustaining employment. Short-term interest rates remained high by historical standards throughout the late twenties. Joint stock banks passed on the curtailment of credit to employers whose frequent response, after suffering losses, was to throw men out of work. The effect was to undermine Britain's ability to operate the gold standard with any measured success since its stability depended ultimately on the country's industrial strength, a strength which the pre-war parity severely undermined by damaging exports and intensifying depression. As the Macmillan Committee put it in 1931, no matter what the supposed gains of restoration, 'it is not likely that they have gone even a fraction of the way towards compensating for the losses of wealth through unemployment in recent years'.[38]

It is clear, in retrospect, that the fundamental mistake of 1925 was not so much a narrow miscalculation of a workable exchange rate[39] as the presumption that the return to gold would restore a smooth system of domestic and international adjustment. However, neither London nor the Bank of England succeeded after 1925 in achieving anything like a commanding influence over events; Bank Rate never rose high enough to secure sufficient leverage in the international money market nor did it fall low enough to afford material help to jobs by stimulating industrial enterprise. The difficulties facing the authorities were formidable. With a given exchange rate and the absence of active policies to increase demand at home and abroad, the achievement of 'full employment' on any orthodox

[37] For a discussion of the scope and effectiveness of such devices see Moggridge, *British Monetary Policy*, 169–227.

[38] Report of the Committee on Finance and Industry, Cmd. 3897, para. 252.

[39] It is extremely difficult to judge what an 'appropriate' exchange rate would have been for Britain in the 1920s. The debate on overvaluation is predicated on the presumption that sterling's 1913 parity was somehow 'right' for the long-term growth of the economy.

reckoning would have entailed massive wage reductions. But by 1929 wages lacked the required flexibility. The 1926 General Strike indicated the extent of trade union opposition to deliberate wage-cutting; British unit wage costs fell by only 5 per cent during the period 1925–29 compared to 10 per cent in the United States and 20 per cent in Sweden. Active policies to increase demand, on the other hand, would have been compatible with the existing parity only if accompanied by import restrictions. Achieving improved employment in 1929, therefore, involved conflict with the goals of official policy, namely wage stability, maintenance of the gold parity and free trade.

The Conservative government was not unaware of the serious doubts surrounding its financial policy. Steel-Maitland, Minister of Labour, warned the Cabinet in 1929 of the serious impact which deflation was having on unemployment and industry. In a memorandum in reply the Treasury vented its own frustration:

It is a complete mistake to suppose that we should have had no unemployment if we had *not* gone on to the gold standard. Unemployment was practically as intense in the period before we reverted . . . as it is to-day . . . A policy of definite devalorisation of sterling (assuming that had been practicable) might no doubt have averted some of the troubles we have had with organised labour, but it would certainly not have solved the problem of unemployment as a whole . . .

The restoration of the gold standard . . . not only benefited our industries directly, by giving them a stable basis for the purchase of their raw materials, but indirectly . . . by leading the way to the restoration of European currencies generally . . .

There is not a shadow of a doubt that, taken as a whole, reversion to the gold standard has already contributed materially to the national well-being; and as a practical matter, there is no possibility of going back on it.[40]

Such confident posturing proved difficult to sustain following the collapse of international prices and production after 1929. Although falling import prices partly offset the effects of declining British competitiveness and the falling overseas demand for British goods, the catastrophic decline in international trade wreaked havoc with British invisible income, plunging the balance of payments into deficit. To make matters worse, countries which had previously placed their surpluses in London began to reduce their sterling holdings in order to meet their own severe trading difficulties. Foreign central banks became less willing to lend at the same time as Britain found herself increasingly unable to attract funds from abroad by raising interest rates. International reflation on a co-ordinated basis was blocked by France and the United States, devaluation continued to be ruled out as a deliberate act of policy, because it was thought likely to invoke a crisis of

---

[40] Cab 24/202, Unemployment. Memorandum by the Chancellor of the Exchequer Covering Treasury Memorandum, 23 February 1929.

confidence and even greater unemployment, whilst protection remained anathema to the Chancellor of the Exchequer. The only available option compatible with the maintenance of the existing parity was deflation, this at a time when registered unemployment exceeded 20 per cent.[41]

The headline of Lord Melchett's article in the *Sunday Express* in September 1930 – 'Unemployed – By Order of the Bank!'[42] – reflected growing concern amongst manufacturers that the government's internationalist stance was being safeguarded at too high a price. Six months earlier the FBI, in evidence to the Macmillan Committee, had expressed serious apprehension over the working of the gold standard. 'British monetary policy during the past five years', it wrote, 'cannot be acquitted of an important share of responsibility for the lamentable condition of trade and employment during that period, and for the lack of expansion of our overseas activities'. Whereas in the USA, France and Germany financial considerations had in the main been subordinated to the needs of industry and jobs, 'in our case the aim [of monetary policy] has been primarily financial'. It was pointless seeking a lasting remedy through industrial reorganization and rationalization. A permanent cure would not be possible 'unless . . . financial arrangements are set up to replace the system destroyed by the war',[43] preferably through central bank co-operation on an international level. Like the FBI, the TUC also deplored the ten years of deflation that had yielded steadily falling prices, industrial unrest and intensified unemployment. Monetary action was required to raise the price level by lowering the exchange rate. Though such a step, it informed the Macmillan Committee, would be 'criticized as a departure from [the gold] standard' it would mean 'simply a readjustment of the relation between our currency and gold, and not a severance of that relation'.[44]

But few had the nerve even to consider voluntarily breaking with gold. Keynes had continually emphasized that the high interest rates which the Bank of England felt were necessary to limit overseas investment to the amount permitted by the current account balance also held down home investment, with the result that both fell well below the level required to offset full employment savings. Hence chronic unemployment. In his view it was too dangerous, however, to abandon gold in the prevailing circumstances; what was needed was a measure of international co-operation to secure a reduction in discount rates to make borrowing and investment more attractive. But this was a pipe dream. Without practical alternatives before them, the financial authorities clung tenaciously to their orthodox

[41]   D. Moggridge, 'The 1931 Financial Crisis – A New View', *The Banker*, 120 (1970), 832–9.
[42]   Cited in Boyce, *British Capitalism at the Crossroads*, 215.
[43]   Cmd. 3897, Minutes of Evidence, Vol. I, 188–9.   [44]   Cmd. 3897, 286.

belief that the fundamental problem lay not with monetary policy but with the uncompetitiveness of British industry.

By the early spring of 1931 the impact of an unbalanced budget on foreign confidence had alerted the Treasury to the difficulty of defending the existing parity. Britain already faced a substantial balance of payments problem; when an international scramble for liquidity developed only months later, precisely at the time Britain required fresh inflows of funds to finance her balance of payments deficit, the pressure on sterling became intense. The Bank of England found itself in an almost hopeless position but remained reluctant to raise Bank Rate, partly because of its continued sensitivity towards unemployment and the state of industry. Panic demands on Britain's official reserves coincided with a worsening budget deficit at home. The government refused either to pursue a severe retrenchment programme, involving substantial cuts in unemployment benefit expenditure, or to secure medium-term credits to support sterling.

The details of this debacle have been told in chapter 2 and need not be repeated here. What is clear is that the authorities remained determined to defend the exchange rate for as long as possible. As late as May 1931 the Bank of England sought to encourage lower interest rates for the sake of easing the burden of unemployment and domestic decline. As the currency crisis developed during the summer, the Bank remained reluctant to impose sharp rises in interest rates, fearing further instability. But by then Britain's vulnerability as an international trader and financier in the midst of a world recession had been cruelly exposed. Since 1929 exports had fallen by 30 per cent in volume, and prices by approximately 10 per cent. The volume of imports fell by less than one-tenth and despite a fall in the price of raw materials and imported foodstuffs, the current account slid into deficit in 1931. By September of that year unemployment was over 2 million (some 15 per cent of the entire labour force and over 20 per cent as officially measured). The deterioration in Britain's trading position and the budgetary crisis engendered by persistently high unemployment so weakened sterling that neither Bank Rate increases nor borrowing from abroad could halt the capital outflow. Withdrawals continued throughout September 1931, exerting constant pressure on the exchange rate. Bank of England efforts to defend sterling finally collapsed in the wake of fresh financial crises and bank failures abroad. Defeated by a crisis of confidence, Britain was forced to suspend the gold standard on 21 September 1931.

The problem of unemployment loomed large in these events because of the effect which Britain's budgetary imbalance had on confidence in sterling, the erosion of which fuelled the scramble for liquidity and helped precipitate the 1931 devaluation. But as we have seen thus far, the symbiotic links between unemployment and the exchange rate were not born of the 1931 crisis; they had been forged during the essentially unstable international environment of the post-war decade. Their future in a world freed from the discipline of gold had yet to be determined.

To recap. The return to gold at a fixed exchange rate in 1925 meant that the activities of the monetary authorities within the domestic economy had been severely constrained by external conditions, insofar as the Bank of England was obliged to maintain currency convertibility. In practice, the pressure of heavy and persistent unemployment prompted a degree of discretion in the conduct of monetary policy which prevented the most beleaguered sections of British industry and society from bearing the full brunt of international monetary stabilization. Nonetheless, monetary policy had remained inherently restrictive and deflationary prior to the world slump and proved incapable in the immediate aftermath of safeguarding domestic interests when faced with dwindling confidence in sterling and a succession of banking crises abroad.

The abandonment of gold removed an important element of rigidity in policy and provided the authorities with substantially more scope to pursue deliberate objectives, both internally and externally. The pre-1929 desire to insulate the domestic economy (particularly the export sector) from undue external pressure was replaced in a surprisingly short time by a positive desire to expand economic activity, output and employment. Immediately after the suspension of gold convertibility the pound depreciated sharply on the foreign exchanges, falling by March 1932 to $3.40, some 30 per cent below par. By that time the Treasury, now more formally in control of monetary policy than hitherto, had begun to look favourably on a low pound as a direct means of promoting prosperity. In its view a low exchange rate would raise British export competitiveness overseas and encourage a rise in wholesale prices sufficient to boost domestic capital formation, all to the benefit of output and employment.

Officials recognized, however, that widespread currency speculation or undue appreciation of sterling would threaten the recovery of exports and jobs and the Treasury acted swiftly to instigate a measure of exchange rate management to avoid either danger. In co-operation with the Bank of England, it established the Exchange Equalization Account (EEA) in 1932 to provide a means of managing the floating pound in such a way as to deliberately keep down the exchange rate or, at the very least, to reduce the amplitude of its fluctuations in order to protect the domestic economy from the destabilizing effects of short-term capital flows. Monetary policy, in other words, was deliberately geared towards domestic objectives. When funds flowed inwards to Britain and the pound was strong, the EEA purchased foreign exchange with sterling obtained from the release of Treasury Bills in an effort to prevent the pound from appreciating too rapidly. In principle, such a 'dirty float' enabled balance of payments problems to be met by controlled exchange rate movements rather than by Bank Rate changes, thus permitting a low interest rate policy to dominate for the sake of raising employment at the existing level of wages.[45]

Domestically, the National Government kept Bank Rate at a historically low level from 1932 for a number of reasons. Cheap money helped to prevent the accumulation of speculative balances which threatened official exchange rate policy and London's financial stability. It also assisted in keeping government expenditure within strict bounds by reducing interest payments on the National Debt. Indeed the conversion in 1932 of the 5 per cent War Loan, 1929–47, to a new 3.5 per cent loan repayable after 1951, coupled with an embargo on all new overseas loans, signalled the authorities' commitment to low interest rates. Bank Rate was held at 2 per cent from June 1932 to the end of 1938 in the hope that the decline in British exports (which had fallen 30 per cent since 1929) would thereby be checked and employment boosted through the stimulation of domestic investment.

Debate still continues over the centrality or otherwise of cheap money as the initiating force behind domestic economic recovery after 1932. There is little doubt that low interest rates helped to raise the demand for and supply of houses, a crucial element in the revival of Gross Domestic Product in the mid-thirties. At the same time, economic recovery was affected in different and varying degrees by the improvement in the real income of those in employment, by tariffs and by exchange rate depreciation. Nonetheless, the shift in the direction of monetary policy from 1931 was certainly more favourable to domestic economic growth than had hitherto been the case. From the authorities' point of view, reasonable stability of the exchanges combined with low interest rates offered the appealing prospect of controlled, non-inflationary price rises and raised industrial profitability, each of which, by easing the rate of increase of unemployment and encouraging commercial investment, promised to reduce pressure on a budget already burdened with the cost of transitional payments to the uninsured out-of-work.[46] Nor was this merely Treasury policy. The Bank of

---

[45]   S. Howson, 'The Management of Sterling, 1932–1939', *Journal of Economic History*, 40 (1980), 53–60; 'The Managed Floating Pound, 1932–39', *The Banker*, 126 (1976), 249–55.
[46]   A. Booth, 'Britain in the 1930s: A Managed Economy?' *Economic History Review*, 2nd ser., 40 (1987), 499–522.

England strove purposely during 1932/33 to create a credit base sufficient to stimulate a rise in prices, at least to pre-slump levels.[47]

Following the creation of the EEA, the exchange rate became 'both a target to be aimed for and an instrument for the promotion of satisfactory, if not optional, price and employment levels'.[48] Certainly the Treasury's attitude to internal balance in 1932 had become strongly influenced by the prevailing unemployment situation. Officials hoped that within three years exchange rate and cheap money policies would arrest the decline in exports and raise prices by about 25 per cent, back at least to 1929 levels.[49] They anticipated further that these effects, when combined with a balanced budget, would reduce unemployment to the official 1927 rate of just under 10 per cent, the lowest since 1920.[50]

In the event, the gains to the unemployed from this redirection of monetary policy proved far from substantial. If overvaluation of sterling worked to the disadvantage of the regions of 'Outer Britain' in the 1920s, depreciation in the early 1930s produced at best only marginal benefits to those areas harbouring the heaviest concentrations of unemployment. Though currency depreciation removed some of the competitive disadvantages under which British exporters had previously laboured, it did not stimulate a substantial rise in export volumes. Nor were the advantages of depreciation sustained; the early competitive edge which Britain enjoyed was partly eroded thereafter by the subsequent devaluations of the dollar and the French franc.[51] Even the extent of Britain's initial advantage can be exaggerated if one focusses on the sterling/dollar rate only; she certainly gained more in relative terms compared to other foreign countries, but the transitory benefits thus obtained have to be weighed against the losses arising from the general collapse of world trade. Exports, moreover, began to face an increasing amount of non-price competition in the early thirties as economic nationalism abroad fostered retaliatory measures. 'The depreci-

---

[47] Sayers, *Bank of England*, 461.

[48] S. Howson, *Sterling's Managed Float: The Operations of the Exchange Equalisation Account, 1932–39* (Princeton, 1980), 34.

[49] The Treasury firmly believed that the fall in world prices had caused much of the depression of recent years and it remained determined to seek a mild inflation as a means of reviving trade and employment. Keynes and Henderson proposed in 1932 that an international authority should issue gold notes to foster general domestic expansion and a rise in world prices. The Treasury adopted a similar idea at the time of the World Economic Conference in 1933 but neither proposal won any significant support.

[50] Howson, *Sterling's Managed Float*, 26.

[51] Eichengreen and Sachs have argued that though the foreign repercussions of individual devaluations in the thirties were generally negative, in the sense that they improved a country's position at the expense of its neighbours, recovery from the Great Depression may have been more rapid had competitive devaluations been more widely adopted and co-ordinated internationally. B. Eichengreen and J. Sachs, 'Exchange Rates and Economic Recovery in the 1930s', *Journal of Economic History*, 45 (1985), 925–46.

ation of sterling . . . has . . . not been followed by the expected benefits', complained the Minister of Labour towards the end of 1931 '. . . While there is a great deal to be said for grabbing as large a share of the existing cake as is possible, the vital need (especially from the point of view of Great Britain) is a larger cake.'[52]

The success of Treasury intervention to prevent an undue appreciation of sterling – such as occurred, for example, during the spring of 1932 and from 1935 to 1938 – is reflected in the considerable stability of the sterling/dollar exchange rate from late 1933 through to mid-1938. Sterling's 'effective' exchange rate, moreover, measured against a basket of 28 other foreign currencies weighted by shares in world trade, rose slowly and fairly steadily during the same periods and remained below its 1929–30 level until 1937.[53] But the management of sterling failed to induce anything like the export-led recovery or reduction in unemployment which Treasury officials eagerly anticipated following the collapse of gold. By 1935 British domestic prices were no higher than they had been in 1931, the balance of payments remained in deficit until the mid-thirties, whilst registered unemployment remained over 13 per cent of the insured population (and never less than 10 per cent of all employees during the entire period 1931 to 1936).

Nevertheless, Treasury officials continually refused to be drawn into a mechanistic defence of the exchange rate for fear of its effects on the labour market. 'The overriding consideration', stated a memorandum in May 1936,

is that we should continue the policy of cheap money so long as we have so grave a problem of unemployment to face. There might always come a time if we committed ourselves to stabilisation when we should have to choose between going back on our promise to stabilise or committing economic suicide by a policy of deflation.[54]

Thus, when the French franc was devalued in September 1936 following the election of a socialist government and a major flight of capital, the British Treasury co-operated with their French and American counterparts, under the terms of a Tripartite Agreement, to reduce exchange rate fluctuations and avoid competitive devaluation. But the British authorities insisted throughout that they should not be further obliged to support a fixed rate for the pound. Likewise, when the Bank of England threatened to allow the pound to appreciate in 1936 following substantial inflows of capital from France and elsewhere, Hopkins and Phillips at the Treasury warned that such a reaction:

[52] Cab 27/468, ET8, Employment Policy. Survey of the Effect of Industrial Development on Employment, No. 10, 19 December 1931.
[53] J. Redmond, 'An Indication of the Effective Exchange Rate of the Pound in the Nineteen-Thirties', *Economic History Review*, 2nd ser., 33 (1980), 83–91.
[54] T160/840/F13427/3, 28 May 1936, cited in Howson, *Sterling's Managed Float*, 27.

quite overlooks the effect on trade . . . To us it seems that it would be altogether wrong at this time to give a new impetus to imports and to impose further difficulties on exports because of a temporary crisis in regard to the movement of bad capital money . . . It is wrong to contemplate any serious increase in the value of the pound with unemployment at the present level [1.7 million].[55]

This evident change in the authorities' concept of management should not blind us, however, to the continued limitations of monetary policy so far as the relief of unemployment was concerned. The insistence on sustaining cheap money and intervening to depress the exchange rate whenever practicable undoubtedly safeguarded any substantial worsening of Britain's export performance during the thirties. Each strategy, moreover, preserved confidence, raised the level of capital formation in both the housebuilding and consumer durables sectors, and assisted economic revival in areas such as the midlands and the south, already buttressed by the rising real incomes of those in work. Yet it is doubtful whether low interest rates had much effect on investment in manufacturing. More to the point, the distorted nature of domestic recovery, as chapter 8 indicates, deflected attention away from long-term unemployment in the depressed regions until political pressure forced a limited response from government in the shape of the 1934 Special Areas Act. Both the direct and indirect effect of housebuilding on the overall growth of employment can be exaggerated. Moreover, the prospective stimulus to demand, output and jobs in the more favoured regions could never be guaranteed, dependent as it frequently was upon future expectations rather than upon the volume and price of available loan capital. And it was fear of upsetting such expectations that reinforced the National Government's determination to resist any progressive unemployment programme that threatened either the 'natural' impulses towards economic recovery, or the stability of the Budget. Even when it became evident by the mid-thirties that monetary policy had had less positive effects on prices and employment than originally expected, the government felt little compunction to alter its declared priorities of policy or to lessen its opposition to fiscal expansion.

Though monetary policy took on an uncharacteristically vigorous air following the collapse of gold, it did little to weaken the authorities' search for stability and neutrality in the conduct of economic affairs. Cheap money and a managed pound survived against a background of non-expansionary fiscal policy. The motivating force throughout was the protection of Britain's longer term interests, particularly the maintenance of foreign confidence in sterling and British credit. Whilst the Treasury proved

---

[55] T175/94, 'Position of Exchange Equalisation Account', 1 December 1936; note by Hopkins, 2 December 1936; note by Chancellor 2 December 1936, T160/1174/F8759/05/3, cited in Howson, *Sterling's Managed Float*, 30.

unwilling after 1931 to divorce exchange rate policy from the needs of the domestic economy, it retained a basic desire to defend the nascent sterling area and Britain's credibility within it. This elevated the maintenance of domestic and international confidence to the forefront of the authorities' economic policy. Insofar as cheap money and a stable value of the pound reduced the risks of expenditure destabilization, international payments default and intensified unemployment, they worked nonetheless to strengthen the pillars of economic and financial orthodoxy, albeit by relatively unorthodox means.

6 * Trade, tariffs and the stimulation of exports

In their faltering efforts to understand the complex origins and nature of the unemployment problem confronting them, interwar governments remained wedded to one essential belief: that its emergence was primarily the result of the failure of Britain's traditional export industries. From that perspective, the natural corrective to the unemployment crisis appeared to lie in a revival of Britain's export performance by whatever means seemed most appropriate. As subsequent chapters will indicate, lower unit wage costs and an improvement in the structure and efficiency of the staple export trades were regarded with varying degrees of enthusiasm during the twenties as valuable means of improving Britain's fortunes in international trade. Likewise, as we have seen, 'sound money' and stable exchange rates were tantamount in the official mind to a positive employment policy inasmuch as they were considered the prerequisite of a lasting trade revival.

To the authorities, however, it seemed sheer folly not to take more direct steps to restore Britain's trading supremacy. Whether that supremacy was or ever would be in reach was not an issue which troubled governments unduly. Attempting to reduce the prevailing pattern of industrial unemployment through expanded trade was after all a far less fearsome prospect than trying to create new jobs through vigorous and untested schemes of national investment. In truth, neither the Conservative nor the Labour governments had any coherent strategy for recouping Britain's losses overseas. This did not prevent them from implementing policies overtly designed to stimulate exports and thereby, they hoped, employment. But throughout, the expectation remained that some combination of national and international circumstances would stimulate trade on a world-wide basis, carrying with it the prospect of reviving the most troubled sectors of the economy. Before we turn to the nature and fate of these policies, it would be instructive to examine briefly the trading difficulties facing Britain between the wars.

THE PROBLEM OF EXPORTS

A dominant element in Britain's post-war economic decline was the marked fall in the volume of her export trade, both in absolute terms and in relation to the foreign trade of the outside world. Old established export industries lost an important fraction of their overseas business, without there accruing any compensating advantage from newer trades, many of which were in their productive and competitive infancy compared with countries such as Germany and the United States. Although in 1929 British exports reached their highest level between the wars, they were 19 per cent lower in volume than in 1913. Export volumes rose by 1.2 per cent per year between 1920 and 1938, but this compared unfavourably with a 4.2 per cent annual increase during the period 1900 to 1913.

In the very early 1920s Britain's share of a much shrunken world trade in manufactured exports exceeded that of 1913 as she benefited from the dislocation of new European rivals. After 1924 it fell rapidly. From 30.2 per cent in 1913, Britain's share declined to only 20.4 per cent by 1929, reflecting relative losses in twelve of the sixteen major manufactured commodity groups in world trade. Substantial reductions in shares were recorded, moreover, in those sectors expanding most in world trade, such as motor vehicle and aircraft, industrial equipment and electrical goods.[1] Although there was some slight improvement in the 1930s (gains in trade shares were made in one-half of the major manufactured commodity groups in world trade) the advantages Britain obtained from a brief period of currency devaluation, from extended Empire preference and from the growth of bilateral trading agreements[2] proved neither sufficiently long lasting nor substantial enough to stem the continued decline in her share of total world exports down to 1937.

As we have emphasized already, the staple export sector fared particularly badly. Coal exports, including ships' bunker coal, had accounted for almost one-third of all output in 1913, but they remained substantially below that level for practically the entire interwar period. Cotton textile exports had peaked prior to the First World War, accounting for one-quarter of Britain's exports by value. But the volume of international trade in cottons fell thereafter, despite an increase in the world consumption of raw cotton and Britain's share of the diminished total declined dramatically. Total cotton exports in the 1920s were on average about 60 per cent of their 1913 level. Iron and steel exports also slumped during the 1920s and even in the best years of recovery in the 1930s reached only one-half of their pre-war level by volume.

[1] Aldcroft, *The Inter-War Economy*, 248–50.   [2] See below pp. 172–5.

Although Britain's export losses were concentrated in the interwar period, they were the result of a number of unfavourable developments, both long term and short term in origin. Her share of world trade had been declining steadily for several decades before the First World War, even though the absolute volume of British exports had continued to expand. The annual average volume of manufactured exports increased by over 70 per cent from the late 1890s to the period 1911–13. This growth, however, disguised the extent to which the largest categories of British exports were in those commodities expanding least in world trade. Although Britain had made some slight progress since the end of the nineteenth century towards shifting the composition of her manufactured exports from textiles, coal and consumer goods towards producer goods, the adjustment was not rapid enough. By 1913 the country was seriously overcommitted to the export of cotton manufactures, coal and steel. By then Britain was providing some 70 per cent of the entire world's exports of cotton manufactures, 80 per cent of the world's coal exports and practically the entire volume of the export of ships. The scale and direction of overseas investment, moreover, enabled the demand for such staples to be sustained in old established markets and to be created in new ones.

Although of some considerable immediate advantage, this manufacturing and trading structure was inherently fragile and by the eve of the First World War it was displaying signs of the strains which had beset it since the late Victorian period. Other countries had increasingly shifted resources away from primary production to industry and were developing manufactures at the very time Britain was losing her comparative advantage in international trade. Britain's share of the world trade in manufactures fell as self-sufficiency abroad became more pronounced; in 1913 her share was less than one-half of what it had been in 1870 and 6 per cent below its 1900 level. Furthermore, although Britain continued to export a higher proportion of her manufactured output than did many other countries, her relative performance declined, principally because of the predominance within those exports of goods, such as textiles and ships, which were suffering a declining rate of growth in world trade, paralleled by a comparative neglect of other goods, such as machinery and metal manufactures, which were among the fastest growing sectors of world trade.[3]

Serious though these problems were, the more damaging aspect was the rise of international competition. Indeed so far as changes in overall shares

[3] S. B. Saul, 'The Export Economy 1870–1914', *Yorkshire Bulletin of Economic and Social Research*, 17 (1965), 5–18.

of world trade are concerned, the evidence is that before 1913 Britain's losses were due more to a loss of market shares because of the intensification of overseas competition than from unfavourable shifts in the commodity and area composition of trade. And it was the continuation and deepening of such competitive losses that were to prove so devastating between the wars.

The havoc which the First World War wrought upon the volume and pattern of international trade was clearly of major significance. The war acted as a catalyst, accelerating and strengthening tendencies in world industrial production, technology and competition of considerable disadvantage to British exporters. It enabled other countries, particularly the United States and Japan, to solidify their position as manufacturing competitors in British markets. More generally, it gave a further fillip to industrial self-sufficiency overseas, boosting industrial development in precisely those product sectors previously supplied by British exporters. At the same time, the exigencies of war made substantial demands upon key industrial sectors within Britain, notably coal, iron and steel and shipbuilding, expanding their capacity and workforces in response to immediate needs but with scant regard to their future viability.

The predominant problem became the absolute loss of markets by those industries which had accounted for the unique importance of exports in the pre-1913 economy. The coal industry suffered a severe loss of overseas markets as competition increased and as former overseas customers developed their indigenous sources of fuel. The American coal strike in 1921 and the French occupation of the Ruhr in 1923 offered some small respite but the losses subsequently intensified; the disruption of the General Strike allowed Germany and Poland in particular to capitalize on Britain's inability to supply her traditional markets overseas. That said, it is clear that coal's fundamental problems arose from technological progress, which encouraged fuel economy and substitution, and, more significantly, from a secular decline in demand which rendered producing countries capable of supplying more coal than the market could absorb at prices sufficient to meet production costs.

Import substitution and competition created similar difficulties for textiles. The spinning and weaving sections of the cotton industry, trading in cheaper coarse piece goods, proved incapable of holding markets in the Far East against intense Japanese competition. The volume of British exports fell by about 34 per cent between 1910–13 and 1924–26. Likewise, the iron and steel industry lost heavily to overseas countries whose operations had benefited, unlike their British counterparts, from postwar reconstruction and a stable or rising home demand. Britain's share of the world iron and steel market fell from 35.6 per cent in 1913 to 25.1 per cent in 1929, partly because of an unfavourable market dependence but principally because of her failure to compete.

The competitive failings of the staple export sector were magnified by other developments. The decision to return to gold at the pre-war parity in 1925 undoubtedly over-priced British exports abroad at a time when other European countries were recovering with undervalued rates of exchange. Moreover, it helped to restrict the growth of new industries and new exports, the conspicuous absence of which mirrored Britain's vulnerability in international trade.[4] In addition, the spread of tariff protection (as distinct from the raising of existing tariffs) reduced the opportunities British exporters had of finding equivalent outlets for the products of those industries which had previously held a predominant place in world markets.

Britain suffered the extra handicap of having concentrated her exports in previous decades upon the markets of low income, primary producing countries. It was those countries which suffered most from rapidly declining incomes as commodity prices fell, particularly in the twenties, and whose ability to import British manufactured exports was thereby seriously impaired. It was particularly unfortunate, too, that in the 1920s Britain came to depend more heavily on the Empire than she had done in the past. On the eve of the First World War the greater proportion of British trade had been conducted with non-imperial countries. The share of the Empire in British domestic exports increased thereafter, from 35.8 per cent in 1910–13 to 43.1 per cent in 1927. But this shift operated increasingly to Britain's disadvantage; imperial customers began to draw a decreasing proportion of their imports from Britain at the same time as they became less dependent on her as an outlet for her exports.

EXPORT COMPETITIVENESS AND THE RESTORATION OF TRADE

Although official efforts to improve Britain's foreign trade as a guarantor of stable employment preceded the acknowledged crisis in her export performance, they proved rather perfunctory. During the First World War, committees of enquiry frequently emphasized the need to improve the administrative and financial foundations upon which trade could be expanded after the cessation of hostilities. A new Department of Overseas Trade was created in 1917 under the dual control of the Foreign Office and the Board of Trade in an effort to improve commercial intelligence. In the

---

[4] For discussion of the impact of British monetary policy on trade and employment see chapter 5.

same year the British Trade Corporation was created to galvanize financial interests at home in an effort to displace German finance in the international market place. Neither of the latter two initiatives lived up to expectations. The two government departments overseeing trade intelligence remained antagonistic towards one other throughout the interwar period. And such was the hostility of merchant banks and issuing houses in the City of London to the BTC that it failed to achieve anything like the degree of corporatist spirit among bankers, traders and the government as was evident, for example, in Germany. Whitehall support was noticeably lukewarm. As a result the Corporation's priorities were never properly defined. Alien to the vested interests of British finance, it ceased to exist in 1926.[5]

During the early years of peace protracted discussions took place over the urgent need to recapture lost export markets, but policy making remained too diffused and unco-ordinated to produce tangible results in the immediate term. Having undertaken at the Prime Minister's request an enquiry into unemployment and the state of trade early in 1919, Sir Auckland Geddes, Minister of Reconstruction, diagnosed 'acute anxiety concerning future Government action', concluding that there had 'not been a clear, coherent Government policy with regard to trade'. Geddes favoured a controlled system of export bounties 'limited in amount to the cost which might otherwise have fallen on the Exchequer for unemployment benefit to the workers'.[6]

Although nothing came of this proposal, parallel efforts were made to repair by financial aid some of the damage inflicted on foreign trade by the war. In 1919 the Treasury and the Board of Trade devised a scheme, embodied in the Imports and Exports Regulation Bill, whereby advances could be made to exporters trading with Eastern Europe for whom bank credits were unavailable because of their involvement with countries thought to constitute an unacceptable high risk. The Bill failed but it was replaced in August 1920 by the Overseas Trade (Credit and Insurance) Act which empowered the Board of Trade to grant credits and to undertake insurance against shipments of goods exported to the countries of Eastern Europe, excluding Russia. The scheme operated retrospectively from September 1919 until July 1921, when it was abandoned as costly and unsuccessful.

An amending Act in the following October continued the spirit of the legislation but altered its financial implications. The revised scheme was

---

[5] R. P. T. Davenport-Hines, *Dudley Docker. The Life and Times of a Trade Warrior* (Cambridge, 1984), 147.
[6] Cab 27/58, G 237, Unemployment and the State of Trade, 14 March 1919, paras, 2, 4, 68.

designed to improve the ability of traders to obtain ordinary bank advances for the purpose of financing exports. Drafts drawn by traders against shipments of goods exported to buyers in specified countries abroad[7] were guaranteed by the Board of Trade up to a total credit of £26 million. The scheme had the advantage of making no immediate call on public funds, which could only be drawn upon in the event of default by the importers. In its original form the scheme lasted until July 1926 during which time guarantees were given for £6,258,000, representing perhaps £10 million of exports.

Industrialists found the scheme to be overly cautious and bureaucratic, and bemoaned the fact that the government refused to share more of the risks in promoting overseas transactions. But the Treasury would not be drawn. It refused to consider guaranteeing advances through banks or to countenance supplying 'derelict' countries with manufactured goods they could not afford. In its view the scheme could do little for unemployment since 'its main effect is to enable existing stocks to be sold at prices rather above the current cost of production'.[8] A new scheme of credit insurance began in July 1926. Exporters were able to insure bills of exchange drawn by them upon approved importers overseas in respect of goods produced in the United Kingdom. Such credit insurance was renewed by the second Labour administration in 1930, continued by the National Government in 1934 and made permanent in 1939.

Neither the guarantee scheme nor credit insurance was extensively used between the wars, primarily because each had to conform to the strictest rules of prudent banking practice. Moreover, when it was decided after a decade of benign neglect to extend export credit guarantees to Russia in July 1930, it became clear that what the Soviets most desired were long-term credits to finance heavy industrial exports from Britain. Such requests pleased the Liberals who had for some time been demanding similar guarantees as a means of reducing unemployment. But although much was made at the time of the diplomatic and political obstacles involved in responding to such requests, there was little enthusiasm for recasting financial policy specifically for industrial ends, least of all without Treasury approval.

The dogmatic defence of trade revival as a forerunner of labour market recovery obliged governments to continue an almost relentless search for

---

[7] The scheme initially applied to Europe (except Russia), North and South America and the Empire. Later in 1921 it was widened to cover all countries except the British Indies, Ceylon, the Straits Settlements and the Far East, and Russia. In 1925 it was opened to all these countries except Russia. A limited extension of export credits to Russia was finally agreed to in August 1929 and extended further during the following year.

[8] Cab 27/120, CU 274, Cabinet. Unemployment Committee. Memorandum by the Treasury, 11 October 1921.

alternative ways of stimulating exports. 'Whatever policy may be adopted for the restoration of trade within the borders of this country', reported the joint TUC/Labour Party Committee on Unemployment in 1921, 'there is a limit to its scope. The root problem lies in the revival of industry and commerce abroad'. What was required, the committee urged, were policies aimed at 'sweeping away all barriers to international co-operation' and 'the revival of healthy economic life in the impoverished countries'.[9]

Expanding trade with Russia proved a particularly popular idea. Apart from compensating for lost markets elsewhere, it could enable Britain to reduce stocks of surplus commodities and secure a measure of stable employment. Sir Allan Smith, Chairman of the Industrial Group of MPs in the House of Commons, warned Bonar Law in December:

America and Germany are at the moment and will be to an increasing degree trading with Russia and while we indulge in the old shibboleths of foreign diplomacy, other countries are reducing their unemployment . . . It may be . . . we are cutting our own throats in the matter of present and future trading.[10]

Smith was a shade premature. A trade agreement had already been signed with the Soviet Union. But little was done thereafter to develop the initiative, partly because of official fears over Russian credit worthiness, but mainly because there was little incentive on the part of the Soviet Union to develop trade with Britain.

The Labour Party nevertheless continued to preach the doctrine of internationalism. It urged action to reverse the impoverishment of defeated countries abroad, the poverty and growing indebtedness of which were regarded as prime sources of unemployment at home. The presumption, throughout the twenties at least, was that abnormal domestic unemployment could only be substantially reduced if the old-established export industries were permanently revived to enable them to reap the benefits of any future trade expansion. Unfortunately this perspective, shared by the Conservatives and by the most vociferous spokesmen of industry and the City, focussed attention on precisely those policies thought likely to improve exports in the long run – such as cutting wage costs, reorganizing industry and restoring the gold standard – even if they were less likely to check rising unemployment in the short term. It was with some confidence therefore that the Board of Trade, reporting on the state of trade in relation to unemployment in 1921, could suggest that:

---

[9] *Unemployment: A Labour Policy. Being the Report of the Special Committee on Unemployment appointed by the Parliamentary Committee of the Trades Union Congress and the Labour Party Executive (January 1921)*, 27–8, 31.

[10] Cited in T. Rodgers, 'Sir Allan Smith, the Industrial Group and the Politics of Unemployment 1919–1934', *Business History*, 28 (1986), 111.

Nothing should be done to retard the fall in British values to the rock bottom which brings them to a level with what are reasonable values in view of existing circumstances in competing countries.

Subsidizing the export sector, therefore, should be firmly resisted since any financial aid:

by depriving the producer . . . of any stimulus to reduce the cost of production . . . does nothing to diminish, but tends rather to stereotype, the difference between English and foreign values, which is the fundamental cause of the slackness of our export trade at present . . . Any action taken to postpone the readjustment of value is fundamentally unsound.[11]

By deliberately pursuing deflationary policies, governments of the twenties thus believed themselves to be promoting the required 'readjustments of value' in the interval before an upturn in world trade. No permanent solution to unemployment would be found until normal political and economic relations were established throughout the world. A Cabinet Committee on Unemployment put it thus in 1924:

All schemes for the artificial creation of employment or for relieving unemployment by payment of benefit can only be regarded as palliatives . . . The only real cure is such a revival of normal trade activity as will automatically re-absorb unemployed workmen into their accustomed occupations.[12]

In the meantime any relevant and unobtrusive action to enhance Britain's presence overseas had to be welcomed. Consular agents overseas were encouraged to investigate the condition of key indigenous industries in order to discover fresh ways of increasing British export penetration. Worthy individuals traipsed around foreign lands in the hope of drumming up orders for beleaguered sections of British industry. Trade delegations visited South America, Scandinavia and the Far East during 1929/30, extolling the qualities of British manufactures. The Lord Privy Seal J. H. Thomas, 'the first British Cabinet Minister to have transformed himself into a commercial traveller', visited Canada in 1929 in a valiant effort to improve British exports of coal, steel and motor cars. But the country had an infinitely bigger and more accessible market on its doorstep. Thomas reported on his return that he had 'a lot of things up [his] sleeve' and that he had 'created an atmosphere for the Old Country in Canada'.[13] Precious little else transpired.

As world trade contracted severely during 1930 grave doubts began to be expressed about the recuperative power of British staple exports. Hope

[11] Cab 27/119, CU 210, Committee on Unemployment. Trade in Relation to Unemployment. Memorandum by the Board of Trade, 26 September 1921.
[12] Cab 27/242, CP 26, Unemployment Committee. Interim Report on Unemployment, 7 February 1924.   [13] Skidelsky, *Politicians and the Slump*, 123.

lingered nonetheless. In August the Economic Advisory Council appointed a committee to investigate the potential of the Chinese market. During the previous month Clement Attlee, Chancellor of the Duchy of Lancaster, implored the Cabinet to appoint a Minister of Industry, among whose first duties would be the formation of a series of export selling agencies 'to handle the whole export trade of the country'.[14] This preoccupation with restoring Britain's export industries to the point where they would be able to take advantage of any sudden improvement in world activity had dominated postwar policy, not only in relation to trade but also in the fields of industry, wages and finance.[15] By 1930 this concern seemed to be hopelessly misguided. For many years past pressure groups inside and outside of the government had clamoured for varying degrees of protection within Britain, aware that the rise of economic nationalism elsewhere had seriously reduced her prospects of gaining any substantial foothold in export markets. This movement attacked the very essence of orthodox commercial policy, but it drew increasing strength and influence from the government's paltry efforts to evoke a national revival in exports. What is frequently overlooked is that the postwar challenge to free trade was merely enhanced by the crisis of the early thirties and not launched because of it. It is thus to the issue of tariffs as a remedial policy for unemployment that we now turn.

THE RISE OF PROTECTIONIST SENTIMENT

Throughout the second half of the nineteenth century Britain viewed the symbiotic links between trade, industry and employment as largely synonymous with the virtues of free trade. Even when the country's comparative industrial and trading supremacy suffered a severe setback in the years before 1914, Edwardian tariff reformers proved incapable of convincing public opinion that economic progress would benefit from the adoption of protective duties. The first formal breach of the doctrine of free trade came during the early part of the First World War, but it was never intended to pose a fundamental challenge to fiscal orthodoxy. The McKenna Duties of 1915, which imposed a 33.3 per cent *ad valorem* duty on gramophones, clocks, watches, cinematograph film and certain types of motor car, were levied more for revenue than for protective purposes. They were designed primarily to preserve foreign exchange and to curtail expenditure on imported 'luxuries'.

Nevertheless, there were already signs that the government was

---

[14] Cab 4/214, CP 293, The Problems of British Industry. Memorandum by the Chancellor of the Duchy of Lancaster, 29 July 1930.
[15] The issues are discussed further in chapters 5, 8 and 10.

concerned over the effects which the dislocation of trade would have upon the stability of the peacetime economy, a concern which threatened to re-open the pre-war cleavage between protectionists and free traders. A wartime committee under the chairmanship of Arthur Balfour, charged with examining future commercial and industrial policy, was set some exacting questions: what industries were essential to the future safety of the nation, and what steps could be taken to maintain or establish them? What steps should be taken to recover home and foreign trade during the war, and secure new markets? To what extent and by what means could the resources of the Empire be developed and rendered independent of foreign supplies?[16] The Committee's answers reopened doubts about the philosophy of free trade. Although it rejected the idea of a general tariff, it argued in favour of preferential Empire duties and for the safeguarding of 'key' or 'pivotal' industries whose products had proved indispensible to wartime production but for which we were traditionally dependent upon overseas suppliers.[17] The principle of granting imperial preference on Empire goods was formally accepted at the 1917 Imperial War Conference. At the same time support grew for finding some way of reducing Britain's dependence upon imports from belligerent countries.

These developments proved significant inasmuch as they coincided with a growing preoccupation within government over whether new departures in commercial policy were required to safeguard industrial employment in the post-war period. The Minister of Reconstruction, reporting to the Cabinet in March 1919 on unemployment and the state of trade, pleaded for the adoption of protective measures against manufactures produced 'by industries which require to be shielded from foreign competition while re-establishing themselves; or while passing from war work to peace work'.[18] The Federation of British Industries went further. Unless 'reasonable control of the restriction of imports' was maintained, the FBI informed Lloyd George in 1919, the resumption of normal industrial activity 'would be gravely prejudiced'. Moreover, if employment was to be adequately safeguarded it was absolutely necessary 'that products which compete with those of any industry in this country should not be imported'.[19] The Cabinet sympathized with the sentiment, even if it was reluctant to pursue such an all-embracing policy. A general relaxation on import prohibitions began in September 1919, but articles forming the products of 'key' industries, such as zinc,

[16] Cab 37/50, Reconstruction Committee, Conclusions, 23 June 1916.
[17] Final Report of the Committee on Commercial and Industrial Policy After the War, Cd. 9035, 1918.
[18] Cab 27/58, Unemployment and the State of Trade. Sir Auckland Geddes's Report, 14 March 1919.
[19] FBI *Bulletin*, 13 March 1919, 99, cited in M. Dintenfass, 'The TUC, the FBI and British Economic Policy Between the Wars', M.Phil thesis, University of Warwick (1980), 41.

tungsten and synthetic dyestuffs, were excluded. In addition, the McKenna Duties were reduced by one-third on all articles manufactured within the Empire.

By 1920, in other words, reconstruction policy had already embraced the idea of imperial preference and industrial protection on a selective basis. Free trade orthodoxy, however, still reigned supreme. Although certain interest groups within the FBI, notably those representing heavy industry in the midlands, had campaigned since 1916 for protective duties as a way of combating German industrial rivalry, distrust and jealousy amongst British manufacturing groups, to say nothing of the powerful free-trade lobby of Lancashire cotton producers, forestalled the emergence of any united pro-tariff campaign within the business community prior to 1920.[20] Though the 'trade warrior' rhetoric of Dudley Docker, President of the FBI, was couched in pragmatic, non-doctrinaire terms in an effort to win general support for a more aggressive commercial policy, a notable reaction set in towards the end of the war against the idea of business corporatism shaping economic reconstruction. This was clearly expressed by the Imperial Association of Commerce, representing financial and shipping interests, whose members announced their firm opposition in 1918 to 'any form of restriction or control of trade which threatens to crush and eventually destroy that splendid and undivided enterprise which has in the past so largely contributed to the strength of the Empire'.[21]

Within government the Board of Trade steadfastly opposed any idea of seeking industrial revival through the imposition of a general tariff. Protection, it feared, would raise costs and subsidize inefficient plant and thereby hamper the proper reorganization of industry. Yet the war had demonstrated Britain's vulnerability in relying upon imported sources of raw materials and, by emphasizing the need to nurture strategically important industries, had boosted the appeal of protectionism. Moreover, with the collapse of the postwar boom and the dramatic rise in unemployment after 1920, the need for a substantial rise in trade grew most urgent just at the time when it was least likely to occur. As a consequence discussion of appropriate commercial policy fluctuated between an ideological commitment to free trade as an ultimate panacea and a plea to counter industrial and economic decline by a more deliberate and pragmatic use of protective duties.

[20] S. Blank, *Industry and Government in Britain. The Federation of British Industries in Politics, 1945–65* (Saxon House, 1973), 15–16.
[21] Davenport-Hines, *Dudley Docker*, 112–19. The National Union of Manufacturers (formerly the British Manufacturers' Association), the representative voice of small businesses, withdrew from the FBI in August 1918 in order to campaign for a full-blooded tariff policy. Dintenfass, 'The TUC, the FBI and British Economic Policy', 29.

The Safeguarding of Industries Act of October 1921 reflected the latter viewpoint. It expanded the range of articles upon which a 33.3 per cent import duty could be imposed (save for goods consigned from or produced within the Empire) principally to protect the products of 'key' industries.[22] In addition, the Board of Trade was equipped with emergency powers to impose a similar levy on any goods suddenly imported from countries whose currency depreciation in relation to sterling allowed them to sell at prices below cost of production, especially if such imports were likely to increase industrial unemployment.

Despite their industrial bias, these defensive measures received a noticeably cool reception amongst the very groups the Coalition government thought would most welcome some form of discriminatory assistance. The Executive Committee of the Labour Party and the Parliamentary Committee of the TUC complained in 1921 that the tariff policy being pursued was:

detrimental to the occupational interests of the workers and disastrous to the best interests of the community. It will decrease the amount of employment by restricting the free exchange of commodities . . . and will increase the cost of living by restricting the available supplies.

Each was convinced, furthermore, that in promoting selective duties:

an attempt is being made, influenced by the operation of commercial and financial groups, to fasten upon industry the shackles of a near protectionism on the plea of safeguarding the interests of workers by providing more employment . . . Experience demonstrates that where high prices are secured, which is the main object of the protectionist, restricted demand follows and the possibilities of employment are correspondingly reduced.[23]

Keynes added his own voice to the passionate defence of free trade. Speaking in Manchester in October 1922 he declared that:

every scrap of experience which accumulates emphasises the blindness and disastrous folly (of protection). Formerly free trade was a desirable end to increased wealth. It has now become a necessary and essential defence against a crushing poverty. Unless we direct our reserves into the directions where they are most productive, we shall not be able to gain a living at all.[24]

As unemployment increased towards the end of 1921, criticism of protectionism as the death-knell of export revival and economic prosperity deepened. Far from helping matters, contemporary critics maintained, the Safeguarding of Industries Act had actually worsened the situation. Certain

[22] Imports of dyestuffs had been completely excluded under the terms of a separate Act nine years earlier.
[23] *Safeguarding of Industries Bill. Manifesto by the Parliamentary Committee of the Trades Union Congress and the Labour Party Executive* (1921).   [24] *JMK*, Vol. 19, 3–4.

manufacturers had found that many of the listed goods subject to duty were required at different stages in their production process, the effect of which was to raise operating costs precisely at the time the government was urging producers to be more competitive for the sake of creating jobs. Moreover, so exhaustive was the general classification of key industries (over 6,500 items were subject to duty in October 1921) that there was a suspicion that many products had been included for revenue purposes only or, even more worrying still, purely as a means of gaining support for a measure of more general protection. Employers, critics argued, were turning to the trade unions to support them in the claim that their industries were being unduly threatened by foreign competition in the hope of pressuring the government into granting protection under the Act.[25]

Such criticisms widened the breach between Liberal free traders and Conservative sections of the Coalition government. Baldwin, President of the Board of Trade, fanned disenchantment when he confessed to parliament that with the Safeguarding Act nine months old he could still make no statement as to its effects on industry and employment, except to say that it had encouraged some manufacturers to keep in operation works which might otherwise have been closed down.[26] This growing disquiet over commercial policy had a notable impact upon protectionist sentiment. When internal disruption finally brought down the Coalition government in October 1922 in favour of a purely Conservative administration under Bonar Law, the pledge which rallied greatest support was that no new tariffs would be imposed as a means of tackling the growing menace of unemployment.

Bonar Law's pledge was initially endorsed by Baldwin on his appointment as Prime Minister in May 1923. But thereafter the Premier grew sceptical of any economic revival occurring within Europe or the Empire sufficiently vigorous to combat rising unemployment. Continued industrial recession at home laid bare the hopelessness of awaiting any 'natural' recovery of trade and exports. The stimulus to employment in coalmining following the French occupation of the Ruhr in 1923 proved fortuitous, but offered no lasting solution to the industry's formidable problems. With public works officially regarded as mere 'palliatives', pressure mounted during the summer of 1923 for the government to offer more tangible relief to industry and the unemployed.

Some Ministers dared to suggest further, if limited, doses of protection. In August 1923 Lloyd-Greame, President of the Board of Trade, pleaded for the Safeguarding Act to be amended to allow duties to be imposed in favour of

[25] S. Shaw, 'The Attitude of the TUC towards Unemployment in the Inter-War Period', Ph.D. Thesis, University of Kent (1979), 216.

[26] R. K. Snyder, *The Tariff Problem in Great Britain, 1918–1923* (Stanford, 1944), 99.

any industry threatened with increased unemployment as a result of foreign competition. Leopold Amery at the Admiralty pressed a similar case with characteristic dogmatism. Additional duties were tantamount to increased employment, he contended; any decline in imports following the adoption of a tariff would increase purchasing power at home and thereby create additional demand for labour.[27] And within industry there emerged a significant change in sentiment more favourable to protectionism than hitherto, particularly in the midlands and in the north. In September 1923 Bradford woollen and worsted trade manufacturers, traditional free traders, sought protection under the Safeguarding Act on the grounds that intense foreign competition was forcing them to shed a substantial volume of labour. A month later the Midland Council of the National Union of Manufacturers publicly advocated the protection of the home market as a remedy for unemployment. Within iron and steel, support for a protective tariff had hardly waned since the war years, but it grew noticeably stronger in the early twenties as public concern focussed upon the need to maintain employment and production in pivotal industries.

Towards the end of 1923 Baldwin, driven by the fear that mounting unemployment might actually wreck the government's chances of survival, grasped the initiative and decided to make protection an immediate political issue. 'Since the war', he informed his Cabinet colleagues in October 1923:

the environment in which industry has carried on has changed. The whole economic system of Europe . . . has broken down. The economic recovery of Germany is inevitably delayed . . . Consequently new factors have entered into the problem of industry, including currency bounties and low wages abroad . . . Uncertainty as to the direction and extent of competition paralyses industry . . . To these difficulties and handicaps to trade, must be added those of reparations. In order to pay for the increased imports which she requires . . . Germany must export more. Similarly, reparations can only be paid by increased exports. Except in the event of a boom . . . – and no such boom is in sight – the world can only absorb such exports by a great dislocation of trade, which must be disastrous to this country.

All that the Government has done for unemployment will be deemed insufficient. There is only one way, not to cure, but to fight unemployment, and that is to protect the home market against foreign manufactures. Without machinery for this, we are impotent to meet any of the dangers described. The alternatives, viz: to do nothing or to temporize by putting on the McKenna duties on a few more articles, are of no value.[28]

Baldwin's conviction – that the economic and political situation had changed dramatically since the time of the pre-war Tariff Reform campaign and that protection was now the only effective weapon against unemploy-

[27] K. Middlemass and J. Barnes, *Baldwin. A Biography* (1969), 215–16.
[28] Middlemass and Barnes, *Baldwin*, 225–6.

ment – was carried to an unsuspecting public with growing confidence and enthusiasm. Free trade, he argued, would render England the 'economic shock-absorber' of the entire industrialized world. Although Bonar Law's pledge bound the existing parliament, he told a Plymouth audience on 25 October 1923, he could not see 'that any slight extension or adoption of principles hitherto sanctioned in the legislature is a break of that pledge'. The Board of Trade, he continued:

> has been investigating certain distressed industries, and if the case is made out that on account of the grave unemployment and the nature of the competition to which they are subjected, special help is needed, I shall have no hesitation in asking . . . the Chancellor of the Exchequer . . . to . . . safeguard those industries . . . This unemployment problem is the most crucial problem of our country. I regard it as such. I can fight it. I am willing to fight it. I cannot fight it without weapons . . . If we go pottering along as we are, we shall have grave unemployment with us to the end of time . . . I have come to the conclusion myself that the only way of fighting this subject is by protecting the home market.[29]

Three weeks later Baldwin dissolved parliament in order to seek a mandate for protection as a remedy for unemployment. The Tories were forced to tread carefully in their appeal to the electorate. They assiduously refused to consider duties on wheat or meat, knowing that a tax on workers' living standards would play straight into the hands of their political opponents. What Baldwin had in mind was to seek a tax on imported manufactured goods, particularly those which he believed to be the cause of the greatest amount of domestic unemployment. Imperial preference would continue, but the move to a fully fledged system of protection would be gradual; indeed, it was felt that duties might more profitably be used to negotiate a reduction in foreign tariffs in those directions most beneficial to the export trade.

Neither the industrial malaise nor the scourge of unemployment convinced free trade critics that the adoption of tariffs was the most effective means of securing economic revival. Although the Liberals were as badly divided as the Conservatives on economic policies to combat unemployment, they wallowed in the opportunity which Baldwin had given them to champion the cause of free trade. Unemployment, they insisted, resulted more from a decline in foreign customers than it did from increased competition. Tariffs would merely aggravate the situation and could only benefit the smallest fraction of the unemployed, perhaps 140,000 at the most.[30] Protection, furthermore, would safeguard the inefficient, strengthen the existing obsolescence of plant and encourage the immobility of labour. Keynes, a staunch Liberal supporter, was particularly dismissive.

[29] Middlemass and Barnes, *Baldwin*, 228–9.
[30] R. Lyman, *The First Labour Government. 1924* (1957), 27–9.

'By cutting off imports we might increase the aggregate of work; but we should be diminishing the aggregate of wages', he wrote towards the end of 1923. 'Is there anything that a tariff could do, which an earthquake could not do better?'[31]

Within the Labour Party MacDonald, Snowden, Thomas, Clynes and Henderson resolutely defended free trade, firmly convinced that protection was both irrelevant and obsolete as a strategy for creating work. In their view, tariffs could not cure unemployment since they impeded the free interchange of goods and services so essential to Britain's economic well-being. In addition, they were likely to encourage trusts and monopolies and to impoverish through raised prices those sections of the working class least able to defend themselves, thereby perpetuating the inequality of wealth. Rising unemployment could best be countered by trade expansion, sound money and increased industrial efficiency.

Voters apparently agreed. The mandate for protection as a remedy for unemployment was decisively rejected by an electorate fearful of any deliberately induced inflation. Although Baldwin had strenuously denied that tariffs would raise the cost of food to any appreciable extent, it proved a difficult argument to sustain given the Empire's insistence on reciprocal preferences. As it turned out, those of the British public with jobs voted for a lower cost of living rather than for increased assistance to the unemployed.

In such circumstances it is not surprising that the orthodoxy of free trade gained strength after 1923. During the brief interlude of the first Labour government the McKenna Duties and the imperial preferences attached to them were abolished, almost as a matter of principle. They were reintroduced by the Conservatives in July 1925 but by then Baldwin, already pledged not to impose food taxes or to modify the fiscal system in any radical way, had installed Churchill, a committed free trader, at the Exchequer; the cause of tariff reform seemed doomed for the foreseeable future.[32]

Nevertheless, the fear of alienating free trade voters did not prevent the Baldwin administration from continuing as an exceptional move to safeguard those industries which complained of serious unemployment, aggravated by excessive foreign competition. The Tory election manifesto in 1923 had declared that the party:

would be unfaithful to its principles and to its duty if it did not treat the task of grappling with . . . unemployment . . . as a primary objective. While a general tariff is no part of our programme, we are determined to safeguard the employment and

---

[31] J. M. Keynes, 'Free Trade', *The Nation*, 1 December 1923.
[32] Though the Conservative administration was now bound by its election pledges, it offered nevertheless to increase imperial preference in order to promote the sale of British Empire products. An Empire Marketing Board was established for this purpose in 1926.

standard of living of our people in any efficient industry in which they are imperilled by unfair foreign competition.

Thus the Board of Trade was empowered in 1926 to judge whether particular goods were being imported in such quantities and sold at such low prices as to establish a case for protecting particular domestic industries for the sake of maintaining profitable production and stable employment.

Few at the time feared that such assistance would prove substantial enough to raise the thorny problem of general tariff protection. But the crisis in the basic staple industries deepened noticeably towards the end of 1928, creating pools of surplus labour too large to be eradicated by any immediate upturn in the trade cycle. The grim reality of structural unemployment revived protectionist sentiment both inside and outside of government in the critical months prior to the 1929 general election. Amongst government ministers Leopold Amery, Secretary of State for the Dominions, became especially alarmist. In a forthright memorandum to Cabinet in July 1928 he warned colleagues of the disastrous consequences of adhering too strongly to previous pledges on fiscal policy. 'For a time', he wrote,

we may have deluded ourselves with the idea that we were suffering from the unsettled state of Europe, and that our difficulties were of a temporary character . . . But . . . our difficulties are neither temporary nor due to purely external causes, but are fundamental and inherent in our own national policy . . . Both on merits and on grounds of political self-preservation we have got to face the facts, find practical remedies and carry them into effect. Further fumbling with the situation will mean well-merited political extinction.

Since it was 'politically impossible' and 'economically unsound' to seek a substantial reduction in total taxation or wage costs to restore British industrial competitiveness, there remained:

the one obvious remedy, no doubt controversial politically, but incontrovertible as common sense, of giving our industries some measure of shelter in the home market . . . At this moment we are importing iron and steel at a rate equivalent to the full-time employment of 135,000 men a year, of whom, at least, 40,000 would be coalminers required to produce the 100,000,000 tons of coal represented in that import. The imposition of a duty which would restrict those imports by 75 per cent would employ 100,000 men in the most depressed industries and in the hardest hit localities. It would do more in a year than migration could do in five years, or domestic transference in twenty years. Last year the retained imports of foreign manufactures . . . were about £230,000,000. If safeguarding duties at an average of 25 per cent excluded half of these, they would provide employment, direct and indirect, for at the very least 500,000 people.

Nor would the perceived benefits end there:

An increase of employment of 500,000 people would involve an increase in the yield of our national taxation of, say, £20,000,000. It would involve a saving of at least £30,000,000 to the community in employment benefit and relief.

Combining tariff protection with extended Imperial Preference, moreover, could only strengthen the situation; any advance, Amery contended:

> which we can make in Imperial Preference in this country that will encourage the Dominions to maintain or extend their preferences . . . is of the greatest importance to the employment position.[33]

Amery was not alone in his strident support of the protectionist cause. By the late twenties interest groups within the Federation of British Industries were calling for greater protectionism in order 'to keep the home market for the home industries' and offered to assist individual producers in their claim for safeguarding status.[34] Similar support was evident in the textile trades and particularly so in the iron and steel industry, a sector which had long regarded tariffs as an important means of safeguarding employment. Convinced of the virtue of its case, the industry worked diligently throughout the twenties to convince Ministers of the need for special assistance, appealing in 1928 and again in 1929 for protection under the Safeguarding Act. Even this substantial effort was but part of a wider campaign by business interests to promote the claims of tariff protection. The National Union of Manufacturers is known to have been active in this direction early in the decade. But it was the Empire Industries Association which conducted a particularly vigorous propaganda campaign from 1924 onwards, cultivating public and government opinion in favour of expanded Empire preference and the extended safeguarding of domestic industry.

Significant though this flurry of protectionist sentiment was, it would be misleading to suggest that it had any immediate impact upon official commercial policy. Of the 49 industries which applied for protection during 1925–29, only nine were successful. Baldwin firmly resisted the lobbying of iron and steel interests fearing that the protection of such a large industry would foster demands for defensive tariffs elsewhere. Tariff protection for steel was likely to raise input costs to large parts of British industry, particularly shipbuilding. In addition, it risked aggravating internal divisions between the 'heavy' and 'finishing' branches of steel, the latter dependent upon cheap imports, and upsetting the consensus required to effect industrial reorganization.[35]

Free traders were plainly aware of the mounting crisis of unemployment, but remained unconvinced that a major change in fiscal policy was either a

---

[33] Cab 24/196, CP 210, Unemployment. Memorandum by the Secretary of State for Dominion Affairs and for the Colonies, 2 July 1928.

[34] A. J. Marrison, 'Businessmen, Industries and Tariff Reform in Great Britain, 1903–1930', *Business History*, 25 (1983), 148–78.

[35] F. Capie, 'The Pressure for Tariff Protection in Britain, 1917–31', *Journal of European Economic History*, 9 (1980), 435–6; S. Tolliday, 'Tariffs and Steel, 1916–1934: The Politics of Industrial Decline' in *Businessmen and Politics*, ed. J. Turner (1984), 56–9.

necessary or an appropriate response to it. In industries such as mining, transport, distribution and shipbuilding there was no 'import' problem as such, whilst the bulk of unemployment in industries open to protection was to be found in those sectors engaged in manufacturing exports. By confining themselves to the direct benefits likely to accrue to remaining trades, critics were able to regale protection as wantonly misguided. *The Economist* put it thus in 1929:

If we indulged in the experiment we should be risking immeasurable damage to our export trade and our whole economic structure which might instil great increases of unemployment on the off-chance that a tiny fraction of unemployment might be removed in certain areas.[36]

Pigou argued that:

A good case for restricting competitive imports as a means of alleviating unemployment can only be made out in respect of commodities for which the home demand is considerably urgent or inelastic. A delicate discrimination would be needed, for which neither the available data nor the economic education of governing persons are at present adequate. If unemployment is to be successfully attacked, some device of more general application and more fool-proof in nature is required.[37]

The Balfour Committee on Industry and Trade, struck by the complexity of the industrial malaise, seriously doubted that protection could neutralize the formidable range of factors influencing variations in international competitiveness:

There is as yet no . . . generally accepted body of doctrine as to the precise conditions under which . . . the imposition of an import duty on competing manufactures would be likely on balance to give rise to higher prices through restricting competition, or to lower prices through decreasing overhead costs.[38]

If unemployment was to fall significantly, the Committee argued, it would be the result of restoring the competitive power of British trade overseas by means less damaging than the hasty erection of tariff barriers. The Liberal Party was rather more specific. Whilst it accepted that a particular industrial sector might gain from protection, it rejected the idea of any general betterment. 'A country cannot restrict imports without restricting exports or increasing its foreign investments', ran one of its official statements: 'In other words, tariffs are not a device for increasing the employment and protection of a country but rather a means of diverting it from one direction to another'.[39]

[36] 'Unemployment and Protection', *The Economist*, 2 February 1928.
[37] A. Pigou, 'Wage Policy and Unemployment', *Economic Journal*, 37 (1927), 362.
[38] Final Report of the Committee on Industry and Trade, 1929, Cmd. 3282, 275.
[39] J. Roberts, 'Economic Aspects of the Unemployment Policy of the Government, 1929–31', Ph.D. Thesis, University of London (1977), 77.

Any lingering hopes that the renewed sympathy for protection would capture the popular imagination were quickly dashed on the election of the second Labour administration in June 1929. Within weeks of taking office the government confirmed its long-standing commitment to free trade. It rejected an application for safeguarding by the worsted and woollen industry and informed parliament that existing safeguarding duties would not be renewed on expiry.

At the time continued economic recovery was still a distinct possibility and efforts to expand world trade were therefore afforded the highest priority within government. In February 1930 Graham, President of the Board of Trade, initiated a conference amongst thirty countries to arrange a two-year tariff truce and to establish a programme of non-discriminatory tariff reductions. Eleven countries agreed in principle not to increase their tariffs until April 1931. For the agreement to become effective, it had to be ratified by the governments concerned by 1 November 1930.

Unlike the majority of his colleagues, MacDonald did not regard the fiscal question as a crucial matter of principle. For some months past he had been seriously considering protection as a means of expanding domestic industrial production and employment. But when Graham's proposals came before Cabinet, the Premier shrank from challenging the free trade lobby. British ratification of the tariff truce proposals duly came in September, effectively ruling out protection for at least eight months.

But deep pessimism was brewing over the future of free trade. The Dominions had promptly denounced the tariff truce. Elsewhere the pressure of continually falling commodity prices had intensified protectionism, particularly in America. Although an export-led recovery under a free trade regime retained some theoretical credibility, it appeared increasingly unlikely in the face of intense economic autarky abroad and accelerating industrial decline at home. With continued Liberal support, MacDonald and his colleagues could champion the free trade cause politically, but the rising tide of tariffs and the speed by which depression was sweeping across Europe forced those less slavishly bound to the ideals of nineteenth-century capitalism to adopt a more pragmatic view of the proper course of commercial policy. By the end of 1930 no fewer than thirteen participants in the first tariff truce conference had raised their tariffs; economic internationalism was fast proving to be an embarrassing burden.

Support for protection grew stronger both inside and outside of government during 1930/31 as the need to respond to the deepening industrial crisis grew more urgent. Hubert Henderson's plea in April 1930 for the government to accept a 10 per cent revenue tariff on manufactured imports stemmed partly from his desire to provide resources for industrial rationalization and to forestall financial chaos by subsidizing the growing debt on the Unemployment Fund.[40] It derived much of its strength, however, from a conviction that large-scale unemployment would never be solved by awaiting the recovery of lost export markets. He explained his position to the Economic Advisory Council in April 1930:

In recent years we have been losing ground relatively to other competing countries in world markets . . . The tide of demand has turned throughout the world against some of those industries in which we largely specialized. Some of our staple industries have reached a stage of development at which it is possible for countries with a comparatively low level of skill and standard of living to carry them on almost as efficiently as ourselves . . . We are faced in a steadily increasing degree with the competition of other countries as efficiently equipped as ourselves in respect of business management and technical skill. Moreover, the trend of tariffs throughout the world is still upward, and will probably remain so for so long as the trend of world prices is downwards.

In these circumstances we still probably do well if . . . we succeed in maintaining our export trade at the level of recent years, and adding to it a modest annual increment. The importance of the export trade remains fundamental . . . but it would seem idle to look to the export trade to supply much positive contribution within any reasonable space of time to the problem of increasing employment.[41]

It would be absurd, moreover, to worry about the likely effects of tariffs on British trade as a whole. People might expect the diminution of imports to turn the exchanges in Britain's favour, helping to boost gold reserves, credit, wages and prices to the detriment of our competitiveness. But it was pointless being apprehensive:

of such reactions, under present conditions, when the prevailing *weakness* of the foreign exchanges, and the danger that gold may at any time flow out on a formidable scale, are actually among the main sources of anxiety regarding our underlying position. I venture to doubt whether a single economist in the country would dispute that, under conditions such as now obtain, the effects of a 10% tariff on manufactured imports would be beneficial to employment; and I also doubt whether many businessmen, whose general position is that of Free Traders, would dispute that such a tariff would have a materially beneficial effect on business psychology.[42]

Keynes had defended free trade for most of the 1920s. He remained convinced for many more years of the inherent difficulties of ever trying to remove tariffs once they had been introduced. But the pressure of unemployment gradually converted Keynes into a reluctant protectionist.

[40] See above chapter 2.
[41] Cab 58/10, EAC(4), The Economic Outlook. Memorandum by H. D. Henderson, 3 April 1930. Similar sentiments were expressed in H. D. Henderson, 'The Falling Price Level and Its Implications'. Memorandum written as Secretary of the Economic Advisory Council, 24 April 1930, reprinted in H. Clay (ed.), *The Inter-War Years and Other Papers* (Oxford, 1955), 53.
[42] Cab 24/212, CP 196, Unemployment Policy – Industrial Reconstruction Scheme. Note by Mr. H. D. Henderson, 30 May 1930.

By February 1930, as chapter 10 demonstrates, he had become convinced that the cost reductions customarily regarded as a necessary pre-requisite to industrial and trade revival could not be achieved for practical and political reasons by enforced cuts in money wages. The virtue of protection, on the other hand, was that it was much more likely to bring down real wages and to relieve the pressure on the balance of payments. The foreign balance, Keynes maintained, could be increased just as effectively if imports were reduced as if exports were increased, once it was recognized that one of the underlying assumptions of free trade – that wages would always fall to their strict economic level – no longer held. In his view a tariff, by raising import prices relative to wages, could reduce real wage costs in an equitable way with the minimum of social strife. Moreover, it would stimulate foreign investment and thus help to offset the damage inflicted by the government's refusal to expand domestic investment on a scale sufficient to absorb the prevailing excess of domestic savings. A moderate degree of protection, in other words, would relieve the pressure on the exchanges, boost the foreign demand for British goods and expand output for use at home, without adverse reactions on the price of exports, given the prevailing surplus of men and plant.[43]

Increasingly, Keynes found himself unable to defend free trade as vehemently as he had done in the past. The critical question, he reminded the Macmillan Committee:

is how far one is prepared to be governed by short [period] considerations . . . If we are jammed for some time I think we should get some immediate relief by well-adjusted tariffs . . . If it is essential for equilibrium that we should invest abroad on a larger scale than at present, the protectionist way of doing it may be the method of least resistance because it does not require a reduction of money wages and has less effect . . . in turning the terms of trade against us . . . With protection we should have lower real wages but less unemployment; with free trade, if it works, we should have no unemployment. But free trade assumes that unemployment is an abnormal break in prosperity of which one should not take account. It assumes that if you throw men out of work in one direction you re-employ them in another. As soon as that link in the chain is broken the whole of the free trade argument breaks down. The protectionist method serves to restore equilibrium by seeking some way of increasing the volume of foreign investment without reducing money wages.[44]

The misgivings expressed by Henderson and Keynes over the prospect of a beneficial revival in staple exports clearly influenced the Economic Advisory Council in its reports to government. Although it was universally accepted

---

[43] Keynes's call for increased public spending to help combat unemployment itself threatened exchange rate stability, but he anticipated in 1930 that there would be sufficient international co-operation, particularly from America and France, to neutralize the supposed damage that domestic reflation might bring. B. Eichengreen, *Sterling and the Tariff, 1929–32* (Princeton, 1981).   [44] *JMK*, Vol. 20, 115–17.

that a major boost in exports would be desirable, the Council pointed out in May 1930:

> to expect an increased efficiency in these trades sufficient to absorb within a moderate period of time the bulk of the persons now unemployed, both in these industries and in other industries, would be quite unreasonable.

Rationalization schemes for the export trades, it confessed, would be likely:

> for the time being to increase profits, but they are not so likely to increase exports or employment. The remaining possibilities seem to be tariffs, bounties, import control and the like, on the one hand, and a programme of home development on the other . . . We see no third alternative, so far as the near future is concerned, except a policy of inactivity in the hope of some favourable development turning up in the outside world.[45]

It was the Report of the Committee of Economists in October 1930 that alerted the government to the real possibility of adopting a revenue tariff to ease the economic malaise. The Committee proposed a uniform 10 per cent tariff on all imports, including food, and a bounty of an equivalent amount on all exports. Tariffs would remain only until such time as 'abnormal unemployment' had ended or until prices had recovered '(say) to the 1925–8 standard'.[46] Keynes contended that the effect of such a tariff on the foreign balance could be equivalent to that obtained from a 20 per cent average reduction of money wages, but without the 'guerilla warfare' that would result from any concerted effect to cut workers' incomes directly.[47]

Not all contemporary economists agreed with this prognosis. Indeed, the final report of the Committee of Economists failed to reflect the bitter opposition amongst some of its members to the policy proposals being pressed upon the government. Robbins, for example, maintained that a tariff could only help unemployment if money wages were rigid in both an upward and downward direction. If they were flexible in an upward direction, then increased import prices would encourage trade union demands for wage increases, thereby exacerbating the unemployment problem. Pigou and Beveridge were equally sceptical, fearing that a 'temporary' tariff would quickly become a permanent feature destined to raise prices relative to costs, thereby eliminating any stimulus to activity. Moreover, Beveridge complained, it was ludicrous to presume either that the surplus unemployed were in the trades likely to be stimulated by protection or that the labour and plant in the export trades destined to lose markets through a reduction in international trade could immediately be

---

[45] Cab 58/10, EAC(H)85, Economic Advisory Council, Committee on Economic Outlook, 1930, paras 9, 10.
[46] Cab 58/11, Economic Advisory Council, Committee of Economists Report, 24 October 1930, para 105.   [47] *JMK*, Vol. 20, 418–19.

used to meet the demands of a protected home market. 'The existence of prolonged widespread unemployment', wrote Beveridge, 'is by itself no reason for trying protection as a remedy . . . The plight of Britain's principal industries to-day is due, not to more imports, but to fewer exports, not to an increase of our international trade, but to the decrease of it. Almost certainly it could only be made worse, not bettered, if international trade was hampered still further by a British tariff.'[48]

The rapid deterioration in the economic climate during 1930/31 convinced Keynes that, such criticisms apart, the case for a revenue tariff as an anti-unemployment measure was stronger than ever. In an addendum to the Macmillan Committee's report drafted largely by himself, and in various articles and speeches, he argued during 1931 for comprehensive import taxes averaging 10 per cent (15 per cent on manufactured and semi-manufactured goods and 5 per cent on foodstuffs). As in earlier months, Keynes maintained that a revenue tariff represented the only reflationary initiative available which could improve confidence and employment without threatening to gold standard. Although he had previously denied that protection could reduce unemployment, he now regarded the imposition of a tariff of as a 'second-best' solution necessary to defend the fixed parity of sterling. The views he spelled out in the *Daily Mail* in March 1931 are worth quoting at length. Unqualified free trade, he wrote:

is part of an austere philosophy which depends, and indeed insists, on things being allowed to find their own levels without interference. But if economic changes are very violent and very rapid, human nature makes it impossible for some things to find their proper levels quick enough . . . When a free trader argues that a tariff cannot increase employment but can only divert employment from one industry to another, he is tacitly assuming that a man who loses his employment in one direction will lower the wage rate which he is willing to accept until he finds employment in another direction. When small changes only are in question, there may be much long-run truth in this. But in present circumstances it is sheer nonsense. Nevertheless, even so, I should be afraid of the long-run effects of introducing the whole apparatus of discriminating protection. It would be much wiser to keep to a measure of a general all-round character, dictated by the requirements of the present emergency, and to employ other measures for the protection of particular industries . . . What are the troubles in our way? There is a lack of confidence – that subtle, intangible, priceless quiddity – at home and abroad. There is a pressure on our foreign exchanges, a tendency for what we lend abroad to exceed the surplus that we have to lend, which makes us nervous and uncomfortable. There is a lack of profit for home producers. And because of this lack of profit men are unemployed who are capable of producing goods which we are now importing. Above all, we have an unbalanced Budget. Yet we need not only to balance the Budget by means which will not upset business confidence or put new burdens on industry, but to provide ourselves with a financial margin under cover of

[48]   *The Times*, 26 March 1931.

which we can make progressive, constructive plans for more far-reaching remedies to improve the demand for our products. Then we should reduce business losses and unemployment without serious detriment to our standards of life.

Observe how appropriate a revenue tariff is to all these objects. Assuredly there is no other tax which, so far from diminishing confidence, will actually increase it. At the same time a tariff of 15 per cent on all manufactured and partly manufactured goods will keep out some goods which we now import and cause home-produced goods to be substituted for them. In so far as this happens, the pressure on our exchanges will be relieved, while profits and employment will be increased in the industries which are thus enabled to supply the home market. And finally, from the revenue levied on the goods which would still be imported – some part of which might, in the exceptional conditions of today, be paid in effect by the foreign exporter – we could put the Budget on a thoroughly sound basis. I regard a revenue tariff as a high card in hand which we have not yet played.[49]

Given the pressure of circumstances, Keynes explained to readers of the *New Statesman and Nation* some days later, it was essential to adopt measures to facilitate internal expansion and industrial recovery.

If I knew of a concrete, practicable proposal for stimulating our export trades, I should welcome it. Knowing none, I fall back on a restriction of imports to support our balance of trade and to provide employment. Moreover, even if we were to agree that we cannot recover a sufficient volume of exports without a large cut in wages, what exactly one does about it I do not know. I wish that someone, who relies on this alternative, would tell me.'[50]

Colin Clark, secretary to the Cabinet Committee appointed in April 1930 'to survey the trade position in the light of changes . . . that had taken place in world trade since the war', estimated that if all the manufactured goods imported in Britain in 1930 had been produced at home, unemployment would have fallen by 875,000.[51]

Nor was it only the economists who were questioning the fate of the unemployed under a free-trade regime. Members of the Federation of British Industries, who had retained a noticeably neutral stance over protection in the 1920s for the sake of institutional unity, later declared their conversion to tariffs. A committee of the FBI enquired in October 1930 'whether or not a more general application of safeguarding duties would contribute materially to the restoration of prosperity to British industry and a consequent alleviation of the unemployment problem', and reported an overwhelming majority of Federation members in favour of a policy which combined industrial protection with the widest possible extension of imperial preference.[52] The Federation's first public declaration in support of

---

[49] *The Daily Mail*, 13 March 1931, reproduced in *JMK*, Vol. 20, 489–92.
[50] 'Economic Notes on Free Trade', *New Statesman and Nation*, 28 March 1931.
[51] Howson and Winch, *The Economic Advisory Council*, 84.
[52] Dintenfass, 'The TUC, the FBI and British Economic Policy', 161–2.

tariffs in March 1931 made it clear that employers accepted the protectionist case essentially as an employment policy. The classical assumptions
underlying free trade, it argued, were not applicable to conditions of less
than full employment. A tariff, scientifically applied, could stimulate output
and jobs, particularly if it enabled a larger volume of domestic production to
be marketed. It could act thereby as a buffer, permitting the rationalization
of industry to proceed without generating still further unemployment.[53] By
1930 it was clear that doubts over Britain's internationalist stance had
spread to otherwise erstwhile supporters of free trade. Regional Chambers of
Commerce and City bankers were calling for a preferential extension of the
market for British goods as a means of shoring up the domestic economy,
thereby assisting sterling to hold its own as a world currency.[54]

The trade union movement, by contrast, remained divided over the issue
of protection, having within its ranks representatives of trades already
suffering from import-induced unemployment and others in the export
sector who feared increased retaliation if Britain adopted tariffs. In its
evidence to the Macmillan Committee, the TUC modified its staunch free-
trade outlook slightly, offering to investigate further the case for a general
tariff. Bevin's Transport and General Workers' Union had pressed the
General Council in 1927 to investigate the effect of tariff movements on the
stability of trade and unemployment. And three years later, at the Congress's
Annual Conference, Bevin himself delivered a blistering attack on the
concept of Free Trade:

> There is a correct analysis of Free Trade and which is called the open monetary
> system operation. You have a price level X. That price level tends to rise, a boom
> follows, you get increased imports with rising purchasing power. When imports rise
> to a certain level gold begins to leave the country. When gold begins to leave the
> country it makes the Bank Rate effective on the discount market in the City of
> London. When the Bank Rate is made effective you restrict credit. When you restrict
> credit you increase unemployment. When you have increased unemployment you
> reduce wages and start at a new price level. This is Free Trade.[55]

But none of this did much to alter majority opinion within the TUC. Rather
than encourage friction within its ranks, Congress adopted a policy of
'calculated ambiguity', refusing either to declare its explicit support of free
trade or to endorse general import restrictions.

In any event, the betrayal of free trade principles by some economists,
industrialists and trade unionists during the bleak years of 1930–31

[53] Federation of British Industries, *The Passing of Free Trade*, 1931. See also R. F. Holland,
'The Federation of British Industries and the International Economy, 1929–1939',
Economic History Review, 2nd ser., 24 (1981), 287–300.
[54] Boyce, *British Capitalism at the Crossroads*, 250–8.
[55] TUC, *Annual Report*, 1930, 283.

seemed of little consequence so long as Snowden dominated Labour's discussion of fiscal policy. Yet even his fetish for free trade orthodoxy did not go unchallenged. It was Vernon Hartshorn, Lord Privy Seal, who raised the unmentionable in a Cabinet memorandum in August 1930. 'If reduction of costs of production by reorganization, modernization, etc. are not sufficient to enable certain industries to retain their home market', he asked, 'or if present fiscal conditions are unfavourable to the expansion of certain established industries . . . ought we not to be prepared to consider a modification of our fiscal policy?'[56] And as we note in chapter 13, Oswald Mosley was committed by the early thirties to reducing unemployment through a vigorous policy of home development. He grew increasingly exasperated, however, by Labour's insistence that economic recovery should ultimately come from a revival in exports, a revival which trends in demand and technology, together with rising protectionism abroad, threatened to delay for some considerable time.

Like Keynes, Mosley recognized that a policy of home development incorporating national public works was incompatible with free trade. Such a policy was neither safe nor practicable unless it was accompanied by measures designed to neutralize its potentially damaging effects upon confidence, the trade balance and the budget. Thus, he argued, a revenue tariff, by rendering the country less dependent upon exports and by providing some means of stemming a demand-induced increase in imports, would provide the breathing space within which domestic expansionist policy could develop. The supposed ill effects of reflation, in other words, would be offset by the favourable impact of protection, each working to expand employment.[57] It was hopeless in his view to pursue a policy of internationalism when intense competition in world markets from countries with cheap, semi-mechanized labour enabled them to undercut the best efforts of British industry and labour. It would be far better for the country to seek within the Empire a self-contained economic system, insulated from low wage competition, and to pursue a bold policy of domestic industrial expansion to assure home market recovery.

A similar re-appraisal of fiscal policy occurred within the Conservative party. Prior to the 1929 election Baldwin had sternly refused to abandon his pledge not to consider a general tariff though, as noted above, he agreed somewhat reluctantly to allow individual industries to be considered on

[56] Cab 27/440, CP 293, Unemployment Policy. Memorandum by the Lord Privy Seal, 18 August 1930.
[57] Skidelsky, *Politicians and the Slump*, 200. Mosley's reaction against the official preoccupation with the export industries pre-dated the world slump. In his policy statement, *Revolution by Reason*, published in 1925, he called for increased domestic production and for the bulk purchase of food and raw materials as a way of lowering total imports, thereby enabling Britain to reduce her volume of necessary exports.

their merits for a limited measure of safeguarding. Nevertheless, he still afforded priority in the assault on unemployment to other expedients, such as the reduction of surplus capacity in the depressed trades, de-rating and labour transference. By 1930, however, the situation had changed considerably. In June MacDonald obtained Cabinet approval to invite both Lloyd George and Baldwin to participate in advisory conferences on agriculture and unemployment. Though Lloyd George accepted the invitation Baldwin refused, on the grounds that protection had been ruled out for discussion. Four months earlier he had reputedly expressed the view 'that industry must have a general stimulus' and he was therefore going 'to put forward a policy of bolder safeguarding extended to all industries great or small, provided that they could show a case for increased employment'.[58]

It soon became clear that this statement reflected rather more than the earlier commitment to selective industrial protection. The Tory Research Department began work on the structure and operation of a general tariff in December 1931. By the following spring it was reported that a 'complete tariff scheme was . . . ready to be rushed through Parliament at a moment's notice'.[59] The staple industries, Baldwin was arguing in 1931, would never be able to compete effectively nor reorganize adequately without protection; nor could Britain hope to bargain with the rest of the world or to develop a new industrial base without a fundamental change in the fiscal system sufficient to reduce the pressure of taxation, boost confidence and stem the rise in unemployment.

THE COMING OF THE TARIFF

Although support for protection had risen noticeably both inside and outside of parliament by 1931, it would be wrong to suggest that the final break with free trade was primarily the result of successful lobbying over the anticipated role of tariffs in the reduction of unemployment. As the previous chapter indicated, economic policy in the late summer of 1931 had become dominated by the financial crisis. At that point protection was regarded less as a means of reducing unemployment than as the least objectionable means of balancing the budget and restoring confidence in sterling. The critical point is that protectionist sentiment grew significantly before and after Britain was forced off the gold standard; before it because tariffs were seen as a valuable means of restoring confidence and stemming the loss of gold in the midst of a worsening international liquidity crisis, and after it because of continuing fears that a floating exchange rate would work only

[58] Middlemass and Barnes, *Baldwin*, 560.
[59] Capie, 'The Pressure for Tariff Protection', 438.

imperfectly as a guarantor of balance of payments equilibrium and stable prices.[60] As the metropolitan economy deteriorated, stability was sought in a general tariff and in the exploitation of the Empire. The obligations of the newly formed National Government, MacDonald reminded his colleagues in September 1931, were to balance the budget, to create a favourable trade balance and to seek powers to deal with problems as they arose. 'Quite specifically amongst those powers must be that of using a Tariff should the financial and industrial conditions require it.'[61]

The suspension of the gold standard made it rather more difficult to justify protection on grounds of stimulating employment. With the exchange rate floating and the external constraint no longer binding, there were risks that a tariff-induced appreciation of the pound would reduce export demand, invite retaliation and so disrupt international trade that the stimulus to employment, production and prices that Keynes and others had argued would result from tariff protection under fixed exchange rates would be lost. In short, imposing a tariff in a world of floating exchange rates could prove self-defeating.

Recognizing this, Keynes, in a characteristic re-think on policy, argued in 1931 that currency depreciation could achieve what he had previously argued tariffs could do, only better. After all, with the suspension of convertibility, the authorities were free to adopt reflationary measures so long as they were prepared to allow sterling to depreciate.[62] Beveridge, his former critic, argued in similar terms. 'As soon as a country is off the gold standard the balance of exports and imports gets adjusted rapidly and automatically by the exchanges', he wrote in the *News Chronicle* in September 1931, and 'to impose a tariff when the exchange is fully free to fluctuate is to deprive ourselves of the one obvious benefit which the break with gold confers – the stimulus to export.'[63]

But given the authorities' growing fears as to the consequences of exchange-rate depreciation for budgetary and trade equilibria, the pressure for an emergency tariff spread, despite its anticipated effects on jobs. Key members of the Tory 1922 Committee declared themselves in favour of a revenue tariff in September 1931, principally because of the adverse turn in trade and finance. A reported 30 Liberals pressed for a fundamental change in commercial policy after the break with gold, contrary to their party's vehement defence of free trade.[64]

[60] For further discussion see chapter 5.
[61] Cab 24/233, CP 247. Notes by the Prime Minister on a General Election, 29 September 1931.
[62] B. Eichengreen, 'Keynes and Protection', *Journal of Economic History*, 44 (1984), 367.
[63] *News Chronicle*, 22 September 1931, cited in D. Abel, *A History of British Tariffs 1923–1942* (1945), 80.   [64] Middlemass and Barnes, *Baldwin*, 641.

By late 1931, the employment-generating effects of a general tariff were not of primary importance to the government. The outlook of politicians, Eichengreen has reminded us:

was conditioned by the European inflations of the 1920s, and few had faith that a floating exchange rate represented a solution to the problem of external balance. They supported the imposition of the General Tariff in order to guard against the dangers of hyperinflation and unbounded exchange-rate depreciation, and they made this choice knowing that the tariff might exacerbate the problem of domestic unemployment. This possibility, however, was the price to be paid for exchange-rate and price stability.[65]

It was ironic, nevertheless, that although the critical balance of payments situation proved to be the major determinant of commercial policy, its effect in raising political support for protection was to rekindle those conventional arguments for a tariff that had found support during the later twenties. Three months after devaluation, the adverse net balance of trade stood at £113 million; over 2.5 million men were recorded as unemployed and world trade showed no signs of early recovery. The election of a Conservative-dominated National Government in October 1931 noticeably strengthened the protectionist movement. Chamberlain, chairman of the committee established in December 1931 to study the balance of trade, openly declared that tariffs were the only means which remained 'to reverse the balance, swell the revenue, and assist unemployment'.[66] To Baldwin, tariffs remained a necessary evil in a wicked world, but he defended them as a means of cheapening British production, stimulating home demand, and increasing Britain's bargaining strength in export markets, particularly for staple goods.

This 'catch-all' sentiment was clearly evident in the passing of the 1932 Import Duties Act. Tariffs, the government maintained, would not only assist the balance of trade, improve revenue and prevent a rise in the cost of living following depreciation, but would increase employment, encourage industrial efficiency, enhance trade bargaining with foreign countries and foster Imperial Preference. Guided by such considerations, a general 10 per cent *ad valorem* tariff was imposed from March 1932 on all imports except those on a free list, which included most raw materials and foodstuffs. Thus ended almost 80 years of free trade. Imports from the Empire were granted free entry on a temporary basis pending further discussion. An Import Duties Advisory Committee was established to consider revisions in the tariff structure. As a result of its recommendations in April 1932, duties on manufactured goods were raised to 20 per cent. By that time, only 30 per cent of imports came in free of duty, one third paid a nominal rate of 10 per

[65] Eichengreen, *Sterling and the Tariff*, 38.   [66] Middlemass and Barnes, *Baldwin*, 658.

cent, almost 15 per cent duties of 11–20 per cent and around 5 per cent of goods paid duties in excess of 20 per cent.[67]

Although it is difficult to separate the effects of the tariff from other factors influencing the progress of the economy after 1932, there was little firm evidence at the time, and there has been little advanced since, to suggest that the tariff had as positive or as wide ranging an effect as government officials had earlier predicted. The alleged benefits of protection so far as output and employment were concerned – namely, its influence in diverting expenditure to domestic goods, in raising prices and profits, and in stimulating confidence and investment and thereby jobs, found some contemporary support. The economist F. Benham believed that employment 'was probably greater than it would have been under free trade'.[68] One contemporary observer claimed that protection had:

proved a far greater stimulus to business in the short run than had ever been expected and a considerable proportion of the nation's manpower and equipment soon began to find employment in industries which had hitherto failed to make headway against foreign competition under free trade.[69]

The reality was far more complex and uncertain. Capie's examination of the workings of the tariff suggests that nominal tariffs did not have any general or significant impact upon imports, or by implication upon domestic production and employment. By determining the 'effective rate of protection' afforded to individual industries (expressed as margin of protection on value added in the production process),[70] he has tentatively suggested that industries such as cotton and woollen goods enjoyed a high effective rate of protection whilst others such as iron and steel, building, shipbuilding, and certain of the so-called new industries, were handicapped by a lower degree of protection. The inference to be drawn is that protection probably exerted a greater check on falling output and employment in the former group of industries than it did in the latter.[71] Both Foreman-Peck and Eichengreen

---

[67] F. Capie, *Depression and Protectionism: Britain Between the Wars* (1983), 44. The 1932 Act had been preceded by the Abnormal Importations (Customs Duties) Act in November 1931 in an effort to curb the surge in imports anticipated before more permanent legislation was introduced. This Act empowered the Board of Trade to impose duties up to 100 per cent *ad valorem* on imports which were thought to be entering the country in abnormal quantities. The maximum imposed was 50 per cent.

[68] Cited in Capie, *Depression and Protectionism*, 101.

[69] E. V. Francis, *Britain's Economic Strategy* (1939), 178; cited in Capie, *Depression and Protectionism*, 100.

[70] The essential point being that to assess the real level of protection available to an industry it is necessary to consider the *effective* rate applicable to the value added in the competing British industry rather than the nominal rate of duty imposed by the government on the final value of goods imported.

[71] Capie, *Depression and Protectionism*, chapter 8. See also F. Capie, 'The British Tariff and Industrial Protection in the 1930s', *Economic History Review*, 2nd ser., 31 (1978), 399–409.

have gone further, suggesting that the tariff probably raised total Gross National Product by just over 2 per cent, providing a useful if undramatic stimulus to employment.[72]

These findings cannot be pressed too far since they depend upon a complex set of assumptions and upon the robustness of differing econometric models. They are also misleading insofar as they suggest that the tariff itself gave an additional boost to output and employment. It is difficult in the period of floating exchanges in the mid-thirties to distinguish between the effects of the tariff in improving the trade balance from its offsetting effects in exerting upward pressure on the exchange rate. Certainly we lack any firm estimates of the employment-generating effects of the tariff *per se*. Some workers may have benefited from a certain stability of employment inasmuch as the tariff spared them from the immediate consequences of enforced structural change within the staple sectors. Others, on the other hand, could well have been denied the opportunity of employment because of the effect that the tariff had in distorting the efficient allocation of resources. And yet, to the extent that the tariff prevented Britain from becoming the dumping ground for competing countries with excess capacity, it might plausibly be argued that some of the older staple industries escaped even greater depression than they had already suffered. Perhaps the most that can be said with any confidence is that the forces that boosted employment in some industries from the mid-thirties onwards and yet condemned thousands of workers in others to long periods of unemployment are too complex to attribute predominantly to Britain having finally abandoned free trade in 1932.

BARGAINING FOR TRADE

One of the declared objectives of the tariff was that it would provide Britain with an effective bargaining weapon with which to secure a larger share of the dwindling volume of world exports. With heavy concentrations of unemployment in the staple trades, it made political sense to encourage the belief that protection could stem Britain's trading losses overseas, if only in part. The spread of bilateral trading agreements during the thirties reflected this strategic approach. Since the enforced shift of labour and capital from the cotton, coal, and shipbuilding industries to those manufacturing sectors most likely to benefit from any general expansion of home demand was always likely to be a slow and difficult process, the government felt it

[72] J. Foreman-Peck, 'The British Tariff and Industrial Protection in the 1930s. An Alternative Model', *Economic History Review*, 2nd ser., 34 (1981), 132–39; B. Eichengreen, 'The Macroeconomic Effects of the British General Tariff of 1932', Mimeograph 1979.

worthwhile in the medium term to use the tariff to bargain for greater concessions for particular British exports in foreign markets.

As a result, commercial agreements between Britain and some 15 countries were concluded between 1933 and 1935, predominantly with overseas producers who were more dependent upon our market for the export of their agricultural produce than we were upon their market for our exports. Britain's declared policy of providing a minimum margin of imperial preference to the Dominions provided little scope for substantial bargaining over duties; on the whole, therefore, the bilateral trade agreements were based on a British commitment not to increase existing duties or not to reduce existing quotas in return for preferential treatment in overseas markets.

The most important agreements from our point of view were those concluded with Scandinavia, the Baltic States, Poland and Germany since they offered specific assistance to two troubled sectors: textiles[73] and, more particularly, coal. Since 1926 Britain had lost important coal export markets in Scandinavia to Poland and Germany. To help redress the situation, the government deployed its comparatively strong bargaining position in 1933 to regain a significant foothold for British coal in Scandinavia and within the Baltic. A series of bilateral trade agreements secured for British coal exports the following minimum share in each respective market:

Norway	65%	Latvia	70%
Sweden	47%	Lithuania	80%
Denmark	80%	Estonia	85%
Finland	75%		

In addition, Germany agreed in 1933 to establish a minimum coal quota for Britain of 180,000 metric tons per month in return for specified reductions in British import duties, a relatively rare concession at the time. As for other products, Poland reduced textile duties in favour of Britain in 1935, whilst Denmark and Finland agreed to increase their share of other purchases, including jute, salt and iron and steel.

Despite the tangible benefits on offer, it is difficult to be precise as to the effects of the agreements upon employment in the trades affected.

---

[73] It is worth noting in this context that Britain continued to secure a preferential duty on her cotton imports to India during the 1930s compared with the amounts levelled against other countries. But India had become increasingly protectionist by this time. Britain had agreed in 1919 not to interfere with Indian tariff making and subsequently witnessed a steady rise in the level of duties imposed on British cotton exports. Though differential aid continued, therefore, it did so on the basis of tariff levels that were by the mid-thirties considerably higher than they had been in 1915 or in 1929.

Contemporary estimates put the rise in the number of coalmining jobs generated by the guaranteed additional tonnage at 11,600; 5,300 from Denmark, 2,120 from Norway and 4,180 from Sweden. Denmark's concessions over iron and steel were optimistically judged to have provided an extra 1,500 jobs, and over salt and jute an extra 360. The German coal quota was expected to employ an additional 3,800 miners.[74]

So far as the coal concessions were concerned, it was obvious that the marginal benefits on offer could do little to expand the net volume of exports and employment. Although the percentage of British coal exports to Scandinavia and the Baltic almost doubled between 1928 and 1937, the effect of securing for Britain a privileged position in those markets was to force previous suppliers to compete elsewhere. To that extent, therefore, what the north-eastern coalfield gained the south Wales coalfield lost as Germany and Poland displaced her coal in French, German, Italian and other European markets. Nevertheless the importance of this diversionary effect should not be exaggerated. British coal was in fundamental trouble and it is doubtful if trade agreements could ever have been particularly effective in withstanding the intensification of competition. Cut-backs in coal imports by the Germans, the Dutch and the Belgians, together with the cumulative effects of changing technology in the use of fuel and the rise of competing sources of power, had already dampened any real prospect of substantial economic betterment within the mining industry.

To the extent that the bilateral trade agreements enabled Britain to increase her share of exports in particular markets (especially Denmark and Finland) they helped her to offset retaliation against the Import Duties Act and to mitigate a decline in British exports that might otherwise have aggravated the balance of payments and prompted restrictive fiscal and monetary policies. But they were of only limited value as a means of reducing unemployment. The agreements were concluded with the very countries which had suffered most from the earlier collapse of primary product prices and the cessation of international lending. Thus impoverished, such countries, already subsidizing the British by supplying cheap food and raw materials sufficient to boost the real incomes of those in work, could hardly have been expected to raise the demand for Britain's staple exports to a level sufficient to provide a second substantial stimulus to output and employment. As Rooth points out:

When exports reached their peak in 1937 they were still below their 1929 level and represented a smaller share in national income. With the trade gap tending to

---

[74] For a detailed account of the negotiations see T. Rooth, 'Limits of Leverage: The Anglo-Danish Trade Agreement of 1933', *Economic History Review*, 2nd ser., 37 (1984), 211–28 and Rooth, 'Trade and Trade Bargaining: Anglo-Scandinavian Economic Relations in the 1930s', *The Scandinavian Economic History Review*, 34 (1986), 54–71.

widen, the current account obstinately in deficit, and with the staple industries still scarred with heavy unemployment, it is difficult to argue that exports (and the trade agreements) played any more than a permissive role in an incomplete economic recovery.[75]

Moreover, so long as the trade agreements – combined with imperial protection – encouraged autarky and retaliation, there was less hope of expanding the total volume of world trade upon which the British basic industries depended. Therefore, however much the break with free trade and the deliberate pursuit of a nationalistic commercial policy were couched in terms of their latent impact upon prosperity and jobs, their ultimate effect was to retard the expansion of international trade.[76] The irony was not lost on the unemployed. For years past they had witnessed the rejection of alternative economic policies on their behalf for fear of their effect upon the normal course of trade.

RESORT TO EMPIRE

Despite being a free-trade nation, Britain had accorded preferential treatment to Empire goods on various occasions before 1932. Such concessions, however, were predominantly on a unilateral basis rather than the result of negotiated bargains from which we gained some benefit in return.[77] But by exempting Empire goods from the general tariff, pending the conclusion of a more permanent arrangement at the Ottawa Conference in June 1932, Britain was provided with an opportunity of consolidating imperial preference as a bulwark against increased foreign competition elsewhere.

Although the second Labour government had steadfastly refused to extend preferential tariffs to the Empire, the National Government regarded imperial preference as a means of increasing trade and employment. Few of its members believed any longer that Britain could successfully adjust to world competition in the short term by lowering wage costs or by trying to enforce changes in capital utilization or productive practice. International co-operation in commercial policy was conspicuous by its absence. The supposed benefits of a floating pound, moreover, looked increasingly suspect given the ease with which competitors could eradicate its export-boosting effects.

Recourse to trade bargaining within the Empire seemed, therefore, a

[75] Rooth, 'Limits of Leverage', 227.
[76] World trade, measured in billions of 1934 gold dollars, stood at $59bn in 1928, fell to $24bn in 1932 and to around $20bn in 1935, rising only to $24bn in 1938.
[77] The minor exceptions were noted above, pp. 151, 156, 170. When the UK introduced Imperial preference in 1919, it lowered duties on Dominion and Empire goods which were subject to the McKenna Duties of 1915 but it did not admit the goods duty-free.

worthwhile expedient. Though there was a threat that imperial protection would raise the total import bill, it might in the short term protect employment if the Dominions lived up to their promise of tariff reductions on UK goods.[78] Thus the British delegates went to the Ottawa Conference in 1932 not in a highly protectionist mood but with the specific intention of expanding British sales of manufactured goods to the Dominions and to India in order to boost exports and jobs. The idea was to have Dominion tariffs lowered against British goods but maintained against foreign produce. The policy backfired. Delegates to Ottawa 'acted as representatives for their national industrial or agricultural interests, not as imperial politicians planning a glorious common future. Divergent national interests were temporarily linked together by a set of fragile arrangements which had no real prospect of creative evolution.'[79]

The origins and course of the Ottawa proceedings have been exhaustively detailed elsewhere.[80] So far as the substance of the Agreements is concerned, the upshot was the refusal of the Dominions to give British imports any improved position against their home manufactures. The Dominions agreed to protect their most potentially successful industries at a level high enough to offset lower British costs without providing home producers an advantage over British ones. Britain, on the other hand, promised continued free entry into the British market to all Dominion products (except meat) and guaranteed margins of preference by the imposition of new duties on a number of foreign foodstuffs including wheat, maize, butter, cheese and other dairy products. The only real concession obtained was Britain's right to lower the duty on foreign wheat if Empire wheat prices rose above world prices, or if Empire production proved deficient for British needs.

It was clear, however, that whereas Britain had hoped to gain some reduction in tariffs and other barriers to inter-Imperial trade, the series of bilateral arrangements concluded in August 1932 granted little direct extension of British preference. Instead of lowering duties in Britain's favour the Dominions simply raised still higher duties on goods from non-British sources; a form of preference no doubt but one which, far from promoting freer trade, merely rivetted tariffs more firmly than before on all concerned. The Dominions simply refused to risk increasing urban unemployment in their own countries by narrowing the band of protectionist duties between their domestic industries and those of Britain.

[78] R. F. Holland, *Britain and the Commonwealth Alliance* (1981), 137–8.
[79] R. Skidelsky, 'Retreat from Leadership: The Evolution of British Economic Foreign Policy, 1870–1939', in *Balance of Power or Hegemony?* ed. B. M. Rowland (New York, 1976), 180.
[80] See in particular I. Drummond's two books, *British Economic Policy and the Empire 1919–1939* (1972) and *Imperial Economic Policy 1917–1939*, (1974).

Although the British delegation had been trying ostensibly to divert trade in order to create employment, it is clear that the government's presentation of the Ottawa Agreements as a 'solution' to domestic problems was hopelessly optimistic. Whilst the UK's declining share of the Dominions' imported manufactures was halted between 1932 and 1935, the effect on the domestic economy was minimal. Certainly the Dominions benefited more from the preference system than did Britain. Drummond tentatively estimates that the Agreements raised British output by £26 million in 1933 and £56 million in 1937 – 0.5 per cent and 1 per cent of total British output in the two years.[81] It is notoriously difficult to gauge the effects of trade shifts on jobs during the thirties, or even to be certain that any improvement in trade or employment resulted from commercial bargaining as such, compared for example with the beneficial effects of sterling movements. What is clear is that the outcome of the 'imperial' branch of tariff bargaining proved as vacuous and disappointing for job creation as the Import Duties Act and the bilateral trade agreements with European countries had previously done.

This is not altogether surprising. Despite the rhetoric of the 1932 Conference, the government was never much concerned to press the Dominions to improve substantially the meagre concessions on offer, purely for the sake of boosting domestic employment. The authorities had more pressing concerns. If the preference system which emerged at Ottawa accorded more generous treatment to the Dominions than it gave us, it provided, as the 1932 tariff had done, an important means of sustaining Britain's role as an international financial centre. As noted above, a principal motivating force behind Britain's abandonment of free trade was the belief that protection would help to stabilize sterling by improving the trade balance. Likewise, Britain soon realized that if the Empire countries heavily in debt to Britain were denied generous access to British markets and to sterling they could find it increasingly difficult to meet their debt obligations. Thus preferences were framed with a view to preventing default by Britain's debtors in the Empire and as a means thereby of protecting the stability of sterling. The glaring inadequacies of the Empire strategy at Ottawa, in other words, had to be officially accommodated for the sake of orthodox financial security.

It became clear by the mid-thirties that the British and Dominion economies could no longer be matched along 'imperial' lines and that refugee imperialism was unable to secure for Britain the size and range of concessions likely to promote sustained economic recovery. The Dominions had little incentive to be drawn into a unified trading bloc; their industrial

[81] Drummond, *Imperial Economic Policy*, 286.

activity was destined to grow without generating the expansion of British exports or the decline in unemployment previously anticipated. In earlier years, however, the idea of the Empire providing a partial solution to domestic unemployment, via its capacity to accommodate migrant unemployed workers and to create secondary demands for British staple exports under the stimulus of orchestrated schemes of colonial development, had been thrust upon the political scene by 'imperial visionaries' intent on stemming what they perceived as a dangerous drift towards narrow-minded apathy in the formulation of public policy on behalf of the unemployed. It is to those additional aspects of the 'Empire solution' to unemployment that we now turn.

7 ✳ Men, money and markets: the 'Empire solution' to unemployment, 1919–1931

The search for immediate and practical responses to wartime demobilization – and more particularly to the rapid deterioration in unemployment after 1920 – introduced into the complex and protracted discussions of post-war imperial and Empire policy considerations of domestic economic problems which might not otherwise have achieved such prominence. This is not altogether surprising since the interruption of war had re-invigorated the 'Empire visionaries' and had emphasized afresh the desirability of securing the most appropriate and beneficial development of the Empire on political, economic and social grounds, to the mutual benefit of Britain and her associated territories.

We cannot do justice here to the vast detail and range of argument surrounding interwar imperialism. Specialist studies of the Empire are concerned principally with two problems: the management of nationalism in the Colonies and economic relations with the Dominions, centred on the Ottawa negotiations. Our present concern is more limited; namely, to examine the extent to which a growing preoccupation with and changing perception of the unemployment problem directly influenced the content, timing and likely success of policies towards emigration and colonial development.

ESCAPE FROM THE DOLE? EMIGRATION AND UNEMPLOYMENT

The marked reversal in official policy towards overseas migration after 1919 cannot be explained solely by the vicissitudes of employment. But despite contemporary pronouncements to the contrary, there seems little doubt that the vigour of the 1920s campaign to achieve a 'proper' redistribution of the population within the Empire was sustained by the somewhat uncertain relief it was expected to bring to domestic unemployment. Before 1914 governments had remained aloof from emigration, preferring to leave its ebb and flow to the multitudinous and spontaneous decisions of private individuals. This situation might well have continued after 1914 had it not been for the persistent pressure put on government by the Royal Colonial Institute whose members feared that the wartime disruption of migration would eventually erode the 'organic' nature of the Empire.

Towards the end of the war the Colonial Office was persuaded after much hesitation to reconsider its opposition to state-sponsored emigration.[1] One of its own consultative bodies (the Tennyson Committee) had recommended free passages to Empire destinations for ex-servicemen[2] and by the end of 1917 other positive proposals aimed at reversing the state's neglect of emigration had emerged from the Dominions Royal Commission and the Imperial War Conference.[3] Although the formation of an Overseas Settlement Committee (OSC) in 1919 confirmed the government's willingness to assist demobilized persons who urgently wished to establish a new life abroad, emigration policy was still very much in a state of flux. Uncertain as to whether the country was likely to be faced in the near future with a surplus or a shortage of labour, government officials resisted any general scheme of overseas settlement. Instead ex-servicemen intending to live and work in the Dominions were allowed free passages from April 1919, provided they were selected as approved settlers under an agricultural scheme or that they were going to guaranteed employment.

But by the end of 1920 'the management of migration'[4] had become a much more urgent issue. The collapse of the post-war boom spurred interest in a more active policy of overseas settlement. Lord Milner, Colonial Secretary, urged his Ministerial colleagues on 15 October to remember:

that all money expended on the overseas settlement of suitable settlers . . . relieves to that extent the housing problem here and also tends to relieve in still greater proportion the problem of unemployment.[5]

Five days later the government committee appointed to consider unemployment problems in the ensuing winter pressed the Colonial Office to prepare a rigorous scheme of large-scale emigration as a direct means of relieving distress at home.[6]

As yet, however, few within the Cabinet were prepared to pursue such a calculated policy. When Britain agreed in January 1921 to join the Dominions in allocating extra funds towards the cost of assisted passage and

---

[1]   The transformation in official attitudes during the war is briefly outlined in J. A. Schultz, 'Finding Homes Fit for Heroes: The Great War and Empire Settlement', *Canadian Journal of History*, 18 (1983), 99–110.

[2]   Report of Committee Appointed to Consider the Measures to be Taken for Settling Within the Empire Ex-Servicemen Who May desire to Emigrate after the War, Cd. 8672, 1917–18.   [3]   Drummond, *British Economic Policy and the Empire*, 72

[4]   Drummond, *British Economic Policy and the Empire*, 77

[5]   Cited in Drummond, *Imperial Economic Policy*, 62.

[6]   Drummond, *Imperial Economic Policy*, 64.

land settlement schemes, it stressed that the gesture was in the interests of bringing about 'the best distribution of man-power of the Empire' and emphatically not 'a means of dealing directly with the abnormal unemployment in the United Kingdom at any given moment'.[7]

Although the idea of overseas settlement as a way of promoting the development, stability and defence of the Empire over the long term gradually gained wider Ministerial support during the early twenties, it fell short of what the more determined strategists had in mind. Leopold Amery, Chairman of the OSC, firmly believed that emigration could prove an effective anti-unemployment device if pursued as a priority of policy. In a report to the Colonial Secretary in May 1921 he warned that:

Unless the Cabinet is prepared to encourage and to help the Overseas Governments to adopt a policy of Empire development by means of primary settlement (i.e. the settlement on the land of primary producers) those governments will soon reach the limit of their powers to absorb our unemployed.[8]

But the Treasury refused to be drawn. Settlement schemes involving increased government expenditure would only worsen employment if financial commitments, expanded to meet temporary economic distress, raised taxes or harmed British credit.[9] In any event, the issue was purely academic. The British government had not by 1921 approved any *general* scheme of free passages; assistance was restricted to ex-servicemen and to the relief of civilians during the winter of 1920/21, measures to which the Treasury did not object. Moreover, neither the Empire Settlement Conference nor the Imperial Conference of 1921 had produced any definite plans of inter-Empire co-operation over emigration. There was no reason to believe that the question would gather any significant momentum.

That it did so was due mainly to the impact of mounting domestic unemployment. When the Australian Prime Minister appealed to the British government in November 1921 to pay half the interest on a £50 million development loan, he found an enthusiastic supporter in Amery who suggested to Churchill, Secretary of State for the Colonies, that such initiatives would have a direct and beneficial impact upon the British labour market, both by increasing emigration and by stimulating the demand for British machinery.[10] Some 70 per cent of the ex-servicemen and women who had so far been granted free passages to the Dominions, Amery informed the Cabinet in October 1921, had been unemployed or in casual

---

[7] Cab 24/123, CP 2943, State-Aided Empire Settlement. Memorandum by the Secretary of State for the Colonies, 6 May 1921.   [8] Cab 24/123, CP 2943.

[9] Drummond, *Imperial Economic Policy*, 71.

[10] Drummond, *Imperial Economic Policy*, 76–8.

employment, 'while of the remainder few did not create vacancies for fresh employment by their departure'.[11] A month later Churchill himself argued that:

> The problem of unemployment is essentially a problem of the right distribution of population . . . The key to the employment situation is the shifting of British population . . . to the Dominions . . . Such a policy . . . would necessarily cost money. But it would secure a real and lasting improvement at far less cost than the present system of relief works and doles . . . The whole of this great expenditure affords a purely temporary relief. It effects no permanent cure.[12]

By the autumn of 1921, the Ministers of Labour and Health and the Board of Trade were agreed that more serious attention should be paid to state-aided Empire settlement as an immediate way of reducing an already abnormal volume of unemployment.[13]

But however enthusiastically put, the 'emigration cure' was compromised from the start. The OSC itself conceded that the overriding need of the Dominions was for agricultural labour and that potential emigrants would stand little chance of being 'approved' if they sought employment other than on the land. In addition the Treasury, though not opposed in principle to schemes offering some potential relief to unemployment, insisted on vetting in advance any migration proposals that involved increased government expenditure, convinced that Colonial Office exuberance, if unchecked, would prove not only counter-productive but positively dangerous.

The legislative backing eventually given to subsidized emigration in the 1922 Empire Settlement Act reflected these concerns. The government's contribution to assisted settlement was made subject to the prior consent of the Treasury. Grants or loans were not to exceed half of the total cost involved, nor be greater than £3 million per year. Despite these strictures a significant shift in the emphasis of policy had occurred. Within a very short period a wartime concern to control and limit emigration had given way to an official scheme to encourage it, a transformation due largely to the urgency with which the problem of persistent and increasingly costly unemployment had to be tackled.

As an anti-unemployment device, the 1922 Act proved bitterly disappointing. Had it operated according to plan, some £7.5 million would have been spent on Empire settlement up to the second quarter of 1925; by the end of 1924 actual expenditure amounted to just over £679,600.[14] The

[11] Cab 24/131, CP 3582A, Overseas Settlement and Unemployment. Memorandum by L. S. Amery, 29 October 1921.
[12] Cab 24/131, CP 3582, Overseas Settlement, Memorandum by the Secretary of State for the Colonies, 23 December 1921.   [13] Drummond, *Imperial Economic Policy*, 78–9.
[14] W. H. Dawson, 'Empire Settlement and Unemployment', *Contemporary Review*, 127 (1925), 576–83.

number of potential settlers proved far fewer than anticipated, and a
significant proportion of those affected by the Act had never belonged to the
unemployed population. In 1923, 199,000 people emigrated from the UK,
of whom 113,000 went to the Empire; the OSC had hoped to 'export' up to
600,000 people per year. Although assisted emigration rose during the
subsequent three years, total emigration fell between 1926 and 1929.[15]
There were some limited achievements. Under an agreement concluded
with Australia in April 1925 the British government undertook to raise
loans of up to £34 million for issue to Australian states at low rates of
interest for the purpose of settling 450,000 migrants within ten years. By
the mid-twenties passage agreements had been entered into with Canada
and New Zealand and a few settlers were sent to Rhodesia.

But few of the Dominion governments were very enthusiastic about
assisted settlement. South Africa refused to co-operate. Canada remained
stubborn and suspicious throughout the twenties, fearful that any major
influx of British unemployed labour would lower average wages and
actually encourage emigration from its own country. Overseas governments became increasingly defensive in their attitude, screening potential
immigrants on physical and educational grounds and discriminating in
favour of nominated immigrants likely to be guaranteed jobs on their
arrival.[16] Only Australia showed any keen interest in land development and
organized migration. Even there schemes of overseas settlement quickly ran
into serious difficulties. The diversion into capital projects of much of the
£34 million allocated in 1925 for expanded migration raised the per capita
costs of settlement and embittered relations among those early settlers lured
by the promise of subsidies and readily available land.[17]

Since the Dominions would not contribute to the cost of training British
workmen for the disproportionate number of agricultural openings available overseas, little could be done under the Empire Settlement Act to
enhance the prospects of the industrial unemployed. Although government
financial assistance was now statutorily available in contrast to previous
years, few of the unemployed in Britain had either the resources to begin the
process of migration or sufficient faith in their ability to acquire regular and
remunerative employment to persuade them to accept interest-bearing
loans. The organized trade union movement, moreover, was cautious and
suspicious, reluctant to encourage any initiatives which might threaten
labour standards in the Dominions or which might, by diverting resources

[15] Drummond, *Imperial Economic Policy*, 94.
[16] G. F. Plant, *Overseas Settlement. Migration from the United Kingdom to the Dominions* (Oxford, 1951), 88.
[17] Holland, *Britain and the Commonwealth Alliance*, 106.

abroad, forestall the adoption of alternative and possibly more effective economic policies at home.[18]

Yet despite the shortcomings of the Empire Settlement Act, both the Labour and Conservative administrations of the 1920s continued to foster the belief that sponsored emigration could be an effective 'employment policy' if only it was pursued more vigorously. The first Labour government openly encouraged the idea of 'exporting' the unemployed, but it was Amery's sympathetic role as Colonial Secretary in Baldwin's second administration that kept the issue firmly on the political agenda. Support for sponsored emigration grew as economic conditions deteriorated. By 1926 the Minister of Labour was urging the government to persuade the Dominions 'to base their internal development on a better balance between industry and agriculture' and 'to take a wider selection of migrants' in order that any increased expenditure on migration might be reflected in 'an improvement in our unemployment position'.[19] The trade union movement, or more precisely the TUC, began to popularize the 'economic' benefits of assisted migration, especially for those workers whose jobs might be threatened by industrial reorganization, a policy which Congress had embraced in 1927 as a quid pro quo for avoiding competitive wage reductions.[20] Employers even suggested that lump sum payments could be made available to potential migrants presently unemployed who might wish to capitalize on the value of their expectations under the state insurance scheme, thereby enabling them to make a fresh start overseas.

Few of the more publicized initiatives augured well for the future. The 'Harvester Scheme', introduced in the aftermath of the General Strike to encourage the transportation of British miners to Canadian farms, proved a disaster. It soon became apparent that overseas farmers had overstated their labour requirements to ensure low wages and many migrants found themselves unemployed in a society with social and political mores vastly different from those to which they were accustomed. But once it became apparent that any cyclical recovery, however imminent, would do little to relieve persistent unemployment in Britain's staple industries, the official attitude towards emigration on economic grounds grew noticeably more sympathetic and urgent in tone. By 1927, writes Drummond:

Neither tariffs nor exchange rates could be manipulated. With the commitment to the gold standard went the paralysis of monetary policy. Unemployment was diminishing but only slowly; and more people were convinced that much of the remainder was structural – confined to the old staple trades of cotton, coal,

[18] P. Gupta, *Imperialism and the British Labour Movement, 1914–1964* (1975), 28–9; Trades Union Congress, Annual Report, 1925, 139, 206.
[19] CO 57/13, 'Migration as Relief to Unemployment', July 1926.
[20] See below chapter 8.

shipbuilding, iron, steel. Emigration, it seemed, was the only answer. It was no longer simply a question of exporting people so as to create export markets. The task now was to export those whom structural change had made unemployable.[21]

The pressure exerted on the Tories in the later 1920s to accord emigration a more vital role in their economic strategy derived much of its strength from the Industrial Transference Board's trenchant diagnosis of acute regional unemployment and of the existence, particularly in coalmining areas, of large pools of able-bodied workmen permanently surplus to competitive needs.[22] Extended migration came to be regarded as a particularly valuable weapon in the breakup of concentrated unemployment in the depressed areas. It was doubtful, warned the Minister of Labour in 1928:

whether we can safely assume that large numbers of miners will come forward for overseas settlement if the agricultural qualification is insisted upon; in any event, so long as effort has to be devoted to giving him this qualification the numbers moved in any given year cannot . . . be adequate for new immediate and urgent needs. We ought, therefore, to consider also the question of the migration of men who wish to seek their future in non-agricultural occupations.[23]

Since there was little prospect in the short term of training the unemployed in the basic trades to meet the predominantly agricultural requirements of the 1922 Settlement Act, much depended upon securing Dominion support for cheaper travel. The Cabinet's Unemployment Committee thus endorsed the Transference Board's recommendation that the state should subsidize third-class passages beyond the strictures of the Act. But although Canada agreed in 1929 to encourage emigration from Britain with a low third-class fare, other Dominion governments baulked at the idea of becoming a dumping ground for Britain's unemployed. Worsening economic conditions thereafter put most countries on the defensive. By mid-1930 even Canada and Australia had put a stop to all assisted migration and, together with New Zealand, had begun to retract much of their support for grandiose schemes of agricultural settlement. Although Britain had demonstrated her keenness to encourage the migration of the unemployed by freeing Canada from any obligation under the Empire Settlement Act to contribute to the cost of the low passage fare from the UK, little else was done subsequently to stimulate voluntary movement of the workless from the depressed areas. In the event, total emigration between 1926 and 1930 continued its

[21] Drummond, *Imperial Economic Policy*, 99.
[22] Cmd. 3156, 1928. In the late 1920s official efforts were made to encourage unemployed labour in areas of chronic industrial decline to seek work elsewhere in the country. The origins and fate of this initiative are discussed in more detail in chapter 9.
[23] Cab 27/374, CP (28)3, Cabinet Unemployment Policy Committee. Unemployment and Migration. Memorandum by the Minister of Labour, 9 July 1928.

downward trend and neither subsidized fares nor deteriorating industrial conditions at home proved sufficient to induce unemployed workers in the staple trades to migrate in any substantial numbers.

Deepening depression at home and abroad during the early thirties quickened the demise of an emigration policy which had already been seriously undermined by the recalcitrance of Dominion governments. Though the second Labour administration flirted briefly with George Lansbury's idea of settling unemployed coalminers as wheat farmers in Australia, socialist politicians came to view emigration as an inadequate, indeed almost irrelevant, response to an unemployment problem infinitely more widespread and complex in origin than had previously been acknowledged. An elaborate scheme for land settlement in Western Australia initiated by the previous government was treated with humorous indifference as a matter not worth a moment's consideration.[24]

Support for sponsored migration on economic grounds was on the wane even before world depression choked off any remaining sympathy abroad for encouraging an inflow of foreign labour. From the outset the 'emigration' response to unemployment had assumed a degree of complementarity between the interests of Britain and the Dominions which had rarely been in evidence. And with the primary producing countries bearing the brunt of tumbling prices and economic insolvency a substantial amount of return migration occurred, partly because the conditions faced by the unemployed in Britain no longer appeared by comparison to be such a deterrent.

The Committee on Empire Migration conceded in 1931 that there was a case in better economic times for increasing the proportion of financial assistance to migrants provided by the British government relative to that provided by the Dominions.[25] It was doubtful even then if the Dominions would be interested in accepting migrants purely as a short-term gesture. Historically the economic value of emigration had been to protect living standards in the long run from the pressure of numbers; the validity of this argument had been seriously weakened, however, by the steady fall in the birth rate over the postwar period. Insofar as there remained a substantial surplus of labour relative to the absorptive capacity of highly localized industries, emigration retained some definite economic advantage to the state. But, warned the Committee, the advantage should not be exaggerated. Even if problems persisted in the staple export sector, new industries and occupations were developing 'on an important and steadily growing

[24]   Cab 24/211, CP 143, Unemployment Policy (1930) Committee. Memorandum by the First Commissioner of Works, 6 May 1930.
[25]   The Empire Settlement Act was amended in 1937 to permit the government to pay 75 per cent of the cost of assisted migration.

scale' sufficient to allow the country to 'succeed in establishing a new industrial equipoise'. Should the return to economic progress prove more faltering and uncertain than expected emigration would still:

provide no satisfactory remedy . . . for under conditions of a stationary or declining population large-scale emigration, drawing, as it must tend to do, primarily on the young and the adventurous, would exert an effect on the average quality of those left behind which would only be viewed with the most serious misgivings.[26]

To all intents and purposes emigration as an 'economic' policy was dead. For the remainder of the thirties 'the masses of British people remained constant in their assumption that the chapter of imperial migration was closed'.[27] Part of the reason why it had remained open for so long was because of the passionate desire of key political visionaries to encourage a redistribution of population, transplanting men, women and children of 'good British stock' to areas of untapped opportunity abroad to the mutual benefit of everyone concerned. Yet such instincts would never of themselves have given rise to new policies of state financial assistance nor have succeeded for so long in keeping the issue of Empire settlement alive within Cabinet had this 'imperial vision' not been firmly harnessed to the needs of the ailing British economy. Leopold Amery in particular saw rising unemployment as the principal justification for continuing with assisted migration. Even if Dominion governments remained suspicious of accepting the visibly unemployed, he argued, extended settlement would nonetheless ease the pressure on the domestic labour market by reducing the competition for the few jobs ever likely to become available.

Although such reasoning brought the Empire Settlement Bill to the statute book it ignored certain fundamental difficulties in the way of pursuing an active emigration policy for the sake of boosting employment. Protagonists severely underestimated the cyclical instability of the Dominion economies, the heavy reliance which sponsored schemes placed upon agricultural expansion in an era of surplus capacity and low prices, and the entrenched opposition of organized labour abroad, all of which limited the opportunities available to any unemployed worker in Britain finally able to overcome the fear and uncertainty of uprooting from his native land.

As the thirties wore on emigration policy came to be regarded at most as a partial and haphazard means of improving the prospects of those out of work. This was due in part to its limited achievements during the previous

---

[26] Cab 24/224, CP 297, Economic Advisory Council, Committee on Empire Migration, Report, 11 July 1931.

[27] W. K. Hancock, *Survey of British Commonwealth Affairs*, vol. 2, *Problems of Economic Policy, 1918–1939* (Oxford, 1940) 175.

decade, but more especially to the growing realization that its success depended upon the existence of a healthier international economic environment than had prevailed hitherto or was ever likely to emerge in the foreseeable future. As an inter-departmental committee noted in 1934, the question of migration:

cannot be considered in isolation from the general economic conditions with which it is inextricably interwoven. There is no foundation for any idea that because there may be, at the moment, a surplus population in this country, and vast areas of unoccupied land in some of the Dominions, a simple act of transference of the former to the latter will of itself solve the problems involved. There must be such economic conditions and prospects in the country of settlement as are calculated to provide a livelihood for the newcomers . . . The history of migration in modern times proves that migration is a symptom of prosperity and not a cure for depression.[28]

DISTANT HOPES: JOBS, MARKETS AND THE DEVELOPMENT OF THE COLONIES

The encouragement given to assisted emigration from Britain in the 1920s was not the only manifestation of the belief that within the Empire there lay some remedy for Britain's economic malaise. As unemployment deepened within the export and heavy manufacturing sections during the decade, support grew for the idea of fostering the economic development of the Colonies as a direct means of stimulating import demand for the products of those British industries hardest hit by continuing depression.

The notion of 'constructive imperialism' – that is, the development of colonial resources to serve national economic self interest – was not a product of the post-war crisis. It had found its most celebrated advocate in Joseph Chamberlain who campaigned vigorously at the turn of the century in favour of colonial development as a means of protecting and promoting the interests of the metropolitan economy. Economic competition from abroad and social unrest at home, he argued then, could be partially assuaged by nurturing colonial markets and by securing important sources of raw materials, such as cotton. But although such visionary ideas were further championed by Chamberlain's successors, contemporaries proved particularly resistant to the notion of state-aided colonial development. A major retarding influence was the persistence with which the Treasury upheld the virtues of financial orthodoxy, carefully scrutinizing claims for cash grants or loans for development purposes. This was the result less of perverse or habitual obscurantism than of the widely held belief that only by

[28] Report to the Secretary of State for Dominion Affairs of the Inter-Departmental Committee on Migration Policy, Cmd. 4689, 1934, paras 196–7.

holding spending in check could the credit of the imperial government be adequately safeguarded.

Another obstacle arose from the Colonial Office's narrow vision of the purpose and nature of colonial expansion. This was limited in its view to the need to improve the ability of the Colonies to supply the primary product needs of the industrialized United Kingdom. Bereft of any Empire-wide strategy of economic development, the Colonial Office merely waited upon dependent territories to initiate schemes of capital investment should they so desire, and upon private enterprise to exploit what profitable opportunities might thereby result. Any more vigorous pursuit of economic self-interest, it was felt, would conflict with the more immediate objectives of colonial administration. When financial aid on any significant scale was made available to the Colonies before 1914, therefore, it was usually for the purpose of securing some strategic advantage or for upholding colonial governments whose financial stability was suspect or threatened.[29]

Little might have changed in this respect had the outbreak of war not rekindled the hopes and aspirations of those imperial enthusiasts determined to proclaim the economic worth of the Empire. As a free-trade nation Britain was particularly vulnerable to any post-war economic offensive; the feeling grew that imperial consolidation could prove critical to the future recovery of trade and industry. Wartime proposals to increase government aid for the improvement of the infrastructure in the Colonies and to create a British Trade Bank to help traders acquire fresh markets reflected the urge for a more radical innovation in imperial economic policy. Milner and Amery, in charge of the Colonial Office in 1919, continued such pressure in peacetime, urging the government to become more financially involved in colonial development for the sake of boosting the demand for British goods.

The Ministers' determination to break with convention achieved some limited success; they gained Cabinet approval for the preparation of colonial development schemes and persuaded some businessmen to join in discussions over the benefits which colonial economic expansion might bring to the British economy as a whole. But despite their drive and enthusiasm, Milner and Amery proved unable to win substantial support from other quarters, either inside or outside of government. The expectation of a continued trade revival, Treasury anxieties over the size of the National Debt, inflation and the stability of credit, plus the demand for increased investment for peacetime reconstruction, severely hampered any sympathetic discussion of broad-based schemes of colonial development. 'Victory and the economic boom', writes Constantine, 'eradicated the

[29] For a thoughtful account of British colonial development policy before and after 1914 see S. Constantine, *The Making of British Colonial Development Policy, 1914–1940* (1984).

phobias which had made the new development proposals popular. The financial detritus of war made their application impossible'.[30] When exceptions were made, they were usually for the sake of protecting the Treasury from the consequences of leaving financially vulnerable territories unaided. Thus, development loans were granted to Uganda in 1920 and to Kenya in 1921, not for the purpose of boosting the overall interests of the imperial economy, but to sponsor such *ad hoc* public works schemes as might generate sufficient colonial revenues to remove the need for embarrassing grants-in-aid from the British Exchequer.

This conventional concern with the financial stability of the Colonies rather than with their potential for improving Britain's economy was rudely shattered by the onset of economic depression and deepening unemployment in the early 1920s. Politicians sought ways of boosting the purchase of British manufactured materials in areas nominally under British influence, primarily to enhance the prospects of the ailing staple industries at home. In October 1921 the government was pressed to raise a National Development Loan to assist the promotion of capital works within the Empire as a direct way of stimulating British industry. Churchill, Secretary of State for the Colonies, estimated that capital projects costing almost £8 million were unable to be implemented abroad because of the difficulties Colonies had either in obtaining funds or in meeting interest charges on loans raised in London. Convinced that such schemes could stimulate orders for goods to the value of £4 million, he implored the British government to underwrite some of the initial costs of works that could 'develop markets for British goods, and enhance the purchasing power of individual inhabitants in the Colonies with future benefit to British trade'.[31] At first the Cabinet demurred but then relented, at least in part. It refused to undertake any special development expenditure in the Colonies, but agreed to authorize the Treasury under the terms of the 1921 Trade Facilities Act to guarantee the payment of interest and principal on loans raised for capital undertakings at home and abroad to a maximum of £25 million (subsequently raised to £50 million in 1922).

It is unlikely that this departure from financial orthodoxy would have arisen had it not been for the politically urgent need to launch some initiative on behalf of the unemployed. Nevertheless there were still formidable obstacles in the way of colonial development programmes being regarded as an appropriate means of alleviating Britain's short-term domestic crisis. The Colonial Office in particular remained deeply suspicious of any suggestion that policy towards the Colonies should have as its

[30] Constantine, *The Making of British Colonial Development Policy*, 56.
[31] Cab 24/129, CP 3415, Imperial Development and Unemployment. Memorandum by Mr. Churchill, 17 October 1921.

primary objective the immediate reduction of domestic unemployment. Its permanent officials retained very specific ideas as to the 'proper' purpose of colonial development. Although they conceded in 1922 that a large development loan would prove 'less costly and far more remunerative ultimately, than money thrown in the sink of unemployment insurance and other forms of unproductive relief',[32] what they had in mind was not an emergency scheme on behalf of those currently unemployed, but rather the planned development of the poorer Colonies over the longer term, involving the annual commitment of substantial Exchequer sums for programmes which would stimulate employment over a period of, say, ten years.

The Treasury on the other hand preferred cautious advance within the strictures of responsible budgetary control and was only prepared to offer grant aid in relief of interest payments on loans. This could only be attractive to the richer Colonies already capable of raising capital; the Colonies able and willing to undertake projects at a speed and of a type likely to be of any benefit to the British unemployed were precisely those which required more generous financial assistance. But it was this assistance which was least likely to be forthcoming from a Treasury firmly committed to reduced capital expenditure in the interests of economy and exchange rate stability.

Pressure continued nonetheless to enhance colonial development in the interests of the metropolitan economy. The Board of Trade campaigned in 1923 for up to £2 million a year to be made available for development work overseas, convinced that such expenditure could materially assist beleaguered sections of British manufacturing. The only concession wrested from the Exchequer, however, was the offer of a maximum grant of three-quarters of the interest for five years on loans raised for public utility schemes in the Colonies inaugurated within a three-year period and in advance of normal requirements. Metropolitan interests were not entirely forgotten: interest relief was restricted to that part of the capital which would be spent directly on orders placed in Britain.

Such grudging assistance was hardly likely to induce accelerated development abroad, but it fell to the incoming Labour administration to squeeze whatever political advantage it could from the offer. The 1924 Trade Facilities Act set aside £1 million to meet the share of loan interest on public utility development schemes in the Empire principally, the House of Commons was told, 'to stimulate orders for goods which will be supplied from this country to help to some extent the unemployment from which we are now suffering'.[33] The Act had some redeeming features. It arose, not in response to the particular needs of the Colonies, but on the initiative of the

---

[32] Constantine, *The Making of British Colonial Development Policy*, 99–100.
[33] HC Debs., 5th ser., vol. 170, 27 February 1924, cols. 560–1.

metropolitan authorities and had as its specific objective the relief of British economic distress rather than restoration of colonial financial independence. Yet it failed to inspire any major response mainly because colonial governments found it almost impossible to meet its strict requirements. Expenditure on development schemes had to be in anticipation of that which would have normally been incurred at a later date and be calculated to promote employment in the United Kingdom. Altogether only five schemes were approved in the three years during which the Act operated, involving an expenditure in the UK of only £0.5 million. Minor adjustments were made to the terms of the Act in 1925 and again in 1926 but it was allowed to expire in the following year. In June 1925 the Labour Party proposed the establishment of a National Empire and Development Board charged with preparing a co-ordinated policy of national and imperial development as a means of boosting British employment. The Board was to obtain funds from an annual appropriation of £10 million, thereby relieving it of the need to seek Treasury approval for each scheme proposed. The Prevention of Unemployment Bill, incorporating these ideas, failed to secure a second reading.

What the Trade Facilities Acts demonstrated was the eagerness of each major political party to embrace the principle of promoting public works schemes abroad in aid of the unemployed without commiting sufficient resources to achieve worthwhile results. Financial aid remained restricted to short-term interest relief on loans which the Colonies most favourably placed to undertake development schemes were reluctant to seek in London. Staff at the Colonial Office continually spurned capital projects hastily improvised to meet British economic needs, whilst the Treasury remained sceptical and unenthusiastic, unconvinced that colonial development would accelerate the purchase of essential materials from Britain on a scale or at a speed that would materially assist the unemployed.

If the urgent need to respond positively to rising unemployment produced in the Trade Facilities Acts such ineffectual and compromised results, the case for promoting colonial development on economic grounds was not entirely lost. Considered schemes of capital expenditure designed to satisfy the longer term interests both of the Colonies and of the metropolitan economy, but only incidentally the immediate needs of the unemployed, occasionally managed to circumvent Treasury opposition. The decision in March 1924, for example, to grant Kenya and Uganda a £3.5 million loan free of interest for five years to aid railway development resulted partly from demands made within those territories for improved communications and partly from the belief that benefits would thereby accrue to the British iron and steel industry. More critical, however, was the government's conviction that such improvements would offer greater security of markets and longer term guarantees of increased raw material supply, in this case cotton, thereby providing an acceptable basis upon which to commit imperial resources. The fact that a further £10 million scheme of transport development in East Africa was sanctioned by parliament in 1926 was a further reflection of the relative ease with which political support could be won for initiatives designed to improve the country's longer term economic prospects by creating markets and securing raw material supplies.

None of this, however, did much to relieve British unemployment in the immediate term. The disappointments and shortcomings of the Trade Facilities Acts had shifted attention towards longer term initiatives. These promised future stability and economic betterment but little by way of emergency improvisation on behalf of the unemployed. And even they were subject to strict financial monitoring. Although the Treasury failed to block the grant of financial aid to East Africa in 1926, it ensured nevertheless that there was no imperial subsidy of interest charges and that the desirability of particular development projects continued to come under the scrutiny and administrative control of an advisory committee.

It was apparent by the end of 1927 that colonial development had ceased to be regarded seriously in official circles as an effective device for improving British employment in the short term. And yet within two years the same policy was being hailed as a singularly relevant and workable strategy for relieving Britain's industrial and trading problems. This transformation in attitude can be explained partly by the persistence with which committed imperialists worked to evoke a more sympathetic response to their cause within government. Writing in November 1928 Amery, Secretary of State for the Colonies, vented his frustrations on Churchill and Baldwin:

Four years bitter experience have convinced me that any attempts to help the employment situation here by accelerating Colonial development is hopeless as long as matters are left to the Treasury, which is at bottom against all expenditure, whether on development or anything else and whose powers of obstruction are infinitely greater on an Imperial subject than on a domestic issue where there is constant parliamentary pressure . . . The truth is that the attempts the Government have hitherto made to combine Colonial development with relief of unemployment lead to little but correspondence, committees and delay.[34]

The crux of the problem, he warned the Cabinet five months later, was that:

We have asked too much of the Colonies, and have offered too little ourselves for what is, after all, our problem . . . Each time the Colonial Office has been asked to produce material in connection with the unemployment problem it has been treated as if it were an exceptional emergency or crisis to be dealt with by special measures taken in a hurry. On the one hand, we have been asked to produce proposals for putting in hand large Public Works . . . to enable the Home Government to deal with

[34] CO 323/1016/51165, November 1928.

the problem of distress in the coming winter. On the other hand, we have been offered terms which have never seemed to us to have been sufficient to induce Colonial Governments to make additional efforts, the effect of which would be appreciable. I am convinced that it is of no use looking for such help if the British Government are going to ask the Colonies to accept liabilities in the shape of debt charges, for enterprises which are not ripe for execution.

What was required, Amery contended, was the establishment of a Colonial Development Fund free from Treasury control and able to meet for at least five years the full interest charges on development schemes undertaken with the definite purpose of boosting demand and jobs within British heavy industry. 'I am reluctant', he declared,

to accept the Treasury argument that 'private enterprise is more likely than the Government to direct investment to purposes which are economically justified', and that, therefore, we live in the best of all possible worlds, in which unemployment is a blessing in disguise. It is clearly the duty of the Government to use all means in its power to direct the monies available for investment into channels where they will create a demand for British goods and employment for British labour.[35]

But although the unemployment problem had sharpened the sensitivity of politicians to criticism of inactivity and ineptitude, there was still a powerful reluctance in key quarters towards exploiting the economic potential of the Colonies. Amery's campaign of persuasion failed to shake the prejudice of permanent officials within the Colonial Office against development programmes which they viewed as a direct threat to the stability of colonial revenues.

Treasury condemnation of Amery's proposed Development Fund was as blunt as it was predictable. 'The scheme is sheer financial immorality', ran one memorandum:

a temptation to the Colonial Governments to embark upon premature and ill-conceived enterprises by financial inducements which blind them to the ultimate risk . . . Mr. Amery's financial philosophy is based on the assumption that idle funds are available in the market for colonial investments and that the Exchequer has surplus cash for subsidies to attract them into enterprises which offer no early return.[36]

Few within the Treasury were prepared to entrust the Colonial Office with any responsibility for expenditure ('There is not a glimmering of financial sense in the place'); thus the defence of fiscal probity remained paramount. Officials at the Exchequer distrusted the vulgar 'Keynesianism' implicit in many of the development programmes. Though they did not actually obstruct agreed policy they sought diligently to educate over-zealous

---

[35] Cab 24/203, CP 110, Colonial Development In Relation to the Problem of Unemployment. Memorandum by L. S. Amery, 10 April 1929.
[36] T161/291/S33978, 1 January 1929.

Ministers of the likely consequences of any hasty development policy. The increased employment which might follow from any induced trade revival, they argued, could be seriously retarded if such expenditure was permitted to distort the money markets, to compromise alternative productive investment, or, most alarming of all, to threaten the fixed exchange rate regime of the gold standard.

This struggle between advocates and opponents of more generous colonial development expenditure lasted well into 1929. As such it became subsumed in electioneering politics, much to the advantage of the colonial 'visionaries'. Conservative MPs approaching a General Election were painfully aware of their dismal record in reducing unemployment and of the vigour with which their political opponents, particularly the Liberals, were canvassing policies for industrial revival. The electorate had to be wooed. In the circumstances, Tory Ministers proved less inclined to ponder the subtleties of the Treasury's case or to weaken their party's platform by rejecting out of hand policies whose alleged shortcomings could easily be dismissed as idle or biased speculation. As Holland notes: 'The bulk of bureaucratic opinion . . . was, as it always remained, suspicious and ultimately antagonistic towards "Empire development". It was the politicians who were drawn towards this concept because it provided them with at least the appearances of a policy'.[37]

Suddenly, though not altogether unexpectedly, Amery's campaign for expanded imperial development on economic grounds, previously undermined by both the Treasury and his own permanent staff, found new recruits. Both the Home Secretary and the Minister of Labour urged the Cabinet in February 1929 to support guaranteed loans for Empire development, with interest charges met by the Exchequer. 'On a general review of the situation', wrote the Home Secretary in an impassioned Cabinet memorandum in February 1929:

it is not easy to escape the conclusion that the Government schemes for the assistance of migration and for the transference of workers, which cannot on the most optimistic reckoning embrace more than 60,000 of the unemployed during the current year, will not afford in the near future any substantial relief to the unemployment problem . . . We must, I submit, find a comprehensive policy . . . of quickening migration . . . and of increasing the wealth-producing capacity of the Empire . . . In the Dominions and Crown Colonies there are vast areas of undeveloped country which at present are potential sources of wealth . . . If these areas were to be opened up, they would attract immigrants and traders and become wealth-producing centres. Such development, whether it were to take the form of the building of railways, dams, irrigation works, electric power plants, harbours or the like is unlikely to be undertaken by private enterprise . . . But if those works were to be undertaken in the near future, were to be constructed so far as practicable

[37] Holland, *Britain and the Commonwealth Alliance*, 18.

of British materials . . . a substantial contribution would have been made to the provision of productive work for the unemployed in those industries which are at present suffering most severely, to the stimulation of migration, to the expansion of the national revenue, and to the productive power of the Dominions and Colonies . . . It will no doubt be urged that if we are going to embark on major works of relief in this country it would be better that we concentrate our attention exclusively on our own needs and drop any idea of overseas development on a large scale. But to take this stand is wholly to ignore . . . the benefits which British trade and shipping will ultimately derive from an increase in the population and wealth-producing capacity of the Dominions.[38]

The memorandum brought a swift rebuff from the Treasury. Any 'superficial results' of the Home Secretary's proposals, it complained, 'would be so inconsiderable that they could not plausibly be represented as making any appreciable contribution towards relieving the existing volume of unemployment'. It was by no means certain that further guaranteed loans would produce financially sound schemes likely to stimulate British industry. A loan of £10 million for overseas railway development over a period of five years, Treasury officials maintained, would only increase the annual export of iron and steel from Britain by about 1 per cent. 'It is more than doubtful', ran one memorandum, 'whether, even in the long run, the wealth producing capacity of the British Empire would be increased by the premature adoption of uneconomic schemes. It is certain that in the meantime the economic and financial difficulties of this country would be enhanced'.[39]

But support was growing elsewhere for the development of the Empire as a means of securing short-term economic benefits. Representatives of the employers and the trade unions engaged in the Mond–Turner talks during 1928–29 called publicly for increased capital investment in the Crown Colonies as an anti-unemployment measure. The Commission on Closer Union of the Dependencies in Eastern and Central Africa went further. Its report of October 1928 condemned the rigidity of the financial aid hitherto offered by the British government and recommended either the raising of interest-free colonial loans by the imperial government or the creation of a development fund to provide grants direct to the Colonies (or loans to meet interest charges). Unlike Amery's parallel proposal there was no suggestion, however, that expenditure from such a fund should be left to the complete discretion of the Colonial Office.[40]

The Report of the Industrial Transference Board issued in 1928 delivered

[38] Cab 24/201, CP 27, Unemployment. Memorandum by the Home Secretary, 7 February 1929.
[39] Cab 24/202, CP 53, Unemployment. Memorandum by the Chancellor of the Exchequer covering Treasury Memorandum, 23 February 1929.
[40] Constantine, *The Making of British Colonial Development Policy*, 177.

a further sombre message to Ministers. Heavy concentrations of unemployment in industries and regions could not be wished away – every effort had to be made to expand activity and to raise the prospects and morale of labour. But although investment programmes overseas were regarded thereby as a possible source of amelioration, the Chancellor of the Exchequer warned that:

all the work of construction on bridges and railways that can reasonably be undertaken is already in progress, and that there can really be little advantage in the long run to any party concerned if Colonial Governments are obliged to undertake costly and ambitious new projects in advance of normal requirements, as the financial burden thus imposed upon them is more than likely to bring them in time to a condition of stagnation and inactivity, unless the Imperial Exchequer would be prepared to bear the cost of carrying out their development programmes indefinitely.[41]

The Conservatives were not prepared to go that far, but it was a reflection of the haste with which an effective political response to the unemployment crisis had to be mounted that Baldwin agreed in April 1929 to the establishment of a colonial development fund.[42] Even the Treasury accepted the principle of annually underwriting such a fund to enable Colonies to raise capital for approved schemes of work likely to benefit the British economy. Yet it still insisted that Exchequer subsidies should be within the limits set by the condition of the nation's finances and that the fund should be administered by a board of commissioners as a safeguard against excessive or unwise expenditure.

The Tories fell from power before any of these developments could be carried further. MacDonald's second Labour government was just as hard pressed to take immediate action against unemployment as its predecessor had been, though it was scarcely better equipped to do so. Thomas, Lord Privy Seal with special responsibility for unemployment policy, eagerly adopted the Tories' colonial development proposals without any real idea how they might affect the situation. Intuition, optimism and auto-suggestion were no substitutes for reasoned analysis and informed judgement, but they could always be relied upon to sustain an image of positive action. Certainly the attitude of the Labour Party towards colonial development schemes had in the past been rather lukewarm and ambivalent. Many of its members shared the Colonial Office's disquiet over using colonial policy to pursue economic self-interest, principally because they felt

---

[41] Cab 24/202, CP 53.
[42] Baldwin remained suspicious of the value of Empire development on economic grounds. He rejected advice to bring the issue more to the centre of his 1929 election campaign. The electorate was not to be swayed by 'specious promises'. 'Democracy . . . is on trial', he wrote, 'I trust the fight may be a fight on the basis of fact and not of fable.' Middlemass and Barnes, *Baldwin*, 514.

it threatened the rights and status of native labour. Trade unions likewise argued against any strident pursuit of colonial development, urging that any available resources should be invested at home for social and economic reconstruction. Arthur Greenwood dubbed the Chamberlainite tradition of constructive imperialism 'anti-socialist'.[43]

But with unemployment the pressing economic and political issue of the time, the Labour government was desperate to increase trade and so stimulate investment and exports. Shortly after a month in office and after only the barest departmental and parliamentary debate, the Colonial Development Act was rushed into being. It empowered the Treasury to advance grants or loans up to a maximum of £1 million a year for agricultural or industrial development in the Colonies 'thereby promoting commerce with or industry in the United Kingdom'. Interest on any loan could be defrayed in whole or part for a maximum of ten years.[44] The importance of the measure lay in the fact that, rather than having as its prime objective the furtherance of long-term colonial development, it was designed specifically to effect an immediate expansion of British exports as a way of reducing domestic unemployment. The Act created machinery for the systematic examination of any scheme forthcoming from within the Empire. A deliberate effort was made, moreover, to expand the scope and range of financial assistance and to dispel the idea that aid was restricted only to particular and immediate cases of urgent need. It had been introduced, Thomas explained, 'not only because we believe in Colonial Development . . . but because I think it will assist me in carrying out my idea of dealing with unemployment'.[45] It was, in other words, 'another weapon in the government's armoury . . . a means rather than . . . an end in itself'.[46]

Thus the customary preoccupation with the financial self-sufficiency of the Colonies was transformed by the pressure of economic events into a deliberate political campaign to popularize colonial development as a direct means of alleviating unemployment. Central to this campaign was the presupposition that there existed a natural division of interest between Britain and her Colonies, the latter remaining primary producers with relatively undiversified economies free of any major industrializing tendencies. Dependent thus upon imports of machinery and capital equipment, their development would stimulate employment and income in the British market directly responsible for supplying their needs.

[43] Gupta, *Imperialism and the British Labour Movement*, 80–6.
[44] The Act also allowed the interest on loans passed under the East Africa Loans Act 1926 to be paid out of capital for a maximum of five years.
[45] HC Debs., 5th ser., vol. 224, 12 July 1929, col. 1300.
[46] G. C. Abbott, 'A Re-Examination of the 1929 Colonial Development Act', *Economic History Review*, 2nd ser., 24 (1971), 68–81.

Viewed in these terms, the 1929 Act proved a dismal failure. Skidelsky estimates that by January 1931 it was responsible for providing work for 13,000 men at a time when registered unemployment stood at 2.7 million.[47] It has to be remembered that the Act was introduced shortly before the onset of the world slump and in a sense hardly had an opportunity to prove itself. Certainly the unemployment levels it was designed to relieve were not those to which the country was about to be subjected. Moreover, the financial crisis which accompanied the depression evoked a stern determination within government to secure substantial economies in national expenditure, thereby limiting severely the funds available for colonial development. In no year during the thirties was the £1 million nominally available under the Act ever allocated. The average disbursement amounted to only £645,000 per year, of which only a fraction was actually devoted to the funding of new development schemes.[48]

Damaging though these facts are, they do not entirely explain the limited impact and achievements of the Colonial Development Act. It was subject to severe constraints in other directions. A development fund had been created on a permanent basis with an annual grant and with unusually wide terms of reference, redeeming features in themselves. But the advisory committee established to administer the fund, though possessed of a fair amount of independent discretion, responded only to plans initiated directly by colonial governments. Unfortunately the number of acceptable applications from the Colonies proved disappointingly low. Minor *ad hoc* projects rather than coherently argued and carefully specified development programmes characterized the submissions. Colonial governments felt inhibited about forwarding development plans which might subsequently be judged to be inadequate as a means of stimulating employment and British manu- factured exports; others recognized the dangers of expanding the produc- tion of primary products in a saturated world market characterized by tumbling prices. Few colonial governments were anxious either to engage in accelerated development works which posed a further risk to their already precarious national finances. In the event, the whole cost of approved schemes over the decade 1929–39 amounted to £17.3 million, involving an expenditure in the UK of only £5.8 million.[49]

It is questionable whether a more positive response from the Colonies would have brought forth innumerable schemes of proven economic worth capable of alleviating British unemployment to any significant extent. Almost from the start of its deliberations the Colonial Development

[47] Skidelsky, *Politicians and the Slump*, 304.
[48] Constantine, *The Making of British Colonial Development Policy*, 199–201.
[49] Constantine, *The Making of British Colonial Development Policy*, 211.

Advisory Committee began to abandon the pragmatic, almost panic-induced search for schemes to improve domestic employment. Although both the Treasury and the Committee on National Expenditure (the May Committee) urged the advisory body to concentrate its recommendations on schemes 'likely to give the greatest and speediest benefit to this country',[50] their appeals were quietly disregarded. The priorities of the Labour administration were effortlessly brushed aside in favour of development projects judged more likely to serve the wider and more diversified economic interests of Britain. Policy priorities characteristic of the previous decade – the desire to secure future supplies of essential raw materials and to expand colonial purchasing power over the medium to long term – were given a new lease of life. Neither the advisory committee nor the Colonial Office displayed any real enthusiasm during the thirties for accelerated industrial growth overseas. They remained fearful that metropolitan interests would emerge ascendant, thereby delaying the infinitely more complex process of colonial development. Adverse shifts in the terms of imperial trade in the 1930s, moreover, wrecked any tendency towards complementarity, integration and development within the Empire. In the circumstances, the National Government's enthusiasm for colonial development schemes withered noticeably. Further industrialization abroad, it feared, would merely exacerbate the competition and disunity that already existed between the primary satellites and the industrial metropolis. Relief for the unemployed in the wake of the world depression would have to be sought in other directions.

[50]   Cmd. 3920, 134.

PART IV

Structural unemployment, industry and the regions

8 * Industrial revival and reconstruction

THE PLIGHT OF INDUSTRY

Official efforts to revive those staple sectors harbouring the greatest concentrations of unemployment were continually confounded between the wars by the sheer scale of industrial decline.[1] Both the coal and cotton industries suffered severely in the 1920s from a loss of overseas markets, an intensification of international competition and growing self-sufficiency abroad. The problems in coalmining were further aggravated by technological change, which encouraged greater fuel economy and substitution, by a reduction in domestic demand as a result of recession in Britain's heavy industries, and by a more general decline in the demand for coal which rendered producing countries capable of supplying more output than the market could absorb at prices sufficient to meet production costs. The spinning and weaving sections of the cotton industry, trading in cheaper coarse piece-goods, proved incapable of holding markets in the Far East against intense Japanese competition. In both coal and cotton low productivity, a tradition of labour immobility and an aversion to internal structural change went hand in hand with an ill-fated optimism that revival in competitive efficiency and trade was but a matter of time.

Similar problems were faced in other basic trades. Despite the rise of German and American competition, British iron and steel exports had exceeded imports before 1914. With the collapse of the post-war boom the industry found itself producing well below its potential capacity, losing heavily overseas to countries whose operations had benefited, unlike their British counterparts, from reconstruction and a stable or rising home demand. There were 'too many firms and plants, operating inferior and often outdated equipment of less than optimum capacity, and frequently in poor locations'.[2] The lag in the domestic demand for steel was influenced

---

[1] For a survey of Britain's industrial problems in this period see N. K. Buxton and D. H. Aldcroft (eds.), *British Industry Between the Wars* (1979).

[2] K. Warren, 'Iron and Steel', in Buxton and Aldcroft (eds.), *British Industry*, 113.

directly by stagnation in the shipbuilding industry. Britain had joined other countries in expanding shipping during the war but the industry failed in subsequent years to respond to the problems of surplus capacity. Persistent over-supply and the determination of other countries to protect their industry at Britain's expense by tariffs and subsidies put a high premium upon improved technique, design and organization. Unfortunately British shipping displayed little enthusiasm for reorganization or improved technique and its obsession with avoiding demarcation disputes with labour actively discouraged the search for more efficient working practices.

The burdens of excess capacity, intense competition, falling prices and rising fixed charges offered scant hope in the twenties of any sudden rehabilitation of the basic sectors. As we have already seen, governments looked to sound currency and to the revival of trade to foster economic recovery and refused to be drawn into any direct interventionist policy, least of all on behalf of industry. Ministers believed that downturns in trade such as occurred during 1920/21 would, like pre-war depressions, be of relatively short duration; the most appropriate response, therefore, was to offer industry only such assistance as would enable it to overcome its temporary difficulties. They were opposed to direct subsidies, save in exceptional circumstances. The flax and sugar beet industries benefited from limited financial aid and wage subventions were made to the coal industry during 1921/22 and 1925/26. For much of the first post-war decade, it was difficult to discern an 'industrial policy' as such; the government was inclined to proffer only such limited and specific assistance as was thought likely, in one way or another, to revive industry along normal channels.[3]

Two examples can suffice. The Trade Facilities Act of November 1921 acknowledged that some inducement might be needed to accelerate schemes of industrial capital expenditure which might otherwise be held up by high interest rates or by the expectation of a fall in productive costs. It empowered the Treasury to guarantee the interest and principal on loans for capital works at home and abroad that were calculated to stimulate employment. The intention was not to increase the sum total of jobs but rather to provide them earlier than might otherwise be possible. Even so the scheme was designed as an emergency initiative and offered only meagre assistance (totalling £75 million). It operated until March 1927, largely to the advantage of the shipping, iron and steel, engineering and transport industries. At the time of its cessation the government had become disillusioned, aware that many applications for aid had been made with

---

[3] One measure additional to those discussed below which falls in this category is that of selective protection. For details see chapter 6.

scant reference to the operating capacity or viability of the industries in question. Thereafter it was for businessmen to shoulder the preliminary costs of capital investment.[4]

De-rating was another government 'enabling policy' designed in part to ease the burden on industry of rising and uncompetitive production costs. Since 1896 agriculture had been relieved of the full burden of local taxation but the concession had not been extended to industry in general. Once the cost of unemployment relief began to bear heavily on local government finance during the 1920s, the poorest and most disadvantaged areas faced a scale of rates sufficient to deter all but the most adventurous entrepreneurs. Though various forms of compensatory relief were discussed within Whitehall during the early twenties, it was not until 1928 that a formal scheme of industrial de-rating emerged, relieving 'productive' industry of 75 per cent of its rate liability.[5] But the scheme proved of limited value mainly because it was insufficiently discriminatory towards those regions whose local finances were being ravaged by the cost of able-bodied pauperism due to unemployment. Relief was too widespread and too arbitrarily distributed to make any noticeable difference to the costs of heavy industry.

Direct government assistance to industry during the 1920s was, therefore, severely limited both in its scale and in its effects. Neither major political party abandoned its inherent opposition to Treasury-funded industrial revival, despite pressure to do so. The Federation of British Industries argued in favour of Treasury grants to the basic trades, especially heavy industries where the loss of substantial contracts, as in shipbuilding and engineering for example, could endanger the very existence of firms and thereby further increase unemployment.[6] Likewise the Conference on Industrial Reorganisation and Industrial Relations pleaded in 1929 for a substantial measure of government financial assistance to industry in order to stimulate and encourage employment. And earlier in 1925 the President of the Board of Trade argued in Cabinet that industries suffering from an abnormally high rate of unemployment might attract a subsidy for each man

---

[4] T161/303, Trade Facilities, 26 March 1929. The Treasury was later empowered under the terms of the Development (Loan, Guarantees and Grants) Act, 1929 to meet the payment of principal and interest on any loan raised for accelerated development projects connected with a public utility undertaking. It was also able to make grants to local authorities carrying out acceptable public works schemes.

[5] Railways, canals and docks were also included in the scheme, their relief being passed on to the freight carried. In essence, the scheme transferred part (in the case of agriculture the whole) of the existing liability of industrialists for local taxation on to the shoulders of the general body of taxpayers. Under the terms of the Local Government Act, 1929, the Exchequer made good the consequent deficits of the local authorities by means of a Block Grant.   [6] Dintenfass, 'The TUC, the FBI and British Economic Policy', 58.

employed in excess of a 'Datum Line of Minimum Employment', the amount to be subsequently repaid from net profits.[7]

This latter suggestion paralleled a contemporary plea that unemployment insurance benefit should be used as a subsidy for wages. The proposal usually took one of two forms – either that unemployment benefit should be applied in part payment of wages on relief work provided by local authorities or, more usually, that such payments should be made to private employers to enable them retain or expand their existing workforce.[8] The effect of such wage subsidies, the Director of the National Federation of Iron and Steel Manufacturers informed the Minister of Labour in 1922, would be to:

enable lower prices to be quoted in competition with low exchange countries and thus increase the volume of employment possible by increasing the volume of work in the country. This again would be likely to reduce production costs and the increasing number of workers employed at full wages would have further repercussions through industry and trade by the distribution of those increased wages within the country.[9]

The government doubted that such schemes could do much to improve trade, prices or employment and thought them impossible to implement without serious risk of inequity and abuse. What worried Ministers most was the suggestion that funds designated for the payment of unemployment benefit should be earmarked for any alternative purpose. By undermining the contributory principle of insurance, the idea threatened to weaken the very cornerstone of the government's anti-unemployment strategy. It was far more palatable in the immediate term to continue to meet the needs of the unemployed by cash payments than to be forced to consider ways of creating jobs.[10]

Despite government misgivings, the idea of using benefit payments for the relief of industry continued to attract support during the twenties. Its principal exponent was Sir Alfred Mond. Having pleaded unsuccessfully as Minister for Health for a wage subsidy policy in 1922, he produced a plan in 1925 'to provide work for those workers who are prepared voluntarily to surrender their (unemployment) benefits in return for definite employment'. Under the 'Mond scheme', industries suffering long-term depression were to notify the Employment Exchanges of the number of new workers

---

[7] Cab 27/197, Cabinet Unemployment Committee. Subsidy in Aid of Wages, 27 April 1925.
[8] For a detailed review see Ministry of Labour, *Memorandum on the Proposal to Use Unemployed Benefit in aid of (A) Wages on Relief Work, or (B) Wages in Industry* (1923).
[9] Cab 27/124, Unemployment Committee. Note by the President of the Board of Trade, 30 December 1922.
[10] Cab 27/120, Cabinet Unemployment Committee. Suggestions for the Payment of Unemployment Benefit to Employers Willing to Employ Men at the Balance of Wages, 27 October 1921.

they would employ for a fixed period (e.g. six months) in excess of the average number fully employed by them during the six months preceding an agreed fixed date (the appointed day). The employers in return would receive, in respect of 75 per cent of the workers thus engaged, the amount of weekly unemployment benefit normally due to each man. Preference was to be given to those persons who had been continuously unemployed for three of the six months prior to the 'appointed day'. In order that the scheme should end 'when the greatest need for it had been met', the number of men and women for whom the employer would receive payment was to be reduced at the end of a six month period after the 'appointed day', and subsequently at the end of every three-month period. The entire venture would terminate automatically when the level of unemployment had reached an agreed level of 'normality'.

In a vague anticipation of the multiplier process Mond stressed the likely cumulative advantage of the scheme in stimulating additional employment:

Say, for example, that in the first six months period no more than 100,000 workers were employed under the scheme, in that time, and from one source alone, there is a total saving to the [Unemployment Insurance] Fund alone of £747,500. The purchasing power of those engaged under the scheme will be very much greater than at present, and this will provide employment for many in other industries who are at present in receipt of Unemployment Benefit. Besides subsidiary and ancillary trades which would immediately benefit by the supply of raw materials, semi-finished materials and plant, the industries concerned with transport and communication, with building, textiles, food and distribution would benefit.[11]

The 'Mond scheme' failed to attract any substantial support. Governments remained opposed in principle to any cross-subsidization of industry, least of all from an Insurance Fund falling deeper and deeper into debt. Far from having any cumulative effect, the President of the Board of Trade warned in April 1925, the scheme would shelter the uneconomic firm and thereby hinder recovery. 'Nothing is saved', he maintained, 'when . . . a man who would have got work is kept out of work and brought on the dole in order that a man already on the dole should be given employment'.[12] Since it was only those firms working below capacity on the 'appointed day' that would benefit directly from the proposals, the scheme appeared to encourage inefficiency. Steel-Maitland, Minister of Labour, put it thus:

Costs are at present needlessly high in the Coal trade, the Shipbuilding trade and the Engineering trade. In each of these three trades Masters and Men are slowly and with much reluctance being brought to face the hard facts and to realise that these

[11] Sir Alfred Mond, *The Remedy for Unemployment. Get the Workers Back to Work* (1925), 2–6.
[12] Cab 27/197, Cabinet Unemployment Committee. Subsidy in Aid of Wages. Note by the President of the Board of Trade, 29 April 1925.

wasteful and unnecessary costs must be reduced. If, however, the belief should become current that another dose of dope is obtainable of a new brand, it would make those engaged in the trades in question still more reluctant than they are to face the facts and take the necessary steps to meet them.[13]

Hawtrey at the Treasury warned that Mond's proposals would spread financial ruin among ineligible firms forced to compete at subsidized prices with unsubsidized labour.[14] Employers, moreover, objected to the use of insurance contributions to subsidize competitors. The Federation of British Industries foresaw nothing but confusion and disaster. 'By rewarding firms which had laid men off, rather than those which had struggled to keep men on by production, the subsidy scheme threatens to undermine the incentive to reduce costs.' How, it asked, would such subsidies be terminated without reproducing the conditions which had first called them into existence? Would subsidizing employment give rise to further unwelcome state involvement in the conduct of private business?[15]

The TUC and the Labour Party were particularly disturbed by the implied emphasis that British labour costs were the principal source of the nation's trade and employment difficulties. 'In the case of shipbuilding', read a Congress committee report in 1925:

the difficulty is primarily a glut of existing ships . . . In the steel trades the output is not much below pre-war production: and though the [wages] subsidy might increase employment and output, it would not necessarily provide a market which would absorb the new output. It is clear that the Mond subsidy would not touch the real problem in many industries.[16]

Both the Blanesburgh and Balfour committees opposed wage subsidies as a means of aiding employment. The policy received some sympathetic attention from the economist Pigou, though he too finally rejected it on the grounds that it was likely to hinder labour mobility and to compromise the determination of wages in any subsequent recovery.[17] Ramsay MacDonald attempted to revive the idea in 1930 but with little success. As Prime Minister he asked the Economic Advisory Council to consider whether it would be possible to use the money then being spent on transitional benefit for the purpose of stimulating industrial activity and employment.[18] Pigou, Stamp and Keynes, members of the Council's Committee of Economists, were wary:

[13] Cab 27/197, Cabinet Unemployment Committee. Subsidy in Aid of Wages. Memorandum by the Minister of Labour, May 1925.
[14] T208/94, Hawtrey on Mond's Unemployment Scheme, 1925.
[15] Dintenfass, 'The TUC, the FBI and British Economic Policy', 98.
[16] TUC, *Annual Report*, 1925, 207–8. Cited in Dintenfass, 'The TUC, The FBI and British Economic Policy', 199.   [17] Pigou, 'Wage Policy and Unemployment', 364–5.
[18] Howson and Winch, *The Economic Advisory Council*, 42.

Should it prove possible by a low rate of subsidy to absorb a large number of unemployed, it might happen that the whole cost of the subsidy would be off-set by the associated reduction in the amount of unemployment benefit. In this event, if the wage-earning classes did not, in consequence of the subsidy, demand and secure higher rates of money wage, unemployment would be much reduced and no off-setting disadvantage would occur. It would, however, be slightly optimistic to suppose either that a general wage subsidy at any given rate would in fact reduce the volume of unemployment sufficiently to pay for itself out of unemployment benefit, or that, if it did so, the wage-earners would refrain from demanding increased rates of wage. Hence in practice it is to be feared that this policy, if the subsidy were at all substantial, would involve a heavy additional charge on the Budget even when allowance is made for savings on the Unemployment Insurance Fund; and in the present state of the national finances there can be no doubt that this would have very unfavourable repercussions. Moreover, a general system of wage subsidies would appear to many persons as a plunge into the abyss: and business confidence might be so shaken that employment would suffer through that cause an indirect injury much greater than any direct gain that might fall to it.[19]

Although the Committee of Economists acknowledged that in principle wage subsidies could be used to encourage the employment of additional workers at a rate less than the prevailing level of unemployment pay, they warned of the attendant difficulties. Such subsidies could hasten the demise of unsubsidized business by providing a bounty to the inefficient; moreover, it would prove almost impossible to assess the economic value of a subsidy without knowing how many workers were employed in addition to the number that would have been taken on without the subsidy.[20] Although similar proposals to use transitional payments to finance employment creation were put before the Royal Commission on Unemployment Insurance in 1932, they attracted so much criticism on practical and administrative grounds that they too fell by the wayside.

RATIONALIZATION: A REMEDY FOR SUCCESS?

By the late 1920s hopes of a rapid and substantial cyclical recovery had begun to fade even within the most optimistic quarters of Whitehall. Employers, economists and trade unionists joined MPs of all political persuasions in bemoaning Britain's lack of industrial (and especially export) competitiveness and in complaining that the reduction in costs urgently required to restore supremacy was being hindered by deficiencies in the organization and rational conduct of business.

As dissatisfaction with the market mechanism deepened, the micro-

---

[19] Economic Advisory Council, Committee of Economists, *Report*. October 1930, para 52.
[20] Committee of Economists, *Report*. October 1930. For an alternative view see N. Kaldor. 'Wage Subsidies as a Remedy for Unemployment', *Journal of Political Economy*, 44 (1936), 721–42.

economic philosophy of seeking a solution to industry's problems through a process of 'rationalization' gained increasing support and popularity. Few contemporary observers agreed on what precisely was meant by 'rationalization' but this did little to check their enthusiasm. To some, the concept involved the application to industry of a greater degree of scientific organization and management, akin to that deployed in other fields of endeavour; to others, it implied widespread merger and amalgamation aimed at altering the scale and efficiency of industrial enterprise; to others again, it involved a commitment to technical advance and the scrapping of obsolete plant. There was agreement on one point – rationalization would provide, if not the complete answer to the complex economic problems confronting industrialists, at least a major impetus to restoring the competitive power of British industry by affecting a necessary reduction in working costs.

An active will to reorganize and the power to carry the policy through were essential to British industrial progress, reported the Balfour Committee on Industry and Trade in 1929. 'We do not believe', it judged:

that any of our basic industries have been so weakened . . . as not to have the power within themselves to take the first measures towards their own rejuvenation, provided that they are thoroughly convinced that such measures are essential and unavoidable, and that they must be taken by themselves without reliance on any outside authority.[21]

Liberals were in no doubt that a significant amount of remedial inefficiency existed within the basic industries. The failure year after year in certain sections of the coal, textile and steel industries:

to deal with the problem of surplus capacity and a continued acquiescence in the wastes of working many plants partially instead of securing the economies of concentration does not seem creditable . . . Some of these industries . . . could operate effectively on a suitable scale, but, as the result of abnormal stimulus received during the War and afterwards, [they] are trying to maintain an inflated equipment of plant and workers.[22]

To many industrialists rationalization simply meant the elimination of competition by amalgamation. The 1920s proved to be the 'merger-intensive decade'.[23] Outside the basic trades the wave of industrial concentration was seen as a conscious reaction against the disadvantages of the prevailing industrial structure and as evidence of a determined effort to remedy some of its more outstanding deficiencies. 'If the owner of anthracite coal-mines suffers from the competition of other Welsh anthracite mines, some of which may be over-capitalised', wrote A. Baumann in

[21] Cmd. 3282, 297.   [22] Liberal Party, *Britain's Industrial Future* (1928), 42–3.
[23] L. Hannah, *The Rise of the Corporate Economy* (1976), 94.

1928, 'the rational way to avoid losses is to combine, restrict output, agree upon a uniform price and damn the consumer'.[24] Alfred Mond, Chairman of Imperial Chemical Industries, viewed amalgamation as the first vital step 'in the wider process . . . of rationalization'.[25] Sir William Seager was convinced that successful competition in world markets depended upon 'the amalgamation and fusion of our manufacturing and industrial capacity'.[26]

By the late twenties the TUC had also grown sympathetic towards rationalization primarily because it offered a safeguard against renewed attacks upon wage costs and a means thereby of extending the scope and content of collective bargaining. Within government Cunliffe-Lister, Conservative President of the Board of Trade, sought to dispel any doubts among his Cabinet colleagues as to the purpose and value of industrial reconstruction. Its immediate effect, he wrote in February 1929:

must be to reduce the numbers employed . . . in proportion to the output. In the long run a rationalised industry will benefit employment. The industry becomes a more efficient competitor with foreign industries, and it employs the maximum number that can find work in the industry. But the true way of putting the position is this. Without rationalisation, our competitive power will diminish, and therefore fewer people will be employed. Given rationalisation, while we shall employ fewer men per unit of output, we shall, in fact, employ as many as an efficient industry can economically employ.[27]

But though the rationalization movement gained strength from a ruling consensus that British industry required a large measure of reorganization merely to survive, there was little considered judgement as to how such reorganization could be successfully implemented. The presumption reigned that different industries and even separate firms within an industry would act sufficiently quickly to effect workable schemes of internal reconstruction. But pride and prejudice were enduring obstacles. Many businessmen baulked at the idea of sharing power with others, preferring to exercise the 'feudal' right to pass on their business to their family. The *status quo* retained an attraction all of its own.

Few industries anyway had either the financial resources or the incentive to seek out sufficient aid to sustain any planned rationalization scheme. They were handicapped, moreover, by the fact that, unlike their counterparts in the United States or Germany, neither the City, the joint-stock banks nor the Bank of England entertained any formal working relationship with the industrial sector. The development of the British banking system

[24] A. Baumann, 'An Attack [on rationalisation]', *Business*, March 1928.
[25] Sir A. Mond, 'Amalgamation – Rationalization – Imperial Arrangement. The Latest Phase in Industry', *System*, October 1927.
[26] Sir W. Seager, 'British Industry Must Nationalise or Rationalise', *Business*, May 1932.
[27] Cab 24/202, CP 57, Government Assistance to Rationalisation. Note by the President of the Board of Trade, 24 February 1929.

since the nineteenth century had been closely associated with the progress of the world economy, permitting British banks a greater degree of autonomy from the domestic industrial base than those in younger industrial economies, where economic growth was more dependent upon a systematic mobilization of funds. Despite changes in industrial structure and an increasing demand from businesses for longer-term investment capital in the late Victorian and Edwardian periods, the British financial system remained wedded to the pursuit of stability and 'sound money', preferring to involve itself in low-risk overseas dealings rather than with industrial capital formation. The overriding faith in the stability of sterling permitted the world economy to operate on what was effectively a gold-pound standard. This, combined with the ability of the majority of businesses to raise finance from sources other than the London money market, ensured that in Britain down to 1914, in contrast to German experience, there was little intervention by the banks in the affairs of industry.

This situation was seriously undermined after 1919, however, by the rapid deterioration in British industrial competitiveness and by the decline of London as the dominant force in the international monetary system. The erosion of the traditionally distinct relationship between banking and industry began during the brief but intense speculative boom of 1919–20. Advances and overdrafts to businesses were freely given, often without due regard to the profitability or stability of the firms receiving them. When the boom collapsed many banks found themselves having to shoulder in-dustrial indebtedness, especially in the cotton and steel sectors, principally to safeguard their original loans.

It was in these circumstances that there developed a degree of mutual dependence between banks and industry which was to prove of critical importance to the government's rationalization strategy in the late 1920s and early 1930s. The pre-war pattern of autonomy between banks and industry was not, of course, transformed at a stroke. Although the wave of bank amalgamations in 1918, which produced the dominant 'Big Five', was regarded as necessary to keep pace with the growth of large firms, it did not alter the banking sector's reluctance to provide long-term advances to industry.[28] Nonetheless both the Bank of England and the clearing banks began progressively to devote more energy to industrial matters than hitherto, mainly because many firms had become increasingly dependent upon the goodwill of their bankers to forestall liquidation. The more or less continuous increase in advances for industrial and commercial use between 1923 and 1929 did not amount to any conspicuous 'managerial'

[28] W. A. Thomas, *The Finance of British Industry, 1918–1976* (1978), 54–6.

involvement in industry along American or German lines. It reflected rather a gradual accumulation of outstanding and frozen loans as the banks sought to safeguard the financial security of the firms with which they had dealings.

The Bank of England's overriding concern with the role of sterling in international money markets left it with neither the will nor the institutional means to shape domestic industrial investment and for most of the 1920s it remained content to avoid any fusion of its financial interests with those of industry. However, its involvement with the steel firm of Armstrong–Whitworth – an ordinary commercial customer whose wartime and post-war expansion had been heavily financed by the Bank's Newcastle branch – soon committed to it a series of advances which by 1925 could not readily be withdrawn without precipitating the firm's financial ruin. In the event, the Bank became a controlling shareholder in the newly formed company of Vickers–Armstrong. The move – unprecedented at the time – proved an important breach in the Bank's customary aloofness from industry and an important step in its evolving concern with the financial difficulties of depressed staple industries. In Lancashire, for example, the decline of the cotton industry had so weakened the local banks, whose financial interests were not so widely spread as were those of banks in other parts of the country, that the Bank of England intervened in 1929 to form the Lancashire Cotton Corporation in an effort to encourage a systematic reduction of industrial capacity and thereby greater financial stability.[29] Some contemporaries feared that increased bank intervention in industry, forced by financial and economic necessity, would seriously damage the country's future prosperity. The much-needed reduction in British manufacturing costs, the Liberals maintained, was being impeded by 'a financial position in which businesses are ... dominated by overdrafts' and by banking practices which were becoming 'a dead hand upon development'.[30] Reconstruction, in other words, was being forced upon firms by their financial difficulties and not as a result of any rational plan.

The fact that the state provided little in the way of central direction or funding for the purposes of industrial revival in the twenties did not mean that the principle of competitive individualism reigned supreme. The First World War had already fostered closer association among many manufacturers and both the Committee on Trusts in 1918 and the Committees of Enquiry under the Profiteering Acts of 1919–20 had called attention to the wide extension of arrangements for restricting competition and controlling prices. The post-war slump provided industrialists with a further incentive

[29] The activities of the Corporation are briefly discussed below, pp. 227–8.
[30] *How to Tackle Unemployment. The Liberal Plans as Laid Before the Government and the Nation* (1930), 12, 22.

to resort to defensive, restrictive practices aimed at maintaining prices, spreading output and arresting the decline in profits. By the end of 1928 marketing schemes had developed in the coalfields of Scotland, south Wales and in the midland counties. Coal owners in the midlands agreed to impose output quotas on members operating the 'Five Counties Scheme' and to raise a levy on each ton of coal mined. The money thus raised was used to subsidize exports of coal from the area in order to counteract the extra competition which had arisen from the invasion of their markets by other disadvantaged regions (such as Durham). When, in cotton, the traditional policy of meeting falling demand by organized short-time working was found to be a woefully inadequate response to secular decline,[31] the spinners resorted to forming a cartel. The Cotton Yarn Association of 1927 aimed to fix minimum prices and to regulate output by a system of transferable quotas. The hope was that weaker mills would sell their quotas to the stronger, helping thereby to stem the increasing tide of financial indebtedness by concentrating output on the more efficient units.

Such ventures covered only a portion of the operating firms in an industry and few had any lasting impact, largely because they were unable to prevent 'weak sellers' from undercutting prices as demand continued to fall. In steel, market imperfections and the smaller number of producers made price fixing more feasible, but here the possibilities were severely circumscribed by the pressure of foreign imports. The cartel arrangements in the cotton industry likewise rested upon the ability of those concerns most heavily burdened with fixed costs being able to raise prices to a level sufficient to meet their outstanding charges; those firms with relatively small loan charges, however, chose either to ignore the policy or to sell at prices low enough to enable them to market their full-time output. In any event, restricting output in the most beleaguered basic trades could do little to equate supply and demand at a profitable level of prices, given the scale of surplus capacity and the degree of international competition to which they were subjected. More drastic remedies were required.

When it became clear by the late 1920s that cartelization was unable to provide any swift or adequate assistance to industries suffering permanent contraction, attention turned towards planned reconstruction and the elimination of firms. With the reality of heavy structural unemployment before them, government officials realized that the task of purging basic industries of their excess capacity could no longer be left to market forces or to the enterprise and energy of private businessmen. Previous government initiatives by way of limited subsidies, de-rating, selective protection and the

---

[31] The policy of short-time working as a 'solution' to unemployment is discussed above in chapter 4.

overt encouragement of voluntary schemes of amalgamation and price and output control, had remained essentially incidental and supplementary to a declared faith in the capacity of private capitalism to find a way out of the prevailing industrial malaise. The time had arrived for a fundamental rethink of policy.

REORIENTATION OF POLICY: GOVERNMENT, BANKS AND
INDUSTRIAL REVITALIZATION IN THE EARLY 1930S

The reluctance of industry to pursue internal reconstruction and moderniz-ation, the growing recognition of the political and social obstacles to enforcing substantial cuts in money wage costs, and the emergence of vigorous demands for expanded credit to finance large-scale public investment, combined by the end of the first post-war decade to increase the pressure on government to intervene more directly in industry, not to supplant private activity but to reinvigorate it for the purpose of industrial revival. 'There was a time', the Conservative administration confessed in 1929:

when perhaps a reduction in the costs of production was looked upon as largely synonymous with the reduction in wages. In present conditions, it must be sought in the improved organisation and efficiency of all elements of industry, in the adjustments of businesses of the country to the changes that have taken place in world demand and in the supplies from different countries, and in all that is implied in the term 'rationalization'.[32]

Following Labour's second electoral victory, Thomas, Secretary of State for the Dominions, was echoing similar sentiments:

Until industry is profitable it will never . . . be able to give a satisfactory volume of employment, and there are wide areas over which there is little prospect of this until comprehensive reconstruction has been effected . . . The choice does not lie between rationalisation and the continuance of the existing organisation – or rather lack of organisation – in industry. Industry is coming to realize more and more that it must rationalise if it is to survive at all . . . The question before us as a Government is whether we are to help rationalisation with advice and co-operation . . . or whether we are to stand aside while the process is prolonged with much unnecessary dislocation and loss.[33]

Vernon Hartshorn, Lord Privy Seal, issued his own warning to Cabinet colleagues in August 1930:

We cannot look to our staple industries, built up so largely on export trade, to give employment in the future to all those workers nominally attached to them. At the

[32] Memoranda on Certain Proposals Relating to Unemployment, Cmd. 3331, 52.
[33] Cab 24/213, CP 227, The Attitude of the Government to Industrial Reorganisation, 3 July 1930.

same time it is clear that our staple industries are crying out for reorganisation and modernisation . . . But the money needed for new plant and equipment cannot be found by our staple industries because the investor is not unnaturally shy . . . and rightly assumes that he can do better with his money elsewhere. How are we to break through this vicious circle? Reorganisation is imperative if we are to stop the rot.

But he warned Ministers not to expect too much. By itself reorganization of industry could never restore foreign export markets 'to the full extent which we have supplied them in the past. Some of the causes which have deprived us of trade . . . are permanent in character and largely beyond our control'.[34]

Having declared its faith in rationalization as a more practicable and workable device for promoting industrial recovery than any large-scale programme of government-financed investment, the second Labour administration went to considerable lengths in 1930 to quicken interest within industry. Although Ministers were anxious to display a measure of public concern over the plight of industry they were determined nevertheless to safeguard the government from any financial or executive involvement in the rationalization movement. The best service the government felt it could render was to impress upon the industrial world the need for rationalization, whilst leaving the responsibility for it – particularly in terms of finance – to the private sector. During a speech in Manchester in January 1930 Thomas, Lord Privy Seal, announced on the basis of assurances given to him by the Governor of the Bank of England that the City was 'deeply interested in placing industry upon a broad and sound basis' and was willing to extend 'the most sympathetic consideration and . . . co-operation' to firms proposing schemes of reorganization and modernization which would enable them to produce at prices competitive in world markets.[35] In the eyes of the government, industrial revitalization was being impeded by the reluctance of creditors to face loss; it was imperative, therefore, for industrialists to take advantage of the supplies of credit on offer and for them to utilize the expertise available in the City for judging the commercial prospects of any venture. As the Cabinet Committee on Unemployment explained:

The task of prevailing upon proprietors, shareholders and debenture holders to accept the reduction – sometimes event the complete writing off – of their nominal claims is necessarily long and difficult. Heavy bank overdrafts are a common feature in these cases, and the anxiety of the Banks to save a higher proportion of their loans than the situation warrants is not the least formidable obstacle. The conflicting

---

[34] Cab 27/440, CP 293, Unemployment Policy. Memorandum by the Lord Privy Seal, 18 August 1930.
[35] Cab 27/418, The State and Rationalisation, Appendix B, 1930.

claims of these various interests can only be adjusted to economic facts as a result of experience, and as reductions are resisted as long as hope remains, the process naturally takes time.[36]

Labour's task was made easier by certain institutional developments within the banking sector. The Bank of England's anxiety to ensure that the financial problems of industry were entrusted to individuals least likely to compromise action for the sake of political expediency had already led it to establish the Securities Management Trust in November 1929 to supervise the provision of funds for those rationalization schemes the bank itself supported. Four months later, the Bankers' Industrial Development Company (BIDC) was created as a co-operative venture involving the Bank, leading issue houses and the merchant banks to expand the supply of credit for mergers and the re-equipment of the basic industries. Norman, Governor of the Bank of England, regarded this development as 'his most effective contribution to the revival of industry and the reduction of unemployment'.[37] It was, in truth, an attempt to head off a somewhat exaggerated fear of increased (socialist) government intervention in the affairs of private industry and to protect the interests of those banking houses which had provided credit for businesses already in financial difficulties. In theory, the BIDC offered firms sufficient economies of scale in finance to make large-scale enterprise a more realizable goal. But in the City it was regarded merely as a temporary measure, necessary only to 'nurse' particular companies until such time as economic conditions permitted them to market their shares on the Stock Exchange.

The readiness of Ministers to entrust much of the vigour of the rationalization movement to the financial and banking fraternity did not escape criticism. It was preferable, the Liberals urged, for the government itself to finance schemes of reorganization 'calculated permanently to raise the efficiency and competitive power of . . . industry' to an extent equivalent to the resultant 'estimated savings on unemployment costs'.[38] Within government Mosley, Henderson and Attlee fought a losing battle to drive a thicker wedge between outside interests and industrial reconstruction by the creation of some form of central funding agency. Mosley proposed the establishment of a state 'Finance House or Industrial Bank' in which City interests would be invited to participate. It was a fundamental mistake, he argued, to leave the effective control of industrial reorganiz-

[36] Cab 27/418, CP 134, Unemployment Policy (1930). Committee Report, 1 May 1930. Although both Ministers and industrialists tried during 1927 and 1929 to have the Trade Facilities Act revived for the purpose of financing schemes of industrial reconstruction, their efforts were stifled by the government's continued reluctance to become directly involved in the reconstruction of particular industries.
[37] Sayers, *The Bank of England*, 323.   [38] *How To Tackle Unemployment*, 31.

ation in the hands of banks. Past experience suggested that they would salvage their own financial commitments as a first objective or, at the very least, continue to aid ailing industries faced with 'ever diminishing and elusive demand' rather than develop new and possibly more competitive ones.[39]

By 1930 Henderson, who only a year before had defended public works expenditure as potentially beneficial to industry and employment, had grown convinced of the positive relief to be gained from industrial reorganization and reconstruction. He foresaw 'a real danger of the development of a vicious circle, economic and psychological in character, which will retard recovery for long after world conditions have taken a favourable turn'. As he put it:

The growth in unemployment and the accentuated deficit in the Unemployment Fund will threaten the prospect of a deficit in the next Budget and a further increase of direct taxation. This prospect will discourage business confidence and intensify unemployment still further. It is therefore very important to consider in advance, freely and without regard to the limitations set by preconceived doctrines, whether it is not possible to do something to break through this circle of reactions.[40]

Henderson called upon the Cabinet in June 1930 to establish an 'Industrial Reconstruction Fund' of £15 million out of the revenue from a 'special temporary' 10 per cent duty on imported manufactures. Part of its purpose would be 'to stimulate immediate capital expenditure on approved ration-alisation schemes' by subsidizing interest costs on a scale which gave preference to projects put in hand at an early date. This idea reflected Henderson's newly declared preference for a microeconomic rather than a macroeconomic approach to remedial policy and his growing belief that rationalization plans were being unnecessarily retarded by the lack of central direction, encouraging businessmen merely to await 'better times' or further cuts in interest rates. The proposal was passed over by Cabinet without discussion. Attlee, too, tried to foster new policy initiatives. As Chancellor of the Duchy of Lancaster, he echoed Mosley's plea for some form of deliberate industrial planning, calling in 1930 for the appointment of a Minister of Industry and for the creation of an Industrial Development Board to encourage compulsory amalgamations in industry in return for a measure of public control.[41] None of these interventions, however, had much impact. MacDonald's administration remained determined to act

---

[39] Cab 24/209, CP 31, Unemployment Policy. Copy of a letter from Sir Oswald Mosley to the Prime Minister, 23 January 1930.
[40] Cab 24/212, CP 196, Unemployment Policy – Industrial Reconstruction Scheme, 30 May 1930.
[41] Cab 24/214, CP 283, The Problem of British Industry. Memorandum by the Chancellor of the Duchy of Lancaster, 29 July 1930.

purely as a bridge between finance and industry and as a powerful advocate but not initiator of schemes of industrial reconstruction.

The government's ability to remain a dispassionate observer of privately inspired industrial revival financed from outside the Treasury was seriously compromised, however, by the setbacks which the rationalization movement suffered in the early thirties, before it had gathered even a limited degree of momentum. Although, according to its official historian, the Bank of England 'entered the 1930s with an unprecedented willingness – and, in a small way, an organisation – for taking an active part in the reorganization of British industry',[42] the new financial institutions designed for the purpose showed little promise of becoming vital agents of industrial rejuvenation. The willingness of the Securities Management Trust to offer advice and funds to particular industrial concerns was compromised by the Bank of England's declared intent from 1930 to reduce its direct involvement in schemes of reorganization. For its part, the BIDC failed to usher in a new era in the finance of British industry. In the absence of any agreed reappraisal of the relationship between the financial sector, industry and the government, its operations became increasingly dictated by the force of circumstance rather than by the weight of principle. Until 1931 the belief reigned within the Bank of England that the intensity of international competition and the relative (in some cases the absolute) decline of industrial fortunes would together provide a sufficient incentive for industry to reorganize; easier access to available funds would merely benefit the process. As the industrial and financial crisis deepened in 1931, however, the Bank's attitude changed. The essential requirements of industrial aid were seen less in terms of marshalling capital resources from a broad base to assist industry in general than of confining activity to tactical manoeuvres designed to keep the government at bay. The Bank even toyed with the idea of financing a few projects out of its own resources although this was never pursued. It had been made plain from the beginning 'that no government money was involved . . . The BIDC was to be nothing more than a vetting and guaranteeing body . . . As the money of its own subscribers was involved in this second function, it was bound to make sure that none but the very "soundest" schemes received its imprimatur.'[43]

This emphasis upon traditional fiduciary practice was more attractive to the Bank than any involvement in wider schemes of reconstruction. From the early thirties, therefore, the 'industrial policy' of the Bank of England began to mirror that of the Labour and National governments – a preference for *ad hoc* intervention in particular industries, for particular reasons and in particular circumstances.

---

[42] Sayers, *Bank of England*, 330.   [43] Skidelsky, *Politicians and the Slump*, 174.

INTERVENTION IN INDUSTRY IN SLUMP AND RECOVERY

Circumspection within the financial sector coincided with growing disenchantment elsewhere over the capacity of rationalization to offer any early or rapid relief to an unemployment problem exacerbated in the extreme by world economic recession. There were economists, trade unionists, and businessmen deeply sceptical of the belief that rationalization, after inducing a spell of 'temporary' unemployment, would expand future employment through its beneficial effects upon industrial costs, efficiency and productivity. Much depended upon the type of rationalization undertaken, the elasticity of demand for the end product and the consequent impact upon the derived demand for labour.[44] Urwick, one-time Director of the International Management Institute in Geneva and a consistent advocate of industrial reorganization, confessed that it was 'quite impossible, in the present state of our statistical knowledge and resources, to produce adequate evidence to prove either that rationalisation does or does not increase unemployment'.[45]

To expect rationalization to increase efficiency in basic trades 'sufficient to absorb, within a moderate period of time, the bulk of the men now unemployed, both in these industries, or in other industries', the Committee of Economists maintained in October 1930, 'would be quite unreasonable'. Even if improved methods and techniques were more widely adopted, they could be quickly matched by overseas competitors. Moreover, the kind of rationalization schemes so obviously favoured by industry would improve neither productivity nor employment since most of them were designed simply 'to arrange an orderly contraction of output . . . with a minimum of financial loss to the firms concerned'.[46] Co-ordinated attempts to eliminate excess capacity were likely to be confounded in the Council's view by the vested interests not only of management and trade unionists, but also of owner-proprietors, banks, outside stockholders and other customers. Keynes conceded in 1930 that rationalization 'was not of itself likely to do much in the way of increasing employment',[47] a view to which Mosley readily subscribed. Indeed, Mosley's vigorous support for emergency schemes of public works was based on his belief that longer term industrial

[44] See for example T. E. Gregory, 'Rationalisation and Technological Unemployment', *Economic Journal*, 40 (1930), 551–67; J. A. Hobson, *Rationalization and Unemployment* (1930), 64–89; Hobson, 'The State as an Organ of Rationalization', *Political Quarterly*, 2 (1931), 30–45.
[45] L. Urwick, 'Rationalisation', *British Management Review*, 3, 1938.
[46] Cab 58/11, EAC (H) 127, Economic Advisory Council, Committee of Economists. Report, 24 October 1930, para 42.
[47] Howson and Winch, *The Economic Advisory Council*, 74.

reconstruction, though vital, was unlikely to offer any positive relief to unemployment for at least three years. 'At present', he informed MacDonald in January 1930:

We are concentrating on Rationalisation schemes and holding out hope to the country that we are thereby reducing immediate unemployment. We are, in fact, doing immediately exactly the reverse and if our pledges to deal with present unemployment are to be implemented we must also devise a far larger immediate policy . . . National reconstruction involving modernisation of British industrial methods . . . in the first instance will generally mean an actual discharge of labour. That condition of weakness must be expected before the benefits of surgery can be realised.[48]

Although at the time of the Mond–Turner talks the TUC supported 'progressive rationalization' as a means of releasing otherwise redundant resources of capital and labour for newer and more productive uses, it was unable with the onset of world slump to view with equanimity the prospect of creating additional redundancies. Its qualified support for the rationalization movement of the twenties gave way in the early thirties to a growing disenchantment with a policy it feared could be a source of rising unemployment. In previous years, the General Council had believed that careful scheduling of reorganization, combined with labour transference, reduced working hours and the provision of financial compensation for workers made redundant, would reduce the problem of labour displacement to manageable proportions. By mid-1930 its mood had changed significantly. Rationalization, it claimed, remained too unco-ordinated to be effective and offered no assurance that any unemployment thereby created would only be of short duration. Neither the employers nor the government, moreover, was prepared to consider offering special financial assistance to the victims of industrial reorganization. Such compensation, preached MacDonald, was both impracticable and unnecessary since rationalization would ultimately add to the volume of employment generally available. Ernest Bevin rejected this view as crass nonsense; rationalization, he told the Economic Advisory Council in June 1930. would only be effective in creating jobs if it was associated with a simultaneous expansion of consumer demand:

Behind all this idea of reorganisation appears to be the conception that, by the cheapening of production, the concentration of labour, and the introduction of scientific methods, wealth will be provided in such vast quantities that it will cause *the creation of new industries*; and therefore, the total volume of people employed as a result of the new outlets will more than compensate for those displaced. I think,

[48] Cab 24/209, CP 31, Unemployment Policy. Copy of a letter from Sir Oswald Mosley to the Prime Minister, 23 January 1930.

however, it is well to remind ourselves that . . . unless there is a shortening of the hours of labour, raising of the school leaving age, pensioning, an increase of purchasing power, and the creation of demand by adding to leisure, new outlets in other industries cannot be provided.[49]

The Labour government remained undeterred by such gloomy prognoses. It was as convinced as the Conservatives had been that rationalization, after creating on initial period of dislocation and increased unemployment, would increase total employment in the long run. Its declared aim was to increase aggregate productivity to allow a greater volume of employment without a reduction in real wages. The implicit assumption was that favourable price elasticities of demand at home and abroad would permit lower prices to be translated into increased revenue and greater demand for labour, with 'new industries and services and the expansion of other sectors' stepping into the breach.[50] 'It is perfectly true that in the course of rationalisation it is often necessary to close down works', Thomas reminded his Cabinet colleagues in July 1930:

On the other hand, rationalisation usually involves re-equipment, which means increased employment elsewhere; more important still it will generally be the only alternative to industrial decay, with a still greater decline in employment. Rationalisation may be the only way of making industry once more remunerative, and it is only by making industry remunerative that a basis for future expansion can be created. I believe that rationalisation is in the best interests of employment.[51]

The Liberals concurred. Short-term unemployment consequent upon the industrial reorganization was 'no argument against the pursuit of greater efficiency'. In the longer term, there was 'no doubt . . . that the . . . policy . . . would ultimately mean a dramatic cut into our present core of permanent unemployment'.[52]

Confounding the critics was one thing: promoting an effective policy to achieve economically desirable results was quite another. Though the Cabinet proved adept during 1930 at defending the rationalization movement, it proved singularly unwilling to discuss its substantive content. As we have noted already,[53] the appeals by Mosley and Attlee for some form

[49] Cab 58/10, EAC (H) 92, Effect of Rationalisation on Employment. Memorandum by Mr. Ernest Bevin, 17 June 1930.
[50] Cab 27/390, DU (29) 58, Interdepartmental Committee on Unemployment. Notes on the Direct Effects of Accelerated Rationalisation upon the Volume of Employment in Manufacturing Industries, 30 September 1929.
[51] Cab 24/213, CP 227, The Attitude of the Government to Industrial Reorganisation. Memorandum by J. H. Thomas, 3 July 1930.
[52] *How to Tackle Unemployment*, 85.   [53] See above, pp. 217–19.

of centralized industrial planning failed to evoke any positive response in Cabinet. Yet falling profits and the burden of over-capacity had clearly proved insufficient to impel the squeezing out of inefficient firms. Government officials were being pressed into taking a more active role in industrial reconstruction, but were instinctively inclined only towards the use of moral suasion to encourage voluntary action within the industrial sector. The necessity for short-term action conflicted with the promotion of longer term objectives. On the one hand, the government wanted to distance itself from any direct responsibility for rationalization because of the risk of being directly associated with the creation of short-term unemployment; on the other, it recognized that by leaving industry to impose its own forms of reorganization the longer term benefits to employment and enhanced competitiveness at home and abroad would be painfully slow to materialize.

By the end of 1930 the internal debate over whether industrial revival was to come through state planning or *ad hoc* government intervention on a case-by-case basis was resolved in favour of the latter; what had yet to be decided, however, were the possible modes of intervention (suasion, direct subsidy, nationalization or legislative coercion) and, perhaps more significantly, whether the proximate ends of state intervention were to be the furtherance of efficiency or the bolstering of uncompetitive industries by restrictive and protective practices. The official responses to these various alternative strategies and their impact upon policy in the 1930s are best illustrated by examining subsequent progress in the industries most affected.

Coal

The persistence of heavy structural unemployment, the legacy of bitter industrial relations and an almost continuous decline in trading performance had done nothing by 1930 to encourage coalowners to seek economic salvation through industrial reorganization and amalgamation. The multiplicity of ownership and the fragmented structure of the industry had been roundly condemned by the Coal Industry Commission as early as 1919. The state, however, had consistently refused to develop a positive and unambiguous strategy in defence of one of the country's most important yet economically vulnerable industries. At the same time the coalowners were openly suspicious of the scale of commercial economies that might be derived from the enforced amalgamation of mines. They argued with some justification that continued economic depression, combined with enforced wage subsidization in the early twenties, had depleted profits to levels far below those required for adequate re-equipment, let alone substantive reorganization.[54]

Although by 1930 the government was, by its own admission, anxious to secure export revival in the basic industries as a way of reducing unemployment, it had already fudged the issue within coalmining. The payment of subsidies in 1921 and 1925–26 had eased the financial difficulties of marginal pits and so allowed them to remain in being. Although this afforded some protection to employment it undermined the process of voluntary amalgamation and the elimination of inefficient collieries which the Mining Industry Act of 1926 tried in vain to encourage.[55] Collective action in south Wales, Scotland and the midlands to restrict output and maintain prices in the mid to late twenties suggested, moreover, that without some form of compulsion efforts at self-survival were doomed to failure. However, the prospects for industrial reorganiz-ation were anything but propitious. Miners understood very well that rationalization was likely to increase unemployment and were understand-ably reluctant to offer themselves as the victims of 'short-term' adjustment. They directed their energies instead towards securing lower working hours, opposing pit closures and seeking a guarantee against wage reductions based on district proceeds. The owners proved equally insistent that any reduction in working hours should be met by wage cuts.

In the circumstances the government's only hope of making progress was by trying to satisfy, if only partially, the divergent interests of the parties involved. The result, the Coal Mines Act of 1930, was a shabby compromise, yet one which illustrated very well the difficulty of trying to 'solve' unemployment by schemes of reorganization. The 1930 Act perpetuated the ambiguity of state policy evident in the earlier decade – a willingness on the one hand to entrust industry with some control over output and prices as a way of responding to national and international market forces, and a desire on the other to raise operating efficiency through rationalization to a level sufficient to render defensive cartelization obsolete in the long run. As an employment policy, however, the strategy was doomed to failure, principally because of its own inconsistency. Part I of

---

[54] The literature on the coal industry in this period is extensive. The views of the miners, owners and government towards industrial reorganization are discussed in N. K. Buxton, 'Coalmining' in *British Industry Between the Wars*, ed. Buxton and Aldcroft; N. Buxton, *The Economic Development of the British Coal Industry* (1978) and M. W. Kirby, *The British Coalmining Industry 1870–1946* (1977).

[55] The Act was essentially 'permissive', designed to encourage voluntary amalgamation in the industry, though compulsory powers were embodied within it. By the end of 1928, 17 schemes of amalgamation had been effected, involving 126,000 workers. M. W. Kirby, 'The Control of Competition in the British Coal-Mining Industry in the Thirties', *Economic History Review*, 2nd ser., 26 (1973), 282.

the Act introduced statutory marketing schemes aimed at establishing output quotas as a way of controlling prices. Part II created the Coal Mines Reorganization Commission charged with promoting and assisting amalgamations within the industry. Price and output regulation were regarded as no more than stepping stones on the way to scientific reorganization of the industry.[56] Within the official mind, the two policies were mutually consistent, as the Secretary for Mines Ernest Brown explained in Cabinet in 1934:

The economic and social effects which would ensue on the revocation of Part I cannot be over-emphasised. Although its operations have tended to maintain wholesale coal prices at a time when other commodity prices have been falling the financial position of the industry remains bad. Its productive capacity is greatly in excess of any demand than can reasonably be foreseen. Unleashing the excess capacity would result in a severe fall in prices which the finances of the industry could not bear and would inevitably lead to attacks upon wages. In the absence of statutory regulation of output and prices, extensive cut-price competition would be embarked upon. Part I has enabled the available employment to be spread among the greatest possible number of men. If it were revoked, the available employment would be concentrated and I estimate that there would be an addition of nearly 150,000 to the number of workpeople totally unemployed.[57]

Part I of the 1930 Act had been enacted prior to the onset of a further and severe contraction in the domestic and international demand for coal. It made no provision for effective inter-district price co-ordination and thus, far from preventing 'cut-throat' competition, it openly encouraged low-cost districts to invade markets in high-cost coalfields, further accentuating their relative decline. On the other hand, the output quota system worked to the advantage of the efficient and the inefficient mine alike, perpetuating the existence of collieries which, in the normal course of events, might have closed down. Moreover, the system paid scant regard to the prevailing level of demand and permitted exporting districts to operate quotas far in excess of the amounts needed to satisfy their established markets. In the short term this acted as a brake upon the potential decline in employment in coal-producing districts by helping to preserve the existing structure of the industry. But it lessened the incentive towards amalgamation, either on the basis of private initiative or state compulsion, which the Reorganization Commission had been designed to promote. Not surprisingly the policy of compulsory amalgamation in coalmining proved a complete failure. The coalowners remained inherently hostile to any form of state intervention in their affairs, especially when it threatened to impose upon them unwieldy

[56] Coal Mines Reorganisation Commission, *Colliery Amalgamations*, July 1931.
[57] Cab 24/247, CP 6, Part I of the Coal Mines Act, 1930. Memorandum by the Secretary for Mines, 1 February 1934.

and unworkable schemes of reconstruction which were required to serve 'the national interest' without inflicting financial injury on any affected concerns. To the miners, rationalization threatened the customary device of spreading employment among as many workers as possible, increasing instead the risk of redundancy without compensation in districts already burdened with heavy localized unemployment.[58]

As far as unemployment was concerned, therefore, the effects of the rationalization movement in coal were somewhat ambiguous. It clearly failed to promote the structural readjustments thought most likely to preserve employment and financial stability in the long run, through the elimination of excess capacity. Cartel arrangements became a far more permanent feature of the organization of the industry than was anticipated. Although this weakened the impulse towards amalgamation, it neverthe-less afforded the industry some protection, allowing it to arrest slightly the process of structural decline and to meet continued depression instead with costly short-time working, but with fewer redundancies than might otherwise have proved necessary. No government could afford to look with equanimity upon the prospect of intensifying unemployment in coalmining districts. For political and social reasons, officials came to regard a more efficient industry as less important than the preservation of jobs.[59]

Cotton textiles

The highly fragmented nature by which the cotton industry developed prior to 1914, based largely upon specialization of function, proved particularly unsuited to fostering the degree of technical and structural change required to accommodate the drastic loss of export markets in the post-war period. By the early thirties, cotton's international trading problems had already intensified domestic decline by increasing short-time working among an expanding pool of surplus and predominantly immobile workers. Structural adjustment had been painfully slow during the previous decade, partly because the banking sector retarded the enforced liquidation of firms. The 'orgy of speculative re-flotations'[60] and the financial reconstruction of existing mills which accompanied the re-stocking boom of 1919–20 were based predominantly on fixed-interest borrowing from the commercial

---

[58] The Miners' Federation of Great Britain had supported 'progressive rationalization' during the twenties as an extension of its demand for nationalization of the coal industry and because it felt that reorganization would help to protect wages.

[59] For more detailed discussion see Buxton, 'Coalmining'; M. W. Kirby, 'Government Intervention in Industrial Organization: Coal Mining in the Nineteen Thirties', *Business History*, 15 (1973), 160–73.

[60] R. H. Tawney, 'The Abolition of Economic Controls 1918–1921', *Economic History Review*, 2nd ser., 13 (1943), 16.

banks at a time of heady but ultimately short-lived prosperity. The greatest volume of company reflotation occurred in the 'American' sector spinning coarse yarn and this suffered the most during the subsequent collapse. Firms threatened with imminent collapse because of the growing burden of interest and depreciation charges came increasingly to depend for their survival upon further extensions of bank loans.[61]

It proved imperative for spinning firms to seek some means of forestalling bankruptcy. Short-time working, the industry's traditional response to economic recession, operated almost continuously between 1921 and 1925, but was by itself a totally inadequate means of restoring profitability and export competitiveness. Various attempts to reinforce it with voluntary price-fixing schemes foundered, largely because of the refusal of minorities to co-operate. In 1927 an attempt was made through the Cotton Yarn Association to organize a voluntary cartel in American spinning, but again a number of producers stood aloof and wrecked the scheme.[62] It was the failure of such devices that made the search for alternative strategies to counteract financial instability all the more urgent.

Besides cartel arrangements there were three possible ways in which the industry could seek to improve its position, by technical re-equipment, by voluntary amalgamation, and by the elimination of surplus capacity. These approaches were not mutually exclusive. A smaller, profitable industry could conceivably allow amalgamation and re-equipment to occur in the medium term under the stimulus of normal market forces. To the beleaguered spinners the answer seemed to lie in fostering a greater degree of industrial concentration via horizontal amalgamation. Since this required capital the spinners sought the advice and support of the Bank of England. Not only did the Bank encourage this process, but it helped to create the Lancashire Cotton Corporation in January 1929 to quicken the pace of amalgamation of the spinning sector. Whereas the Cotton Yarn Association had been a cartel designed predominantly to avoid financial loss, the LCC aimed to effect economies in production 'by providing a highly concentrated entity under centralized control with the financial ability to re-equip . . . and force inefficient producers out'.[63] Commercial banks were encouraged to use their influence over debtor firms to persuade them to offer themselves as candidates for absorption. The hope was that, in its initial

---

[61] J. H. Porter, 'The Commercial Banks and the Financial Problems of the English Cotton Industry, 1919–1939', *International Review of the History of Banking*, 9 (1974), 1–16; G. W. Daniels and J. Jewkes, 'The Post-War Depression in the Lancashire Cotton Industry', *Journal of the Royal Statistical Society*, 91 (1928), 153–92.

[62] B. Bourker, *Lancashire Under the Hammer* (1928), 80–7; G. W. Daniels and H. Campion, 'The Cotton Industry Trade', in *Britain in Depression*, British Association (1935), 340–1.

[63] W. Lazonick, 'The Cotton Industry', in *The Decline of the British Economy*, ed. B. Elbaum and W. Lazonick (Oxford, 1986), 31–2.

stages at least, the Corporation could acquire 10 million spindles. This boost to rationalization within cotton arose, however, less from the bank's concern for the planned reconstruction of an ailing industry than from a calculated desire to proffer emergency relief to Lancashire banks threatened under the pressure of mounting industrial debt with a breakdown in credit.[64] The motivation was borne out by the failure of the bank to promote any further mergers and by the fact that of the first 29 companies absorbed by the LCC most were recapitalized concerns dating from the post-war boom.[65]

The rate at which the LCC acquired firms (almost 100 between 1929 and 1932) made it 'not only the largest merger between the wars but the largest on record in Britain at any time'.[66] But the Corporation's intervention created severe managerial diseconomies in an industry characterized by highly fragmented ownership and vertically specialized management. Neither the threat of bankruptcy nor enforced amalgamation was able to overcome the fundamental problem of matching working capacity to demand. By 1931 both the government and the banks believed that a significant reduction of capacity was necessary to restore a measure of profitability before wider schemes of reorganization could be contemplated. But, despite the efforts of the Joint Committee of Cotton Trade Organizations, the industry itself proved unable to formulate an effective scheme whilst the government remained unprepared to impose any alternative against the wishes of large sections of the trade.

Behind the scenes Horace Wilson, Chief Industrial Adviser to the government, sought to stimulate the regeneration of the industry by a policy of industrial diplomacy. He worked tirelessly to persuade businessmen to secure the required measure of rationalization. When cotton-spinning requested statutory powers in 1935 to raise a levy on working spindles, to enable it to buy up redundant spindles, the move was presented as evidence of the industry's spontaneous desire to remedy its own problems. In fact, the resultant Cotton Spinning Act of 1936 was but the culmination of five years' work by Wilson to unite opinion within the industry against amalgamation and in favour of the reduction of surplus capacity.[67] The fear of exacerbating unemployment had encouraged all

---

[64] Sir Henry Clay, *Lord Norman* (1957), 335, cited in M. W. Kirby, 'The Lancashire Cotton Industry in the Inter-War Years: A Study in Organizational Change', *Business History*, 16 (1974), 149n.

[65] Kirby, 'The Lancashire Cotton Industry', 151. The support given by the banks to the idea of amalgamation was echoed in 1930 by the sub-committee of the Economic Advisory Council appointed by Labour in the previous year to report on the problems of the cotton industry.   [66] Hannah, *The Rise of the Corporate Economy*, 75.

[67] R. Roberts, 'The Administrative Origins of Industrial Diplomacy', in *Business and Politics*, ed. J. Turner, 93–104; J. H. Bamberg, 'The Government, the Banks and the Lancashire Cotton Industry 1918–39', Ph.D. Thesis, University of Cambridge (1984), chapters 9–10.

concerned to tread warily, but as the Joint Committee of Cotton Trade Organizations stressed in 1935, it was hoped that the removal of surplus capacity would ultimately benefit the worker:

As the main purpose of [such] schemes is to provide a foundation for more positive measures their adoption should be followed by an increase in employment and activity . . . Even in the preliminary stages of their operation, total employment in the sections concerned will not suffer. The closing of particular mills or works should be offset by increased employment in others which would be able to work nearer to full time.[68]

Although both the Cotton Spinning Act of 1936 and the Cotton Industry (Reorganization) Act which followed in 1939 were designed to facilitate the reduction of industrial capacity, each came too late to be of any major assistance. It is true that structural readjustment in cotton was more apparent in the 1930s than it had been in the 1920s – the number of spindles fell from 60 million in 1924 to only 58 million in 1931, but then fell further to 41.8 million by 1938; likewise the number of looms declined from a total of 792,000 in 1924 to 658,000 in 1931 and to 461,000 by 1938.[69] However, both the cotton entrepreneurs and the government had for too long held out the hope that export markets would revive sufficiently to provide an immediate source of economic betterment. The enforced adjustment to market conditions in the 1930s was noteworthy but partial; by 1938 the much reduced capacity was still far from fully employed.

Iron and steel

The chronic depression which affected iron and steel for almost the whole of the twenties resulted largely from an intensification of the competiton from continental Europe and the USA which had beset the industry before 1914. Steel was not in the grip of secular decline; it fed into both rising and declining industries and its record of output in the interwar period compared favourably with that of its European competitors. But it faced an acute problem of overcapacity. The industry was characterized by fragmented ownership and by a degree of integration and size of operation that prevented it from operating at maximum efficiency. Wartime expansion, often on the basis of old existing works, had merely compounded steel's competitive disadvantages.

The boost to trade and demand which the post-war boom gave to the basic trades was shortlived, laying bare in subsequent years inherent problems of high costs, structural deficiencies and problems in marketing.

[68] Joint Committee of Cotton Trade Organisations, *Report by the Executive on Remedial Measures Applicable to Present Position of the Lancashire Cotton Industry*, March 1935.
[69] Kirby, 'The Lancashire Cotton Industry', appendix, 159.

As Britain's share in the world market for steel fell during the twenties, a wide discrepancy emerged between output and productive capacity, compounded by the slow growth in domestic steel demand as stagnation spread to engineering and shipbuilding. With demand and prices falling, unit costs increased as profits declined. A simultaneous process of contraction and modernization was required. However, the industry was characterized by a multiplicity of firms, smallness of plant and pattern of location which hindered structural reorganization and technical reconditioning. In addition, the proliferation of cartel and price-fixing arrangements which developed within it down to 1931 acted as a further obstacle to structural change.

By the second half of the decade many steel companies found themselves increasingly dependent upon the goodwill of their banks to avoid liquidation. Overdrafts had been freely given during the brief post-war boom and, as in cotton textiles, further lending became necessary to support the original advances. At first bankers acted defensively, nursing their loans until, as we have seen, there emerged a new relationship between finance and industry with the establishment of the Bank of England's Securities Management Trust (SMT) in 1929 and the Bankers' Industrial Development Company (BIDC) a year later.

Determined to pre-empt government aid for industrial rationalization, which it viewed as a dangerous first step towards bringing industry under state control, the Bank of England became involved in large steel restructuring projects. The SMT played a pivotal role in the reorganization of Armstrong Whitworth, hiving off their extensive iron and steel interests to the English Steel Corporation and the Lancashire Steel Corporation, whilst the bank became embroiled in plans to build a large-scale Bessemer plant at Corby in the east midlands. But the Bank's insistence on the promotion of widespread amalgamations frequently conflicted with management's wish to pursue more limited policies of modernization (as in Lancashire Steel), whilst its fear that extensive developments elsewhere (as at Corby) could compromise its own blueprint for reorganization drove it to curtail such ventures to sub-optimal levels. Devoid of the industrial or managerial expertise to devise flexible strategies of reorganization or to shoulder the burdens of entrepreneurial leadership, the bank was increasingly driven towards the defence of traditional financial practice. As Tolliday points out, to Governor Montagu Norman, 'the SMT and the BIDC were all ultimately committed to profoundly orthodox economics which left no space for the idea of absorbing short-term losses for long-term advantages'.[70]

---

[70]   S. Tolliday, 'Steel and Rationalization Policies, 1918–1950', in *The Decline of the British Economy*, ed. Elbaum and Lazonick, 83.

If the banks were reluctant to act as a coherent force for rationalization so too were the steelmakers. Scottish entrepreneurs, for example, remained convinced that the nature of the raw materials indigenous to particular districts, together with the specific demands of local steel-consuming industries, particularly shipbuilding, called for flexibility and for the preservation of small-scale units in the face of a hostile market environment. Thoroughgoing reorganization within the industry, most steel entrepreneurs agreed, had to await more favourable economic and trading conditions. Meanwhile, piecemeal cost-reducing improvements which offered some amelioration of immediate distress would be sought in preference to regional amalgamations.[71]

Apart from a severe loss of exports in the twenties, iron and steel also suffered increased foreign competition in the home market. The volume of imports from 1924 to 1931 annually exceeded the pre-war maximum of 2.2 million tons, and in 1927 was twice as high. To some it seemed essential, therefore, to check the flood of steel imports via tariff protection before large-scale reconstruction could be seriously considered.[72] At first the government favoured active rationalization to defensive protectionism; it was not entirely convinced that a monopolized home market protected from high import penetration was required before costs could be reduced and reorganization made feasible. Governments in the late twenties believed that tariff protection could actually hinder rationalization by bolstering inefficient production, reducing competition, distorting investment and raising prices and profits. Rather than risk being held directly responsible for such developments Ministers insisted that reorganization should precede any state aid to steel.[73] Thus, both the Conservative and Labour administrations strove purposely during 1925 to 1931 to foster rationalization via merger and amalgamation, to eliminate excess capacity and to lower costs through increased capacity utilization.

However, the question of whether private schemes of reorganization would emerge within the industry and produce the anticipated results at the level of the plant and the firm was rarely asked, let alone answered. But improving long-term employment prospects within a revitalized steel industry was never much of a real possibility. In most of the firms there were conflicting and overlapping interests hindering the emergence of desirable strategies. The lack of a single centre of power within the industry was

[71] N. Buxton, 'Efficiency and Organization in Scotland's Iron and Steel Industry during the Interwar Period', *Economic History Review*, 2nd ser., 29 (1976), 107–24.

[72] For fuller discussion see S. Tolliday, 'Tariffs and Steel, 1916–1934: The Politics of Industrial Decline', in *Businessmen and Politics*, ed. Turner, 50–75 and Tolliday, *Business, Banking and Politics. The Case of British Steel, 1918–1939* (Harvard, 1987).

[73] See chapter 6.

mirrored by the absence of any effective political lobby amongst steel industrialists.[74]

Even when import duties arrived in 1932 they were regarded as insufficient in themselves to foster a thoroughgoing regeneration of industry. Although granting tariff protection to steel was originally designed to encourage industrial reorganization, it had not been made conditional upon it. Officials at the Treasury and the Bank of England feared that tariffs would actually hinder reorganization unless protection remained temporary. Yet the government acquiesced in pleas for tariff renewal for a further two years from October 1932, given the vague assurances from the industry that planned reconstruction would follow. But the National Committee established within steel to produce reorganization proposals proved unable to suppress the power of vested and conflicting interests and spent much of its time during 1932–33 devising stronger industry-wide price associations as a means of reducing competition rather than formulating any reasoned scheme of industrial reorganization. The Committee warned that the work of reconstruction would be 'a process of evolution' and not one which could be 'completed at a stroke'. Its success, moreover, would depend not upon the operation of rigid centralized authority, but upon the continuation of adequate protection in the home market and 'the vigour and single-mindedness' of steelmakers.[75]

National reorganization, however, proved an unattractive prospect both to the expanding steel firms and to the backward and depressed ones; each wished to strengthen its own autonomy and monopoly position within the existing industrial structure. The government was forced to compromise. Having refused to introduce compulsory powers in an effort to enforce structural change, it acknowledged that tariff protection for steel would need to stay as a first line of defence against worsening trade and employment. Since the government regarded the industrialists as being better equipped to run the industry than were Whitehall officials, it sponsored a cartel over which it had little control. The tariff proved singularly inadequate as an instrument of industrial reconstruction and as a consequence the steel industry was able to operate in the 1930s much for its own private ends, the more so once it joined the European Steel Cartel in 1935.

This benign neglect of the fundamental problems facing the industry

---

[74] Tolliday, 'Tariffs and Steel', 56–9.

[75] The struggle between the Import Duties Advisory Committee, established to report on the progress of protected industries, and the National Committee in the steel industry to secure practical progress towards industrial reconstruction during the 1930s is detailed in Sir Hubert Hutchinson, *Tariff Making and Industrial Reconstruction* (1965).

illustrated the inherent difficulty of trying to impose a comprehensive programme of reconstruction upon a large sector without a wide measure of public control. Neither the clearing banks nor the Bank of England was inclined to use financial leverage to achieve effective reorganization; the government similarly lacked the will to intervene positively. In the absence of organized intervention the interests of individual producers were allowed to take priority over the needs of the industry as a whole. And yet, although 'effective' reorganization was thereby retarded, so too, as with coal, was the high social cost of increased short-term unemployment.

Shipbuilding

The condition of British shipbuilding in the 1920s, like that of other basic sectors, stood in direct contrast to the experience of the war years and to the progress achieved before 1914. British shipyards had built around 60 per cent of the world's tonnage before the First World War and the need to replace war losses and to build new types of ships kept activity and employment buoyant down to 1918. The substantial rise in shipping freight rates during the short-lived postwar boom raised the price of existing ships and encouraged owners to place orders for new ones. British yards launched the greatest tonnage of shipping in the history of their industry in 1920 and in March 1921 the tonnage under construction exceeded the pre-war maximum.

But the reduction in the volume of international trade between 1920 and 1925 reduced the demand for new ships and a serious problem of over-capacity arose. British shipbuilding capacity had increased by about 25 per cent during the war. During the immediate post-war period investment increased further both in Europe and America. By 1923 world mercantile tonnage had risen to 65.2 million tons compared with 49.1 million tons in 1914. This proved far in excess of what was required in the early 1920s to carry the volume of goods moved by sea.

Persistent over-supply and the difficulties of competing with overseas countries placed Britain in an unenviable position. Her share of world shipping production fell from its pre-war level of 60 per cent to 49 per cent in 1922–25, rising to 53 per cent in 1927–30. Although this latter improvement reflected the rapid recovery of world shipping during the late twenties, Britain proved unable to recover her pre-war position in output and exports. By the end of the decade, writes Slaven, 'the high levels of war time production and profitability had evaporated, leaving an industry that was over-extended in capacity, over-capitalised in relation to the earning power of its assets, and over-priced in relation to its continental competitors'.[76] World slump in 1930 severely damaged international trade and further intensified depression in the industry. The volume of gross registered tons launched in the UK as a percentage of world output, which had fallen from 64 per cent in 1924 to 51 per cent in 1930, fell further to only 27 per cent in 1933, sufficient in the latter year to employ only 5,000 men.[77] At no time during the twenties was unemployment in shipbuilding less than twice the recorded national average. It reached 43.6 per cent of the insured workforce in 1923 and at its lowest point in 1927 stood at 22.3 per cent. Almost two-thirds of the industry's insured labour force were idle in 1933. Although shipbuilding revived as the world climbed out of depression, both British output and exports during 1937–38, at least of merchant ships, were below their 1929–30 levels.

Governments were not unmindful of the plight of British shipbuilders in the 1920s – the industry, for example, received favourable treatment under the Trade Facilities scheme – but they relied ultimately upon a revival of Empire and foreign trade to boost the industry's fortunes. Both the Conservative administration in 1925 and the Labour government in 1929 considered assisting the scrapping of obsolete tonnage but made little progress. Despite the immense difficulties before them, few shipyards were ready to cease operation and it was left to the industry itself to try to accelerate a reduction in shipbuilding capacity.

A Shipbuilders' Conference in 1928 considered organizing a fund for the purpose of purchasing redundant yards. In the following year Sir Andrew Duncan, then a Director of the Court of the Bank of England, raised with Montagu Norman the possibility of finance being made available in advance of any accumulated fund to facilitate the elimination of surplus berths. Shipbuilders' representatives met the Governor and appealed for a long-term loan of around £2 million.

Both the shipbuilders and the Bank of England favoured a thoroughgoing scheme of liquidation aimed at removing redundant and financially parlous yards and agreed in 1930 to the formation of National Shipbuilders' Security Ltd. Shipbuilders who became members of the new company[78] covenanted to pay NSS a levy of 1 per cent on the price of vessels commenced after 1 November 1930 in order to facilitate by purchase and closure a reduction of capacity to meet anticipated demands.

---

[76] A. Slaven, 'Self-Liquidation: the National Shipbuilders' Security Ltd. and the Rationaliz-ation of British Shipbuilding in the 1930s', in *Chartered and Unchartered Waters*, ed. S. Palmer and G. Williams (1982), 127; Slaven, 'British Shipbuilders: Market Trends and Order-Book Patterns Between the Wars', *Journal of Transport History*, 3 (1982), 37–61.

[77] J. R. Parkinson, 'Shipbuilding', in *British Industry Between the Wars*, ed. Buxton and Aldcroft, 81–2.

[78] The company was registered on 27 February 1930 with an authorised capital of £10,000 but with borrowing powers of up to £3 million.

Most operations were completed by 1935. In all, some 1.4 million tons of shipbuilding capacity were sterilized, involving 38 yards – more than one-third of the capacity of the entire industry.[79] The effect was to increase the workload available to those remaining, enabling the burden of the 1 per cent levy to be met. But with demand so low the industry's capacity remained far in excess of requirements. Operating costs were hardly reduced. The effect of diverting orders into fewer yards, moreover, meant permanent closure for others. Such closures had a devastating effect on particular localities, adding a new shock-wave to the depression of the thirties. Indeed, had the industry attempted to form NSS in the later thirties, when regional unemployment had become a more discernible issue of political concern, there would doubtless have been considerable pressure to curtail its development.

The National Government did a little to ease the plight of the industry. In 1935 it introduced a 'scrap and build' scheme for the construction of tramp shipping under which Treasury loans were made available to shipowners on favourable terms if they undertook to scrap two tons of existing tonnage for every one ton built. Having already agreed in 1934 to subsidize the construction of the *Queen Mary* and the *Queen Elizabeth* for transatlantic service, the government also agreed to assist tramp shipping by direct subsidy and to encourage owners to avail themselves of the limited finance available. Direct subsidies, however, discouraged the scrapping of tonnage. As in coal, the government almost ensured by default that progress towards self-induced revival would be hesitant and limited. In any event, the problems of persistent overcapacity and severe competition were too widespread to be overcome so easily. And the will to overcome them was not always there. Despite the severity of insured unemployment in the industry, seldom falling below 20 per cent during the interwar period, there was often stern resistance on the part of employees to any remedial policy which upset existing working practices. Labour demarcation was rife, strengthened by a legacy of sub-contracting.

RATIONALIZATION IN RETROSPECT

It is clear from the foregoing that there were innumerable obstacles in the way of rationalization ever making much progress in the fight against structural unemployment in the basic industries. Governments on the whole feared being held directly responsible for the unemployment consequences of industrial reconstruction. They exhausted the due processes of enquiry and consultation, but rarely considered coercing private

---

[79] Slaven, in *Chartered and Unchartered Waters*, ed. Palmer and Williams, 136.

industrialists, preferring instead to await the formulation and execution of plans from within industry itself. Industrialists on the other hand remained sceptical of the assumed benefits to be derived from greater amalgamation and were often reluctant to bear the cost of reviving weaker firms for the benefit of industry as a whole. The intense individualism which character-ized producers in coalmining, shipbuilding, iron and steel and textiles seriously retarded plans for industrial reorganization or the rationalization of capacity. Conflicts between rival interests within firms and the diffusion of decision-making powers proved to be a serious hindrance in steel. Elsewhere, in coal and cotton textiles for example, there was no effective way of securing joint action by industry as a whole. Employers in the staple industries remained openly hostile to planned reorganization. Few were prepared to relinquish managerial control over their enterprises. As a general rule they had neither the incentive to participate in nor the ability to promote enforced reconstruction. Many businessmen remained sceptical of the assumed relationship between size and efficiency, doubtful that the managerial problems of large scale production could easily be overcome. As a result, traditional methods of operation within such industries remained virtually intact throughout the interwar period.

A more fundamental reason why so little was achieved by way of rehabilitating the staple trades was the recurring idea that there was within them some simple defect of organization that could be cured by a simple measure of reform. The rationalization movement of the 1920s reflected the belief that reliance upon the 'invisible' hand of market forces was a costly and risky means of correcting the perceived failures of the capitalist economy. Excess capacity led to price cutting which destroyed profits without stimulating demand. Real improvement, it was therefore assumed, required some form of consistent, centrally co-ordinated policy pursued over a period of years. However, this merely intensified the confusion within government as to whether it should be facilitating the long-term re-construction of industry or meeting the crisis needs of depressed trades by short-term palliatives. The dilemma was clearly identified by Mosley. 'The confusion between long term planning and short term unemployment schemes arising from our failure to divide two quite distinctive objectives in our minds', he wrote in 1930, 'is responsible for a policy which in one sphere is ill-considered and dangerous, and in the other sphere is hesitant and ineffective.'[80] Lloyd George too recognized that in the absence of co-ordinated planning on a national scale most worthy schemes of industrial reconstruction would wither. 'Financial stringency has doubtless combined with lethargic administration to hold up progress', he noted in 1935. 'The

---

[80] Cab 24/209, CP 31, Unemployment Policy. Copy of a letter from Sir Oswald Mosley to the Prime Minister, 23 January 1930.

interests of national industry demand that the situation should be tackled without delay'. His preferred solution was the establishment of a National Development Board to act as a controlling and co-ordinating authority responsible for a measured degree of planned reconstruction in iron and steel, coal, cotton and shipbuilding. The state would determine what industrial developments were desirable and under cover of its guarantee would direct capital resources to such productive uses.[81] But it was precisely the spread of such control and responsibility that Ministers were anxious to avoid. The attendant difficulties were spelled out in an official reply to Lloyd George:

If the state takes the initiative and, above all, if in taking the initiative it holds out the attractiveness of public subsidies or wields the weapon of compulsion, voluntary reorganisation will cease, for the private *entrepreneur* will naturally sit back and await the State decision likely to be thrust upon him.

Not that the state would have no part to play in the matter. Results would come 'not by compulsion, nor yet by bribing businesses into plans in which they had little or no part', but rather by stimulating spontaneous development 'through varying methods fitted to the actual circumstances of each case'.[82]

The idea of rationalization was thereby able to be interpreted in whatever way best suited the limited needs and aspirations of the participants – from a planned reduction in unit costs through amalgamation, to the pursuit of monopoly pricing power via marketing agreements, to the co-ordinated scrapping of redundant capacity, the broad significance of which remained sufficiently ambiguous in each case as to stifle any speedy or effective progress. Moreover, by attempting to reverse a long-term loss of industrial competitiveness during a period of intense economic contraction the reconstruction programme put the pursuit of increased efficiency directly at odds with the need to protect employment and profitability in the declining sectors. Consequently governments chose to deal with specific industries on a case-by-case, non-coercive basis, treating them as specific instances of depression. This gave rise to ill-directed and unco-ordinated policies which lacked authority or perception and which often generated programmes to shelter the depressed sectors by protecting them from the losses of internal competition. Although this hindered the remedial processes which the various policies were designed to promote, it saved many workers from having to suffer immediate unemployment as the 'inevitable' price of safeguarding jobs in the future.

[81] Cab 24/254, CP 59A, Revised Text of Mr. Lloyd George's Memorandum on Unemployment, 12 July 1935.
[82] Cab 24/256, CP 150, Statement by His Majesty's Government on Certain Proposals Submitted to them by Mr. Lloyd George, 19 July 1935.

The idea of restoring competitive prosperity through increased efficiency gained currency in the late twenties but soon disappeared as a deliberate object of policy. It was quickly replaced after 1930 by the more urgent desire to check mounting unemployment within the basic trades. Attention was directed therefore to the adoption of restrictive practices as a prelude to any thoroughgoing reorganization. The reluctance of the National Government to abandon its *ad hoc* approach to industrial revitalization was illustrated by its stern opposition to Lord Melchett's 1935 Enabling Bill which sought to permit any industry in which the majority supported a reorganization scheme to obtain the necessary administrative powers to compel the support of the minority. The result was that public attempts at rationalization 'left British industry with the worst aspects of both competitive and monopolistic worlds. Productive structure remained highly fragmented and inefficient, while quasi-cartelization and tariff barriers . . . protected existing producers from competitive pressure. Rather than achieving its objective of promoting . . . rationalization, interwar policy inadvertently reinforced pre-existing institutional rigidities'.[83] Indeed, by sponsoring self-governing producers' associations, as in steel and coal, the National Government effectively reduced its power to exhort such industries by persuasion to alter their increasingly anachronistic industrial structures.

Although this pragmatic approach helped to delay the deterioration in unemployment which could have followed from a more abrasive and successful industrial 'shake-out', it did nothing to foster economic progress within the depressed areas, which remained disadvantaged in the absence of any external stimulus to recovery. What is striking about the official attempts to revive industrial prosperity is the absence of any coherent strategy for fostering greater diversification through the active stimulation of new enterprises. 'Unemployment cannot be resolved merely by Rationalisation of our basic trades', Mosley warned the Cabinet in 1930, 'a great necessity evidently exists for the promotion and encouragement of new trades . . . By some means or other we must secure a mobilisation of the wealth of scientific intelligence in this country for the capture of a leading position'.[84] New industrial developments were being hindered, he argued, not only by inadequate scientific and industrial research, but also by deficiencies in the industrial banking system which created a 'hiatus . . . between the short-term credit on collateral security and the long-term loan market'.

Yet although the Bank of England became involved in the later 1930s in the creation of the Special Areas Reconstruction Association to help

[83] B. Elbaum and W. Lazonick, 'The Decline of the British Economy: An Institutional Perspective', *Journal of Economic History*, 44 (1984), 579–80.
[84] Cab 27/418, The State and Rationalization. Note by Sir Oswald Mosley, 29 March 1930.

promote industrial diversification in the depressed areas, it remained intent, as it had done in previous dealings with the rationalization of the older basic industries, upon preserving the limited relationship between the banks and industry. It continued to avoid any substantial involvement in the problems of industry, preferring instead to act only to forestall such government intervention in industrial affairs as was thought would interfere with ordinary market mechanisms. The policy measures which emerged from SARA proved relatively ineffective, offering only partial aid to small, diverse light industries rather than to new industries proper.[85]

Nor were these the only obstacles in the way of easing chronic unemployment by measures of industrial revitalization. No effective agency existed to co-ordinate government policy towards industry. What was required at best was a determination by central government, industry and the banks to face the political, financial, administrative and social implications of trying to improve Britain's economic and labour market crisis through a radical transformation of its industrial structure. It was the conspicuous absence of such political will that allowed the endemic problems of the 'old' industries to remain largely unresolved between the wars and the full potential of the newer growth sectors to be discovered only in a subsequent generation. Meanwhile, regions heavily dependent upon the basic export trades were forced to bear the burden of unemployment to a considerably greater degree than elsewhere; it is to the remaining policies government adopted on their behalf that we now turn.

[85] For further discussion see chapter 9.

9 ✳ *Uneven development: regional policy, labour transference and industrial diversification*

It is clear from the evidence presented so far that interwar Britain faced a major problem of economic adjustment. Even before 1914 her relative share of world production and trade in manufactured goods had begun to decline; after the First World War she faced the added problem of an absolute stagnation in staple exports. For years past, Britain had lagged behind her major rivals in the development of those industrial sectors gaining the fastest hold in world markets (namely engineering, metal manufacturing, vehicles and chemicals). The potential for revitalizing uncompetitive and technologically backward industries by deliberate schemes of rationalization and reorganization was never fully realized; nor as we have seen would it have proved in itself a sufficient remedy, even at its best.

As chapter 1 indicated, the clearest manifestation of this struggle to contain the secular decline of traditional trades was to be found in the varying fortunes of Britain's oldest industrial regions. Their nineteenth-century developments had been based primarily upon a high degree of localization and specialization in precisely those sectors hardest hit by the post-1920 depression. Unemployment in areas such as Northumberland, Durham, Lancashire and Cheshire, Wales and Scotland remained disproportionately high throughout the interwar period, both in absolute terms and relative to the more favoured areas of the midlands and the south. In 1924 over 83 per cent of the net value of total cotton spinning production and 88 per cent of cotton weaving was to be found in Lancashire; in the same year that region, together with those of Northumberland, Durham, the North Riding of Yorkshire, Wales and Scotland, were responsible in total for almost 65 per cent of the net value of total coal production, 56 per cent of iron smelting and rolling, 47 per cent of mechanical engineering and 75 per cent of shipbuilding.[1] Ministry of Labour data on fluctuations in the number of insured persons during the period 1923–37 (as a percentage of

---

[1] C. Heim, 'Uneven Development in Interwar Britain', Ph.D. Thesis, Yale University (1982), 90.

240

1923) show that of the sectors suffering a decline in numbers some 86 per cent of the total was accounted for by the coal, shipbuilding and ship repairing, cotton and iron and steel industries, themselves heavily concentrated in particular regions.[2]

During periods of depressed economic activity, therefore, regions which contained a larger share of declining industries suffered particularly badly. But their plight did not occasion any systematic search for a discriminatory regional policy as such. Centres such as Birmingham, Coventry and London experienced severe unemployment during the collapse of the post-war boom during 1920–22 without any suggestion that they would remain permanently debilitated. And although the struggle of local authorities to contain the financial burden of rapidly rising unemployment spawned persistent demands down to 1927 for central government aid for 'distressed' and 'necessitous' areas, their special pleading achieved little of substance. The Exchequer remained fearful of relieving Poor Law Guardians of their existing financial responsibilities, given the prevailing cost of the national insurance scheme and the perceived threat which any intervention on behalf of needy areas posed to the structure of local government finance.[3]

Likewise, there was little enthusiasm before 1928 for relieving local authorities of any major part of the contributory cost of public works on behalf of the unemployed. Both the relief works programme and the policy towards Poor Law finance had to conform to the government's minimalist stance, pending the return of cyclical recovery. New manufacturing industries and services already established in the south and the midlands, moreover, tended to utilize locally available sources of labour and capital to meet the needs of a growing market, without ever having to consider the industrial needs of the more disadvantaged areas.[4] So long as it was believed that the recovery of the more depressed areas lay in the revival of staple exports, ideally through systematic reductions in unit costs and by appropriate measures to reduce dislocations in international trade and currency, the government felt little compunction to introduce discriminatory policies on their behalf.

STRUCTURAL UNEMPLOYMENT AND THE ORIGINS OF LABOUR
TRANSFERENCE

The emergence of intense structural unemployment in the late twenties wrecked this complacency. A somewhat bland statement in the Ministry of

---

[2] Royal Commission on the Distribution of the Industrial Population, Minutes of Evidence, 1937–39, 292–4. See also S. Dennison, *The Location of Industry and the Depressed Areas* (1939).   [3] See above chapter 1.   [4] Heim, 'Uneven Development', 136.

Labour's Report for the Year 1927 pointed ominously to the emerging problem. 'There is some ground for thinking', it noted, 'that the problems of employment and unemployment which have revealed themselves during the year ought to be considered, not merely as residual difficulties of the war period, but as problems of a new industrial and commercial era.'[5] One striking manifestation of this 'new era' was the concentration in particular industries and areas of a substantial volume of labour surplus to productive needs.

The situation was particularly acute in the coalmining industry. By March 1927 the national unemployment rate had fallen below that of December 1925 and December 1924. At the time coal was the only major industry with increasing unemployment and the outlook was bleak. Rising productivity within the industry had enabled the average rate of output to hold up even in the face of job losses; this bode ill for employment prospects in the near future given any reasonable estimate of the market demand for coal, especially in those coalfields which were not, as Lancashire for example was, contiguous with larger industrial areas offering some meagre hope of alternative work. Steps had already been taken towards shifting the balance of demand for and supply of labour in the industry. Section 18 of the Mining Industry Act, 1926 restricted employment in mines (except for boys) to those already in the industry in April 1926. In addition, training schemes for unemployed miners began in 1925 as a means of promoting emigration and overseas settlement.[6] And it was in 1926 that the Minister of Labour urged the need 'to restore the fluidity of the labour market' by encouraging the dispersal of surplus mining labour to other less stricken areas.[7]

The potential for distributing unemployment more evenly across the country was not lost on Baldwin's government. It established an Industrial Transference Board in January 1928 with a seemingly self-evident purpose. 'Until recently', the Board declared,

national policy has assumed that industries and areas would return, broadly speaking, to the position they held before the war; and unemployment policy has been largely one of 'tide-over', the aim being to maintain the labour force required for the industries in the areas in which they were normally conducted in a state as free as possible from demoralisation . . . However . . . our considered opinion is that from now onwards the first aim of policy should be the dispersal of the heavy

---

[5] Report of the Ministry of Labour for the Year 1927, Cmd. 3090, 1928, 13–14.
[6] J. Sheldrake and S. Vickerstaff, *The History of Industrial Training in Britain* (1987), chapter 3. Until 1925 government activity in this field had been limited primarily to providing training for ex-servicemen and to supporting industry's efforts to encourage the growth of apprenticeship.
[7] Report of the Ministry of Labour for the Year 1926, Cmd. 2856, 1927, 23. Cf. a similar appeal by Sir Alfred Mond in a letter to *The Times*, 21 November 1927.

concentration of unemployment by the active encouragement of movement from the depressed areas to other areas, both in this country and overseas.

Nothing therefore should be done to hinder the process of voluntary migration. Relief works which held out 'an illusory prospect of employment' in depressed areas should be avoided; likewise, the administration of poor relief and unemployment benefit should be monitored so as not to weaken artificially 'the economic stimulus to transfer'. After all, there was little risk to those already in jobs. As the Board explained:

There is a ceaseless ebb and flow of employment, and at all times the employed personnel is constantly changing. Each man taken on is adding to a flowing stream, not driving another out of a space of fixed dimension. The existence of local unemployment does not make it unnecessary or uneconomic to bring labour in from other areas. It is quite normal to find simultaneously in the same area unemployment and an unsatisfied demand for labour, because the labour available is not suitable for the vacancies . . . In drawing upon the depressed areas for their workpeople, employers need not fear that they are being called upon to subordinate economic efficiency to sentiment.

On the contrary, there were substantial gains to be had. It was:

positively uneconomic, to judge it from this standpoint alone, to leave in areas where a trade revival is unlikely, a reserve of labour which could be made available for industrial development in areas where general trade activity is much more brisk.[8]

Although its terms of reference were broader, the Transference Board chose from the outset to concentrate on the 'tragic problem' of the coal industry. The difference between the existing insured workforce and the number who could count with any certainty upon obtaining their livelihood within the industry was put at upwards of 200,000 men, a surplus unlikely to be affected by any of the existing schemes for controlling labour supply. But transference posed particular problems, however laudable in aim. Coalminers had a strong, almost immutable, tradition of local community. Industries that required heavy labour, moreover, were not expanding fast enough to absorb the available labour surplus; those that were expanding, such as artificial silk, printing, electrical engineering and motor manufacture, had low labour–output ratios.

Nonetheless, the severity of depression in the coalfields kept transference high on the political agenda. By the time the official report of the Transference Board appeared in June 1928, unemployment in coal mining had reached 25.7 per cent, two-and-a-half times the national rate. Furthermore, the increased duration of unemployment amongst miners, combined with levels of insurance benefit which were by no means

[8] Cmd. 3156, paras. 35–6, 45–6.

generous, had publicized evidence of need – of children apparently lacking clothes, shoes and even food – the impact of which was heightened by its concentration within isolated, almost forgotten communities.

Charitable responses laid bare both the capacity of local authorities to cope and the paucity of government remedial policy. In April 1928, only weeks after emotive revelations in *The Times* of social deprivation amongst the unemployed in Durham and south Wales, the Lord Mayors of Cardiff, Newcastle and London appealed for contributions to a Lord Mayors' Fund to assist women and children in mining areas. The government had long argued that it was for voluntary agencies alone to alleviate the worst manifestations of local distress whilst Ministers worked to promote economic betterment for all. But public disquiet was mounting. Despite Treasury misgivings, the Cabinet agreed to make a pound for pound grant towards the cost of feeding schoolchildren in the worst stricken areas of Wales and Durham. More generally, there seemed little option but to encourage even greater voluntary migration. 'The only alternative', the Minister of Labour Steel-Maitland reminded his Cabinet colleagues in November 1928, 'is to continue to maintain the surplus by some form of State relief, while it is slowly driven out by economic pressure. This alternative is uneconomical and wrong in itself and politically impossible to sustain.'[9]

As Ministers gradually lost faith in the recuperative powers of the market, labour transference was embraced with embarrassing alacrity since the only real alternative was to create jobs for the indigenous workforce in the staple export regions. Public works, truncated in the mid-twenties, were revamped in the autumn of 1928. 'Transfer grants' were made available, offering discriminatory financial aid to relatively more prosperous areas, on condition that a fixed proportion of the labour employed on such projects was drawn from depressed regions.[10] 'The idea lying behind this', the Unemployment Grants Committee informed the Scottish Board of Health, 'is that some of the men should "stick" once the relief works have been completed and so return no more to the impoverished districts whence they came.'[11] In August 1928 Baldwin appealed by letter to 15,000 employers, urging them whenever possible to employ men from areas of excessive unemployment. And together the Admiralty, the Postmaster-General, the

---

[9] Cab 24/198, CP 324, Industrial Transference Scheme. Memorandum by the Minister of Labour, 1 November 1928.
[10] For details of this policy shift see below chapter 11.
[11] Lab 4/183, Correspondence with Ministry of Labour in Connection with Schemes Subsequent to Issue of UGC Circular, 19 November 1928, cited in D. Pitfield, 'Labour Migration and the Regional Problem in Britain, 1920–1939', Ph.D. Thesis, University of Stirling (1973), 165.

First Commissioner of Works and the Secretaries of State for War and Air pleaded for government contractors to respond in a similar fashion.

Such appeals were scarcely able in themselves to foster labour mobility on anything like the required scale. Yet the speed with which social conditions were deteriorating in certain parts of the country made the search for a more effective transference policy all the more urgent. In the hardest hit areas of south Wales, the Minister of Health informed the Cabinet's Distressed Areas Committee in December 1928:

> the food with which people are now able to provide themselves is insufficient to keep the workers in a fit condition to take up work when this is made available . . . The morale of the people appears to be suffering from this state of affairs and from a long continuance of lounging about in idleness. The only permanent policy which is of any real use is to get the people away from the workless areas.[12]

A Household Removal Scheme, introduced in the same month, sought to boost the transference programme by avoiding the break up of families. Grants were paid towards the lodging expenses of transferred males and towards the cost of removing their dependants. But even this initiative had limited application. Most transferees were young, single men. Moreover, financial aid was confined to depressed mining areas at a time when transference policy, in principle at least, was meant to apply equally to declining iron and steel and shipbuilding areas.

The major responsibility for improving the scope and vitality of transference fell upon the second Labour administration. It was abundantly clear by the end of the twenties that bolder action would be required to maintain the momentum of policy. Although the demands of receiving areas for labour were growing as a result of the programme of transfer relief works the supply of mobile labour was falling off. To stimulate the programme a norm of two months was set, after which labour was to be discharged from such work to provide openings for other transferees. Transfer Instructional Centres, originally established in May 1929 to assist men who found physical work too demanding after periods of unemployment, were increased in number at the end of 1930 in an effort to forestall the decline in the quality of labour. As an additional boost to labour supply the five counties of Lanark, Northumberland, Durham, Glamorgan and Monmouth were included in the transference scheme from September 1929. Other beleaguered areas in Lancashire, Cheshire, Yorkshire and Derbyshire were subsequently brought within the scope of the juvenile transference scheme (in March 1930) and the adult scheme (in June 1930).

[12] Cab 27/381, Distressed Areas Committee. Report, 15 December 1928.

Beyond this, the Household Removal Scheme was extended to people on short-time or in temporary employment and the period of the payment of grants increased to allow a longer search for accommodation. And from October 1929 grants in aid of wages from the Lord Mayors' Fund were amended to encourage a greater migration of younger boys under the age of 16.

THE DEPRESSED AREAS AND THE WORLD SLUMP, 1930–32

Intense depression during 1930 forced other changes in policy as antipathy towards transference grew in potential receiving areas. Local authorities outside the depressed regions began to complain of the difficulty of providing work even for their own unemployed let alone that for transferred men, while trade unionists feared the effects that labour transference might have upon the prevailing level of wage rates. The Labour government responded by permitting all local authorities to become eligible for maximum UGC 'transfer grants' from June 1930. At the same time the condition that a proportion of men from the depressed areas had to be employed on relief works was waived. As a result, though total employment on public works schemes increased (albeit to still insignificant levels in comparison with the total volume of registered unemployment) the beneficial effects on the staple export regions were significantly weakened.

World recession did little to diminish the Labour government's faith in labour transference as an effective means of stemming regional and structural decline. But as unemployment intensified during the cyclical downturn of the early thirties, so too did the 'natural' obstacles to voluntary migration – distance, age, sex, skill and family ties. Despite earlier attempts to raise the quantity and quality of men offering themselves for transfer many of the unemployed resisted the pressure to move. In coalmining districts the strongly developed sense of home and community proved an enduring obstacle. Miners saw little point in seeking an opening in an unfamiliar industry and locale, possibly at a lower level of skill, without any guarantee of success. And once unemployment began to afflict the relatively prosperous trades, the consequent reduction in the flow of vacancies made migration appear an even less attractive proposition since only the most employable workers could risk a move.

The cyclical fall in voluntary migration revived criticism of the unemployment insurance scheme. By cushioning declines in employment, critics argued, the prevailing scale and availability of benefits removed the financial penalties of workers refusing to relocate, thereby immobilizing labour in declining trades and communities. Employers, moreover, were accused of worsening the situation by arranging spells of unemployment in such a way as to afford their workforce the maximum entitlement to benefit that prevailing rules would allow. Steel-Maitland, Conservative Minister of Labour, put it thus:

In a few areas there are considerable aggregations of men who are becoming demoralised by long idleness at the public expense, and who will remain in their present condition so long as they can go on drawing benefit (or poor relief where it is given) . . . There is no work for them where they are. The only hope for them is to get work elsewhere . . . but they lack either the fitness or the energy to seek this for themselves, and so long as they can live at the public expense they refuse to take advantage of any forms of help under the training and transference schemes which are continually being pressed upon them.

It was on these grounds that he tried in 1929, without success, to introduce a tighter contribution qualification for the receipt of benefit by the 40,000 or so men without dependants, of whom about 16,000 were to be found in south Wales, Durham and other depressed mining industries. Such people, he argued, 'most need a stimulus to galvanise them out of their inertia . . . and they are the class most easily handled by the Transference Scheme'.[13] But at a time of deepening unemployment there were enormous political and administrative difficulties in trying to boost labour mobility through strategic changes in the benefits system.

With transference so obviously sensitive to cyclical fluctuation, Ministers began to consider alternative means of assisting the depressed areas. Could new industries be persuaded to develop there? The question had been raised in 1929 by Clement Attlee, Labour's Chancellor of the Duchy of Lancaster, and by the Government Chief Industrial Adviser, Sir Horace Wilson.[14] At first MacDonald's administration was sceptical; little could be done to overcome the prejudice of industrialists against the impoverished and uncongenial character of the depressed regions.[15] After all, business and financial interests in Lancashire and the north east had complained that the depletion of capital and amenities in their areas was such as to deter even the most active entrepreneur.[16]

Attlee disagreed. What was required was 'the correlation of industrial development with the other economic activities of the state', including if necessary the planning and direction of the future industrial location. 'There is', he judged:

[13] Cab 24/202, CP 63, Unemployment Insurance. Memorandum by the Minister of Labour, 2 March 1929. Cf. above chapter 2, pp. 50–1.
[14] See Cab 27/390, Inter-Departmental Committee on Unemployment. New Industries in Depressed Areas. Memorandum by Sir Horace Wilson, 13 July 1929.
[15] Cab 27/219, UP (30) 42, Panel of Ministers on Unemployment. Notes on the Problems of the Depressed Areas, 16 December 1930.
[16] Cab 27/440, UP (30) 58, Panel of Ministers on Unemployment. Industrial Development in Depressed Areas. Note by President of Board of Trade, 2 February 1931.

a sense throughout the industrial world of the inevitability of change, and a remarkable willingness on the part of industrialists to co-operate in attempting the solution of national difficulties, and to accept guidance by the State.[17]

In his view depressed areas were endowed with raw materials, skilled labour, and transport and communication facilities upon which industrialists would readily draw; what they needed was positive encouragement. Similar sentiments were expressed by G. D. H. Cole, a member of the Economic Advisory Council. But when in June 1932 the Council reported on the feasibility of establishing an independent research organization to promote new industrial development for the sake of creating additional employment in declining areas and elsewhere, it rejected the idea as unnecessary and distracting.[18] Yet two years earlier an analysis of structural unemployment by the economist G. C. Allen had emphasized the extent to which industrial diversity had enabled one of Britain's oldest industrialized areas – the west midlands – to counter the depression. 'Where the prospective advantages of alternative sites to the manufacturer do not differ substantially', he wrote:

it would be reasonable for the government to tilt the balance so as to favour the creation of diversified areas by diverting new industries to places at present highly specialised. A national policy of industrial location would thus have as its purpose both the alleviation of heavy localised unemployment and also the shaping of industrial centres which would be less vulnerable in times of change than the old specialised regions have shown themselves to be during the last decade.[19]

Few in government were prepared even to contemplate let alone implement such a policy. Given the widespread intensification of unemployment there was little compunction to introduce measures favouring one region at the expense of another and even less to interfere with the investment decisions of private industrialists. The Chief Industrial Adviser to the Board of Trade, writing in 1931, expressed a generally held sentiment:

There are obvious objections to any suggestion that coercive powers might be taken to regulate the flow of new industrial development throughout the country. So long as industry is organised as it is at present on a basis of private enterprise, any attempt compulsorily to dictate location . . . is much more likely to result in stifling new

[17] Cab 58/12, EAC (H) 138, Economic Advisory Council. National Industrial Planning and Development. Memorandum by the Chancellor of the Duchy of Lancaster, 9 February 1931.
[18] Economic Advisory Council. Committee on New Industrial Development. Report, 28 June 1932; Cab 27/440, CP (30) 66, Panel of Ministers on Unemployment. Proposal for Stimulating New Industrial Development. Note by Chancellor of the Duchy of Lancaster, 25 February 1931.
[19] G. C. Allen, 'Labour Transference and the Unemployment Problem', *Economic Journal*, 40 (1930), 242–8.

enterprise altogether than to achieve the object of diverting it to the depressed areas.[20]

It was far better to encourage local initiative and self-reliance. Regional bodies, a Board of Trade memorandum suggested in January 1931, should demonstrate faith in their local areas by advertising and other forms of publicity, and by maintaining lists of available sites and premises for prospective industrialists.[21] But these were the arguments of expediency; put thus, the government could distance itself from the responsibility of alleviating the industrial problems of the depressed areas, and when results proved meagre or non-existent, could point knowingly to the inherent difficulties of implementing remedial action.

Although nascent pleas for an interventionist industrial strategy failed to evoke positive action, they helped nonetheless to sustain official concern over the regional problem. MacDonald's government realized that the longer private enterprise was allowed by benign neglect to ignore the depressed areas, the greater would be the pressure on government to intervene to stem growing unemployment and industrial dereliction. Anxious as ever to avoid such a commitment, the Cabinet empowered the Board of Trade in 1931 to commission local universities in south Wales, Lancashire, Merseyside, the north east and south-west Scotland to survey the range of facilities potentially on offer to new industrial enterprises. An additional survey of Cumberland and Furness was carried out by a team from Manchester University at the request of the local Employment Committee of the Ministry of Labour. The results of these various investigations were published in 1932 and made grim reading.[22] Each of the Board of Trade survey areas displayed a heavy dependence upon declining staple trades and a dearth of expanding industries. Together they accounted for just over 30 per cent of the total insured population in 1931,

[20] BT 56/38/1800. Industrial Development in the Depressed Areas. Report by the Chief Industrial Adviser to the President of the Board of Trade, 1931.

[21] Heim, 'Uneven Development', 401–5. By November 1931 there were 24 local development boards or councils in existence in England and Wales. The policy of encouraging local development agencies continued after the fall of the Labour government. See Cab 27/468, PE (31) 20, Employment Policy Committee. The Depressed Areas and New Industrial Development. Memorandum by the Chief Industrial Adviser, 3 January 1932.

[22] The published results included *An Industrial Survey of South Wales. Made for the Board of Trade by University College of South Wales and Monmouthshire* (1932); *An Industrial Survey of the Lancashire Area, excluding Merseyside. Made for the Board of Trade by the University of Manchester* (1932); *An Industrial Survey of the North-East Coast Area. Made for the Board of Trade by Armstrong College* (1932); *An Industrial Survey of South West Scotland. Made for the Board of Trade by the University of Glasgow* (1932), and *An Industrial Survey of Merseyside. Made for the Board of Trade by the University of Liverpool* (1932). The Cumberland and Furness survey was not published under official auspices. It appeared as J. Jewkes and A. Winterbottom, *An Industrial Survey of Cumberland and Furness: A Study of the Social Implications of Economic Dislocation* (Manchester, 1933).

but had within them almost 45 per cent of the recorded volume of unemployment. It was evident, too, that declining industries deteriorated at a faster rate and growing industries expanded at a slower rate in these areas than in the country as a whole. Lancashire contained 14 per cent of the country's manufacturing employment, but had only 8.2 per cent of its workers employed in industries which had expanded by more than 10 per cent during the years 1923–29. Moreover, ancillary services such as transport and distribution suffered as a consequence of the decline of other key industries, adding to the overall reduction in the level of demand.

National economic policy, the investigators reported, had produced little beneficial relief. Britain's departure from the gold standard had failed to produce any major stimulus to the declining export trades; and, at best, industrial de-rating had been of only marginal significance. Even labour transference appeared to be of waning importance. Between 40 and 50 per cent of persons transferred from Lancashire, south Wales and Scotland during the period 1928–31 had subsequently returned home and there were clear indications that the composition, family circumstances and attitude of those currently unemployed in the areas made them increasingly unable or unwilling to consider migration. The existence of permanent labour surpluses seemed inevitable, amounting perhaps to upwards of 160,000 men in Lancashire, 64,000 in the north east, between 40,000 and 70,000 in south Wales, 90,000 on Merseyside and 100,000 in south-west Scotland.[23]

Poignant though these disclosures were, they proved singularly ineffective in galvanizing support for a more determined attack on regional unemployment. At the time the reports appeared in the summer of 1932, overall unemployment averaged over 24 per cent. The plight of the depressed areas was worse than this composite figure suggested, but the impact of nationwide recession made it increasingly difficult to focus public attention upon their particular needs. In the event, neither the press nor the House of Commons paid much attention to the survey reports, whose almost fatalistic acceptance of prevailing economic conditions merely reinforced the conventional belief that regional recovery could follow only in the wake of national economic revival.

[23] Each total was highly speculative and was based on the variety of factors thought likely to affect the future supply of and demand for labour. The estimates were not strictly comparable. The figure for south-west Scotland related to a future year (1934) nominated as the 'first normal post-crisis year'. In the north east and Merseyside, the figures related to a five-year period after 1931. In south Wales, the total referred to the surplus existing in 1930, while the Lancashire estimate was made on the basis of the level of unemployment prevailing in 1929.

REGIONAL POLICY AT LAST? THE ORIGINS OF THE 1934 SPECIAL
AREAS ACT

The economic recovery which set in during 1933–34 was characterized by
a marked shift in expenditure towards home market consumer durable
goods and as such produced little short-term benefit to the staple export
areas, already harbouring the greater share of long-term unemployment. In
the country as a whole the number of insured workers out of work for
longer than a year rose from approximately 45,000 in September 1929 to
300,000 in September 1931 and to almost 483,000 in May 1933.

With their electoral survival increasingly in doubt, MPs representing
northern industrial areas called repeatedly upon the government to adopt a
more urgent and sympathetic response to the needs of 'Outer Britain'.
Ministers could scarcely claim that they were unaware of the nature of the
problem. There was a volume of factual material to hand. Unemployed
hunger marches during 1932–33 had at the same time raised to public
view the human dimension of regional decline. The government remained
loath, nevertheless, to implement any form of discretionary or interventionist policy to meet what was regarded as an endemic problem of industrial
decline, especially if it threatened domestic economic revival. Neville
Chamberlain cautioned the Commons thus in 1933:

No thoughtful member of the House now believes that the maladjustments which
have brought about this world-wide unemployment are likely to be corrected as
rapidly and completely that we can look forward with any confidence to the
reduction of unemployment to a comparatively small figure within the next ten
years.[24]

In the circumstances, he maintained, the deliberate promotion of industrial
activity in the depressed regions scarcely merited serious discussion; all that
was required was for agencies such as the National Council of Social
Services to continue to oversee the promotion of voluntary rehabilitation
schemes for the unemployed.

This minimalist approach failed, however, to withstand the surge of
public sympathy which arose in the mid-thirties over the plight of the
impoverished unemployed in industrially derelict areas. It is now generally
accepted that the demand for urgent ameliorative action on their behalf
became more strident following the publication of a series of investigative
articles in *The Times* in March 1934 portraying in graphic and emotive
terms the conditions of unemployed miners and their families in the

---

[24] HC Debs., 5th ser., vol. 274, 16 February 1933, cols. 1218–19.

Durham coalfield. The problem of the depressed areas, wrote *The Times* correspondent, was a 'non recurrent' one. It required specific treatment of an 'emergency type', involving perhaps the appointment of a Director of Operations who would be 'the channel and instrument of a concerted effort to rid the land of these terrible pools of idleness'.[25] The message was uncompromising. Within weeks it attracted support from across the social divide as accountants, clergymen and Lords of the Realm appealed in letters to the press for a more positive government response towards chronic long-term unemployment.

This focus of public concern was all the more significant since it followed in the wake of mounting criticism of official unemployment policy. Less orthodox economists and politicians had already launched a vigorous campaign in 1933 in favour of deficit-financed reconstruction on a national scale as an antidote to the persistent underutilization of capital and labour. The threat that this radical perspective posed to the canons of 'sound finance' merely strengthened the government's appeal to economic commonsense, prompting it to denounce any such strategy as dangerously foolhardy. But the chorus of complaint against official policy grew louder and more persistent. Backbench MPs, able led by Harold Macmillan, pressed the government to expand consumption and to increase the price level as a means of raising output, demand and employment. Local authorities also warned of the dangers of complacency. The burden of unemployment relief expenditure necessitated such a high level of rates in the depressed regions, they complained, that industrialists had little or no incentive to plan for recovery. And the situation could only get worse. The introduction of means-tested transitional payments for the long-term unemployed had prompted Public Assistance Committees to award many applicants the maximum amount of benefit available regardless of family resources, as a deliberate and defiant demonstration of their disapproval of government policy.[26]

Official reaction to such criticism was swift but indecisive. MacDonald and Baldwin urged the Minister of Labour at the end of March 1934 to consider the appointment of Commissioners for the depressed areas with executive powers to initiate policy. Instead the government bought time. Policies aimed at restoring confidence and protecting the domestic market recovery would continue to receive unreserved support; meanwhile, further enquiries would be conducted into the plight of areas suffering abnormal unemployment. At the time Ministers were deeply involved in the fate of the Unemployment Bill, the principal purpose of which was to take

---

[25] See 'Places Without a Future' and 'The Derelict Areas', *The Times*, 20–22 March 1934.
[26] See above chapter 3.

the contentious issue of the relief of the longer-term unemployed 'out of politics' by the creation of an independent means of assessing the real needs of potential applicants.[27] Any accompanying interventionist policy for the economic relief of depressed areas would, to say the least, have been politically embarrassing.

The fact that the condition of most of the areas to which attention was now being drawn had already been surveyed in considerable detail only a few years before was of little consequence. It was of crucial importance from the government's point of view that nothing should be done to disturb the foundations upon which its 'employment' policy was based. Treasury guidelines as to the purpose and scope of the new investigations reflected this concern. Attention was to be focussed upon the wastage associated with long-term unemployment and less upon the economic revival of the depressed areas (though consideration of the opportunities that might exist for attracting new industrial concerns was not entirely ruled out). The able-bodied out-of-work were to be encouraged to make full use of the transference scheme. At the same time a fresh examination was to be made of facilities for recreation and self-help provided by private individuals and organizations for those unable to transfer because of age, skill or domestic circumstances. Four areas were chosen for study. The Chancellor of the Duchy of Lancaster, J. C. C. Davidson, was appointed to report on Cumberland and Captain D. Euan Wallace, Civil Lord of the Admiralty, chosen to investigate Tyneside and Durham. Joining these politicians were two outside businessmen, Sir Arthur Rose, who was to survey conditions in Scotland, and Sir Wyndham Portal, responsible for a report on south Wales. Both Lancashire and Merseyside were excluded from the exercise, reflecting the limited nature of the policy response.

The investigators' reports proved workmanlike but unimaginative, falling short even of contemporary expectations. Their examination of unemployment rates, of housing and health standards, and of the existence of a 'permanent surplus' of labour relative to demand in the foreseeable future provided a mass of factual material which does not warrant detailed summary here. Much was made of the need to encourage labour transference and of the somewhat exaggerated employment opportunities that lay in the expansion of agricultural small holdings. For the sake of speed and homogeneity, all of the investigators limited the scope of their enquiries to areas smaller than those originally allocated to them. None had any clear notion of how to define and thereby identify a 'derelict' area. Captain Wallace provided the only clarion call to more positive action. Depression in the north east, he urged, could not easily be alleviated

---

[27] Cf. chapter 3, pp. 66–81.

without positive assistance, particularly with regard to the location of industry. The time had come:

when the Government can no longer regard with indifference a line of development which, while it may possess the initial advantage of providing more employment, appears upon a long view to be detrimental to the best interests of the country; and the first practicable steps which could be taken towards exercising a measure of control in this direction would seem to be some form of national planning of industry.[28]

Not if the government could help it. On political grounds it was prepared to support those recommendations which buttressed existing priorities, such as increased labour mobility, improved schemes of training and the provision of recreational facilities for older men beyond the lure of transference. But it refused to be swayed by the special pleading of 'expert' opinion, however eminent its source. The idea of greater land settlement, Ministers judged, 'would need careful examination in the light of the Government's general agricultural policy'. Davidson's call to improve Whitehaven harbour in Cumberland to assist the coal export trade was rejected as a scheme 'impossible to justify'; similarly, other special public works identified as likely to afford much-needed employment in their specific areas, such as a road tunnel under the River Tyne in the north east and sewerage schemes in south Wales, were regarded as 'of a low order of priority'. Any attempt to influence the spatial distribution of industry had to be sternly resisted. 'Industry', departmental Ministers preached:

cannot be compelled to go to a locality which the manufacturer does not consider best for his purpose, and in the opinion of the Board of Trade the more far reaching suggestion for what might be called the 'locational control of industry' would require much work and much research before the controlling body possessed the necessary knowledge for giving directions as to how industry should develop; nor would the opinion when formed be likely to command universal consent. Under such a system some industrial development would be prevented unless a guarantee were given to a prospective manufacturer to compensate him for going to what he might regard as an unsuitable locality. It seems probable, too, that the assumption of powers to settle the location of factories (except perhaps on defence grounds) would involve the State in embarrassing questions of management.[29]

But however hard the National Government tried to distance itself from the problems of the depressed areas, it remained under severe political pressure to be seen to be doing something for the victims of industrial recession. The politically astute answer was to co-ordinate the administration of existing palliatives rather than to breach the declared policy of non-intervention. It

---

[28] See Ministry of Labour, Cmd. 4728, 106.
[29] Cab 27/577, CP 220, Reports of the Investigators into the Depressed Areas. Inter-Departmental Committee, 2 October 1934, 3–16, 18–23, 31–9, 52–3.

was not, as Neville Chamberlain put it, 'a question of spending a great deal of money, but of showing that the matter had not been pigeonholed'.[30]

The Depressed Areas Bill presented to parliament in November 1934 was born of such calculated expediency. It made the novel suggestion that two Commissioners should be appointed, one for England and Wales and another for Scotland, to concern themselves with the residual unemployment problem that could not be dealt with by labour transference. This they would do by encouraging land settlement, the greater provision of allotments, local occupational schemes and certain public works, and, more generally, by seeking improvements in the local environment.

The Bill received a stormy reception in parliament. Opponents on both sides of the House saw it as an avowedly political device, designed to deflect criticism of the government's inability, indeed unwillingness, to consider any means of creating jobs. Ministers, critics claimed, had failed to grasp the enormity of the difficulties to be faced in revitalizing the depressed areas. Not only had the Commissioners limited funds at their disposal (£2 million in the first instance), they were prohibited from assisting any undertaking established for profit. Their attention, moreover, was strictly limited to those geographical areas recently surveyed. Thus the growth potential of major centres within the scheduled areas, such as Glasgow, Newport, Cardiff, Swansea, the textile towns of Lancashire, and the Teesside area of County Durham, would continue to be neglected.

But the government had never intended launching a 'move industry' policy or of empowering the Commissioners to experiment with methods of solving regional unemployment beyond labour transference. Unemployment was still regarded as semi-permanent for certain sections of the population; it was necessary in the first instance, therefore, merely to encourage agents outside the reach of party politics to foster greater labour mobility and to sustain the morale of those unable to seek work elsewhere. If there was a larger intent, it was merely the hope that parallel efforts to improve the infrastructure of the depressed areas would remove some of their least attractive features, thereby encouraging fresh industrial activity without the need for direct government intervention. A month of parliamentary debate and an enforced change by the House of Lords in the title of the new legislation to the Special Areas (Development and Improvement) Act did little to alter the substance of policy.

Nevertheless the critics were right. The government had only the barest of policies with which to deal with continuing structural and regional unemployment. It remained hopeful on the one hand that the material

---

[30] F. Miller, 'The Unemployment Policy of the National Government, 1931–36', *Historical Journal*, 19 (1976), 467.

needs of the long-term unemployed would be met without serious contention by a nationalized form of relief payment and assessment under the auspices of the Unemployment Assistance Board, and on the other that the 'temporary difficulties' of the depressed regions (now called Special Areas) would be significantly eased by the timely intervention of its newly appointed Commissioners.

HOPE DEFERRED: THE COMMISSIONERS AND THE SPECIAL AREAS, 1934–36

Almost from the outset a conflict arose between what the Commissioners could actually do to assist the Special Areas and what any superficial reading of their declared functions suggested might be expected of them. Although they were formally charged with the initiation, organization, prosecution and assistance of measures designed to facilitate the economic development and social improvement of the scheduled areas, neither Sir Malcolm Stewart (Commissioner for England and Wales) nor Sir Arthur Rose (Commissioner for Scotland) proved able to develop any fundamentally new approach to the problem of chronic regional unemployment. Their status as extra-parliamentary officials counted for little so far as the determination of economic priorities was concerned. Their working papers were able to be scrutinized by any Ministry with a declared parliamentary interest in the Special Areas. In addition, the Treasury kept a watchful eye on the budgetary implications of any suggested remedial policy, particularly if it threatened to involve Exchequer assistance to local authorities for schemes of 'uneconomic' value.

In the early stages, the Commissioners restricted their expenditure to schemes of health and welfare, to the provision of small holdings and to the inauguration of projects aimed at improving the local environment. This emphasis reflected a developing awareness of the links between poverty, malnutrition and unemployment, and an earnest belief that the social and psychological needs of the longer term unemployed could best be met by encouraging low-cost forms of therapeutic activity. However, within six months of embarking on their task the Commissioners began to suggest a series of additional measures which they considered to be of real value in easing unemployment, but which went far beyond what the government saw as their legitimate areas of concern. They included proposals for shorter hours and later entry into industry, earlier retirement, a system of providing jobs in other parts of the country for youths under 21, a licensing scheme to control the location and movement of factories, and the provision of easier finance for new small industries starting up in the Special Areas.

Neither the Civil Service nor the Cabinet wanted to be troubled by such fanciful nonsense. 'There is nothing in the present position in the Special Areas which suggests that a policy of giving work to the people in the areas can be much more than make-believe', Sir Horace Wilson the Government's Chief Industrial Adviser, penned indignantly:

It is right that Mr. Stewart and Sir Arthur Rose should go on with their efforts to improve the economic position of the areas, to ensure that unemployment and local financial difficulties do not result in the social services becoming dangerously inadequate, in experimenting with land settlements and in encouraging any communal activities which may make life more tolerable for those who may not be absorbed by any local revival that may occur or who – on account of age or other reason – cannot be moved away. But . . . if the coal trade cannot give employment locally, and other industries with a comparable range of employment can find no reason why they should settle themselves round derelict pit shafts, the people who wish to work must go where the work is.

The only effective contribution government could make towards alleviating regional unemployment outside of the social services, he opined, was 'the creation and maintenance of improvement in the position of the country as a whole':

for it both describes the foundation of the Government's employment policy (restoration of general business confidence, cheap money, fiscal policy, etc.) and indicates the limits to which further action can go, namely, that nothing must be done to shake confidence or check business development – for unless the country as a whole is in good trim the plight of the Special Areas will indeed be bad.[31]

And who could disagree? Certainly not the Cabinet Committee appointed to co-ordinate discussions over the fate of the Special Areas. 'We do not believe', it declared confidently in October 1935, 'that the introduction of new industries is going to play any very large part in the near future in solving the problem of those areas'.[32]

The Commissioners, however, grew weary of defending the status quo and continued with renewed vigour to champion industrial diversification within the Special Areas. Precluded by the 1934 Act from granting direct help to private industry, they urged the government to establish factory sites in the Special Areas as a means of inducing fresh industrial development. Baldwin himself struck a discordant note with colleagues when he appealed in July 1935 for businessmen contemplating new industrial ventures 'to show their gratitude to the country' by establishing plants 'where the country needs them most'.[33]

[31] Cab 27/577, Committee on the Report of Commissioners for the Special Areas. Report of Inter-Departmental Committee. Note by the Chairman, 27 September 1935.
[32] Cab 27/577, CP 197, Report of Inter-Departmental Committee on Special Areas, Appendix II. Summary of the Cabinet Committee's Conclusion on the Points Dealt with by the Inter-Departmental Committee, 18 October 1935.
[33] HC Debs., 5th ser., vol. 202, 9 July 1935, cited in Pitfield, 'Labour Migration', 225.

Political expediency finally forced the government's hand. With an election pending and surrounded by the publicity given to Lloyd George's 'New Deal' programme of deficit-financed public works[34] Ministers felt compelled to display a rather more positive concern for the unemployed in derelict regions. In a blatant act of electioneering, the government committed itself in the autumn of 1935 to discriminatory aid to private industry on the basis of geographical location, with the prime objective of reducing local unemployment. The restrictions on financial help to private concerns contained in the 1934 Act were neatly circumvented by permitting Development Boards in the scheduled areas to establish trading estate companies which would buy sites and erect factories for lease or sale at current market prices. This proved the least objectionable way of being seen to encourage industry to settle in the Special Areas without having to offer direct subsidies to private enterprise. The first trading estate to be constructed was at Team Valley, Gateshead, outside Newcastle. Other centres were established at Treforest (South Wales) and Hillington (outside Glasgow). But although they proved to be the most visibly successful of the interwar regional unemployment measures, they had only a limited effect in creating jobs in the immediate term. By May 1939, 273 factories were in production, employing just over 8,500 people. Unemployment in the Special Areas alone, even in July 1939, stood at 226,193.[35]

NEW INDUSTRIES, FINANCE AND INDUSTRIAL DIVERSIFICATION IN
THE SPECIAL AREAS, 1936–39

Although the trading estates initiative represented an abrupt about-turn in policy, exceeding the bounds of previous interventionist activity by the National Government, it failed to contain the rising tide of criticism over the handling of the regional problem. During the early months of 1936 MPs representing depressed regions in the north east demanded that the state should interfere directly in the location of new factory development, rather than rely upon the energy and commitment of private enterprise. In their opinion, there was no reason to suppose that industry would prove footloose merely in response to the employment needs of the Special Areas and in this they were correct. Long before the mid-thirties regional income disparities had distorted the spatial composition of new business formation in favour of the prosperous south east. New firms crowded into the service sector in all

---

[34] See chapter 13.
[35] Heim, 'Uneven Development', 392, 401. For a more general review see G. C. Allen, 'The Growth of Industry on Trading Estates, 1920–39, with special reference to Slough Trading Estate', *Oxford Economic Papers*, 3 (1951), 272–30 and H. Loebl, *Government Factories and the Origins of British Regional Policy, 1934–1948* (1988).

regions, but it was the size of its potential market, both regional and European, and its favourable level of local purchasing power that provided the self-contained economy of south-east England with an almost unassailable advantage over the north and the west.[36] In practice the depressed regions might have benefited more directly from this imbalance in regional growth had branch plants mushroomed to a significant extent, as they did in the post-World War II period. In the interwar years, with abundant skilled labour close to parent firms in the south and with wage rates and trade union densities no lower and sometimes greater in regions of high unemployment than elsewhere, there was little incentive for industrialists in and around Greater London to establish branches in 'Outer Britain', least of all for the sake of reducing regional unemployment differentials.[37]

With unemployment in the Special Areas consistently above the national average, the government could not afford to appear inactive. It wished nonetheless to remain as politically neutral as possible. Perhaps industrialists could be persuaded to move to such areas by the prospect of easier finance. The proceedings of the Macmillan Committee on Finance and Industry had already focussed attention on the difficulties which small and medium-sized enterprises faced in obtaining finance with which to operate or expand (subsequently dubbed the 'Macmillan gap'). If Ministers could persuade outside interests to make finance capital more readily available to private industry, the government could continue its policy of non-intervention, encouraging the belief that the relief of regional unemployment was still possible through the operation of existing market mechanisms.[38] The creation in April 1936 of the Special Areas Reconstruction Association (hereafter SARA) reflected this calculated approach. Initially orchestrated by the Bank of England, its purpose was to establish an experimental scheme whereby loan finance, organized by the Bank and the

[36] J. Foreman-Peck, 'Seedcorn or Chaff? New Firm Formation and the Performance of the Interwar Economy', *Economic History Review*, 2nd ser., 38 (1985), 402–22; C. Lee, 'Regional Growth and Structural Change in Victorian Britain', *Economic History Review*, 2nd ser., 34 (1981), 438–52; Lee, 'Regional Structural Change in the Long-Run: Great Britain 1841–1971', in *Region and Industrialization: Studies on the Role of the Region in the Economic History of the Last Two Centuries*, ed. S. Pollard (Gottingen, 1980), 254–75.

[37] C. Heim, 'Industrial Organization and Regional Development in Inter-War Britain', *Journal of Economic History*, 43 (1983), 931–52.

[38] C. Heim, 'Limits to Intervention: The Bank of England and Industrial Diversification in the Depressed Areas', *Economic History Review*, 2nd ser., 37 (1984), 533–50. Towards the end of October 1935, the Chancellor of the Exchequer was empowered to discuss with the banks a scheme whereby applications for loans for the establishment of industries in the scheduled areas would be sifted first by Local Development Councils and thereafter, on prima facie evidence of suitability, by the relevant Commissioners. Either of the two Commissioners would then be permitted to request the banks to offer more than their usual limit of credit on the understanding that in such cases the Commissioners would guarantee the first 25 per cent of any loss that might be incurred in the long run.

City, would be made available to support industrial development in the Special Areas, particularly amongst small firms. Loans were not normally to exceed £10,000 for a period of five years and were to be made available at rates of interest as close as possible to market rates.

The venture proved disappointing, attracting criticism almost from the outset. Neither the London financial community nor the Treasury was convinced of the need for the new facility and both were sceptical as to its capacity to generate extra employment. The proposed initial capital of the company (£1 million) was paltry in comparison with the existing regional problem and there could never be any guarantee that firms would respond to what was perceived as a charitable gesture. And despite its initial enthusiasm, the Bank of England swiftly circumscribed the scale of assistance it was prepared to encourage through the Association. The Bank's original motivation, as with its earlier involvement with industrial rationalization, was to keep government out of industry; at the same time it remained fearful of becoming involved itself in the internal affairs of industry. As a result, SARA's activities, aimed ostensibly at industrial diversification, became focussed on small, 'light' industries rather than upon the new industries requiring relatively large initial injections of capital. The scheme operated slowly and laid down stringent conditions for loans, demanding that at least half a project's capital had to be provided by its promoters. Total advances agreed by June 1939 amounted to £908,750 for 190 projects; although new capital promised from other sources raised this figure to £1,458,000, the whole was expected at full operation to provide only an additional 14,061 jobs.[39]

SARA was only one of three special finance organizations established with similar aims in the late thirties. One of the others was a private body, the Nuffield Trust, which provided from the beginning of 1937 both share capital and loan capital for projects likely to provide direct and permanent employment in the Special Areas. The Trust, with £2 million at its disposal, proved invaluable in assisting those projects considered to be too risky even for SARA money or where the degree of involvement at industry and firm level ran contrary to the declared objectives of both the government and the Bank of England. The remaining initiative was provided by the Treasury Fund, established by the government in March 1937 to serve the needs of larger firms inside the Special Areas and elsewhere in other depressed regions. It provided finance only by way of loan.

These different forms of assistance to industry were not mutually exclusive; many projects were undertaken with the aid of one or more of the funds. The Nuffield Trust proved the most effective agent in inducing larger

[39] Heim, 'Uneven Development', 443, 534–6.

concerns to locate in the Special Areas. But the total impact of the three organizations was not great. None of them was in existence very long before the outbreak of war. Total funding amounted to only £5 million and the maximum employment expected to be provided by all three was estimated in February 1938 to be only 18,279, this at a time when total registered unemployment exceeded one-and-a-half million and when only two months earlier there were approximately 290,877 out of work in the Special Areas alone.

Trading estates and the provision of special finance originated in response to heightened public criticism of the government's apparent willingness to allow key industrial areas to suffer cumulative decline as other parts of the nation shared in the benefits of economic recovery. The fact that the government regarded the two separate initiatives merely as experimental and extraordinary occasioned only further criticism of its fundamentally *laissez-faire* approach. Throughout 1936 complaints grew over the handling of the Special Areas programme and the Cabinet was forced into making even further concessions to its opponents. Various factors combined to increase public unease about conditions in the depressed areas. A Hunger March on London, the Jarrow Crusade of October 1936, and the visit of the King to south Wales a month later publicized the human dimensions of the regional problem in a way that no official report had ever previously managed to do.

To add to the government's embarrassment both Commissioners for the Special Areas resigned in 1936, Sir Arthur Rose because of ill-health and Sir Malcolm Stewart, by all accounts, because of his growing frustration over the myopic and faint-hearted approach of the Civil Service to economic conditions in the scheduled areas. Stewart in particular vented his anger at the shortcomings of official policy. Despite all efforts since 1934, he wrote in his Final Report:

It has to be admitted that no appreciable reduction of the numbers of unemployed has been effected. This, however, was not to be looked for seeing that the Special Areas Act makes no direct provision for this purpose. Such increased employment as is likely to result from the operation of the many schemes initiated will prove altogether insufficient, in the absence of a spontaneous frontier of new industries and an expansion of existing industries to offset the release of labour brought about by increased mechanisation and rationalisation.

Although Stewart opposed the compulsory location of industry in high-unemployment areas as 'unnecessary and dangerous', he was convinced that the problem of regional decline had to be treated as a national emergency. Since the government had already provided through trading estates a degree of assistance to private enterprise within the limits of the 1934 Act, the time had now arrived, he maintained, to attempt directly to attract industrialists to the Special Areas 'by means of State-provided inducements'. These could include over a period of say seven years, relief from income tax on profits earned, relief from local rates and the granting of long term loans at a low rate of interest.[40]

The English Commissioner's parting words were swiftly interpreted as a damning indictment of official policy. 'The Cabinet's present inertia is seriously out of touch with public opinion', warned *The Economist* in November 1936. It was no longer sufficient merely to press the unemployed to transfer from the Special Areas; what was actually required was 'the deliberate direction of new industries' into the regions.[41] At first the government tried to preserve the status quo, announcing in parliament that transference policy would continue and that the Special Areas Act would be included in the Expiring Laws Continuance Bill. Popular and political pressure, however, forced greater concessions. Towards the end of 1936, further investigation was promised of the problem of unbalanced industrial expansion in and around London.[42] More than that, Commissioners were to be empowered for the first time to offer inducements to industrialists to locate in the Special Areas.

It seemed at first that the regional programme was in the throes of being transformed from a social relief policy for 'derelict'areas into an interventionist strategy for the promotion of more balanced industrial growth. But the political battle was far from won. Civil Service advisers sought desperately to restrain Ministers from over-reacting to Stewart's stinging criticisms of current policy. Inducements of the sort he suggested, warned an interdepartmental committee of civil servants, would not:

in practice attract industry in any appreciable degree. As regards income tax, the waiving or lowering of tax on profits cannot in itself do anything to enable a concern to make profits. It cannot turn a loss into a profit . . . The amount which would be involved to a concern which anticipated making a profit would be small compared with the other factors which might weigh with them in selecting their location – proximity to raw materials, accessibility to markets, availability of labour supply.

Moreover:

The total number of undertakings which are looking for a home or which are ready to move from their present homes and which will be attracted to the Special Areas by any inducements which are within the sphere of practical politics is limited.[43]

---

[40] Third Report of the Commissioners for the Special Areas (England and Wales), Cmd. 5303, November 1936, 3–4, 10–11.   [41] *The Economist*, 14 November 1936.

[42] In July 1937 a Royal Commission was appointed under the Chairmanship of Sir Montague Barlow to consider the geographical imbalance in industrial location, especially in and around London. The Barlow Commission became a landmark in the development of regional policy in the post Second World War period.

[43] Cab 24/268, DA (34) 10, Committee on the Reports of the Commissioners for the Special Areas. Report of Interdepartmental Committee, 11 January 1937.

For once the Cabinet proved more optimistic and adventurous. 'I am ready', the Chancellor of the Exchequer announced in February 1937:

to provide a sum of money which would be available to assist the establishment of new industrial undertakings in the form of a loan of capital on favourable terms. In the Special Areas, the new money would be a supplement to Nuffield and S.A.R.A. In the other areas, it would stand alone but would be worked in co-operation with the arrangements for the provision of sites and buildings.[44]

It was now the business of government, in other words, to help move work to the workers, not only to the Special Areas but also to hitherto neglected areas of high unemployment such as could be found, for example, in parts of Lancashire.[45] Although the significance of this shift in policy can be exaggerated it should not be overlooked. Until the publication of Stewart's Final Report, the government had been able to make marginal changes in its unemployment policy without abandoning its commitment to the free play of market forces. Indeed, the administrative device of allocating responsibility for the relief of the depressed areas to specially appointed Commissioners had originally been designed to relieve the pressure on government to intervene directly on behalf of the unemployed. As it turned out, it had precisely the opposite effect.[46]

The necessary extension of the Commissioners' industrial powers was provided by the 1937 Special Areas (Amendment) Act. Each Commissioner was empowered to let factories to private industry and to grant tax, rent and rate rebates to profit-making firms for up to five years, even in 'certified areas' outside the scope of the original 1934 legislation.[47] This advance on policy owed much to the Ministry of Labour's insistence that unemployment could only be permanently countered by the development of a balanced industrial structure at regional level, necessitating a new relationship between government and industry on the basis of positive discrimination.

Although the provisions of the 1937 Act were helpful in this respect, they left ample scope for the authorities to pursue a more vigorous policy had they wished to do so. After all, the government had not yet assumed any

[44] Cab 27/577, DA (34) 12, Committee on the Reports of the Commissioners for Special Areas. Memorandum by the Chancellor of the Exchequer, 9 February 1937.
[45] Ministry of Labour. Statement Relating to the Special Areas. Including a Memorandum on the Financial Resolution to be Proposed, Cmd. 5386, 1937.
[46] A. Booth, 'An Administrative Experiment in Unemployment Policy in the Thirties', *Public Administration*, 56 (1978), 153.
[47] A 'certified area' was defined as an area which had been 'for a considerable period suffering from severe unemployment, that is an area mainly dependent on one or more industries which are unable to provide sufficient employment by reason of general depression in those industries, and where there will be no immediate likelihood of a substantial increase of employment in the area unless financial assistance is provided'.

direct responsibility for reducing regional unemployment differentials. Policy continued to be vested in the hands of extra-parliamentary officials who were powerless to control the location of industry directly; the most the Commissioners could hope for was that firms would choose to settle in the localities where they were most needed now that greater financial inducements were on offer, and that their decision to do so would not arouse undue opposition from established manufacturers.

In any event, the depressed areas benefited more from meeting the requirements of defence contracts than from private industrial growth. The government resolved not to have the equilibrium of the budget upset by the inflationary consequences of concentrating too much of the growing expenditure on rearmaments in the prosperous south, where wage costs were higher and where there were already indications of a shortage of skilled labour and capacity,[48] and therefore directed rearmament expenditure towards areas of high unemployment in the hope of overcoming each production constraint with the minimum of difficulty. That is not to deny that defence contracts were sometimes placed in depressed areas either because certain engineering and armaments industries were localized there, or for strategic reasons. But, as *The Economist* put it in March 1937, 'Depression and distress are to be bought off by expenditure on guns and battleships. The Special Areas plan pales into insignificance besides the rearmament programme.'[49]

Indeed the whole tenor of government policy towards the depressed areas as such in the two years prior to the outbreak of war presupposed the continued existence of high regional unemployment. Although financial aid continued to be offered to new industries, the Cabinet continued to endorse policies of land settlement, labour transference and organized voluntary work amongst the surplus unemployed. The 1937 Act was regarded within the Treasury as a 'political' device. In its view the Act had not laid the basis for any major extension of state assistance to industry, least of all for the sake of reducing local unemployment. The Chancellor Sir John Simon, put it thus in June 1938:

The State is involved in assisting people many of whom are in competition with other industries in this country. Hitherto there has not been much criticism, no doubt because the assistance has been, in general, confined to places whose condition was such as to excite widespread sympathy. There is not, I think, any great volume of floating industry in this country which is ready to go to places which would normally be inconvenient for it . . . Consequently, any wide extension of financial assistance . . . would . . . be futile . . . The position as I see it, is that the

[48] A. Lonie and H. Begg, 'Comment: Further Evidence of the Quest for an Effective Regional Policy, 1934–37', *Regional Studies*, 13 (1979), 497–500.
[49] *The Economist*, 6 March 1937. For a discussion of the impact of rearmament expenditure upon employment in the depressed areas see chapter 13.

Government have tried an experiment which has up to the present produced good results. But . . . I doubt myself whether more than this is possible without a radical revision of outlook as regards the freedom of choice at present permitted to industrialists which would be fundamentally opposed to the essential basis of our policy as regards industry.[50]

When the future of the Special Areas was discussed in the summer of 1938, the majority of the Cabinet were in favour of allowing discriminatory policy to lapse, ending rate and rent subventions in the scheduled regions. Even the mere continuation of the existing functions of the Commissioners, they feared, would give rise to a strong demand for government support to be extended to other needy areas, threatening an unwelcome increase in non-defence expenditure.[51] It was only the Prime Minister's stern warning of the political backlash that would follow any such decision that ultimately persuaded the Cabinet to reverse its position and allow the Commissioners to remain in office.

EMPLOYMENT AND THE REGIONS

If, as we have argued thus far, there was little evidence before 1939 of an official commitment to 'regional policy' as generally understood, can we presume that those government initiatives ostensibly designed to reduce unemployment in the depressed areas, namely the transference of workers to jobs elsewhere, the promotion of public works and the much-delayed effort to attract new investment, actually created extra jobs?

The question is difficult to answer with any precision. So far as labour transference is concerned, it is generally acknowledged that the population of interwar Britain remained overwhelmingly immobile. London and the south east were the principal recipients of what internal migration occurred, much of it originating in Northumberland, Durham and Wales. On the whole, long-distance (inter-regional) migration was more signifi-cant in the 1930s than in the 1920s. It responded to changing economic circumstances and proved particularly sensitive to the cyclical downturn of the early thirties.[52] The transference scheme sponsored by the Ministry of

[50] Cab 27/578, DA (34) 18, Committee on the Reports of the Commissioners for the Special Areas. Financial Assistance to Industry in the Special Areas. Memorandum by the Chancellor of the Exchequer, 28 June 1938.

[51] Cab 27/578, DA (34) 16, Committee on the Reports of the Special Areas. The Future of the Special Areas Scheme, 13 June 1938; Cab 27/578, DA (34) 19, Areas of Heavy Unemployment, 19 October 1938; Cab 27/578, DA (34) 23, Areas of Heavy Unemploy-ment. Loan Facilities Bill, 13 April 1939.

[52] See D. Friedlander and R. J. Roshier, 'A Study of Internal Migration in England and Wales. Part I: Geographical Patterns of Internal Migration, 1851–1951', *Population Studies*, 19 (1966), 239–79; B. Thomas, 'The Movement of Labour into South-East England, 1920–32', *Economica*, 1 (1934), 220–41; B. Thomas, 'The Influx of Labour into London and the South-East, 1920–36', *Economica*, 4 (1937), 323–6; B. Thomas, 'The Influx of Labour into the Midlands, 1920–37', *Economica*, 5 (1938), 410–34.

Labour from 1928 was but part of this general process of migration and a relatively unimportant one at that.[53] Its original purpose, after all, was not to accomplish all labour transfers, but rather to stimulate at the margin the migration of those surplus workers in the depressed regions who might otherwise have avoided a move elsewhere. Such transfers were only meant, in other words, to complement the spontaneous, unassisted movement of workers that was already under way. Those who moved of their own accord to find work were certainly more numerous than those assisted by government grant. And a proportion of the latter would probably have moved sooner or later even in the absence of direct grant aid.

Ministry of Labour data of the numbers transferred from the depressed areas to employment through the Employment Exchanges and by other means do not, therefore, reveal the scale of total migration. Nonetheless they provide an indication of the scale of assisted migration over the course of the trade cycle; the details are reproduced in appendix 9.1. The total annual flow of all assisted persons of working age varied from over 40,000 in the years 1929 and 1936 to 14,000 in 1932 and 1933, and averaged almost 32,000 over the ten-year period 1929–38. There is no way of knowing precisely how many assisted transferees returned to their native home. If it is assumed that half of those who were helped to move stayed at their destinations at least until the end of the scheme, the ten-year total of assisted movers who did not return would probably be in the order of 150,000. This compares with an estimated 500,000 or so persons accounted for by the excess of unemployment rates in the less prosperous regions in comparison with those in the south and the midlands.[54]

Empirical studies have shown that voluntary labour mobility between the wars was induced by regional differences in employment prospects and by the overall national level of unemployment.[55] Migration was affected by a combination of 'push' and 'pull' factors; the former exemplified by poor employment prospects in one area and the latter by better employment prospects in another. The pattern of assisted migration reflected the tendency of the 'pull' factor to determine the timing of moves. Evidence of

---

[53] According to the Ministry of Labour, only 28 per cent of all people migrating from the depressed areas during 1936–37 were assisted by the various schemes then on offer. Lab 8/218, Report of Enquiry into the Industrial Transference Scheme (Adults), May 1938.

[54] A. J. Brown, *A Framework of Regional Economics* (Cambridge, 1972), 281. The Barlow Commission reported that between 1928 and mid-1937 nearly 190,000 men and women were transferred under the official scheme, but that between 1930 and 1937 almost 56,000 were known to have returned to the depressed areas. Report of the Royal Commission on the Distribution of the Industrial Population, Cmd. 6153, 1939–40, 150.

[55] H. Makower, J. Marschak, and H. W. Robinson, 'Studies in the Mobility of Labour: Analysis for Great Britain, Part I', *Oxford Economic Papers*, 2 (1939), 70–97; G. H. Daniel, 'Some Factors Affecting the Movement of Labour', *Oxford Economic Papers*, 3 (1940), 144–79.

the duration of unemployment before and after moving shows that workers were reluctant to migrate from an area of high unemployment unless they were reasonably confident of securing a vacancy in another area. Social cohesion, family ties, acquired skills, the possibilities of cross-subsidy between earners and the unemployed in larger households, a growing knowledge of the difficulties of obtaining suitable accommodation in other districts, together with the shared experience of unemployment, all served to deter mobility amongst the out-of-work. Such influences played less upon the young, male unmarried skilled worker, and it was they whom the Ministry of Labour particularly encouraged, if only to curry favour with prospective employers.

Beyond this was the effect of the trade cycle. Economic depression, as appendix 9.1 further illustrates, lessened labour mobility. Total transfers through the Employment Exchanges in 1933 were only 30 per cent of their 1929 level. On the other hand, the higher proportion of long-distance moves recorded in the thirties as a whole suggests that some of the inertia of the previous decade had begun to crumble, given continued secular decline in the staple trades. It seems that intense depression during the world slump served merely to restrict labour movement to later years of the decade, at a time when the Ministry of Labour purposely extended the scope of available assistance.[56] The 'cyclical' upturn in assisted transference was most evident after 1934, reaching a peak in 1936. Thereafter the quickened pace of industrial activity in the Special Areas and the reorientation of government policy towards a measure of industrial diversification in depressed areas, rather than the movement of national unemployment per se, weakened the impulse to transference. If anything, the emphasis had shifted by 1938 to intra-regional transfers in an effort to ease the continuing plight of severely depressed districts. There is evidence, too, that such had been the relative success of transference in previous years that fewer and fewer individuals were being judged by the end of the decade to be suitable for transfer, in terms of age, skill and general adaptability.

Although the transference scheme sought to remove the unemployed to jobs in more buoyant regions, the raw data upon which our remarks have so far been based tell us little about the actual impact which transference had upon employment, either in the losing or in the receiving areas. Did transference merely redistribute the unemployed geographically, helping to equalize unemployment percentages across the country, or was it, in effect, an employment policy?

[56] Transference was encouraged from 1935 by the advance of fares to transferees and grant aid towards the cost of lodgings. The Household Removal Scheme inaugurated in December 1928 was extended to allow a family to follow younger transferees. Allowances were provided for dependants and the juvenile transference scheme was also expanded.

One would expect *ceteris paribus* that as out-migration increased, unemployment would fall in the depressed areas; in the receiving areas the direction of impact could vary, depending on whether migrants found permanent or semi-permanent work or whether they simply increased existing unemployment levels. So far as the areas losing population are concerned, it is clear that the scale of migration during the slump years of the early thirties could never have removed the growing surplus of labour in the heavy basic industries. Perhaps the most that can be said is that were it not for transference, unemployment in the depressed ones might have been worse than it was by 1934, though only marginally so in relation to the size of the problem. In the receiving areas, the impact of migration before 1934 was equally negligible and it is not certain from the available evidence whether transference added to unemployment or not.

As national unemployment deteriorated during the world slump, prospective vacancies in London and the south east declined. Though transfers also declined, competition for existing vacancies grew between previously transferred and indigenous labour. Those migrant workers who succeeded initially in finding work frequently lost it after a short time. It is difficult, therefore, to be precise as to the direction of impact of transference on unemployment in the receiving areas. The situation is particularly complicated so far as UGC public works are concerned. After July 1930, local authorities were no longer required to employ a certain proportion of transferred labour in order to qualify for grant aid. This discouraged further migration and made it progressively more likely that transferees would add to unemployment in southern England.

Thanks largely to Pitfield's work, we are able to offer a rather more substantial, if still tenuous, assessment of the influence of a policy on unemployment after 1934, at least within the strict geographical compass of the Special Areas. His analysis of data culled from contemporary sources, reproduced in table 10, gives some indication of the relative impact on unemployment transference, factory development, and public works.

These estimates make no allowance for the income or employment multiplier effects either of Special Areas expenditure or of new factory development. Nor in the case of industrial transference do they account for 'wastage' (returning migrants), estimated by contemporaries to be of the order of 30 per cent.[57] To remedy such deficiencies, Pitfield inflated the direct employment series and deflated the migration series. For industrial transference an allowance was made of one local job lost for every five

---

[57] Royal Commission on the Geographical Distribution of the Industrial Population, Memorandum of Evidence of the Ministry of Labour, 2–3 February 1938; A. D. K. Owen, 'Social Consequences of Industrial Transference', *Sociological Review*, 29 (1937), 331–54.

Table 10. *Reported reduction in unemployment in the Special Areas achieved by regional policy, 1934–38*

	Scotland	England and Wales	Total
Transference[a]	7,774	90,759	98,533
New Factory Employment[b]	4,546	15,630	20,176
Public Works etc.[c]	10,167	40,341	50,508
Total	22,487	146,730	169,217

[a]For the derivation of these figures see note (d) to Appendix 9.1. The cumulative total of Pitfield's own figures of transference from the Special Areas in England and Wales is 10,000 greater than the figure originally quoted in his thesis, table 34 (80,759). A correction has been made above to reflect this error.

[b]Data derived from the Board of Trade, *Annual Surveys of Industrial Development, 1934–38*. The figures reflected the accumulated total of maximum employment at December, created by new and extended factory development less the cumulative employment loss resulting from closures. The accumulations depended on the assumption that no reductions or expansions in the workforce took place over the period after the case was first noted in the Board of Trade data. No other source of data was judged to provide an acceptable indication of the growth of employment in the Special Areas from such activity. Total estimated employment provided on trading estates by 1939 has already been given in the text.

[c]Derived from the Reports of the Commissioners for the Special Areas. Sporadic estimates of the man-years of employment that would be provided by expenditure on public works were assumed to bear a constant relation to the financial commitments actually undertaken during the period and that the same relation held true for both Scotland and England and Wales. It should be noted, however, that there was a divergence between money committed and money expended.

Source: D. Pitfield, 'Labour Migration and the Regional Problem in Britain, 1920–1939', Ph.D. Thesis, University of Stirling (1973), table 34, adapted and revised.

migrants lost to a region. A local income multiplier of 1.35 was used for public works and industrial policy, i.e. for each new job 0.35 new local jobs were created by additional spending power. The adjusted figures shown below suggest an immediate rank order of importance for each type of regional policy pursued. The confidence with which such data can be used is still open to considerable doubt. Public works after all were essentially temporary in nature; and, as we have seen, industrial transference did not peak until 1936. Moreover, the 'move work' policy was only developed in any recognizable form in 1937.

Table 11. *Estimated reduction in unemployment in the Special Areas, adjusted for 'wastage' and income multiplier effects*

	Scotland	England and Wales	Total
Transference	4,353	45,225[a]	49,578
New Factory			
Employment	6,137	21,101	27,238
Public Works etc.	13,726	54,460	68,186
Total	24,216	120,786	145,002

[a] Based on Pitfield's earlier but incorrectly reported total reduction of unemployment of 80,759. See Table 10, note *a*.
Source: Pitfield, 'Labour Migration and the Regional Problem in Britain', table 34.

Pitfield's adjusted figures may even underestimate the influence of Special Areas policies. They make no allowance for the effect which an initial expansion of local purchasing power might have had upon the demand for material inputs from local industry and, thereby, upon the generation of additional employment. There are major methodological problems in trying to use the available data to capture such effects and we are left largely ignorant, therefore, of the full impact of the policies actually adopted. Except, that is, for Jones's highly suggestive work on Durham and Tyneside. He has estimated employment multipliers for 'diverse', 'old', 'new' and 'building' industries in the northern region in 1935, and applied them to the suggested volume of new employment created by the four 'types' of industry during 1934–38 (thereby postulating the total employment generated both directly and by first-round inter-industry effects.) The results suggest the magnitude of the 'effective' regional employment multiplier for each separate industrial classification. When its overall minimum value (0.5) is applied more generally to the reported impact of industrial policy in the Special Areas in the same period (20,176 jobs according to table 10 above), the figure rises to 30,264, reflecting likely direct and inter-industry effects on employment. When Pitfield's suggested income multiplier is added the figure rises further to 40,856.[58]

Insured rates of unemployment in the Scottish and English Special Areas in December 1934 stood at 29 and 35 per cent compared with just over 16 per cent in the country as a whole; by December 1938 the respective rates

[58] For a discussion of statistical method and sources of data see M. E. F. Jones, 'Regional Employment Multipliers, Regional Policy and Structural Change in Interwar Britain', *Explorations in Economic History*, 22 (1985), 417–39.

were still 20, 24 per cent and 13 per cent (see appendix 9.2). Registered unemployment in the Special Areas did improve significantly during the period 1936–38. In the year down to June 1937 the Special Areas, with one-tenth of the country's insured workers, achieved one-seventh of the total improvement in employment; and in the twelve months ending September 1938 they accounted for only 5.8 per cent of the country's rise in unemployment.[59] It would be tempting to suggest that such improvements sprang directly from the changed priorities of government policy in operation at the time. It appears, however, that the improvement in Special Areas employment in 1937 and to a lesser extent in 1938 was due largely to the revival of traditional industrial sectors under the stimulus of rearmament demand.[60]

It is sobering to recall that the total number of jobs expected to be created by advances of capital to industrial concerns and by the operation of firms on trading estates only amounted to between 20,000 and 25,000. So far as industrial diversification is concerned, it remained true throughout the thirties that, with motor cars the partial exception, most new manufacturing and diverse light industries, such as electrical goods, rayon, food, furniture and clothing, did not mop up surplus long-term unemployed men. Such trades, as well as the expanded services sector, tended to draw upon cheaper and less skilled juveniles, agricultural workers and females rather than upon the pool of displaced workers from declining staple industries. Those relatively few assisted firms which located themselves in the Special Areas similarly looked to new sources of labour; they also tended to be situated on trading estates near to the metropolitan centres of the regions rather than near the derelict mining or shipbuilding centres where the largest share of unemployed men were located. Thus, even the limited policy of 'taking work to the workers' did not necessarily take it to the unemployed.[61]

'REGIONAL POLICY' AND THE UNEMPLOYMENT PROBLEM: AN OVERVIEW

Despite the progress made from the mid-thirties in developing differing forms of discriminatory aid on behalf of the depressed areas, the scale of public expenditure committed to the problem remained paltry even at the

---

[59]   M. Daly, 'Government Policy and the Depressed Areas in the Inter-War Period', D.Phil Thesis, University of Oxford (1979), 289–90.
[60]   The scale of such improvements is discussed in greater detail in chapter 13.
[61]   C. Heim, 'Structural Transformation and the Demand for New Labor in Advanced Economies: Interwar Britain', *Journal of Economic History*, 44 (1984), 585–95; D. W. Parsons, *The Political Economy of British Regional Policy* (1985).

outbreak of war. Only £8 million was actually spent by the Special Areas Commissioners between 1934 and 1938; by 1939 only around £2 million had been disbursed as government loans to industry, and a mere £50,000 in contributions towards taxes and rents. In themselves, neither the Special Areas programme from 1934 nor the 'location of industry' policy of 1937–39 proved particularly effective in narrowing regional unemployment differentials.

It is notoriously difficult, of course, to isolate the impact of government policy upon the regional unemployment problem. A range of extraneous influences were at work, such as the vagaries of the trade cycle, the effects on trade and competition of the intensification of economic nationalism, and the thrust of rearmament after 1935. Perhaps the most charitable assessment that can be made of policy is that though it had only a slight effect on the reduction of unemployment and the creation of new jobs, it did at least weaken the orthodox impulse not to take any action at all. From this perspective, the Special Areas initiative remains significant as a link between the established *laissez-faire* ideology of the twenties and the evolution of pragmatic intervention in the thirties. Even so, the official response for most of the time was triggered by external pressure and was aimed at containing the regional unemployment problem at a politically manageable level. Policy lacked direction and was rarely, if ever, coherently formulated. The provision of grants to necessitous local authorities, the encouragement given to voluntary agencies undertaking welfare work amongst the unemployed, and the effort to stimulate labour mobility through the industrial transference scheme represented at best strategic concessions to mounting pressures within and outside the depressed regions. From an official point of view they were necessary to allay discontent until cost reductions in the export trades worked to bring about more substantive and lasting relief.

Transference remained a vital element of policy until 1937, despite the difficulty of securing jobs for migrants and the tendency of transferees to return home within a relatively short time. It suffered a setback during the world slump and was retarded further by the election of a National Government committed to retrenchment. Cyclical recovery from 1933, however, renewed Ministerial faith in spreading unemployment more evenly throughout the country, and as such weakened the already lacklustre search for a more effective remedy to regional decline. Although the combined weight of press and public concern over the worsening condition of the depressed areas forced the government's hand in 1934, politicians were never desperately concerned to reduce unemployment as such. The Special Areas Act, for example, sought only to co-ordinate existing measures of social relief at a time when influential voices in the

National Government – most notably Neville Chamberlain and Horace Wilson – were stressing the inevitability of heavy localized unemployment and the limited prospects of any regional revival based on new industrial enterprise. Whenever the needs of the depressed areas conflicted with the established norms of national economic policy, discriminatory activity was modified, if not abandoned.

It was the Special Areas Commissioners who sustained the demand for an 'industrial' policy as a way of stabilizing employment in the depressed areas. The subsequent thrust of policy in this direction owed more, however, to the pressure of public opinion and the calculation of short-term party political advantage than ever it did to a belief in the inherent value of industrial diversification. However significant the emergence of a 'move industry' policy by 1937 remains in comparison with the passive inertia of public policy in the early and mid-thirties, it should not blind us to the severe obstacles it faced almost from its inception. Ministers continually refused to upset the prevailing relationship between government and industry and baulked at the idea of manipulating public authority to further private ends. With the compulsory location of industry thus ruled out, the fate of the unemployed, so far as new industrial openings in their locale were concerned, came to depend upon the vigour with which appointed agencies pursued their task of exhortation and, later, upon the willingness of industry to respond to the modest financial inducements on offer.

Labour transference and 'move industry' policies rarely conflicted, partly because they did not overlap seriously as priority objectives. Much was made at the time of the supposed ill-effects of transference in robbing stricken areas of their more mobile, adaptable and skilled workforce. But it is difficult to believe that the alleged effects of voluntary and assisted migration upon the attractiveness of the depressed areas would ever have loomed large in the thinking of what remained a small group of footloose industries, the majority of which preferred anyway to remain in the more prosperous part of the country.

It cannot be denied that Ministry of Labour support for labour transference succeeded in persuading the Treasury that unemployment was no longer a temporary, cyclical phenomenon. Between 1934 and 1939, the Ministry did much to shift the emphasis of official policy away from voluntary social service activity towards a measure of industrial rejuvenation in the depressed regions. What was missing, however, was a level of overall effective demand to help sustain either policy. In themselves, measures designed to encourage interregional movements of resources on a predominantly voluntary basis could only prove of marginal significance, given the scale of the regional problem. Although by 1937 financial inducements were on offer to industrialists to locate in the Special Areas, there was no parallel commitment to boost activity in the more prosperous parts of the country to help foster the search for new factory development elsewhere. Such incentives, moreover, were never meant to alter the distribution of industry to any substantial degree; they were seen as a useful means of boosting business confidence and of influencing those marginal investment decisions that might otherwise have been directed to the Special Areas but for the existence of various deterrents. The emphasis, in other words, was upon redistributing a fixed volume of investment rather than upon increasing the total volume of industrial capital formation. The continuation for most of the thirties of a spatial unemployment problem largely unaffected by the cosmetic application of official 'regional' policy reflected the strength of the limiting factors at work. Whilst the Special Areas Commissioners, and particularly the English Commissioner Malcolm Stewart, succeeded in putting the issues of discriminatory aid and industrial policy on the agenda of government regional activity, they inadvertently enabled Ministers to interpret the problem as one amenable to administrative solution.

Appendix 9.1. *Labour transference, 1928–1938*

1 Labour transferred from the depressed areas to employment through the Employment Exchanges, 1928–1938.

	Men	Women	Boys	Girls	Total individuals	Household and family removals[c]
1928	3,600[a]	360[b]	1,840	na	na	—
1929	36,843	2,239	2,622	1,994[a]	43,698	2,850
1930	28,258	1,752	1,313	1,708	33,031	2,100
1931	17,889	2,631	868	1,986	23,374	1,608
1932	8,359	2,651	628	2,502	14,140	990
1933	5,333	4,038	1,117	2,955	13,443	605
1934	6,828	4,420	1,661	3,512	16,421	1,308
1935	13,379	6,350	5,343	4,648	29,720(19,513)[d]	3,718
1936	20,091	8,008	8,699	5,937	42,735(28,383)[d]	10,025
1937	17,585	6,416	7,675	6,450	38,126(24,314)[d]	7,673
1938	11,637	6,214	4,131	5,496	27,478(18,549)[d]	4,000

[a] Part of year only.
[b] Women and girls transferred after training.
[c] The Household Removal Scheme began in December 1928 and the Family Removal Scheme in 1935.
[d] The figures in brackets refer to transference from the more geographically restricted Special Areas of England and Wales and are based on Pitfield's adjustments of quarterly and monthly data to produce estimates for calendar years. Figures available for Scotland refer to non-comparable time periods and are not able to be presented in the same form. An overall estimate of movement under the transference scheme for the Scottish area during 1935–38 puts the total at 7,774. Pitfield, 'Labour Migration', 260–1.

Sources: Ministry of Labour Gazette, 1928–1938; Pitfield, 'Labour Migration', table 31.

2 Subsidiary Schemes.

2.1 Labour transferring from the depressed areas to prospective employment, 1928–1937.

1928[a]	1500
1935	1016
1936	2039
1937	2052

2.2 Labour transferring from the depressed areas to employment found other than through the Employment Exchanges and assisted by the Ministry of Labour (Free Fares), 1936–1938.

1936	4,000
1937	3,000
1938	2,000

[a] Part of year only.

Source: Pitfield, 'Labour Migration', table 21.

3 Numbers of men and women known to have returned to the depressed areas after transference by the Ministry of Labour.

	Men	Women
1929	na	
1930	9,875	
1931	8,298	na
1932	6,080	
1933	6,221	
1934	7,326	
1935	3,935	2,120
1936	5,665	2,764
1937[a]	2,113	733
	49,513	5,617

[a] First six months only.

Source: Royal Commission on the Geographical Distribution of the Industrial Population, Minutes of Evidence, 1937–39, 257.

Appendix 9.2. *Percentage rates of unemployment in the Special Areas, 1934–1938*

	Scottish area	England and Wales	North-East coast	West Cumberland	South Wales	Great Britain
1934	28.9	35.0	32.9	37.9	37.1	16.6
1935	25.3	32.7	30.7	40.7	34.5	14.8
1936	20.5	27.9	24.6	38.6	31.3	12.5
1937	21.5/16.9	23.1	21.8	30.5	24.4	12.6
1938	19.9/17.3	24.1	20.2	25.9	29.0	13.6

Notes:

Figures are for December of each year, except 1938 where June is taken. (Unemployment generally tends to be higher in winter months than in midsummer).

Boundaries: Total for Ministry of Labour local office areas that include any part of the Special Areas.

Percentages. Numbers registered at Employment Exchanges as a percentage of insured persons aged 16–64 of July of each year (except 1938 which is a percentage of insured at July 1937).

Scotland 1937, 1938: Men and women aged 18 and over on the register as a percentage of the insured population aged 18 and over.

Source: Adapted from Pitfield, 'Labour Migration', table 32.

PART V

Macroeconomic policy options: theory and practice

10 ✳ Pricing jobs: the real wage debate and interwar unemployment

During the 1920s few observers inside or outside of government could resist the temptation to blame industrial stagnation, rising unemployment and falling overseas trade upon the failure of money wages to respond freely or adequately to market signals. Accepted economic doctrine taught that the demand for and supply of labour would be rendered equal by the operation of free market forces. The persistence of unemployment convinced contemporaries, therefore, that particular institutional and attitudinal forces were creating market imperfections to the detriment of Britain's economic revival.

This preoccupation with apparent labour market failure proved to be an important element in the evolution of the radical plea for a more interventionist and managed economy in Britain. Mass unemployment convinced Keynes in particular that whatever pure theory might proclaim, once money wages and prices could not and so obviously did not clear markets, for whatever reason, then some alternative strategy had to be adopted. If aggregate demand fell but money wages did not, he was to contend, the labour market would not clear. Even if money wages did fall, there was no guarantee that planned output would settle at a full employment level. This contention raised the intriguing question of whether the unemployment associated with a level of interwar real wages above market clearing levels could have been reduced earlier and more substantially by a mildly inflationary policy of fiscal expansion. The substance of that debate is taken up in subsequent chapters. First we must examine why the 'problem of wages' figured so prominently in the diagnosis of interwar unemployment.

THE NEO-CLASSICAL THEORY OF WAGES AND EMPLOYMENT[1]

Many government officials, industrialists and economists between the wars saw a distinct connection between the crisis of unemployment and the

---

[1] This section draws upon W. R. Garside, 'The Real Wage Debate and British Interwar Unemployment', in *The Road to Full Employment*, ed. Glynn and Booth. The question of stimulating employment by subsidizing wages from money normally paid in unemployment benefit is discussed above in chapter 8.

prevailing level of money wages and prices. There were differing interpreta-
tions, however, as to the precise nature of this alleged association and of its
consequences for public policy. Nevertheless, the contrast between employment conditions and the behaviour of real wages in the pre-war and post-
war periods, and more particularly the co-existence in Britain in the early
1920s of increased labour costs and falling international competitiveness,
convinced many contemporary observers that real wages, already 'too
high', were a fundamental cause of the prevailing economic malaise.

It was generally conceded that before 1914 British nominal wages
possessed a sufficiently high degree of flexibility to prevent excessive
unemployment. Although there is evidence of standard wage rates being
maintained while prices fell during the 1880s and early 1890s, in contrast
to the experience of the previous thirty years, labour unions during the
Edwardian period proved generally unable to prevent wage reductions in
times of rising unemployment. Collective bargaining procedures and
statutory unemployment insurance had yet to be fully developed; thus the
temptation to accept wage reductions rather than endure extreme poverty
was strong. At that time, Clay noted:

it was impossible to maintain wage rates generally at a level that restricted
employment throughout industry; somewhere, usually at many points, wages (in
relation to efficiency) could be reduced to the level at which expansion could take
place.[2]

According to the classical equilibrium theory of the labour market, both
the demand for and supply of labour were functions of the real wage. The
demand price of labour was equal to its marginal product, that is, the extra
increment to total production arising from the employment of an extra unit
of labour. The supply price of labour was that at which the marginal
product of labour equalled the value which the marginal unit of labour
assigned to the leisure forgone by working (the marginal disutility of
labour). Aggregate labour demand was a negative function and labour
supply a positive function of the real wage. It was the real wage, therefore,
which served to equate the supply of and demand for labour. Providing that
real wages were flexible, market forces would ensure that all those willing to
work at a given real wage would in fact be employed; prices would adjust
through market competition to reduce any temporary unemployment,
leaving those not willing to work at the prevailing level of real wages
voluntarily unemployed. As Pigou put it:

There will always be at work a strong tendency for wage rates to be so related to
demand that everybody is employed . . . The implication is that such unemploy-

___
[2] H. Clay, *The Postwar Unemployment Problem* (1929), 154.

ment as exists at any time is due wholly to the fact that changes in demand conditions are continually taking place and that frictional resistances prevent the appropriate wage adjustments from being made instantaneously.[3]

Classical orthodoxy, in other words, maintained that the existence of unemployment beyond the frictional level was due primarily to real wages being too high in relation to marginal productivity.

It was not surprising, then, that contemporary observers judged the rapid rise in unemployment after 1920 to be the result of the destruction of the self-regulating character of the labour market, giving rise to a level of real wages incompatible with full employment. The problem was not just that money wages had been boosted during and immediately after the war, but that in general they proved resilient in the face of subsequent economic depression, at least after 1923. Until then the imperfection and failings of the labour market system to which informed commentators were later to draw so much attention had not become especially apparent. By 1919 average weekly and hourly money wage rates were more than double their 1914 level. They both continued to rise through to the end of 1920, particularly hourly wage costs following the reduction in normal weekly hours of work across industry during the previous year.[4] However, the collapse of the post-war boom and the sharp rise in unemployment which accompanied it caused money wages to fall during 1920–23 by what were extraordinary percentages by historical standards. Sliding-scale agreements operated in many industries permitting wages to follow prices in a downward direction.[5] The index of weekly money wage rates (July 1914 = 100) declined from 276 in December 1920 to 178 in December 1922. Although real wages improved slightly during 1920–21, the pressure on money wages proved greater. Real weekly wage rates (1914 = 100) rose from 104 in December 1920 to 116 a year later but had fallen to 100 by the end of 1922.[6]

Much of the concern over real wages in the 1920s arose from the fact that the wage flexibility exhibited before 1923 gave way thereafter to a marked degree of money wage rigidity. During 1923–32, in particular, the 'normal' inverse relationship between unemployment and wages broke down. Money wages proved to be 'stickier' than money prices. Nominal wages fell at most 2 to 3 per cent per year and actually increased after 1934 in the face of

---

[3] A. C. Pigou, *The Theory of Unemployment* (1933), 252.

[4] For further details see Dowie, '1919–20 is in Need of Attention', 429–50.

[5] The number of people affected by sliding-scale agreements was estimated to have doubled from 1.5 million to 3 million during the period 1919–22. Many of the wage reductions imposed during 1921–22 resulted from the operation of scales attached to the price of the particular industry's product. J. F. Wright, 'Real Wage Resistance: Eighty Years of the British Cost of Living', in *Economic Theory and Hicksian Themes*, ed. D. A. Collard *et al.* (Oxford, 1984), 152–67.   [6] Dowie, '1919–20 is in Need of Attention', 442.

recorded unemployment levels in excess at times of 16 per cent of insured workers. By 1929 money wages were only 1.3 per cent below their 1925 level. The fall in British unit wage costs during the same four-year period, moreover, was only one-half of that achieved in the United States and only one-quarter of that in Sweden.[7] Even the tightly skewed industrial and regional distribution of unemployment did not produce any significant widening of wage differentials between depressed and growing regions or between expanding and contracting industries. The general impression for most of the years after 1923, in other words, was of rather stable nominal money wages in the face of falling prices.

It is not altogether surprising that the apparent 'inflexibility' of money wages occasioned alarm within government and industry, given the pressure of high unemployment and weak international competitiveness. If only real wages could be forced down, the argument ran, the prospects of Britain's staple industries could be improved, workers would be encouraged to seek openings in the labour-intensive sectors of the economy, and costs would be reduced by competitive wage bidding, thereby stimulating profits and investment. What worried so many contemporaries was that the labour market had become more rigid than hitherto, seemingly incapable without corrective action of equating supply and demand and destined therefore to exacerbate Britain's relative economic decline. Whether the pre-1914 cyclical flexibility of wages had actually pertained to the extent customarily believed was rarely discussed; nor did many question whether the substantial wage reductions during 1920–23 were wholly exceptional both in origin and in scope, suggesting wages to have a plasticity they would not normally possess.[8] Neither the frequency nor the amplitude of declines in wage rates in the early twenties differed markedly from those recorded during cyclical downturns between 1885 and 1913. There is no assurance, in other words, that wage behaviour in the inter-war years was necessarily as abnormal or represented such a marked break with the historical trend as was generally supposed. Nevertheless, there was a widespread belief during the early post-war period that wage 'stickiness' was preventing the economy from absorbing a significant proportion of the registered workforce.

There was no shortage of explanations at the time as to why this situation had developed. Trade unionism had to be partly at fault. The problem as

---

[7] Wages did not, of course, remain uniformly stable in all industries. By the end of 1929 wage rates were below their 1923 level in textiles, boot and shoe manufacture, coalmining, railways and shipping and in building there was a gradual reduction in time rates from 1927.

[8] J. F. Wright, 'Britain's Inter-War Experience', in *The Money Supply and the Exchange Rate*, ed. W. A. Eltis and P. Sinclair (Oxford, 1981), 282–305.

perceived was not the spread of trade unions *per se* (total union membership had doubled between 1914 and 1919 but had fallen by one-third on the eve of the General Strike), but rather the maintenance of their defensive power. Important in this respect was the growth of national collective bargaining in highly unionized industries. Before the First World War collective bargaining had directly affected only a minority of manual workers, but by 1920 the majority of such were covered by national agreements dealing with pay and conditions. Thereafter the coverage of collective bargaining, at least down to 1933, continued to increase faster than trade union membership. This spread of national wage bargaining was believed to have upset the traditional function of wage differentials in reallocating labour from declining to expanding industries and regions. The enforcement by Trade Boards of industry-wide minimum wages in less organized sectors, it was further alleged, had checked the downward flexibility of wages rates so vital for a return to equilibrium at full employment. It also required additional expenditure to establish the required administrative machinery, expenditure which could only restrict employment by adding to the burden on the financial community.

And there were other reasons for concern. Social and political rather than strictly economic criteria had crept into the determination of prevailing wage levels; notions of 'fairness' and of what constituted an appropriate 'living wage' were preventing workers from disturbing existing relativities and of undercutting each other's wage in order to secure employment. In addition, commentators anxiously observed, employers after 1926 had proved reluctant to press their advantage against labour, resisting systematic wage cuts in order to avoid costly disturbances and the disruption of mutually agreed bargaining procedures.[9] There was some truth in this. In the aftermath of the General Strike there was no widespread attack on wages by employers, outside of coalmining. Even during the bleak years of 1930–32 employers on the whole sought to maintain good relations with the trade unions and to react according to their assessment of immediate economic conditions rather than in accordance with any general undertaking that wages had to be reduced.[10]

It was self-evident to others that a major cause of labour market rigidity lay in the operation of the unemployment insurance scheme. The extended availability and rising real value of benefit payments down to 1931, critics maintained, had hampered labour mobility, had taxed industry without

---

[9] W. R. Garside, 'Management and Men: Aspects of British Industrial Relations in the Inter-War Period' in *Essays in British Business History*, ed. B. Supple (Oxford, 1977), 244–67.

[10] H. A. Clegg, *A History of British Trade Unions since 1889*. Vol. 2. *1911–1933* (Oxford, 1985), 539–30.

due regard to profitability and had enabled workers to refuse non-customary wage offers without loss of benefit, encouraging them to extend their search for jobs at 'acceptable' rates of pay. More significantly, trade unionists had been encouraged to push their labour market demands even at the risk of jeopardizing their members' jobs. Employers too were being encouraged to dismiss workers rather than promote efficient production knowing that welfare legislation offered some degree of compensation to those displaced.[11] The Economic Advisory Council maintained that:

Unemployment benefit represents money paid without any services being rendered in return. There is necessarily a danger, therefore, that the payment of unemployment benefit will tend in various ways to weaken the incentive of the worker to obtain work, or to diminish the efforts of the employer to keep his workpeople in regular employment. This danger is the greater in proportion as the rates of unemployment benefit per family approach to the wages of individual wage-earners in unskilled occupations, and the regulations for obtaining it easy to satisfy. Largely for these reasons, a generous and easy system of unemployment relief is apt to make for a rigidity of the economic structure, including an inability to effect wage reductions in cases where they are desirable, which may be a serious handicap in meeting rapidly changing conditions. It is indeed difficult to avoid the conclusion that the rigidity of the wage structure in Great Britain in recent years compared with that of other countries is largely attributable to the generous character of our unemployment insurance system.[12]

To put it another way, trade unionists had less incentive to agree to money wage reductions once the responsibility for the employment consequences of their wage bargains could be shifted to the state. The French economist Jacques Rueff had no doubt that the underlying cause of British unemployment was the effect which unemployment insurance had had in immobilizing wages. Trade union discipline would not have been so effective in the 1920s, he claimed, and would certainly have been insufficient to maintain the resistance of the unemployed to 'the inevitable movement of wages', had not a policy of subsidies to unemployed persons, 'as generous as it was costly to the country, enabled them to remain indefinitely unoccupied rather than transgress the trade union rules'.[13] Pigou echoed such sentiments in 1927, maintaining that post-war wages policy had been

---

[11] See for example the views expressed by H. Clay, *The Post-War Unemployment Problem* (1929); H. Clay 'Unemployment and Wage Rates', *Economic Journal*, 38 (1928) 1–15; E. Cannan. 'The Problem of Unemployment', *Economic Journal*, 40 (1930), 45–55; E. Wilson, 'Unemployment Insurance and the Stability of Wages in Great Britain', *International Labour Review*, 30 (1934), 767–96.

[12] Cab 58/12, Economic Advisory Council. Sub-Committee on the Limits of Economic Policy, 18 March 1932, para 19. For further discussion see chapters 1 to 3.

[13] J. Rueff, 'Les Variations du Chômage en Angleterre', *Revue Politique et Parlementaire*, 125 (1925).

responsible for adding some 5 per cent to the volume of unemployment normally brought about by other factors, partly 'through the added strength given to workpeople's organisations . . . by the development of unemployment insurance'.[14] The Committee of Economists agreed. Before the war, they informed the government in 1930, 'if unemployment in any industry went beyond a certain point, it was in the interests of the trade unions to modify wage-rates. Today, the resistance of the unemployment insurance system, divorced as it has become from any actuarial basis, is tending to prevent those adjustments. Yet if such adjustments are not made, it is a matter of common experience that unemployment follows'.[15]

Despite the forcefulness with which such arguments were put, it proved difficult between the wars and has proved difficult since to establish any significant causal link between unemployment, unemployment insurance, institutional wage procedures, trade union strength and wage rigidity. Unemployment insurance did not provide benefits for all the able-bodied unemployed; nor did the changing rules regarding the eligibility for and method of administration of the available benefits induce widespread or substantial voluntary unemployment. Efforts to resurrect a classical perspective on the interwar period, as we have already seen, have proved largely unpersuasive. The strident claim that the interwar insurance scheme was so 'generous' as to induce a considerable degree of benefit-induced unemployment has been roundly condemned on economic, statistical and administrative grounds. There is little substantive evidence to support the view either that money wages held or that competitive clearing of the labour market was hindered because substantial numbers of the unemployed refrained from seeking or accepting available jobs because of the financial gain to be obtained from remaining out of work.[16] Nor was the defence of minimum wage standards as widespread or as damaging as is sometimes suggested. The rapid extension of Trade Boards down to 1921, raising the number from the pre-war figure of 13 to 63, was checked thereafter, only six new Boards being created after 1921. By 1939 the number of workers covered by the Boards had declined from a post-war peak of 3 million to 1.25 million.[17] In any event, as contemporaries observed, there were good reasons for presuming that, far from creating unemployment, the existence of Trade Boards had helped to prevent the

---

[14] Pigou, 'Wage Policy and Unemployment, 355.
[15] Cab 58/11, Economic Advisory Council. Committee of Economists. Report, 24 October 1930, para 14.
[16] For further elaboration see chapter 1. Cf. F. Maurette, 'Is Unemployment Insurance a Cause of Permanent Unemployment?' *International Labour Review*, 24 (1931), 663–84.
[17] Lowe, *Adjusting to Democracy*, 100.

already depressed level of home demand and employment from being further curtailed by safeguarding working-class purchasing power.[18]

As far as national collective agreements are concerned, they had indeed grown apace, but even in the industries where they were developed they did not necessarily encompass the majority of the workforce; nor did they inhibit flexibility in workplace wage bargaining. As for the strength of trade unions, it is noteworthy that the most dramatic fall in nominal money wages occurred during the early twenties when the union share of the labour force was nearly double that of 1930–31 when wages stayed almost constant at a time of considerably higher unemployment. Had the strength of the unions been the dominant factor, the levels of unemployment in different industries would have been positively correlated to the relative rise in wages in those industries. However, wage changes in industry between 1914 to 1927, as Clay pointed out, displayed an inverse correlation with unemployment.[19]

In a deliberate reassertion of classical orthodoxy, some writers have maintained that the substantial increase in unemployment between 1929 and 1932 was due primarily to the exceptionally rapid rise in the real cost of labour to employers and that the economic recovery from 1932 owed much to the subsequent moderation of real wage growth. Beenstock, Capie and Griffiths's estimate of a demand function for manufacturing employment, using the employer's own product real wage, that is, the nominal wage paid deflated by an appropriate price index, in this case manufacturing output, indicates that whenever own product wages rose the demand for labour fell and vice versa.[20] Other research suggests that three-quarters of all job losses during 1929–32 were attributable to real wage growth in excess of the trend rate for 1921–28, whilst one-third of the growth in the population at work during the depression (and one half of the effective job gains after 1932) were the result of real wage moderation.[21] The issue, however, is far

---

[18] The Royal Commission appointed in 1922 to examine the working of Trade Boards reported that they were not a major cause of unemployment. For further discussion see Lowe, 'The Erosion of State Intervention in Britain, 1917–24', 270–86.

[19] Clay, 'Unemployment and Wage Rates'. At the end of January 1930 the recorded unemployment percentage of all insured industry was 12.6. In coal it was 12.9, iron and steel 23.7, shipbuilding 23.4, general engineering 10.1, cotton 20 and woollen and worsted 20.5.

[20] M. Beenstock, F. Capie and B. Griffiths, 'Economic Recovery in the United Kingdom in the 1930s', Bank of England Panel of Academic Consultants, Panel Paper No. 23, 1984. See also F. Capie, 'Unemployment and Real Wages' in *The Road to Full Employment*, ed. Glynn and Booth; A. Newhall and J. Symons, 'Wages and Employment between the Wars', Centre for Labour Economics, London School of Economics, Discussion Paper No. 257, October 1986.

[21] M. Beenstock and P. Warburton, 'Wages and Unemployment in Inter-War Britain', *Explorations in Economic History*, 23 (1986), 153–72; M. Beenstock, 'Real Wages and Unemployment in the 1930s: A Reply', *National Institute Economic Review*, 119 (1987), 76–8.

from settled. Although there is evidence of inverse movements in the later 1930s, real wage variations do not correspond to variations in employment at the critical turning points of 1929 and 1932. Dimsdale's careful reworking of the available data, moreover, suggests that both the scale of the rise and fall of manufacturing product real wages and their alleged relationship with employment in depression and recovery have been considerably exaggerated.[22]

A substantially lower level of wages during the twenties would doubtless have raised the demand for labour and stimulated higher investment. Yet it is by no means certain that wage rates could have been driven to levels low enough to have made a serious impact upon unemployment in the staple industries or depressed regions. The question of whether high labour costs in the 1920s were an independent source of unemployment or simply one unfortunate result of an exchange rate policy which squeezed employers between domestic money wages and world prices, is one which cannot yet be answered precisely. What is more probable, as Matthews and others have pointed out, is that before 1930 'rises in the real cost of labour contributed to increasing unemployment' but that 'the effects are difficult to separate from those of other influences tending in the same direction'.[23] Likewise, the more moderate growth of money wages in the 1930s is likely to have afforded some assistance towards recovery but only to a limited extent.

UNEMPLOYMENT AND WAGES IN THE 1920s

There was a strong temptation nevertheless for contemporary businessmen and politicians, concerned about rising labour costs and mounting unemployment at home and declining international competitiveness abroad, to see in an enforced reduction of real wages a direct and effective remedy for Britain's economic ills. The Chancellor of the Exchequer appealed as early as September 1921 for unemployment relief expenditure to be the lowest minimum possible to prevent starvation in order that it should not interfere with the more important process of effecting a systematic reduction in wage costs. A committee headed by Hilton Young, Financial Secretary at the Treasury, reported to the Prime Minister in the autumn of the same year that although 'the fundamental causes of unemployment are of a world-wide character' the most immediate

[22] T. J. Hatton, 'The Analysis of Unemployment in Interwar Britain: A Survey of Research', Centre for Economic Policy Research, Discussion Paper No. 66, June 1985, 15–20; N. H. Dimsdale, 'Employment and Real Wages in the Inter-War Period', *National Institute Economic Review*, 110 (1984), 94–103.
[23] R. C. O. Matthews *et al.*, *British Economic Growth 1856–1973* (Oxford, 1982), 314–15.

influence in Britain was 'the relatively high costs of production caused mainly by the higher rates of wages'.[24] And in a memorandum to the Cabinet Committee on Unemployment in October 1921 the Federation of British Industries urged the government not to ignore economic reality:

If foreign labour costs are below ours in any trade, either through their workmen accepting lower rates of remuneration than ours or giving higher efficiency for similar remuneration, no artificial measures will enable us to continue to give employment in that trade.

The choice before the country, therefore, was to increase labour productivity or to enforce wage cuts, either by agreement 'or by the sheer force of circumstances – continued unemployment, continued distress and in the ultimate resort starvation for the workmen and bankruptcy for the employer'.[25] Over the course of 1921–22, the most powerful members of the National Confederation of Employers' Organizations, backed by the Federation of British Industries, mounted a determined offensive to reduce the level of money wages in order to reduce costs of production and to protect profits. In doing so, they raised the wage factor from the traditional arena of collective bargaining to the forefront of the debate over the causes of job losses in the staple export trades. In the preamble to the General Strike, Baldwin's reported assertion that 'all workers in this country have got to take reductions in wages to help put industry on its feet'[26] proved sufficient to galvanize TUC support for the miners' struggle.

Protestations that unduly high wage costs were a severe handicap to Britain's industrial, but particularly export, supremacy continued into the thirties. It was neither law nor contract that prevented the necessary adjustment to money wage costs, the Economic Advisory Council's Committee of Economists informed the Government in 1930:

but a strong social resistance to changes which, for the very reason that they would have to take place piece-meal and without any ordered plan, are likely to be open to charges of inequity and injustice. But it is the inevitable result of so many of the items of production costs remaining fixed in terms of money that the residue which forms the inducement to the businessmen . . . is reduced to vanishing point. The result of all this is that money costs . . . are out of line with money prices. Consequently, producers lose money; they are unable to maintain their former labour forces; and unemployment ensues on a colossal scale.[27]

Early in 1931, with Britain already deeply affected by world slump, employers warned that the only practical solution to the crisis was 'to

---

[24] Cab 24/128, CP 3363, Proposals of Commander Hilton Young's Committee Submitted to the Prime Minister at Gairloch, 2 October 1921.
[25] Cab 27/120, Committee on Unemployment. The Trade Depression, 14 October 1921.
[26] *Daily Herald*, 31 July 1925. Baldwin later denied the statement.
[27] Cab 58/11, Economic Advisory Council. Committee of Economists. Report, 24 October 1930, paras 23–4.

reduce wages, to let export industries, not sheltered trades, set the wage pattern [and] to cut unemployment benefit'.[28] Hubert Henderson had warned fellow members of the Committee of Economists in October 1930 that 'in view of the turn which world prices have taken and the extreme slenderness of the chances of substantial recovery . . . we have no alternative now but to face up to the disagreeable reactionary necessity of cutting costs (including wages) in industry . . . That I say is the plain moral of the situation, as plain as a pikestaff'.[29]

Few denied the attractiveness of short-circuiting deflation on an equitable basis by some sort of national consensus aimed at the simultaneous reduction of money, salary and rentier income. But this was a dim prospect, not least because the TUC adamantly refused to sacrifice wages for jobs, arguing that any reduction in working-class consumption would merely intensify falling prices and profits at home, thus further hindering economic revival. This defence of wages it must be said was less an embryonic expression of Keynesianism than an instinct basic to the whole trade union movement. More perceptive observers, however, argued that it was fallacious to attempt to counter unemployment through a direct assault on money wages. It was a mistake, Keynes argued in the late 1920s, to single out real wages as a fundamental cause of unemployment; the prevailing level of real wages was merely the by-product of misguided monetary policy which, under the pressure of exchange appreciation, had exerted a differential pressure on particular industries making profitable operations extremely difficult.[30]

At the heart of Keynes's condemnation of the return to gold at the pre-war parity in 1925 was his conviction that it would be impossible to secure the required reduction in money wages to offset the effect of an overvalued pound without singling out particularly vulnerable groups of workers (he had the coalminers in mind) who shared a common concern to defend living standards and to maintain wage relativities. Keynes did not presume that money wages were fixed or rigid in a downward direction; what he stressed was that, given the institutional and psychological background against which policy had to be framed, deliberate wage-cutting as a way of reducing unemployment would prove socially chaotic, politically impracticable and ultimately self-defeating. As a member of the Macmillan Committee, he expressed serious doubts:

as to whether reductions of salaries and wages are the right way of dealing with the existing international slump. It is not easy to see how we can expect a revival in our

[28] National Confederation of Employers' Organisations, *The Industrial Situation*, 11 February 1931, cited in Dintenfass, 'The TUC, the FBI and British Economic Policy', 169.
[29] Cited in Howson and Winch, *The Economic Advisory Council*, 69–70.
[30] J. M. Keynes, 'The Question of High Wages', *Political Quarterly*, 1 (1930), 110–24.

foreign trade, on a sufficient scale to be of much value to us, by any other means than through a revival of world demand . . . A policy intended to direct increased purchasing power into the right channels at home and abroad with a view to restoring equilibrium at the *present* level of costs, would . . . be much wiser . . . than a policy of trying to cut our costs faster than the rest of the world can cut theirs.[31]

By the late 1920s enthusiasm for money wage cuts as a counter to unemployment had certainly waned. Henry Clay conceded that:

only a concerted and co-ordinated revision of all wage-rates would afford any great stimulus to employment; and for such co-ordinated action there is no machinery. Wage revision therefore offers little chance of reducing costs.[32]

Mosley too rejected the idea that if only workers were prepared to accept a lower wage, production would thereby be rendered profitable and full employment restored. In his view wage reductions on any large scale merely destroyed the purchasing power of the community and threatened to intensify the problem of idle capacity.[33] In his evidence to the Macmillan Committee even Pigou, customarily though unfairly regarded as the arch-spokesman of classical economics, refused to accept that unduly high wages were necessarily the cause of persistent unemployment or that a direct assault on money wages would offer any effective or lasting remedy.[34] 'The more wages are cut down', George Lansbury told Cabinet colleagues in 1930, 'the more the standard of life is depressed, the more unemployment we shall be cursed with'.[35]

Nor was the case against wage-cutting as a means of combating unemployment conducted solely in domestic terms. To some critics the policy was nothing less than a perverted and mistaken form of economic nationalism; a strategic ploy to steal a march on the rest of the world by reducing costs of production, thereby hoping to capture prosperity at the expense of others. But, as the economist G. D. H. Cole reminded the International Labour Office in 1931, such an approach was myopic and dangerous. 'A successful campaign to reduce wage rates in one country is exceedingly likely . . . to usher in a general campaign for their reduction in all countries', he maintained. What was needed in the world was 'a larger amount of income available for spending on consumable commodities and not . . . a contraction of consumers' demand'. There was 'no substance' in

[31] Cmd. 3897, Addendum I, 1931, para 19.
[32] Clay, *The Post-War Unemployment Problem*, 156.
[33] Skidelsky, *Oswald Mosley*, chapters 9 and 10.
[34] Committee on Finance and Industry, Minutes of Evidence, Vol. 2, May 1930, 48. For a succinct analysis of Pigou's views in this respect see T. W. Hutchison, 'Demythologising the Keynesian Revolution: Pigou, Wage-Cuts and *The General Theory*', *On Revolutions and Progress in Economic Knowledge* (Cambridge, 1978), 175–99.
[35] Cab 24/216, CP 390, Unemployment Policy. Note by First Commissioner of Works, 22 November 1930.

the view that unemployment was caused largely by the maintenance of uneconomically high wage-rates. On the contrary, any rigidity in the wage structure was 'a blessing' in so far as it helped to save nations from engaging in competitive wage-cutting in an effort to increase trade. 'In short', Cole wrote, 'the idea that high wage-rates and a high level of employment stand in an antithetical relation is as far from the truth as it is possible for any superficially plausible idea to be'. If the world would only co-operate in order to increase the purchasing power of the worker, instead of competing to reduce it, it was far more likely that depression would be overcome.[36]

The enforced suspension of the gold standard in the wake of the 1931 financial crisis transformed official attitudes towards the wages issue. The floating of the pound provided Britain with a competitive edge in the short term and the hope reigned that when the world economy recovered prices would increase to a sufficient extent to be consistent with profitable trade on the basis of prevailing costs. As the Economic Advisory Council explained in 1932:

So long as the pound remained at gold parity, there was a strong case for holding that all-round reductions of money wages were essential unless British industry was to lose its hold on world markets to a disastrous extent, and upon this assumption it was arguable that the state should lead the way by reducing drastically the pay of its own servants . . . The fall of the pound has served, however, to improve materially the competitive position of British industry in world markets . . . It is reasonable . . . to hope that when world trade recovers, prices will increase to a sufficient extent to be consistent with profitable trade conditions on the basis of the present level of wages. In the meantime, general reductions in wages . . . initiated by Government example, might serve to accentuate business depression by encouraging the belief that prices were likely to fall still further.[37]

Though Britain's trading advantage fast disappeared in the face of the subsequent devaluation of the dollar and the franc, a wave of economic nationalism abroad strengthened trade restrictions and increased the threat of retaliation against any country seeking unilaterally to improve its cost competitiveness.

KEYNESIAN THEORY, UNEMPLOYMENT AND WAGES IN THE 1930S

It was in these circumstances that Keynes, already convinced of the folly of deflation as a cure for depression and deeply suspicious of the free market system as a guarantor of full employment equilibrium, vigorously attacked any notion of reformulating economic policy along strictly classical lines.

[36] G. D. H. Cole, 'Wages and Employment', in *Unemployment Problems in 1931*, International Labour Office, Studies and Reports, Series C, No. 16, (Geneva, 1931), 255–80.
[37] Cab 58/12, Economic Advisory Council. Sub-Committee on the Limits of Economic Policy. Report, 18 March 1932.

The *theoretical* case for attacking real wage costs was as yet intact. In the years before and immediately after the publication of the General Theory Keynes himself accepted the orthodox doctrine that with a given capital stock and state of technology the marginal product of labour would tend to fall as employment expanded. Any reduction in unemployment, in other words, would require a cut in the real wage because diminishing returns would effectively raise the supply price of increased output. There was considerable agreement that a reduction in real wages could do much to ease Britain's industrial and trading difficulties; the contentious issue was how best to bring this about.

What Keynes and others came to realize was that the classical doctrine involved such unrealistic assumptions – of a stable, self-regulating labour market with free competition and perfect mobility of labour – as to render it incapable of providing any policy prescriptions valid in the real world. In the mid-1920s both Pigou and Keynes believed that manipulation of wages could in theory increase employment. But because the existing system of wage determination did not in their view possess sufficient flexibility for practical and procedural reasons to secure the required reductions, action to increase employment had to be consistent with prevailing real wage standards. Faced therefore with the reality of institutionalized wage bargaining, with the potentially high cost in economic and social terms of industrial conflict, and with a labour movement determined to defend the hierarchy of relative wages, it would be foolish, Keynes maintained, to seek a remedy for economic depression through cuts in money wages. There was no guarantee, moreover, that recourse to such a strategy in an open economy would enable Britain to expand its sales or be free from retalitory wage-cutting abroad. In any event, Keynes argued further, wage cuts were an unreliable 'cure' for unemployment because they were incapable in themselves of expanding employment at home merely because producers' costs had been reduced. Behavioural assumptions which might be valid at the level of the individual firm did not necessarily hold at the aggregate level. A cut in the money wage would increase employment only if prices remained fixed or did not fall by as much as the money wage so that real wages were reduced. But since labour costs governed the supply price of products in the short run, a cut in money wages could conceivably lead to product prices falling in the same proportion as the money wage, leaving the real wage unchanged (unless there was a simultaneous increase in demand). Product prices would chase wages down without any stimulus to expanded output or employment. The resultant redistribution of real income was likely, moreover, to prove unfavourable to spending and employment, drawing income away from those whose marginal propensity to consume was high. Furthermore, if such wage cuts increased the expectation of future falls in wages and prices the uncertainty and gloom could depress businessmen's incentive to invest. There had to be a more sensible alternative.

Contrary to what many economists and historians have since chosen to believe, Pigou did not champion the orthodox view. The notion that real wages were 'too high', he informed the Macmillan Committee in 1931, was true only given the existing demand for labour. As he explained:

If you have got unemployment, one can say that the cause of the unemployment is either that the real rate of wages is all right, but there is not enough demand, or if one takes the demand as given one can say that the rate of wages is too high . . . So I do not want to say that unduly high wages are the cause.[38]

For prosperity to be restored, he wrote two years later:

either money costs must fall or money prices must rise. The practical difficulties in the way of the former solution have proved so serious and the friction to be overcome so great that the main body of instructed opinion has turned towards the latter.[39]

'Instructed opinion', in other words, was resolutely seeking some alternative means of stimulating economic activity and employment without recourse to deliberate cost-cutting. Keynes believed that the real wage could only be reduced by an increase in product demand which would raise product prices relative to the money wage. Only then would the real wage fall and employment increase. In his view the government ought to have engaged in deficit-financed public spending to raise the trend level of investment and, at the same time, to have increased the money supply in order to keep the rate of interest low, thereby helping to sustain private investment and business confidence. Without such stimuli, confidence would sag and transactors would hold money instead of real assets. The resultant decline in the money value of real assets would discourage investment but encourage transactors to accumulate money balances by spending less than they earned. The demand for real investment would fall, depressing aggregate product demand.

The inference was clear: it was easier to lower real wages by raising prices than by lowering money wages. Workers after all would be more likely to accept an economy-wide price increase (reducing all real wages proportionately) than they would sectional attacks on money incomes which threatened their relative wage positions. By using fiscal and monetary means, it would be the level of employment determined by aggregate

[38] Committee on Finance and Industry, Minutes of Evidence, Vol. 2, May 1930, 48.
[39] *The Times*, 6 January 1933.

demand that would set the real wage; the classical postulate that the real wage determined employment would therefore be turned on its head.[40]

But the classical postulate still had its supporters. The contemporary economist Lionel Robbins insisted in 1934 that unemployment need not have risen so dramatically during the world slump had wage rates been allowed to fall to much lower levels. The trade unions should have been 'guided by considerations of employment' and should not have sought to maintain wage income. 'A policy which holds wage rates rigid when the equilibrium rate has altered', Robbins wrote, 'is a policy which creates unemployment'.[41] Contemporaries feared that in the long run trade unions had the power to neutralize the effects of any expansionary monetary and fiscal policy by linking money wage settlements to the price level, effectively stipulating a real wage. The critical point, on reflection, was whether a monetary and fiscal stimulus was likely at the time to drive up money wages because of the existence of a real-wage constraint or whether there existed sufficient slack in the labour market for money wages to lag behind prices. Casson's assessment of the 1930s is relevant in this context. During that time, he writes:

The relatively high level of unemployment, coupled with surprisingly good industrial relations, seem to have prevented the trade unions from forcing the issue in this way. Keynes judged that . . . the British economy could be reflated without inducing a substantial increase in money wages, and he seems to have been broadly correct.[42]

Ironically the offensive launched by Keynes and Pigou, denouncing on practical, social and political grounds any immediate recourse to direct cuts in wages as a means of boosting industrial competitiveness and employment, had given way by 1936 to an alternative emphasis upon demand expansion. It was one nevertheless which reasserted the belief that a fall in unemployment required a reduction in real wages. The General Theory implied as much, principally because it remained wedded to the classical view of the diminishing marginal productivity of labour.

But what if in conditions of high unemployment, low output and idle capacity labour's marginal cost did not rise with increased output? The possibility then arose of a positive relation between employment and the

---

[40] G. W. Maynard, 'Keynes and Unemployment Today', *Three Banks Review*, 120 (1978), 3–20; A. P. Thirlwall, 'Keynesian Employment Theory is not Defunct', *Three Banks Review*, 131 (1981), 14–29. The range of policy options was even wider than suggested here. Keynes's support for protection in the late 1920s and early 1930s sprang in part from the manner in which a tariff-induced inflation would help to reduce the prevailing level of real wages. See chapter 6.

[41] L. Robbins, *The Great Depression* (1934), 60–75; 160–72, 186–93.

[42] M. Casson, *Economics of Unemployment. An Historical Perspective* (1983), 162.

real wage. Indeed by the end of the 1930s Keynes, prompted by suggestive evidence for Britain and the United States of a positive relation between money wages, real wages and employment, re-examined the historical evidence for the period 1880–1914 and found a positive relation in the booms and slumps, except over the cycle 1880–86. Cyclical variations in real wages from 1886 had revealed them to be higher in periods of rising employment than in periods of depression. Keynes's assertions in the General Theory had been originally based on Marshall's empirical findings relating to booms and slumps prior to 1886. 'It seems', he wrote, 'that we have been living all these years on a generalization which held good by exception in the years 1880–86, which was the formative period in Marshall's thought in this matter, but has never once held good in the fifty years since he crystallized it!'[43]

The inference to be drawn was that in an economy operating at less than optimum output with plant and labour only partially employed, the marginal product of labour could rise (and its marginal cost fall) as output expanded and as capacity became more fully utilized. Once the possibility of increasing returns to labour was accepted, the classical view that unemployment was high because real wages were too high made little sense since an expansion of output could permit an increase both in employment and the real wage. This at once strengthened the case for a planned expansionist policy since a fall in real wages was no longer regarded as a prior condition for a rise in employment.[44]

By 1937 the economy displayed an exceptional degree of rigidity and there is evidence that the rate of measured unemployment consistent with non-accelerating inflation had begun to rise.[45] Although this prompted Keynes to caution against increased government expenditure[46] it did not deflect him in his belief in the ultimate value of demand-induced expansion as the more positive and socially acceptable way of raising the aggregate level of employment and activity. On the contrary, the persistence of involuntary unemployment mirrored the fact that the labour market did not automatically clear; what was required, according to Keynes, was a rise in aggregate demand engendered by expansionary fiscal policy sufficient to re-employ workers forced through rising prices to accept a decline in real wages. There was little doubt at the time, compared for example to the anxieties so prominently expressed in Britain during the 1980s, that

[43] J. M. Keynes, 'Relative Movement of Real Wages and Output', *Economic Journal*, 49 (1939), 34–51. See also N. Kaldor, 'Keynesian Economics after Fifty Years' in *Keynes and the Modern World*, ed. D. Worswick and J. Trevithick (Cambridge, 1983), 1–48.

[44] Thirlwall, 'Keynesian Employment Theory', 24–6.

[45] N. R. Crafts, 'Long-Term Unemployment, Excess Demand and the Wage Equation in Britain, 1925–1939', Centre for Economic Policy Research, Discussion Paper No. 147, December 1986.   [46] See chapter 13.

organized labour would accept a fall in real wages achieved in this way. So long as there was substantial unemployment, it was believed, trade unions would not respond to the rise in prices caused by an expansion of demand by insisting on a compensating rise in money wages.

This anti-unemployment strategy challenged the very essence of conventional economic orthodoxy. 'Unsound' money, Whitehall preached, threatened both the stability of national and international credit and the existing relationship between private enterprise and central government. The inflationary impact of budget deficits, it was further argued, would hinder economic recovery by wrecking confidence and by undermining all that the authorities were doing to encourage the creation of 'real' jobs through cautious improvements in industrial and trading performance. Economists and politicians of a more radical persuasion were far less sanguine; they doubted the recuperative powers of the free market and pressed for more deliberate interventionist policies aimed at boosting economic activity on a national scale. The substance and fate of these opposing views are detailed in subsequent chapters. But since much of the argument centred upon the alleged need for job-creating schemes of national investment on a scale for greater than governments had previously contemplated, we must first examine the efforts that were officially made to foster public works down to the early 1930s.

11 * Relief or remedy? The development of public works policy, 1920–1932

COUNTER-CYCLICAL PUBLIC WORKS, EMERGENCY RELIEF AND THE UNEMPLOYMENT GRANTS COMMITTEE

Official attitudes towards public works as an appropriate response to interwar unemployment were strongly influenced by the intellectual and administrative precepts of the late Victorian and Edwardian periods. By the late nineteenth century the most generally accepted method of alleviating the distress of the unemployed outside of the Poor Law was by the provision of emergency relief works by local authorities. The work provided was usually labour intensive, required few skills and, by way of a deterrent, attracted wages at less than the normal market rate for unskilled labour. It was aimed primarily at combining the largest increase in employment with the smallest possible capital outlay, engaging the least efficient workmen on tasks of doubtful utility.[1] The principal drawback of such projects, apart from being demoralizing, wasteful, expensive and singularly inappropriate as a means of equipping men for future work, was that they were devoid of any concept of stabilizing employment, merely waiting as they did upon the outbreak of acute unemployment.

Towards the end of the Edwardian period, however, a shift occurred away from this fatalistic emphasis upon less eligibility towards the idea of manipulating by advancement or retardation existing plans for capital expenditure for the benefit of the unemployed with recognized skills. It owed its inspiration to the work of A. L. Bowley and to the influential Minority Report of the Royal Commission on the Poor Laws. Drawing on Bowley's earlier evidence to the Royal Commission, the Minority Report proposed in 1909 that the government should earmark a definite proportion of its normal capital expenditure to finance a programme of public works on an

---

[1] The intention nevertheless was to avoid the stigma of pauperism. From 1905 every local authority with more than 50,000 inhabitants was obliged to establish a Distress Committee to provide such assistance to the unemployed. For further details see Harris, *Unemployment and Politics*; K. D. Brown, *Labour and Unemployment, 1900–1914* (1971).

ordinary commercial basis, attracting the customary level of wages and executed before unemployment became acute, that is, before it rose above 4 per cent, the level then regarded as normal for frictional, seasonal and casual unemployment.[2]

Bowley himself was aware of the limitations of the scheme so readily embraced by the signatories of the Minority Report. 'This is not a proposal to cure or to diminish unemployment', he wrote, 'but only to equalise it over the years'.[3] But, as a means of compensating for swings in private investment activity without committing the state to raising its trend level of expenditure over the business cycle, these proposals held a certain attraction. Pigou, Beveridge and Robertson endorsed them with varying degrees of enthusiasm,[4] though each remained acutely conscious of the 'inevitability' of cyclical fluctuations and of the principal need to improve labour mobility to counter the changing fortunes of industry. 'It is, indeed, true', wrote Pigou in 1913, 'that the State is unable . . . to increase the demand for labour on the whole on the average good and bad times together'.[5]

Nonetheless, the idea of timing the implementation of government contracts to mitigate unemployment, rather than relying upon old-style local authority relief works, gradually took root. The TUC had anticipated such ideas as early as 1905. Its *Special Report on Unemployment* attacked the government's failure to regulate scheduled investment expenditure in a counter-cyclical way and urged officials to encourage both local government and private enterprise to join in a concerted effort to mitigate the effects of the trade cycle.[6] Provision was made under the Development and Road Fund Act, 1909, for the establishment of a Development Commission to assist in the execution of public works, having regard 'to the general state and prospects of employment'. The value of such works was assessed in social and human as well as economic and financial terms; work schemes were not expected at the time to eliminate cyclical fluctuations entirely.[7] Even so, early in 1914 the Commission set aside a reserve for use in depression years and, when war started, drew upon it for works in areas where unemployment persisted.

[2] Royal Commission on the Poor Laws, Minority Report, Cd. 4499, 1909, Part II.
[3] A. L. Bowley, 'The Regularisation of the Demand for Labour by the Advancement or Retardation of Public Works', in *The Regularisation of Industry*, National Movement Towards a Christian Order of Industry and Commerce (Cambridge, 1924), 40.
[4] A. Pigou, *Unemployment*, (1913): W. Beveridge, *Unemployment: A Problem of Industry*, (1909); D. H. Robertson. *A Study of Industrial Fluctuations* (1915). Robertson emphasized the short-fall in the demand for capital goods as the principal cause of unemployment and called for economic policy to create 'an artificial elevation in the demand for construction goods'.   [5] Pigou, *Unemployment*, 172.
[6] Dintenfass, 'The TUC, the FBI and British Economic Policy', 17–20.
[7] Harris, *Unemployment and Politics*, 341.

It was only the outbreak of hostilities that prevented a Treasury Committee from investigating 'what steps might be taken with a view to regularising the total demand for labour from year to year and in different seasons, by adjusting the distribution of public works conducted or given out by Government Departments'.[8] In its anxiety over the likely state of trade and employment after the war the Labour Party called upon the government in 1917 'to maintain at an appropriately uniform level the national aggregate demand for labour, by controlling the giving out of orders by government Departments and local authorities, in such a way as to make them vary inversely with the demands of private employers'.[9] By 1919 the wartime coalition government had accepted a suggestion of the provisional Joint Committee of the Industrial Conference that it should 'undertake the definite duty of stimulating the demand for labour in bad times by postponing contracts of a non-urgent character until it is necessary to promote a demand for labour owing to falling trade'.[10] In the same year the Ministry of Labour pleaded that the principal government contracting departments should decide on the allocation of contracts only after considering the current distribution of unemployment, even to the extent of authorizing work at a cost of not more than 10 per cent above the lowest tender if industrial conditions appeared to justify it. 'One of the dangers of the coming winter', warned the Ministry, 'is that the government will be strongly pressed to open relief works, which would be very expensive and demoralizing . . . It would be much better to pay a little more for contracts.'[11] And over the next two years the Ministry tried, unsuccessfully, to have a permanent committee established to co-ordinate and regulate the flow of government contracts to help reduce fluctuations in employment.

The idea of advance planning of public works as a means of stabilizing output and employment was revived on numerous occasions throughout the first post-war decade but without much success. In its Prevention of Unemployment Bill, 1925, the Labour Party proposed that a National Employment and Development Board should prepare public works schemes for application in times of depression. Any unexpended portion of its £10 million annual grant was to be accumulated year by year for use whenever employment conditions demanded it. The Bill was rejected. It was reintroduced in 1926 and again rejected. Both the conference of employers

---

[8] B. Swann and M. Turnbull, *Records of Interest to Social Scientists: Employment and Unemployment* (1978), 480.
[9] Labour Party, *The Prevention of Unemployment After the War*, 1917, para 4.
[10] Swann and Turnbull, *Records of Interest to Social Scientists*, 513–14.
[11] T1/12414, 'Suggested Placing of Government Contracts with reference to Unemployment', 1919.

and trade unionists on industrial reorganization and industrial relations (the Melchett–Turner Conference) and the Balfour Committee on Industry and Trade suggested in 1929 that a development fund should be established to encourage the acceleration or retardation of public works schemes for the relief of unemployment.

None of this special pleading for counter-cyclical public works made much impact, and for good reason. The 'good times' of the post-war period were so shortlived that it proved virtually impossible to shore up productive work for subsequent periods of depressed economic activity. Indeed it was the substantial rise in unemployment in the autumn of 1920 and the prospect of a further deterioration during the following winter that produced a sudden and marked reorientation of government policy, one which was destined to shape official public works activity for the remainder of the decade. As the recession deepened towards the end of 1920, Ministers realized that they could no longer consider merely how best to postpone public investment programmes for use in a later depression; they were obliged instead to put in hand whatever public works were available to meet the prevailing disorganization of the labour market. Frustration was mounting among many of the younger, unskilled able-bodied within a land supposedly 'fit for heroes'. Given the urgent need to provide immediate employment, the emphasis of policy shifted away from the advance planning of works on a strictly counter-cyclical basis towards the advance execution of public works which under ordinary circumstances would have been undertaken at some other time.

Emergency relief work came to be regarded as the only practicable means of avoiding serious social unrest and political unpopularity.[12] Its success depended largely upon the co-operation of the local authorities. Almost from the beginning of the post-war recession, however, it became clear that, despite the removal of the wartime restrictions on local government borrowing for public works, only the promise of further government financial assistance would encourage local authorities to act swiftly enough to meet the emergency situation. Accordingly, the government agreed in 1920 to subsidize the annual charge on works undertaken by local authorities out of capital expenditure and to meet part of the wages bill for approved schemes of useful work (other than on roads and housing). Ministers noted anxiously that 'the only adequate solution is in the revival of trade' and warned that Exchequer contributions would cease 'as soon as employment is normal'.[13]

The government body entrusted with these responsibilities was the

---

[12] Cab 24/112, CP 1907, Interim Report of Unemployment Committee, October 1920.
[13] Cab 27/190, CP 2202, Cabinet Unemployment Committee. Third Interim Report, 30 November 1920.

Unemployment Grants Committee (UGC), appointed in December 1920 to administer a scheme of financial aid according to the following general principles: expenditure was not to exceed a total of £3,000,000; works would be approved only in areas where the existence of serious unemployment which was not otherwise provided for was certified by the Ministry of Labour; preference had to be given in employment to unemployed ex-servicemen; the grant should not exceed 30 per cent of the wages bill of additional men employed; and the works should be 'of public utility'. The Committee's attitude towards applications for grants varied in accordance with the changing perception of successive governments as to the nature and scale of the unemployment crisis.[14] Those schemes which received assistance were mainly works of sewerage and salvage disposal, the supply of electricity, the extension or improvement of docks and harbours, and the construction, diversion and reconstruction of those unclassified roads ineligible for financial aid from the Road Fund.

The original intention of the grant scheme was to provide temporary relief in localities where severe unemployment had arisen because of the failure of industry to absorb demobilized men from the services. It was not anticipated at first that there would be any need to provide emergency relief work beyond the spring of 1921 but the worsening unemployment situation led to the renewal of schemes for successive winters. Much of the official effort during the first half of the twenties, therefore, went into devising means of encouraging local authorities to respond more positively to an improved range of financial subsidies from the UGC. The grant in support of wages, originally set at 30 per cent, reached 75 per cent by August 1924. From September 1921 local authorities were encouraged to undertake works financed by loans for which government aid on a pound-for-pound basis were made available to meet the cost of repayment charges. And the rule that grants should be conditional upon the issue of a Ministry of Labour certificate confirming the existence of serious unemployment was dropped in March 1924 (although unemployment continued to be a deciding factor).[15]

An official survey of UGC works in March 1922 reported that:

in almost all cases the output is . . . very considerably below normal . . . The effect on unemployment of a particular scheme . . . is usually impossible to estimate but . . . the combined effect is felt in the creation of a better state of feeling amongst the unemployed, and in a stoppage of deputations and demonstrations.[16]

---

[14] For details of the changing terms and conditions attached to the grants in aid see Final Report of the Unemployment Grants Committee, Cmd. 4354, 1933.

[15] The quantitative estimate of what constituted serious unemployment fluctuated during the course of the UGC's activities from 5 to 15 per cent.

[16] Cab 24/134, CP 3812, Unemployment Relief Works, 7 March 1922.

Alfred Mond, Minister of Health, urged the Cabinet in 1921 not to falter in its encouragement of local authority activity and for good reason:

> To turn down ruthlessly hundreds of schemes of Local Authorities in areas where the unemployment is of a grave character would serve but to infuriate the element inclined to violent action and would play into the hands of extremists . . . Apart from Unemployment Insurance and assistance to dependants, the one and only measure which has any result manifest to the man in the street, is that of stimulating Local Authorities by grants to undertake works of public utility.[17]

By the summer of 1923 the UGC had dealt with almost 10,000 schemes and had approved grants in respect of projects costing over £40 million. But there were signs of flagging enthusiasm. Many local authorities were unduly hampered by financial difficulties and had practically exhausted identifiable schemes of work deemed suitable for the reduction of unemployment. The UGC, having surveyed 35 'representative' authorities in June 1924, was clearly conscious that many ventures would lapse under apathy unless the level and availability of grant aid was substantially improved to meet the growing level of local indebtedness. Authorities in recent years, it reported:

> have been putting in hand 'accelerated' works, that is to say, works which would not be done at all at the present time and which indeed need not be done except to relieve unemployment. But they are now rather forced back on work which really ought to be done in the ordinary course but which, owing to the financial burdens they have undertaken for 'accelerated' works, they feel quite unable to proceed with at the present time without state assistance.

The Borough Engineer of Salford informed the UGC that 'if he were given a free gift of half a million pounds to provide schemes he could not think of any'.[18]

As an effective attack on mounting unemployment, the public works programme was doomed from the outset. Its inauguration during the slump of 1920–21 coincided with the beginnings of an economy campaign in public expenditure. The pressure on local authorities to undertake work in advance of existing schedules was singularly inept 'since it implied that assistance could be given to projects the need for which was relatively remote, while more urgent work was being curtailed . . . in the interests of economy'.[19] Even when schemes were proposed and accepted it was

---

[17]   Cab 24/131, CP 3574, Works for the Relief of the Unemployed. Memorandum by the Minister of Health, 21 December 1921.

[18]   Cab 27/190, Local Authority Works 1924/25, 12 July 1924. The towns visited by the UGC were selected to cover various industries and degrees of unemployment in Lancashire, Yorkshire, the midlands, the south of England, the north east, south Wales and 11 areas in Scotland.

[19]   K. Hancock, 'The Reduction of Unemployment as a Problem of Public Policy', *Economic History Review*, 2nd ser., 15 (1962), 336.

impossible to devise any measure of long-term planning, since most works were undertaken to provide employment only for the following winter. Moreover, the UGC had to be convinced that a particular scheme was of real public utility, the criterion being the value of the scheme as a measure of benefit to the ratepayers as a whole, taking into account the expenditure involved. Considerable difficulty was experienced, furthermore, in determining whether non-revenue-producing schemes were being sufficiently 'accelerated' in anticipation of grant aid.

As a result of the deteriorating financial situation of local authorities in the poorer industrial areas, governments in the early twenties became increasingly concerned with the relief of the rates rather than with the relief of unemployment. Anxious to bolster up the finances of depressed areas they came to view any relief works capable of keeping a few families off the rates 'as a loop-hole through which the Exchequer might give a "dole" to the local authorities'.[20] The chief beneficiaries of many schemes, therefore, became the lower classes of labour who had fallen on the Poor Law rather than those best fitted for the job in hand. Critics readily denounced such works as no better than those of the Edwardian period, calculated to impair the industrial quality of the skilled workforce. The government's own regulations perpetuated the difficulties in impoverished areas. In May 1923 the state provided (for non-revenue-producing works) assistance towards interest and sinking fund charges during the first half of a loan period, which could be anything from two and a half to 15 years. Once the first half periods began to fall in, local authorities were forced to find additional funds to meet the whole of the charges for the second period of the loan. They therefore came under growing pressure to obtain as much increased financial aid as possible from the government to enable them to meet future commitments.

By the mid-1920s there was evidence of a growing disenchantment with public works. The Chancellor of the Exchequer reported to the Cabinet in November 1925 that:

however necessary it may have been to assist Local Authorities immediately after the war to undertake works of real acceleration with a view to meeting what was then regarded as a purely temporary unemployment crisis, the justification for the policy had disappeared when all accelerated work had been carried out and unemployment had become almost chronic.[21]

The government could not easily repudiate commitments already undertaken but nor could it resist increasing political pressure to have public

[20] R. Davison, *The Unemployed. Old Policies and New* (1929), 58.
[21] Cab 24/175, CP 487, Educational and Unemployment Relief Expenditure. Note by Chancellor of the Exchequer, 23 November, 1925.

Table 12. *Number and estimated cost of schemes approved by the Unemployment Grants Committee*

	Number	Total estimated cost
December 1920–March 1922	3,523	£26,574,000
March 1922–June 1923	2,917	15,874,000
July 1923–June 1924	2,780	24,222,000
July 1924–June 1925	2,272	20,639,000
July 1925–June 1926	1,240	17,566,000
July 1926–June 1927	63	792,000
July 1927–June 1928	28	319,000

Source: Adapted from Final Report of the Unemployment Grants Committee, Cmd. 4354, 1933, 22.

money directed to possibly more productive uses. Given the lacklustre response of local authorities, the time had come to limit the subsidization of works projects. From December 1925 grants were restricted to schemes undertaken by local authorities in areas where the average unemployment rate of adult males during the previous year had been at least 15 per cent; to be eligible for financial aid, works had to be such as would not normally have been put in hand for some considerable time (ordinarily more than 5 years).[22] The effect of this decision was to curtail drastically the number of 'emergency' schemes approved and aided by the UGC, as shown in table 12. The average number of persons employed directly on approved projects fell from about 57,000 between 1921 and mid-1926 to an average of less than 7,000 during the following two years. At no time since 1921 had total recorded unemployment fallen below one million.

THE IMPACT OF STRUCTURAL UNEMPLOYMENT

Local authorities, trade unionists and representatives of the Labour Party condemned these restrictions but failed to persuade the Cabinet to adopt a more positive attitude. The Minister of Labour judged public works in 1927 to be 'a wasteful use of capital and therefore a mistake'. He refused to abandon them altogether however, since, as he put it, they formed a useful part of the government's political armoury, giving 'tangible evidence of an

---

[22] But as Hancock has noted 'stealing work from the future appeared to be less justified where there could be no confidence that the future could afford it'. 'The Reduction of Unemployment', 375.

effort to provide employment and probably effective in allaying unrest . . . to a degree out of proportion to the numbers actually employed'.[23]

But this circumspect view was about to undergo a radical change, principally because of the emergence of structural unemployment. Despite earlier misgivings, the Conservatives were openly prepared by 1928 to accord public works a more strategic role in the fight against unemployment. For years past many politicians had rested content in the belief that unemployment was a self-correcting cyclical phenomenon, the scale and duration of which would be rendered less serious once parallel policies to stabilize trade and finance worked their way through the economy. However, once unemployment emerged in a more persistent form in the late 1920s, condemning thousands of workers in key staple trades and in entire industrial regions to periods of enforced idleness much longer than previously experienced or anticipated, the same government officials recognized the serious political consequences of failing to respond in a sympathetic and positive fashion.

Initially the government reacted to the growing pool of surplus labour in the depressed areas by encouraging labour mobility under the aegis of the Industrial Transference Board.[24] The public works programme was boosted in November 1928 to help encourage this progress. Local authorities in relatively prosperous areas, who had for some years been ineligible for financial assistance, were permitted to claim UGC grants for non-revenue-producing works that would not normally be undertaken, on condition that half the labour used was recruited from distressed areas. In such cases the rule under which works had to be accelerated by at least five years was waived, whilst the promotion of public works in the depressed areas themselves was purposely discouraged.[25]

Although there was no intention of upsetting the prevailing arrangements for offering grants to areas with exceptional unemployment, the terms available to those authorities willing to receive transferred labour were more favourable than those on offer to the less favoured districts. They also made the government a more predominant contributor to the cost of the schemes than it had been hitherto. The most favourable grant in force until 1928 in respect of any work scheme had covered only the first half of the loan repayment period up to 15 years, and was equivalent to almost half of the total cost. Under the revised terms the grant to authorities employing transferred men covered the whole of the loan repayment period up to 30 years, equivalent to as much as 63 per cent of the total cost.

---

[23] Cab 24/184, CP 46, Unemployment Grants Committee, Memorandum by the Minister of Labour, 11 February 1927.   [24] See above chapter 9.

[25] Cab 24/108, Interdepartmental Committee on Unemployment. Interim Report, 2 November 1928.

The improvizations of the late twenties could do little, however, to strengthen the impact and effectiveness of public works once the country became embroiled in the world slump in 1930. Too much remained to be done. Only £6 million worth of schemes had been sanctioned by the UGC between 1926 and 1929 compared with over £100 million in the previous six years. MacDonald's second administration tried to encourage the further submission of schemes but virtually scuppered any effective public works programme by insisting from the outset that: financially, state aid had to come from current revenue; administratively, policy had to work through the machinery of local govenment and other statutory under-takings; and economically assisted works had to be directly 'useful' and 'remunerative'.[26]

The government still refused to undertake work directly; it merely waited upon local authorities to make use of the financial incentives available to help defray the cost of schemes. Minor amendments to grant aid were conceded to encourage local initiative. The minimum period during which 'non-transfer' work schemes had to be accelerated to qualify for financial assistance was lowered in July 1929 from five to three years so long as the projects were executed in areas of severe and prolonged unemployment; those authorities claiming 'transfer' grants under the arrangements introduced in November 1928 were no longer formally required to take at least 50 per cent imported labour (though acceptance of a certain proportion of transferred labour was still a condition of grant aid), while the minimum annual average level of unemployment under which areas not involved in transferred labour could claim financial assistance was reduced from 15 to 10 per cent. In a somewhat different context the Development (Loan Guarantees and Grants) Act, 1929, empowered the Treasury to aid revenue-producing schemes launched by profit-making public utilities (but not by private industry generally) in order that 'the employment energy generated by . . . assistance should not be dissipated over a large number of small schemes but be focussed upon larger schemes of an economic character'.[27]

---

[26] For detailed discussion of public works policy during 1929–31 see Skidelsky, *Politicians and the Slump*; Janeway, 'The Economic Policy of the Second Labour Government'; J. Roberts, 'Economic Aspects of the Unemployment Policy of the Government 1929–31'. The restrictive attitude to public investment was not limited to local authority works. The Cabinet agreed in principle in 1930 to the construction of a Channel Tunnel by private enterprise, but only on the clear understanding that if the venture run into difficulties there should be no appeal to the government for a subsidy or financial support.

[27] Cab 24/204, CP 183, Assistance to Public Utility Undertakings, 27 June 1929. Non-profit-making public utilities were already under the aegis of the UGC. Part II of the 1929 Act empowered the Minister of Labour to make grants to local authorities on the recommend-ation of an Advisory Committee. The existing Unemployment Grants Committee was appointed for this purpose, its activities placed, for the first time, on a statutory basis.

At first the local authorities reacted positively to the relaxation in the terms of grant aid. Between July 1929 and June 1930 about 1,850 schemes of work were approved, involving capital expenditure of almost £37 million.[28] But MacDonald thought the response was inadequate and called a conference of local authority representatives in London in June 1930 to help increase the volume of work that might possibly be put in hand. To facilitate progress, the terms of grant aid were again amended; from July 1930 all local authorities became eligible for the maximum grants hitherto available only under the 'transfer' scheme. The condition that a proportion of men from depressed areas should be employed was dropped. In addition, the Public Works Facilities Act of August 1930 sought to remedy legislative and administrative delays by conferring simpler and speedier powers for the compulsory acquisition of land for local authority projects. Of course, none of this renewed activity was likely to make public works any more effective in reducing unemployment; the level of grant aid available, the scale and method of implementation of the programmes, and the inevitable delays involved once schemes were submitted to government departments saw to that.

As unemployment increased sharply during 1930–31, from 17.7 per cent of insured workers in July 1930 to 23.6 per cent in March 1931, the government was forced once more to renew its appeal to local authorities to act with even greater vigour, especially in submitting schemes that could be started in advance of the winter months. But it was clear that grant-aided public works were making little impression on overall unemployment. By mid-1931 the work of the UGC had been critically reviewed by the Committee on National Expenditure (the 'May Committee') whose report in favour of substantial reductions in public expenditure preceded by only a few months the outbreak of a financial crisis, the scale and consequences of which helped to circumscribe public works activity for the remainder of the 1930s. With the UGC increasingly regarded as something of a luxury, the May Committee recommended that grants for public works should be substantially reduced and should in no case amount to more than 25 per cent of the cost of any scheme. Although some authorities continued with projects already negotiated and for which advance preparations had been made, the collapse of the second Labour administration effectively brought the work of the UGC to an end. The Committee ceased to approve schemes at the end of January 1932 but remained in being until the Development (Loan Guarantees and Grants) Act 1929, which had provided it with statutory authority to sanction relief work, expired at the end of August 1932. The chequered progress of UGC works following a resurgence of activity in 1928 can be gauged from table 13.

[28] Cmd. 4354, 8–9.

Table 13. *UGC approved schemes of work*

	Number	Total estimated cost
July 1928–10 June 1929	352	£ 6,181,000
11 June 1928–August 1929	147	1,665,000
September 1929–August 1930	2,026	41,770,000
September 1930–December 1931	2,274	35,234,000
January 1932	18	170,000

Source: As for table 12.

NON-UGC PUBLIC WORKS

Public works activity for the relief of unemployment was not confined to schemes aided by the Unemployment Grants Committee. Road construction and improvement, for example, had commended themselves at the very start of the post-war recession as valuable sources of employment for unskilled labour. When the UGC was established in December 1920 classified roads[29] were excluded from its sphere of activities largely because the power to construct new roads and to make grants to local authorities for road improvement already lay with the Ministry of Transport operating the Road Fund.[30] As a contribution to the relief of unemployment, a special fund of over £10 million was created in 1920 to encourage new arterial road construction and the widening of existing roads. The Treasury made a special contribution of £1,200,000, the Road Fund £4 million in anticipation of revenue, and £5,200,000 was earmarked for Treasury loans to local authorities. Over £7 million was spent during the first year of the scheme, consuming half the special Exchequer contribution. This was but a prelude, however, to a series of road schemes in the early twenties financed jointly by the Road Fund, the Exchequer and the local authorities. From 1924 onwards the Road Fund was permitted to use an increasing proportion of its annual revenue to meet its contribution towards capital works of construction or improvement.

The road programmes launched between 1920–21 and 1924–25, some of which were not completed until after 1930, cost £57 million, the

---

[29] Unclassified roads remained the responsibility of the UGC and were eligible for grant aid.

[30] This had originally been entrusted to the Road Board established under the Development and Road Improvement Funds Act, 1909 and derived its revenue from the Motor Spirit and Carriage Licence Duties. The duties were withdrawn during the First World War but were restored in April 1920. A new system of motor taxation took effect from 1 January 1921.

contribution of grant aid to total cost ranging from 50 to 75 per cent. At the beginning of the period the Road Fund had an autonomous source of revenue but a distinct change occurred in central government policy in 1925. New programmes for unemployment relief road works were outlawed by the Ministry of Transport. From April 1926 income to the Fund was gradually drained by the appropriation of part of revenue for other budgeting purposes and by the transfer of the annual liabilities of the UGC for past schemes of unclassified road development. The Fund was thus effectively hamstrung and for the next three years, though total expenditure on roads was fairly constant, expenditure on capital account fell sharply.

It was the Liberals and Oswald Mosley who argued strongly during 1929–30 for a far more rigorous programme of national road development in aid of unemployment. To Mosley, substantial road schemes were critical to the prestige of the government since they offered 'perhaps the one way in which large numbers of unemployed may be rapidly put to work'.[31] The Liberals, too, maintained that a road development programme was particularly suitable at a time of excess unemployment 'because a large variety of labour can be employed, widely spread over the country, and because a very high proportion of the total expenditure represents wages'.[32] Expenditure on road works actually increased during the early months of Labour's administration thanks largely to Morrison's persistent pressure within Cabinet. Having won approval in June 1929 for a £37.5 million road programme spread over five years,[33] he won a further increase of £4 million in the trunk road allocation in March 1930, despite Treasury opposition. The amount was deducted from the remainder of the five-year programme, thus leaving the Road Fund liability intact, but the rate and conditions of grant were improved to attract local authority support. The cut in the five-year programme was quickly restored in June 1930 at the same time as a further £7.5 million was advanced for trunk road schemes.

But although Snowden, Chancellor of the Exchequer, succeeded thereafter in deflecting Treasury opposition to increased road expenditure by promising to seek parliamentary approval to sanction adequate financial guarantees, it proved impossible to overcome the growing opposition within Whitehall to systematic increases in national spending. Expenditure

---

[31] Cab 27/397, Conference on National Schemes. National Road Schemes, 7 November 1929.

[32] *We Can Conquer Unemployment*, 12. The Liberals maintained that for every £1 million spent on roads work would be provided for at least 5,000 men per year. For further discussion see below chapter 12.

[33] £9.5 million was allocated for trunk road development with a 75 per cent contribution from the Road Fund and £28 million was allocated for all other roads with a 50 per cent Road Fund contribution.

on major improvements fell to a minimum in 1933–34, although the National Government did agree in 1933 to complete those road programmes suspended during the 1931 financial crisis. A third period of expansion began in 1935, involving grant aid for trunk road and dual-carriageway developments. The Ministry of Transport eventually took over direct responsibility for trunk roads in April 1937 and embarked upon an extensive policy of improvement.

Two other non-UGC public works ventures deserve mention – land drainage and forestry. Apart from their value as a potential means of expanding Britain's food production, land drainage and reclamation offered an opportunity for mopping up small pockets of unemployment and as such received ministerial support in the post-demobilization period.[34] Reclamation schemes proved relatively expensive in terms of their likely impact on unemployment and few projects survived the 1921 economy campaign.[35] Land drainage and water supply works, however, received Cabinet approval in 1921 as means of alleviating unemployment in rural areas and the success of grant-aided works carried out during the winter of 1921–22 led to similar ventures being sanctioned during the following four years. 'Although all the figures are not yet available', wrote the Minister of Agriculture reviewing the 1922/23 programme, 'it is clear that over 10,000 unemployed were at work for a considerable period, and that by far the greater part were rural workers who would have been in receipt of relief had they not found employment in these schemes'.[36] Drainage schemes continued to attract grant aid during 1928 provided that a proportion of the labour used was recruited from the depressed areas as part of the government's declared policy of industrial transference. The 1929 Labour administration removed this condition but continued to support schemes that were likely to reduce unemployment, until the 1931 financial crisis forced it to withdraw support from those schemes not yet in operation.

The duties of the Forestry Commissioners appointed in November 1919 included not only the provision of an adequate supply of home-grown timber so obviously lacking during the war years, but also the fostering of work in rural areas during periods of unemployment. During the winter of 1920–21 the Committee on Unemployment agreed to allocate £250,000 of the Unemployment Relief Fund to forestry work in order to accelerate road making and the preparation of land for planting in the Commission's

---

[34] Cab 27/118, CU 157, Land Drainage and Reclamation as a Means of Alleviating Unemployment, 24 May 1921.
[35] Cab 27/124, CU 502, Land Reclamation as a Means of Relieving Unemployment, 20 December 1922.
[36] Cab 27/194, CU 557, Drainage Unemployment Relief Works in Rural Areas. Memorandum by the Minister of Agriculture and Fisheries, 18 July 1923.

forests, in Crown woods and forests and on municipal and private estates. Further sums were provided for such purposes in 1922/23 and 1923/24 in the belief that the flow of unemployed men from rural areas to the towns would thereby be reduced.[37] From 1924 greater emphasis was placed on the establishment of forest holdings and the guarantee of forestry work each year to each individual holder. This idea fitted well with the policy of industrial transference after 1928 and became an acknowledged feature of the unemployment programme of the 1929 Labour administration. But, as with land drainage, the expansion of forest holdings was severely curtailed by the 1931 crisis. It was rescued in principle by the National Government as a potential means of relieving unemployment, particularly in the Special Areas. The government encouraged the establishment of a new training estate on Forestry Commission land at Kielder and helped launch forest holding schemes after 1935 which aimed to provide about 1,000 jobs during the subsequent decade.

EMPLOYMENT AND PUBLIC WORKS EXPENDITURE

It is impossible to provide an exact tally of total public works expenditure because the local authority returns available for the 1920s and 1930s do not provide separate financial details of such activities. For its part the UGC sanctioned schemes of work between December 1920 to January 1932 to an estimated total capital value of £191 million, of which only about £67 million was actually spent. Local authorities submitting schemes were required to estimate the average number of men to be employed directly. From such data the UGC claimed that every £1 million of expenditure provided 2,500 jobs in terms of direct employment.[38] It refused to estimate the supposed indirect effects arising, for example, from the manufacture and transport of materials. Contemporaries inside and outside of government claimed that the total primary employment (direct and indirect) created by every £1 million spent was of the order of 4,000 jobs.[39]

Such estimates ignored the secondary effects of expenditure on aggregate demand and employment but, on their own, suggest that the approved schemes and the special road construction programmes together probably employed on average less than 0.3 per cent of the workforce during the

---

[37] Cab 27/124, CU 559, Committee on Unemployment. Forestry Schemes in Relief of Unemployment, 19 July 1925; Cab 27/195, CU 646, Unemployment Committee. Memorandum by the Forestry Commission, 7 February 1924.

[38] Cmd. 4354, 22, 24–5.

[39] See, for example, R. F. Bretherton, F. A. Burchardt and R. S. G. Rutherford, *Public Investment and the Trade Cycle in Great Britain* (Oxford, 1941), 302–6; J. M. Keynes, 'Crisis Finance', *The Times*, 17 April 1939; Cmd. 3920, 139–40.

1920s or 4 per cent of the unemployed.[40] The Cabinet was informed in 1932 that grants in aid of public utility development after 1929 had probably provided a peak total primary employment of just over 50,000.[41] The highest number of workers employed on projects financed by the UGC at any time was 59,000 (March 1931), but for the greater part of the period from 1920 to 1932 the numbers were far smaller (only 10,000 in 1929). The expenditures on road construction under the 1920/25 programmes reached a maximum annual outlay of between £6 million and £8 million during 1926 and 1928, but, according to the Ministry of Transport, provided direct employment each year for only 12,000–16,000 men. The 1929/30 road programme was estimated to have provided direct employment for not more than 16,000 persons during the financial year ending March 1931; the number fell to little more than 2,000 during 1934/35.[42] With the disappearance of the UGC in 1932, the number of public works schemes dropped dramatically and although those previously approved by the Committee were continued thereafter, they were few in number, employing only 6,779 men in 1934 compared with 23,975 two years previously. Only two schemes, employing 303 men, required completion in 1937. Nevertheless, between 1929/30 and 1937/38, local authority capital spending on public works resulted in primary employment of about 400,000 men per year. On the assumption of a multiplier of 1.5,[43] this suggests that over half a million men were employed by such means.[44]

Susan Howson has provided some interesting if highly speculative estimates of the maximum potential effect which public works might have had in reducing unemployment between 1920 and 1932 if they had been carried out as originally planned, that is, ignoring the fact that planned expenditures were in practice severely curtailed. The supposed effects on primary employment are obtained by accepting the official UGC estimate of direct employment (2,500 man-years for each £1 million spent) and assuming an equal amount of indirect primary employment, on transport and raw materials for example. The scale of the secondary effect on jobs is judged to be the result of an employment multiplier of between 1.5 and 2. Howson's data, reproduced below, are necessarily conjectural but they do indicate that the maximum potential reduction of unemployment likely to have resulted from officially sponsored public works schemes was fairly

---

[40] Hancock, 'The Reduction of Unemployment', 334–5. Even this calculation assumes that all planned work was completed. Less than one-third actually was.
[41] Cab 27/479, Employment Policy Committee Report, 25 January 1932, 5.
[42] Burns, *British Unemployment Programs*, 86–7, 133.
[43] There is no general agreement as to the most appropriate multiplier to use to judge the aggregate effects of interwar government expenditure. See chapter 13.
[44] Bretherton *et al.*, *Public Investment and the Trade Cycle*, 306.

small in relation to recorded unemployment. '*If* the second Labour government's expanded public works programme had been carried out as planned', she writes, '*and* if all its potential employment-creating effects had occurred within 12 months, then existing unemployment (3,250,000) would have been reduced by 648,750–865,000. The actual amount of employment created by the public works schemes must have been much smaller'.[45] (See table 14.)

It is worth recalling that the terms and conditions under which the public works programme operated down to 1932 severely restricted its potential as a major remedy for unemployment. The Unemployment Grants Committee itself proudly announced in 1933 that at no time had it 'approved or recommended a scheme put forward purely as a means of providing work without regard to economic considerations'.[46] Although the relief programmes had the appearance of central planning, the effective control was diffuse; local authorities on the whole initiated the work, but were themselves bodies which met infrequently and were often composed of persons whose major interests lay elsewhere. There were inherent difficulties in anticipating wants – capital works had to be 'substantially accelerated' and of strict economic utility in order to qualify for aid. They had to comply at the same time with complex and changing conditions governing eligibility. Approval of a scheme did not preclude expenditure on it being spread over many years. Moreover, in the early years especially, the scale of conditions attached to grants limited the progress of the authorities in depressed areas, for which the aid was then primarily designed. Indeed there were considerable variations in the timing and magnitude of capital expenditure by local authorities in different parts of the country. The level was generally both low and unstable in the poorer regions suffering high unemployment. Although on occasion public investment expenditure worked in the right direction (e.g. during 1929/31), it did not provide anything like sufficient compensation for shortfalls in private investment during periods of severe depression.[47]

Throughout the period of the UGC's operations and beyond, appeals were made inside and outside of government for a more vigorous policy of fiscal expansion to counter rising and increasingly persistent unemployment. Governments of each major political persuasion resisted such calls in the vain hope that economic conditions would improve sufficiently to create job opportunities beyond what local authorities could ever hope to provide.

[45] S. Howson, 'Slump and Unemployment', in *The Economic History of Britain Since 1700*. Vol. 2. *1860 to the 1970s*, ed. R. Floud and D. McCloskey (Cambridge, 1981), 280.
[46] Cmd. 4354, 26.
[47] R. Middleton, 'The Treasury and Public Investment: A Perspective on Interwar Economic Management', *Public Administration*, 61 (1983), 353–4.

Table 14. *Possible employment effects of planned public works*

| | Planned expenditure (£m.) | | | Planned direct employment, man-years $(4)=(3)\times 2500$ | Direct and indirect primary employment, man-years $(5)=(4)\times 2$ | Total primary and secondary employment, man-years $(6)=(5)\times(1.5 \text{ or } 2)$ |
	Unemploy-ment Grants Committee schemes (1)	Road works (2)	$(3)=(1)+(2)$			
Dec. 1920–Mar. 1922	26.6	13.5	40.1	100,250	200,500	300,750–400,100
Mar. 1922–June 1923	15.9	10.8	26.7	66,750	133,500	200,250–267,000
July 1923–June 1924	24.2	5.1	29.3	73,250	146,500	219,750–293,000
July 1924–June 1925	20.6	4.7	25.3	63,250	126,500	189,750–253,000
July 1925–June 1926	17.6	3.7	21.3	53,250	106,500	159,750–213,000
July 1926–June 1927	0.8	3.7	4.5	11,250	22,500	33,750– 45,000
July 1927–June 1928	0.3	2.7	3.0	7,500	15,000	22,500– 30,000
July 1928–June 1929	6.2	2.9	9.1	22,750	45,500	68,250– 91,000
June 1929–Aug. 1930	43.5	12.9	56.4	141,000	282,000	423,000–564,000
Aug. 1930–Dec. 1931	35.2	51.3	86.5	216,250	432,500	648,000–865,000
Dec. 1931–June 1932	0.2	2.3	2.5	62,500	125,000	187,500–250,000

Source: S. Howson, 'Slump and Unemployment' in *The Economic History of Britain Since 1700. Volume 2. 1860 to the 1970s*, ed. R. Floud and D. McCloskey (Cambridge, 1981), 281. Corrected for arithmetical errors in the original.

Critics were convinced that government make-work policies, however much they might be amended in particular circumstances, were no more than a political sham. There were economists and politicians who refused to accept the minimalist approach of central government and who campaigned vigorously for a much-expanded programme of public works expenditure for the sake of boosting demand and employment. It is to the origins and fate of such proposals that we now turn.

12 ∗ The limits of intervention: budgetary orthodoxy and the reduction of unemployment in the 1920s

It has been indicated thus far that the development of an active fiscal policy during the first post-war decade, in terms of a commitment to rising expenditure on works programmes for the sake of creating jobs, was extremely limited. Few of the public works undertaken were ever destined to achieve a substantial reduction in unemployment. They were developed in the early years of the post-war slump purely as emergency measures, necessary to allay social unrest and to ease the strain on both the Poor Law and the revamped unemployment insurance scheme. For the remainder of the decade, governments – whether Labour or Conservative – strove purposely to reduce their commitment to such activity to the shortest period compatible with efficiency and economy, preferring instead to await a substantial reduction in industrial costs and the revivial of normal trade.

Demands for increased public works expenditure violated the contemporary dictates of 'sound finance', themselves an embodiment of the Victorian principle that central government accounts should be balanced at the lowest possible level. Money, it was thought, was best left to 'fructify in the pockets of the people'. It was generally believed that government should aim for a small Budget and for an *ex post* surplus sufficient to permit redemption of the national debt on a regular basis, whatever the state of the economy. Moreover, when revenues fell, as they inevitably did during periods of depression, it was accepted that public expenditure should be reduced in accordance with balanced budget orthodoxy.

The emergence of large-scale unemployment after 1920 posed a serious threat to such conventional thinking. Public expenditure had already grown substantially during the war, both absolutely and as a proportion of Gross National Product. Wartime spending had been financed, not by taxation, but by printing money. This primitive form of deficit financing, though supportive of employment, merely strengthened the post-war urge to restore fiscal orthodoxy, both to eliminate inflation and to secure stability of the exchanges.[1] Even after severe curtailment of spending following the end of hostilities the budget remained abnormally high. Nominal expenditure in 1920, at 20.5 per cent of GNP, was over four times its 1913 level.[2] To restore the situation the authorities embarked on a deliberate and systematic policy of cutting government expenditure (the infamous 'Geddes axe' of 1921/22)[3] and made provision through a Sinking Fund for the reduction of interest payments on the national debt, the burden of which had increased sharply following the collapse of prices and revenues after 1920. 'What is required in order to maintain and stimulate industry and commerce – and secure full and regular employment in the country', wrote the Chancellor of the Exchequer in May 1921, 'is a reduction of . . . the burden of the State's indebtedness as rapidly as possible, a process which can only be achieved by a continuous reduction of expenditure throughout the next five years'.[4]

None of this bode well for unemployment policy. Proposals to facilitate debt redemption by alternative means, such as the imposition of a capital levy on accumulated wealth, found little favour outside the organized labour movement.[5] To weaken the opposition towards borrowing for 'unproductive' purposes, declared the Treasury as early as 1918, 'would be to follow the historical precedent set up by King Canute in relation to the activity of the tides'.[6] Every pound which had to be borrowed to finance expansion, it was held, tended to raise the interest on government loans and prejudice the chances of saving on the national debt charge by conversion operations. Such a policy, wrote Keynes in the late twenties, was 'as short-sighted in its purpose as it was wrong in its choice of purpose . . . So long as this remains "the settled financial policy of the country" we are aiming, whether we realize it or not, at trade depression and unemployment'.[7]

But within the Treasury the antipathy towards unbalanced budgets – on the grounds that they would adversely affect business confidence by withdrawing funds from productive use, be inflationary and increase the

---

[1] The parallel question of how best to conduct economic policy for the purpose of restoring the 'automaticity' of the gold standard is taken up in chapter 5.

[2] R. Middleton, *Towards the Managed Economy* (1985), 37.

[3] In 1921 Lloyd George set up a Committee on National Expenditure headed by Sir Eric Geddes to recommend economies for the 1922 budget. It proposed cuts in military expenditure, a reduction in health and educational services and a dismantling of a significant part of the government's bureaucratic machinery.

[4] Cab 24/123, CP 2919, Cabinet Reduction of Public Expenditure, Memorandum by the Chancellor of the Exchequer, 9 May 1921.

[5] R. C. Whiting, 'The Labour Party, Capitalism and the National Debt, 1918–24', in *Politics and Social Change in Modern Britain*, ed. P. J. Waller (1987), 140–60.

[6] T170/125, Reconstruction Finance, 21 January 1918.

[7] J. M. Keynes, 'Unemployment and Treasury Policy', *Nation and Athenaeum*, 4 August 1928.

deadweight of national debt – only grew stronger as the twenties wore on. There seemed, after all, to be no brake on the natural profligacy of politicians. Public expenditure continued on a rising trend, growing from 20.5 per cent of GDP in 1920 to 24.5 per cent by 1929.[8] Though the authorities tightened their fiscal stance during 1919/20 on both the revenue and expenditure sides, they found themselves engaged thereafter in an almost constant struggle between the demands of financial purity on the one hand and the need to court electoral popularity by raising social expenditure, particularly in aid of the unemployed, on the other. In 1919 the Cabinet had sought to strengthen financial control over Whitehall by making the Permanent Secretary of the Treasury head of the Civil Service, but no one then could have foreseen the powerful forces making for expenditure growth or the strains under which the orthodoxy of balanced budgets would subsequently have to operate.

So far as public works expenditure was concerned, Chancellors in the buttressed by public, business and City opinion, campaigned throughout the twenties for the most prudent and economical use of public money. There was to be no open-ended or future commitment to state expenditure and no disguised assistance in the form of subsidies or direct loans. Appeals for increased spending on public works on behalf of the unemployed rankled not only Treasury officials but also the majority of businessmen who feared rises in taxation beyond levels which, they constantly complained, were already excessive and inimical to productive enterprise. With the Treasury opposed in principle to the idea of reducing income tax to stimulate demand, the fetish for economy focussed primarily on the need to avoid unnecessary capital outlay.

So far as public works expenditure was concerned, Chancellors in the twenties became impressed 'not by the comparison between the cost of works proposals and the total level of government expenditure, but by the comparison between the outlay on works and the precarious margin available for debt reduction'.[9] Whether this damaged the prospects of the unemployed did not worry the Treasury unduly; after all, its responsibilities lay ultimately in the fields of budgetary control and debt management, not in the determination of the level of employment. And though the Labour Party cheerfully urged major programmes of loan-financed works during the early part of the decade, it continued to embrace the ideal of balanced budgets, expecting that the 'good' years would produce sufficient revenue surpluses to finance the 'lean' ones.

---

[8] Middleton, *Towards the Managed Economy*, 3. The percentage in 1913 was 11.9.
[9] Hancock, 'The Reduction of Unemployment', 332.

'UNEMPLOYMENT CAN BE CONQUERED': DEFICIT FINANCE,
NATIONAL DEVELOPMENT AND THE CHALLENGE TO ORTHODOXY

It was against this background of hopeful inertia that there emerged during the early twenties urgent calls for a more progressive fiscal policy to expand opportunities for the out-of-work. Unemployment, which had stood at 5.8 per cent in December 1920, had almost quadrupled three months later. Worst hit were the basic trades. At the end of 1921 36 per cent of the insured workers in the shipbuilding industry were unemployed. In iron and steel the figure was almost 37 per cent and in engineering 27 per cent. Though this major contraction of the economy was not prolonged (by December 1921 aggregate unemployment was down to 16 per cent and to 12.2 per cent twelve months later) the subsequent recovery proved incomplete. At its lowest point in June 1924, registered unemployment remained between 9 and 10 per cent, affecting some one million people.

Industrialists in the House of Commons, led by Sir Allan Smith, pleaded on various occasions during 1922–24 for the government to embark upon remedial work schemes, such as railway electrification and the extension of the London underground. 'If a definite policy of productive employment is formulated', Smith wrote to Baldwin in July 1923, 'unemployment will look after itself'. Any interest charges incurred 'would be very small in comparison with the Unemployment Dole and relief granted by the Guardians'. Failure on the part of the government to adopt a constructive policy on employment 'in place of the present half-hearted temporising and palliatives', he argued, would deal a blow to the economic life of the country 'from which recovery will be impossible'.[10] J. R. Clynes, the railwaymen's leader, expressed a similar sentiment. 'The capital defect of the Government's policy is its refusal to accept the unemployment crisis as a national responsibility', he complained to the Minister of Labour in September 1923: 'Schemes of great national value exist in abundance. All that is needed is the necessary Treasury aid. The government should at once raise a substantial loan to finance approved schemes of national development'.[11]

Imbued with a sense of impending crisis, Lloyd George called in 1924 for a large-scale programme of public works to 'overhaul our national equipment . . . so as to be ready . . . to meet any revival . . . in the markets of the world'. 'A far-seeing manufacturer', he wrote:

[10] Prem 1/30, Unemployment Committee. Letter to the Prime Minister from the Industrial Group at the House of Commons, 26 July 1923; Cab 27/1914, Cabinet Unemployment Committee. The Suggestions of the Industrial Group of Ministers of the House of Commons, August 1923.
[11] Prem 1/34, J. R. Clynes to Sir Montagu Barlow, 27 September 1923.

utilizes periods of slackness to repair his machinery, to re-equip his workshop, and generally to put his factory in order, so that when prosperity comes he will be in as good a position as his keenest competitor to take advantage of the boom . . . No man who has examined the use now being made of our national resources can believe that we are making the best of them . . . Capital and labour are alike strangled by vested prejudices and traditions. Both are capable of producing infinitely more wealth for the benefit of the community than they are now creating . . . The best means of achieving production seems to be the most urgent task for our industrial and political leaders at this hour.[12]

In the same year Keynes argued for a drastic remedy for unemployment, complaining that the prevailing volume of savings, largely untapped because of the lack of domestic investment, was drifting abroad under the stimulus and bias of British legislation and financial institutions. There were no established means beyond free market forces of allocating aggregate savings between home and foreign investment. What was required, he maintained, was a degree of central co-ordination to help organize and distribute the flow of savings towards more nationally productive and employment-generating channels. As he explained:

With home investment, even if it be ill-advised or extravagantly carried out, at least the country has the improvement for what it is worth; the worst conceived and most extravagant housing scheme imaginable leaves us with some houses. A bad foreign investment is wholly engulfed . . . Investment abroad stimulates employment by expanding exports. Certainly. But it does not stimulate employment a scrap more than would an equal investment at home.

With new capital expenditure already severely curtailed by industrial depression and deflation, there was little hope in his view of boosting jobs within the strict confines of sound finance. What was needed was 'an impulse, a jolt, an acceleration'. The Treasury, he urged, should raid the Sinking Fund to the extent of £100 million for the purpose of constructing capital works at home.[13]

Criticism that the slump had been prolonged by a misguided policy of monetary deflation involving high taxation and reduced spending even found expression within government. 'As a nation', the Committee on Unemployment reported to the Cabinet in August 1923:

we have by means of reduced expenditure and higher taxation balanced our budget; we have even paid off debt . . . So we have seen demand reduced and prices dropping. Falling markets have discouraged manufacturers and their output has been curtailed; and opportunities for employment have been greatly contracted . . . Simultaneously many of our foreign markets have been closed to us; . . . Our present

[12] D. Lloyd George, 'The Statesman's Task', *Nation and Athenaeum*, 12 April 1924.
[13] J. M. Keynes, 'Foreign Investment and National Advantage', *Nation and Athenaeum*, 9 August 1924.

unprecedented unemployment . . . is the result of the combined effects of the reduction in purchasing power abroad and at home.

It may well be that if we could stay the course our policy would justify itself by ultimately putting us in a position to engage more successfully in the competitive markets of the world . . . But can we, during a third, fourth and fifth winter, or even longer, carry the financial burden of, say, £2 million a week in dole and relief with ever increasing demands by Local Authorities for rescue from bankruptcy; and can we allow the progressive deterioration of the workless with the further economic loss and the diminished taxable capacity entailed?[14]

The answer the incoming Labour government gave was yes, so long as the nation kept its eye firmly fixed on reducing costs in the export sector, bolstering industrial efficiency, safeguarding the stability of the exchanges and, above all, avoiding inflationary expenditure, whilst endeavouring to meet by cash payments the immediate needs of the genuinely unemployed. Snowden defined his position as Chancellor to the House of Commons in July 1924:

It is no part of my job as Chancellor of the Exchequer to put before the House of Commons proposals for the expenditure of public money. The function of the Chancellor of the Exchequer, as I understand it, is to resist all demands for expenditure made by his colleagues and, when he can no longer resist, to limit the concession to the barest point of acceptance.[15]

To more progressive minds, this was but a counsel of despair. It was not the duty of government to force labour through impoverishment out of depressed occupations but to attract it into prosperous ones; not to crush wages where they were high but to raise them where they were low; not to stifle enterprise by cheeseparing economies in public expenditure but to set it in motion by a courageous diversion of national finance into capital development at home.[16] If, Keynes maintained, the volume of real investment fell short of the savings of the community, purchasing power would be rendered sterile, invoking trade depression and unemployment. It was therefore the duty of the state to guard against such an occurrence, eschewing its slavish regard for settled finance and debt redemption.

Similar ideas were further developed by the Liberals whose advocacy of government-sponsored schemes of national reconstruction and development as the means of restoring prosperity was clearly stated in the 'Yellow Book', *Britain's Industrial Future*, published in February 1928,[17] and even

[14] Cab 27/194, CU 574, Committee on Unemployment. Resume of Measures for Dealing with Unemployment during the Coming Winter, 27 August 1923.

[15] H C Debs., 5th ser., vol. 176, 30 July 1924, cols. 2091–2.

[16] J. M. Keynes, 'Does Unemployment Need a Drastic Remedy?', *Nation and Athenaeum*, 24 May 1924.

[17] This was based on the conclusions of the Liberal Industrial Inquiry initiated in 1925 by a committee of Liberal politicians and economists, including Lloyd George, J. M. Keynes, H. D. Henderson, Herbert Samuel, John Simon and B. S. Rowntree.

more powerfully in their 'Orange Book' election document, *We Can Conquer Unemployment*, issued in Lloyd George's name in March 1929. The former implicitly acknowledged that the crisis of unemployment demanded a degree of enlightened state intervention but one far removed from the extremes of socialism. The existence of structural unemployment, particularly in the traditional export sectors, necessitated the chanelling of a large proportion of the funds destined for capital export into domestic schemes of national development. The state would not itself direct funds into domestic projects; rather a National Investment Board would raise money in the City to finance the requisite investment programme. Requests to export capital would be handled by the NIB and permission would be granted only after domestic claims on capital had been met. Job creation would come from the implementation of broad-based schemes of road construction, new housing, electrification, transport improvements, slum clearance and the rehabilitation of agriculture, all financed by the NIB and by a 'betterment tax' on the increase of land values resulting from transport improvements.[18]

From the Liberals' point of view, it was simply no longer possible to

acquit the timid, unimaginative, unenterprising policy of the present Government of a major responsibility for damming up in the stagnant pool of unemployment so much of the available forces of willing labour which might be employed – if only the stimulus, the encouragement, the central direction, were there to give it the lead.[19]

Like their political opponents, the Liberals conceded that the restoration of economic prosperity in the long run depended upon the gradual improvement of industrial competitiveness and world trade. But their sense of urgency and immediacy transcended that of the two major political parties; emergency plans were needed to meet abnormal unemployment of a quasi-permanent character.

By 1929, with electioneering in the air, the argument was bolder and more precise. An emergency two-year programme of road and bridge construction, housing development, land drainage and expanded telephone and electricity services, the Liberals informed the electorate, was destined to stimulate cumulative increases in employment beyond levels hitherto experienced. Such schemes 'would begin to absorb labour within three months of (their) adoption . . . and would before the end of twelve months reduce the numbers of unemployed workers to normal proportions'. They were expected, as table 15 shows, to employ about 600,000 men a year for two years at a cost of £251 million (some 6 per cent of 1929 Gross Domestic Product).

[18] Booth and Pack, *Employment, Capital and Economic Policy*, 43–4.
[19] *Britain's Industrial Future*, 281.

Table 15. *The Liberal Party's 1929 public works programme*

| | Direct employment (primary) | | |
	Within the first year of the scheme commencing operation (man-years)	Within the the second year (man-years)	Cost (£m)
Roads and bridges	350,000	375,000	145.0
Housing	60,000	60,000	34.5
Telephone development	60,000	60,000	30.0
Electrical development	62,000	62,000	31.0
Land drainage	30,000	30,000	
London passenger transport	24,000	24,000	11.0
Total	586,000	611,000	251.5

Source: Liberal Party, *We Can Conquer Unemployment*, 52.

Finance for such schemes was to be obtained from the issue of a National Development Loan and from economies in 'non-productive' forms of public expenditure (especially on administration). The total outlay would eventually be recovered from a £30 million saving on the money already being paid in unemployment benefit, from funds currently being invested abroad (though this embarrassingly implied a higher Bank Rate), from loans secured on the Road Fund sufficient to finance a £145 million road scheme, from an anticipated £12 million increase in tax revenues, and from those assets lying idle in bank deposits and not being actively used to promote fresh investment. Government borrowing and expenditure, in other words, would help to counteract unemployment arising from the contraction of domestic demand, itself a result of an imbalance between savings and investment.[20]

The Liberals' plans incorporated what might now be regarded as a crude formulation of the multiplier mechanism. They were based on estimates that each £1 million invested in capital production not requiring substantial imports would employ at least 5,000 men per annum. Given the self-liquidating nature of the projects involved, the annual cost to the budget of a £251 million programme was put as low as £2.5 million. The critical point, developed separately by Keynes and Henderson in a supporting

[20] *We Can Conquer Unemployment.* It was expected that works of national development would have to continue for a total of five years to stimulate industry and employment fully.

pamphlet, entitled *Can Lloyd George Do It?*, was that the impact of
expenditure upon indirect employment would be far larger than upon direct
employment, in that it would be spread 'far and wide over the industries of
the country'. A policy of development was almost certain to provide extra
jobs, the authors maintained, because:

The fact that many workpeople who are now unemployed would be receiving wages
instead of unemployment pay would mean an increase in effective purchasing
power which would give a general stimulus to trade. Moreover, the greater trade
activity would make for further trade activity; the forces of prosperity, like those of
trade depression, work with cumulative effect.[21]

On these grounds, Keynes judged, an investment programme of £100
million per year 'might be expected to break the back of abnormal
unemployment'.[22]

Neither the Labour nor the Conservative Party, however, was prepared to
countenance such proposals. The real remedy for unemployment, according to the Tories' 1929 election campaign, was to be found not in hasty and
ill-considered schemes of public works, but in the expansion of trade, in the
increased efficiency of productive industry through rationalization, and in
the restoration of international competitiveness via a reduction of wages
and other costs. The Labour Party's reaction to the Liberal plan was limp, to
say the least. Its manifesto, *How To Conquer Unemployment*, focussed on
long-term plans of national development and the rejuvenation of British
industry, but offered little hope of an early or substantial reduction in
unemployment. The party opposed the specific programmes urged by the
Liberals on the grounds that they did not contain 'a single proposal . . . that
will bring about the reconstruction of industry on a sound and permanent
basis'. Unemployment could not be cured by 'palliatives', but only by a
'lasting restoration of industry'. Thus were promised 'diversified schemes' of
housing, electricity, road and docks development, land reclamation,
improved telephone communications, agricultural improvement and afforestation, and the reorganization and rehabilitation of basic industries,
coupled with appropriate changes in the administrative machinery of
government to help expedite official policy.[23] But such developments were
to take place against a background of steep reductions in public expenditure
and economies in administration. Thus 'development' programmes were
seen in terms of re-allocating expenditure from 'non-productive' to more
productive uses, financed out of redistributive taxation.

[21] J. M. Keynes and H. D. Henderson, *Can Lloyd George Do It? The Pledge Examined* (1929), 25.
[22] 'Mr. J. M. Keynes Examines Mr. Lloyd George's Pledge', *The Evening Standard*, 19 March
1929. Such expenditure was regarded by Liberal sympathisers as very modest given that,
at the prevailing level of recorded unemployment, the waste of unemployment since 1921
(assuming the value of the net annual output of every employed man to be £220)
amounted to almost £2,000 million.   [23] *How to Tackle Unemployment*.

For all its detail, Labour's manifesto lacked any firm statement of the timetable of action or any clear recognition that plans for economic recovery might conflict with the demands of fiscal orthodoxy. The Labour Party was not unmindful of the need to sustain purchasing power, but was clearly less willing that were the Liberals to acknowledge any potential impact which large-scale development programmes might have upon internal demand and employment. Public works were viewed as essentially diversionary, useful perhaps as temporary measures to alleviate the worst periods of unemployment, but not as a means of stimulating economic activity in general.[24] The Independent Labour Party shared the view that domestic demand should be sustained. Its belief in the 'underconsumption-ist' origins of unemployment led it to demand increased family allowances, minimum wages and a state-controlled credit system. But public works on a national scale were not central to its thinking; revival was to come from a redistribution of income via direct taxation in favour of working-class consumption.[25]

The two dominant political parties agreed on one point: unemployment could only be tackled successfully by pursuing cautious policies on a broad front, stimulating industrial efficiency whenever and wherever possible in lieu of a revival of world trade. The influential contemporary economist Professor Henry Clay endorsed such an approach; public works might be an attractive way of providing direct employment in an emergency, but should not 'divert attention from the longer term needs of industry'. There was no alternative 'except to bring down costs'.[26]

THE 'TREASURY VIEW' AND THE FATE OF THE RADICAL ALTERNATIVE

The enormity of the Liberal Party's 1929 electioneering pledge, that it could by a deliberate policy of national development 'abolish' abnormal unemploy-ment in the course of a single year without undue financial repercussions, was roundly condemned in Whitehall. For years past the Treasury had repudiated the notion of seeking domestic economic recovery via government-financed public works in terms so confident and dogmatic as to

---

[24] Such attitudes had even wider currency. The International Labour Office regarded public works as a useful means of compensating for fluctuations in private investment but did not accord them any special significance as a way of stimulating demand, output and employment. They were stop-gap measures to be used while other more important steps were taken to improve the economic situation 'such as rationalisation, lowering of costs, international trade agreements, tariff agreements and so on'. International Labour Office, *Unemployment and Public Works* (Geneva, 1931), 26.

[25] See H. N. Brailsford, J. A. Hobson, A. C. Jones and E. F. Wise, *The Living Wage: A Report to the ILP* (1926). MacDonald dismissed the ILP's plans as 'a collection of flashy futilities'.

[26] Clay, *The Post-War Unemployment Problem*, 136.

constitute a 'Treasury view', neatly summarized by Churchill in his 1929 Budget speech:

> [For] the purpose of curing unemployment the results [of public works] have certainly been disappointing. They are, in fact, so meagre as to lend considerable colour to the orthodox Treasury doctrine which has steadfastly held that, whatever might be the political or social advantages, very little additional employment and no permanent additional employment can in fact and as a general rule be created by State borrowing and State expenditure.[27]

Viewed from this perspective, the Treasury's basic objection to state-sponsored public works on a large scale was that they would be diversionary and unproductive. With a limited (though not necessarily fixed) stock of 'genuine savings' available to finance new investment, it argued, the use of such funds for public works would merely reduce the supply of capital available to finance private investment, helping to lower efficiency and to raise costs throughout the economy.[28] Public works would not increase aggregate employment unless they were financed by credit creation, which ran the danger of encouraging inflation. Borrowing to finance such schemes, the criticism ran, would merely drive up interest rates and pose a direct threat to debt redemption and the stability of the budget. Since a very large proportion of any extra government borrowing could only be obtained, without inflation, by diverting money which otherwise would have been used by private industry, the net addition to employment resulting from any grandiose public works scheme would not be large.[29]

The Treasury argued its case in a memorandum to the Cabinet in February 1929. In a covering note the Chancellor of the Exchequer warned that it would be foolish to be drawn by panic into 'unsound' schemes to cure unemployment or to 'divert national credit and savings from the fertile channels of private enterprise'. His officials were more precise. No government could create resources from which to expand employment unless it was prepared 'to bring about an inflation of banking credits'. The crucial question, argued Leith-Ross, was:

---

[27] H C Debs., 5th ser., vol. 228, 15 April 1929, col. 54.
[28] For a detailed statement of the Treasury's view of the effect of a development loan programme see Cmd. 3331, May 1929.
[29] Cmd. 3331, 48ff. See also G. C. Peden, 'The "Treasury View" on Public Works and Employment in the Interwar Period', *Economic History Review*, 2nd ser., 37 (1984), 167–81. The nature of the contemporary fear of inflation was outlined by R. F. Kahn in 'Public Works and Inflation', *Journal of the American Statistical Association*, 28 (1933), 168–73. Hawtrey helped to convince the Treasury that public works were 'no more than a ritual'; they could only increase employment if they were accompanied by an expansion of Bank Rate, in which case they were not only unnecessary but inflationary. R. G. Hawtrey, 'Public Expenditure and the Demand for Labour', *Economica*, 5 (1925), 38–48.

whether £1000 spent by the Government will give more employment than if the £1000 had been left to the public to spend . . . This is a very difficult problem, and against any success achieved must be set the waste and inefficiency which accompany all hasty Government expenditure. Moreover, there can be little doubt that extensive Government borrowings would tend to increase the cost of production, and thus further aggravate the real evil from which we are now suffering.

On balance it would be far better to persevere with the existing policy of relieving the rate burden on industry, of seeking the absorption of the unemployed into productive industry, and of encouraging their transference from areas of chronic industrial decline.[30]

Liberal claims that they could 'conquer unemployment' were treated with restrained contempt. Not only did their programme lack detailed plans complained the Treasury, it reflected:

a war mentality . . . without much thought of cost or consequences . . . The necessary road works, the necessary telephone extensions, the necessary housing etc. etc. are being undertaken by this Government as and when they are needed. The new Liberal plan insists in going beyond necessary works and spending money on things that will bring little or no return for years to come and therefore for the moment represent a dead loss of capital . . . Mr. Lloyd George would freeze up every dead penny into some profitless work leaving the country no reserve with which to bound forward when the opportunity at last arrives. In so far as his schemes would demand more money than . . . [is] held in suspense they would inevitably compete with other demands for capital.[31]

Wilfred Eady, Principal Assistant at the Ministry of Labour, rejected the supposed benefits of government-financed public works as 'an illusion', arguing that 'all expenditure by the Government must be directed to strengthening the economic structure of the country' so enabling trade 'to give regular employment to men in the ordinary course of business'.[32]

The Treasury never doubted that loan-financed public works expenditure could raise aggregate demand and employment in the short run. What it did doubt was that a works programme could be successfully launched and financed on a scale sufficient to provide a permanent solution to chronic unemployment. In its view the creation of employment during times of exceptional depression could best be achieved by the expansion of bank credit designed to tap those accumulated idle balances lacking profitable outlets, without at the same time displacing normal investment. Public

[30] Cab 24/202, CP 53, Unemployment. Memorandum by the Chancellor of the Exchequer Covering Treasury Memorandum, 25 February 1929.
[31] T161/303, S40504, 'Some Comments on "We Can Conquer Unemployment"', 1929/30.
[32] Lansbury Papers, LSE, Section II Vol. 19 (d), Unemployment. Letter from Sir Wilfred Eady, 10 September 1929.

works would only be necessary if and when business did not respond to a reduction of bank rate to say 2 per cent, as happened in 1894/95.[33]

This received opinion was not without its critics, even within government. Anticipating the public works proposals of their political opponents, Joynson-Hicks (Home Secretary), Steel-Maitland (Minister of Labour) and Amery (Secretary of State for Dominion Affairs) called in 1929 for an extensive trunk road programme to be launched and financed by public money, irrespective of Treasury objections that credit advanced for such a purpose would merely divert funds from ordinary business.[34] 'After 8 years of financial orthodoxy and 8 years of unabating unemployment', pleaded Steel-Maitland in Cabinet, 'ought we not to ask for reasoned proof, for some foundations of belief that the financial policy by which we guide our steps is right?'[35] Hilton, at the Ministry of Labour, called for the appointment of a mixed official and non-official committee to examine the 'theory and practice' of the Treasury's contention that capital raised by the state necessarily influenced the volume and direction of productive private investment. Reflecting on the Liberal programme, he noted guardedly in March 1929:

I still regard it as not conclusively proved that capital can be raised by a state loan without *pro tanto* diminishing the amount of capital that would otherwise have gone to employment creating investment. But it seems to me that Henderson and Keynes have advanced arguments in favour of that view which have not been disposed of, or even faced, by the Treasury.[36]

But the Treasury's concern to quell any support for an active unemployment policy forced it to articulate in dogmatic terms its economic objections to public works.

The essential difficulty with the 'Treasury view' as it was propounded in 1929, however, was that it presumed the existence of full employment as the norm, despite overwhelming evidence of the under-utilization of human and capital resources. The 'diversionary' argument was manifestly absurd in conditions of chronic unemployment and surplus productive capacity and had been rejected by practically all leading economists by the end of the post-war decade. 'There is . . . a presumption', Pigou wrote in *The Times* in June 1930:

---

[33] Peden, 'The "Treasury View" on Public Works', 172.
[34] Cab 24/210, CP 37, Unemployment. Memorandum by the Minister of Labour, 16 February 1929; Cab 24/201, Memorandum by the Home Secretary, 7 February 1929; Cab 25/202, CP 87, An Employment Policy for the Election. Memorandum by the Secretary of State for Dominion Affairs, 18 March 1929.   [35] Cab 24/201, CP 37.
[36] Lab 2/1361, ED 9885, The Liberal Pamphlet and the Melchett-Turner Report. Note by Mr. Hilton, 22 March 1929.

that men set to work in 'artificially created' occupations will not be worth their wage and that the 'artificial creation' of employment is a waste of national resources. Both those presumptions . . . would provide good reasons for deprecating State action designed to reduce unemployment . . . provided there was no unemployment to reduce! When, however, as at the present time, there is an enormous mass of unemployment their virtue and their relevance are lost. If employment is 'artificially created' in these conditions, men are available to come to it, not merely from more useful occupations elsewhere, but from soul-destroying idleness . . . It is important to be sure that our pre-suppositions are adjusted not to imaginary but to actual conditions.[37]

The notion that state investment was either inflationary or diversionary, argued Keynes and Henderson, could logically be applied to all private investment.[38]

The substance of the Treasury's opposition to loan-financed expansion on a large scale was, however, more subtle and wide-ranging than is customarily believed. The final sentences of the Memorandum issued in response to the Liberal Party's election manifesto *We Can Conquer Unemployment* were more temperate than Churchill's earlier Budget utterances:[39]

Seeing that the national savings are less, allowing for the altered level of prices, than before the war, and capital is therefore comparatively scarce and dear, it follows that we cannot afford investments which yield only an uneconomic, or very distant, return, or are of a purely luxury nature. Judged by this test, it is difficult to believe that the greater part of the expenditure proposed would increase the power of industry to provide remunerative employment.[40]

In his evidence to the Macmillan Committee in 1930 Sir Richard Hopkins, Controller of the Finance and Supply Department at the Treasury, countered the abrasive confidence of the Liberals' anti-unemployment strategy not in doctrinaire terms but from the perspective of practical politics, administration and market psychology. He agreed that large development schemes 'deserved the most unprejudiced consideration'. It was not for him to endeavour to place any obstacle in their way 'from the point of view of mere Treasury dogma'. It was, however, 'from a practical aspect' that the real difficulties emerged.

How, for example, could the government market a substantial debt without creating a crisis of confidence? The Treasury accepted that, to a degree, the Liberal programme might prove self-financing by utilizing funds

---

[37] *The Times*, 6 June 1930, cited in T. W. Hutchison, *Economics and Economic Policy in Britain 1946–1966* (1968), Appendix, 285.
[38] Keynes and Henderson, *Can Lloyd George Do It?* 34–5. This argument did less than justice to the Treasury view.
[39] See above p. 328.   [40] Cmd. 3331, 54.

from abroad, by mobilizing idle balances and by reducing the cost of unemployment benefit. It feared, however, that large-scale public works would merely engender disruptive forces sufficient to neutralize any anticipated benefits. A deficit financed by bond sales could raise doubts about the government's overall economic strategy and promote an increased demand for cash. This in turn could prevent idle balances from taking up the additional bonds unless interest rates rose. The business community, aware of a marked shift in fiscal stance and fearful of higher taxation in the short term, was likely thereby to curtail investment, thus exacerbating deflation. And to the extent that foreigners viewed the government's financial policy as 'unsound', stability of interest rates, to say nothing of the gold standard, could be threatened by an unwelcome outflow of sterling.[41] It was the evaluation by the financial authorities of the capital market's likely reaction to a national development loan that helped determine official attitudes to the merits of such a strategy.

Nor were these the only difficulties. An extensive works programme concentrated on a narrow range of industries, Treasury officials maintained, would produce a singularly lopsided form of prosperity, unlikely to be of much assistance to the depressed basic trades most in need of help. With additional employment directed instead to trades which were neither unsheltered nor unprosperous, there was a distinct risk of supply bottlenecks and cost pressures being transmitted throughout the economy, threatening further export uncompetitiveness, import penetration and the stability of the external balance. Few Treasury officials believed that demand impulses created by large-scale investment projects could successfully work their way through to industry as a whole. The advantages were likely to be nullified by the distortion caused to the 'normal channels of trade' and by pressure for yet further rounds of investment to sustain any expanded volume of employment, pressure which any responsible government would have to resist.[42]

The inherent strength and influence of the 'Treasury view', in other words, did not depend upon the theoretical soundness of a 'supply of capital' thesis and it is doubtful whether attacks from within or outside of government on the crude 'diversionary' argument would have necessarily called forth more positive action. It is now recognized that the objections of the Treasury and of other government departments to public works

---

[41] Committee on Finance and Industry, Minutes of Evidence, Vol. 2, 22 May 1930, Q. 5565.
[42] Committee on Finance and Industry, Sir Richard Hopkins, Minutes of Evidence, Vol. 2, 22 May 1930, QQ. 5613–37. See also R. Middleton, 'Treasury Policy on Unemployment', in *The Road to Full Employment*, ed. Glynn and Booth, 109–18; R. Skidelsky, 'Keynes and the Treasury View: The Case for and against an Active Unemployment Policy', in *The Emergence of the Welfare State in Britain and Germany*, ed. W. Mommsen (1981), 167–87.

proposals embraced a range of practical and administrative considerations which were pressed with particular conviction during and after 1929.[43] Much of the criticism was levelled against the road construction programme which constituted nearly 60 per cent of the total proposed expenditure in the Liberal plan. Such schemes, Ministers keenly remarked, were a singularly inappropriate method of dealing with an immediate crisis, given the need for adequate planning and allowing for the multifarious problems of acquiring suitable land, labour and materials. Writing in November 1929, Morrison, Labour's Minister of Transport, cautioned against the state undertaking any large-scale road programme, even for the sake of reducing unemployment:

> Not only would inevitable delays occur in working out a scheme and obtaining the necessary legislation but we should paralyse meanwhile all the local authorities who are at present proceeding actively with a large volume of work. Whatever might be the results of such action, some two or three years hence, the strong probability is that we should have to face a net diminution of employment in the near future.[44]

Indeed, it was not so much the Treasury's as the Ministry of Transport's indictment of the road programmes of Lloyd George that held greatest sway within the Cabinet. The Ministry doubted whether even a centralized agency could find more than £20 million worth of useful projects or be able, for technical reasons, to spend in the first year more than one-fifth of the total value of any road programme. Moreover, a scheme which could be launched quickly could have only the most insignificant effect on registered unemployment; more extensive programmes on the other hand would take so long to plan and to execute that it would be almost impossible to synchronize the peak of expenditure with the appropriate point of the depression.[45]

Nor was it merely a question of what public money was spent on; it was the sheer scale of the Liberal development programme, in relation to what was felt to be economically justified, that occasioned alarm. For government

---

[43] This point is developed extensively in R. Middleton, 'The Treasury in the 1930s: Political and Administrative Constraints to Acceptance of the "New" Economics', *Oxford Economic Papers*, 34 (1982), 48–77 and in Middleton, 'The Treasury and Public Investment', 351–70.

[44] Cab 27/397, 'National Roads'. Memorandum by the Minister of Transport, 13 November 1929.

[45] Cab 24/202, CP 53, Unemployment. Memorandum by the Chancellor of the Exchequer Covering Treasury Memorandum, 25 February 1929. Experience of road schemes during the period 1920/21 to 1924/25 had suggested that each year's programme took at least six years to complete and that the peak of expenditure on and the employment provided by each scheme was reached only in the second and third years from the date of starting. Cab 27/440, CP 293, Unemployment Policy. Memorandum by the Lord Privy Seal, 18 August 1930.

expenditure to do any good, argued J. H. Thomas, Labour's Lord Privy Seal, it had to earn its keep or it would merely increase unemployment. To those critics who believed that the merits of an unemployment programme could be measured by the millions of pounds spent he had 'nothing to say . . . My view is that the root cause of our unemployment is the weakened competitive position of our export trades . . . Unproductive expenditure at home can only add to this weakness'.[46]

Even if *bona fide* schemes were available, judged the Ministry of Labour in 1930, they were unlikely to provide much beneficial employment for men in their normal trades or in areas where they were most needed – indeed indiscriminate public works which failed to increase industrial efficiency or expand the volume of exports were regarded as positively harmful.[47] The Liberals certainly weakened their case by overstating the cyclical character of unemployment and understating the difficulty of matching labour demand with the available supply. Ministry officials doubted whether many more than 250,000 persons of the type normally required for public works could actually be found amongst the army of the unemployed. Although 1.1 million individuals were registered as unemployed in April 1929, there were many among them who could not be regarded as willing or able to accept alternative employment. These included women and girls, boys under 18, men temporarily unemployed, casual workers, men over the age of 50, plus disabled labour. Their exclusion, on official calculations, reduced the total number available for employment on works programmes to 440,000. Even this figure took no account of the number of men incapable of meeting the physical demands of public works or of the substantial difficulties in overcoming the geographical and occupational immobility of the registered unemployed.

The Ministry of Labour was particularly scornful of the Liberal pledge to employ some 380,000 men on roads and land drainage in the first year of any major development scheme. Even if it was assumed, rather generously, that a road programme could be planned and executed in the best interests of the unemployed, there were serious attendant difficulties:

Unemployed miners . . . are gregarious and dislike leaving their mining villages. So long as in one way or another . . . there is enough coming into the household to keep them from starvation, and they have no rent to pay, they will be very reluctant to recognise the necessity of seeking work in other industries away from home. If therefore the road programme is seriously to attempt to absorb most, if not all, the

---

[46] Cab 24/211, CP 120, Unemployment Policy. Memorandum by the Lord Privy Seal, 7 April 1930.

[47] Prem 1/183, Unemployment, 1930. The question of whether there were public work schemes available which could have had such a positive discriminatory influence was never seriously examined.

employable miners and shipbuilders, concerted measures of compulsion will be necessary for an appreciable number.[48]

In 1928 the Ministry had defended public works as a useful adjunct to its policy of labour transference.[49] Now it was less sure; moving men away from familiar if depressed surroundings without the assurance that industries elsewhere required extra 'imported' labour seemed an increasingly less attractive policy option.

And there was a further problem to be faced. Public works of the sort contemplated by Lloyd George and his colleagues were likely to come to an abrupt end without any guarantee that the attached labour would be reabsorbed into 'normal' industrial activity. As officials put it:

Men do not understand that they are given six months' work on a road passing through a prosperous area in order to give them a chance of leaving the road to take more permanent work in the area. They have a six months' job; they work it through, and then they go home and wait for something else to turn up. A Road Programme of the size contemplated for 2 years would simply create a problem of 'demobilisation' at the end of the period.[50]

There was no support here for the idea that public works, by raising demand, might have secondary and tertiary effects on employment, inducing the reabsorption of the labour initially engaged on works projects. But this was no mere oversight. The Treasury had already warned that the deleterious effects of increased public works expenditure on interest rates, confidence and private sector investment could be such as to deny 'normal' industry any permanent benefit.

In essence, the authorities' narrow views as to what constituted 'acceptable' and 'worthwhile' public works virtually ensured that any development programme would have limited potential impact, almost irrespective of Treasury control over expenditure. Both the Minister of Transport's success in the autumn of 1929 in expanding the trunk road programme and the ending of the 'transfer' condition of grant aid for public works in the same year[51] illustrated how Treasury prerogatives could on occasion be breached. But it was the determination of officials to ensure that the parameters of policy were strictly defined that curtailed public works activity to an appreciable extent. Such works had to be capable of being speedily implemented while yielding an economic return sufficient to pay the interest on the sinking fund on any loan. They were expected, moreover, to improve trade, reduce industrial costs, involve no 'demobilisation' problems on their cessation, guard against upsetting traditional wage

[48] Lab 2/1361/ED 9885, We Can Conquer Unemployment. Memorandum by the Ministry of Labour, 1929.   [49] See above chapter 9.   [50] Lab 2/1361/ED 9885.
[51] See above chapter 11.

differentials and prevent labour being drawn away from sectors most likely to provide secure employment in normal times.

Such constraints were powerful because they were self-fulfilling. So long as the authorities insisted that state aid for public works had to come from current revenue, that the origin and execution of any programme had to remain the initiative of local authorities, and that the works themselves had to be directly 'useful', 'remunerative' and be likely to improve industrial efficiency, then the scale on which they could be mounted inevitably meant that they could only be of limited value, incapable of effecting a substantial reduction in recorded unemployment. Given the contemporary predilection to judge public works by only the narrowest business-like measure of 'economic' as against 'social' utility, there was a natural tendency to thwart any programme which did not offer an immediate prospect of profitable return.[52]

The electioneering euphoria of 1929 sharpened the criticism of prevailing budgetary practice and raised expectations amongst advocates of a more progressive policy that the forces of gradualism would be noticeably weakened. It was not to be. Contemporary observers who saw in the rejection of Conservative 'safety-first' policies the possibility of an invigorated employment programme witnessed no dramatic shift thereafter in official attitudes towards the creation of work, even when unemployment rose substantially during the world slump. The deterioration in labour market conditions was undeniable, but so too was Britain's poor standing in international trade and finance. If the spectre of inflation, domestic instability and budgetary chaos as a result of increased government expenditure on works projects could be invoked in the twenties, the ensuing slump served only to deepen ministerial prejudice against interventionist policies during a period of intense uncertainty and introspection. As the thirties wore on, governments became less convinced of the benefits likely to be derived from increased public spending, least of all on national programmes of public works; radical economists meanwhile pressed with renewed vigour for precisely such a policy. The rift that developed between these opposing views is the subject of the next chapter.

---

[52] Keynes had anticipated such arguments. He called in 1931 for work to proceed on well-conceived projects irrespective of the speed by which they could be executed, confessing that 'the main obstacle in the way of reducing unemployment by such schemes is . . . to be found . . . in the practical difficulties of initiation and organisation . . . It is difficult to improvise good schemes'. Cmd. 3897, Addendum 1, para 48. Later in 1933, he confessed that he was 'not unmindful of the delays and disappointments which await those who take the responsibility for an active policy' and that it would be very difficult 'to combine a judicious choice of schemes with speed of execution'. But it was precisely for those reasons that bold action was required since 'there will be so many delays and so many projects . . . which will not survive scrutiny, that the risk of our over-doing it is nil'. *The Times*, 5 April, 1933.

13 ✳ New Deal or no deal? Fiscal policy and the search for stability, 1930–1939

Government economic policy in the major industrialized nations became increasingly defensive and circumspect during the period 1930–32. In Britain the misgivings expressed earlier in Whitehall over radical pleas for deficit-financed expansion grew stronger and gained wider currency. What would be the effect, Treasury officials nervously opined,

> of a sudden reversal of our present policy and the announcement that we were going to embark on a campaign of unrestricted expenditure financed out of loans, with its inevitable concomitants of special powers to coerce labour, landowners, etc., and its attempts to force capital into unremunerative channels or to attract it at the cost of subsequent increases in taxation? The combined effect of all these factors . . . might well be to create a very serious shock to confidence not only in this country but abroad.[1]

The country had to look towards long-term reconstruction based on *laissez-faire* and responsible finance. 'However much we may be criticized', reported the Unemployment Policy Committee in March 1930, 'we must not be rushed into shovelling out public money merely for the purpose of taking what must inevitably be a comparatively small number of people off the unemployment register to do work which is no more remunerative and much more expensive even than unemployment'.[2]

The time had come for a ruthless reappraisal of the value of public works expenditure on behalf of the unemployed. 'The true measure of the success of a policy of development', wrote the Lord Privy Seal in April 1930, 'is not the amount of money raised to finance a hypothetical programme but the amount of work which can actually be put in hand to give an economic return'.[3] A month later he informed the Cabinet:

[1] Cab 24/209, CP 11, cited in Skidelsky, *Oswald Mosley*, 204–5.
[2] Cab 27/418, CP 134, Unemployment Policy Committee. Report, 9 March 1930.
[3] Cab 24/211, CP 120, Unemployment Policy. Memorandum by the Lord Privy Seal, 7 April 1930.

337

It is one thing to construct a paper programme and to quote it as evidence that you have a policy: quite another to work out the details of concrete schemes which will give an economic return, obtain the necessary powers, and get the work put in hand . . . The idea that when we took office there were, and still are, countless projects of economic development all ready and awaiting only the genial influence of a substantial Exchequer grant to set them in instant motion, is a myth.[4]

As the slump deepened even Hubert Henderson, a member of the Economic Advisory Council and co-author of *Can Lloyd George Do It?*, had grown more sceptical of the public works policy he had helped to popularize only a year or so before. 'In light of the world slump', he wrote in October 1930:

I find it quite impossible to maintain such an attitude any longer . . . I should still support pressing forward with roads within the limits of transport requirements, and useful public works generally, by way of a recognised palliative for unemployment in times of depression . . . But to describe the undertaking of such work as an *alternative remedy* for the situation in which we find ourselves, i.e. as something we may reasonably turn to in order to avoid the necessity for reducing costs is . . . misleading.[5]

Exasperated by the limitations of existing policy, politicians and economists of a more radical persuasion relentlessly argued their case for an expansionary fiscal policy. Lloyd George urged Labour's Panel of Ministers in the autumn of 1930 to expand the volume of direct and indirect employment by an accelerated programme of national development, along the lines of the Liberal's 1929 programme. Clearly, he argued,

it must pay a community better, in one way or another, to have its citizens engaged in remunerative agriculture and in equipping the nation to maintain its competitive industrial position in the world on useful work, than to have them deteriorating in idleness; the expenditure which will bring this about is wise investment, and wise investment is true economy. There is nothing inconsistent in cutting down unnecessary and unproductive costs and simultaneously spending freely [on] new equipment. It is the practice of all successful enterprise.[6]

A £200 million works programme spread over three years, combined with strategic changes in pensions and the school-leaving age,[7] Oswald Mosley informed the Cabinet in January 1930, would reduce unemployment within a foreseeable time to considerably below the Government Actuary's estimate of what was 'normal', that is, below 6 per cent. An emergency situation demanded bold action; the dimensions of public works should thus

[4] Cab 24/212, CP 178, Unemployment Policy. Memorandum by the Lord Privy Seal, 26 May 1930.
[5] Economic Advisory Council, Committee of Economists. Memorandum by Mr. H. D. Henderson on the Drift of the Draft Report, 13 October 1930.
[6] Cab 27/439, UP 30, Panel of Ministers on Unemployment. The Liberal Proposals for Dealing with the Present British Unemployment and Agricultural Situation, October 1930.   [7] Cf. chapter 4, pp. 94–111.

be determined, not by accounting estimates of 'economic' schemes, but by the sheer scale and intensity of the unemployment problem.[8]

Keynes meanwhile had become even more convinced that private investment alone would prove insufficiently buoyant to reduce unemployment to any appreciable extent. His advocacy of public works, as we have already noted, dated from 1924, a year before the return to gold. Thereafter, he strengthened this early intuitive appeal for domestic reflation by emphasizing both the political and the social difficulties of attempting to enforce wage cuts and the deleterious effect which the fixed parity had in preventing interest rates from falling sufficiently to restore equilibrium, and this long before he was able to provide any coherent theoretical justification for his views. If the need to protect gold reserves prevented the rate of interest from equating saving and investment, Keynes argued by 1930, it was the government's responsibility to look to public works as a useful 'reserve weapon' to promote internal stability by fiscal means, leaving monetary policy to safeguard the existing gold-standard regime.[9]

Over a wide area of private enterprise, Keynes told the Macmillan Committee in March 1930, prices had already fallen below costs of production, enforcing deflationary declines in business profits and employment. Increased home investment under government stimulus could work to reduce the gap between saving and investment. It was pointless worrying about whether such investment offered a prospective return below that customarily regarded as economically justified. If the prevailing rate of interest fixed by banking policy was 5 per cent, it was still better to employ men and plant to produce an investment to yield 4 per cent in perpetuity than to have both rendered idle. It was not a choice 'between investing at four per cent or five per cent; it is a choice of investing at four per cent and having 80 per cent of the savings wasted and spilled on the ground'. This, Keynes argued, was not a plea for ever-increasing or permanent schemes of publicly funded national investment; it was a call for action to provide 'the first impetus' to break 'the vicious circle'.[10]

As depression deepened in 1930 Keynes tried earnestly to win political support for a more radical economic policy. It would be imprudent, he told the Economic Advisory Council in May 1930, to rule out the possibility that

---

[8] Cab 24/209, CP 31, Unemployment Policy, 23 January 1930.
[9] Keynes was undoubtedly influenced in this context by D. H. Robertson's *Banking Policy and the Price Level* (1925), which had emphasized that voluntary savings need not necessarily be matched by new investments.
[10] Keynes's 'private' evidence to the Macmillan Committee on Finance and Industry. The full text of this evidence is reprinted in *JMK*, Vol. 20, 119–48. His defence of counter-cyclical investment was developed further in an Addendum to the Macmillan Report in 1931. See Cmd. 3897, Addendum I, June 1931. The other signatories were R. McKenna, T. Allen, E. Bevin, J. F. Taylor and A. Tulloch.

unemployment could rise to 2 million by the end of the year. Would it not be wise, therefore, 'to investigate the merits of any diagnosis supported by a responsible section of public opinion' rather than await the pressure of circumstance? MacDonald thought so. It would be 'very interesting', he maintained, if the EAC could have a report on the repercussions on employment, both immediately and in the long run, of a £100 million expenditure on home investment 'over a period of years'.[11]

Prompted by the Advisory Council, the Chancellor of the Exchequer Philip Snowden approached the Macmillan Committee to ask if they would be prepared to draft a private interim report on the following questions:

(i) Does expenditure on capital development at home, stimulated in some way by the Government, tend to increase the volume of employment?

(ii) Or is it offset by reason of it causing a diversion of employment from other capital development which would have taken place or from the production of exports, or in some other way?

(iii) Does it make a difference to the effect on employment whether the increased capital development at home is the result of private enterprise or of Government initiative?[12]

Lord Macmillan responded 'without hesitation' that it would be 'quite impracticable' for his Committee to prepare such a report.

As chapter 5 indicated, it was the gold standard which limited the extent to which even unorthodox economic opinion was prepared to press the case for unbridled domestic expansion for the benefit of the unemployed. Once Britain was forced off gold in 1931, however, interest rate movements were no longer dictated by international considerations. Keynes's initial reaction to the break with gold was to advocate cheaper money to promote domestic recovery. In June 1931, in lectures to the Harris Foundation in Chicago, he called for government-sponsored public works as a recovery agent *alongside* positive efforts to reduce the rate of interest.[13] According to classical economic theory, aggregate demand for the output produced by the employed labour force would always be sufficient to absorb that output since flexible interest rates would ensure that the willingness of entrepreneurs to undertake productive investment would match the community's desire to save out of current income.

By 1932, however, Keynes had grown increasingly sceptical of the view that the capitalist system possessed an inherent tendency towards self-adjustment sufficient to maintain full employment. He recognized that lower interest rates would not necessarily induce sufficient investment to

[11] Cab 58/2, Economic Advisory Council. Conclusion of the Fourth Meeting, 8 May 1930.
[12] Cab 58/2, Economic Advisory Council. Conclusions of the Fifth Meeting, 19 June 1930.
[13] J. M. Keynes, 'An Economic Analysis of Unemployment', in *Unemployment as a World Problem*, ed. Q. Wright (Chicago, 1931), 1–42.

absorb all current saving; in a situation of excess saving over investment, interest rates could settle at a level dictated by the public's desire to hold non-interest-bearing money rather than investment-financing bonds (what we now call their 'liquidity preference'). It could not be assumed, however, that at this level investment would prove sufficiently attractive to employ all unused resources; the economic system, in other words, could be in equilibrium at less than full employment. The interaction of a relatively high interest rate elasticity of demand for money with a relatively low interest elasticity of demand for investment, both of which were influenced by expectations, suggested that any adjustment mechanism based on monetary policy alone would work only very slowly to improve employment.

At this juncture Keynes supported public works 'not because of the "international complications" that would be generated by continued reductions in the rate of interest', but because 'such reductions would not be adequate to the task'.[14] In the short run, Keynes was to argue, monetary policy ought to become subordinate to a progressive policy of government-induced investment, the effect of which, by raising expectations, would be to encourage further investment, output and employment without serious inflation, given the existence of substantial surplus capacity.[15] The contemporary economist D. H. Robertson agreed that during a severe depression fiscal policy should be the more dominant partner in any policy mix; an easier monetary policy, he maintained, was unlikely by itself to boost spending once business confidence had sunk to a low ebb.

The national economy campaign launched during 1931–32 was the very antithesis of this approach. Expenditure on public works by both central and local authorities fell by 35 per cent in the four years after 1929. To Keynes, the veto imposed by the Ministry of Health in September 1931 on local authority borrowing to finance building and other enterprises was 'silly beyond words'. The impact upon the labour market was 'much greater than the direct unemployment, since each man whose purchasing power is curtailed by his being put out of work diminishes the employment he can give to others'.[16]

But with the pursuit of economy and stability to the fore in the aftermath of the 1931 financial crisis, there was little sympathy within government for the view that unorthodox finance could prove an effective remedy for

[14] D. Patinkin, 'The Development of Keynes' Policy Thinking', in *Anticipations of the General Theory?*, ed. Patinkin (Oxford, 1983), 211.
[15] Public works, in other words, would help to 'keep market estimates of the marginal efficiency of capital sufficiently buoyant to allow interest rate policy to operate successfully over the longer term'. D. Moggridge and S. Howson, 'Keynes on Monetary Policy 1910–1946', *Oxford Economic Papers*, 26 (1974), 238–9.
[16] J. M. Keynes in *The Daily Mail*, 1 January 1933, cited in *JMK*, Vol. 21, 144.

unemployment. The Conservative-dominated National Government judged that public works were far too costly in relation to per capita expenditure on unemployment benefit. Critics were keen to point out that it cost the state an average of £324 to employ a man for a year on subsidized works projects but only £78 to support a family of five on unemployment benefit. Public works, moreover, were judged to be both impracticable, in view of the age, sex, physique and geographical distribution of those currently unemployed, and unnecessary, given the prevailing scale of public utility services. The Unemployment Grants Committee was thus terminated, road schemes were postponed and local authority capital programmes severely cut from the autumn of 1931. Fortunately, the lag between the cancellation of a project and the actual cessation of work, plus the need to continue expenditure on previous commitments, meant that the full deflationary effects of the policy were never felt at the depth of the depression.

Towards the end of December 1932 MacDonald brought before a newly created committee on trade and employment a businessmen's proposal that the £120 million currently being spent on unemployment benefit should be used to raise a £4,000 million loan to sponsor public works projects, similar to those championed by Lloyd George in 1929. The idea was treated with contempt, not least because of the implication that emergency measures were required. 'The most helpful contribution which the Government could make in the matter of industrial re-equipment', the Committee judged, was not by way of public works but by 'giving more generous terms in the matter of Income Tax allowances for depreciation'.[17]

Britain refused after 1931 to pursue an active policy of deficit-financed expansion to create jobs, despite the fact that the constraints of previous years, notably the need to sustain relatively high interest rates to sustain gold reserves and her vulnerability as a free trade nation, could no longer be invoked with the same authority once sterling left the gold standard and tariffs were introduced. The opposition in official circles was based in part, not so much on blind prejudice or woolly-headed incompetence, as upon the firm belief that past experience with public works provided compelling evidence of the futility of pursuing any such activity in the future.

Both the Liberals' 1929 programme and the limited public works programme of the second Labour administration had been designed primarily to ease short-term cyclical unemployment. The number of first-round jobs created by such works projects always appeared to officials to be pitifully small, even in comparison with the pre-slump volume of registered unemployment, and the more so following the outbreak of world recession. Primary employment on road works, for example, rose from 12,000 in July

---

[17] Prem 1/126, Committee on Trade and Employment, 29 December 1932.

1929 to only 41,000 by August 1931. During their first full year of operation, the second Labour government's public works schemes provided direct employment for only 61,165 people; if we presume the creation of an equal amount of indirect to direct employment and an employment multiplier of 1.5, such schemes might be credited with raising total employment by 183,495 at most, or 8.9 per cent of recorded unemployment. Even when they reached their peak in 1931 the schemes were likely, on the same assumptions, to have provided employment equivalent to only 10.9 per cent of the total number out of work.[18]

Against the supposed advantages of such works, complained the National Government, had to be set the resulting debt burden involved; considered merely as a means of providing employment, public works expenditure had shown itself unduly burdensome in relation to the very limited results obtained. While the moral and economic effects of 'special action' might prove of some value in certain circumstances, it could not materially help an unemployment problem dominated by the international situation in general. To withdraw money from the taxpayers' pocket to spend it on providing work 'would probably tend to reduce rather than increase the sum total of employment'.[19]

This penurious approach to fiscal policy was shared as much by Labour as by Tory Ministers. Philip Snowden's memorandum to the Cabinet on the financial situation in 1931 was characteristically dire in tone. The country, he preached:

cannot afford a Budget with any sort of deficit. From the internal point of view alone there are compelling reasons for maintaining the country's credit. The falling off in revenue coupled with the constant increase of expenditure on the great demands for new capital resources occasioned by borrowing, particularly for the Unemployment Fund, are bringing back our floating debt to the dangerous high level at which it stood a year ago . . . If in these conditions the public look upon the Budget as unsound, it will become a question whether they can be induced to subscribe for the short term accommodation which is vital to finance and equally whether they can be induced to subscribe to any necessary long term loans . . . Failure to secure the necessary short term accommodation will prejudice the continuation of cheap money with all that that implies. Failure to obtain necessary long term money at reasonable rates will not merely postpone all prospects of successful conversion of the war debt, but will jeopardise the whole improvement in the long term rate of interest which has characterised recent months and which, if maintained, is full of promise for business in the future.

This is not scare-mongering; in present conditions of gloom and anxiety these would be the necessary consequences of unsound State finance: nor is the probability of other graver consequences – a breakdown of our financial organis-ation and the removal of great sums abroad – lightly to be dismissed. . . . It is not

---

[18] Middleton, *Towards the Managed Economy*, 165–6.
[19] Cab 27/479, Employment Policy Committee. Report, 25 January 1932, 9.

enough now to refrain from undertaking fresh expenditure. We must secure substantial reductions in existing expenditure.[20]

Public works were not outlawed entirely during the slump but any suggestion that they might be regarded as a major stimulant to employment was summarily dismissed in light of their anticipated effects. A proposal for a London Outer Circle railway was rejected by a special Employment Committee in 1932 on the grounds that its commercial possibility did not justify the heavy construction costs involved; similarly, various schemes for providing road transport across the River Forth were deemed either impracticable or, if desirable in themselves, judged of doubtful value because of their potential impact upon 'the limited resources of the Road Fund'. And when the Committee agreed not to press for the renewal of the Development (Loan Guarantees and Grants) Act of 1929, it justified its action on the grounds that 'there was little or no effective demand for such assistance', that the Act's usefulness was 'exhausted' and that its renewal 'would be of no material benefit in dealing with the present phase of the unemployment situation'.[21]

Ways had to be found 'of occupying usefully the minds and bodies of the unemployed', reported a Cabinet Committee in September 1932, but assistance was only to be given 'in order to supplement local effort and to the extent strictly necessary for the purpose'. Pressure to introduce large-scale public works had to be resisted. The government's dilemma, claimed the National Government's Health Minister Hilton Young, was that: 'Work could not be provided without capital and capital must be conserved for use in the restoration of industry.'[22]

Few economists by this time shared such a minimalist approach but the views of the minority were music to the government's ears. Towards the end of 1932, Gregory, von Hayek, Plant and Robbins argued in strictly classical terms that:

many of the troubles of the world at the present time are due to improvident borrowing and spending on the part of the public authorities . . . The depression has abundantly shown that the existence of public debt on a large scale imposes frictions and obstacles to readjustment . . . If the Government wishes to help revival, the right way for them to proceed is not to revert to their old habits of lavish expenditure.[23]

[20] Cab 24/219, The Financial Situation. Memorandum by the Chancellor of the Exchequer, 7 January 1931.
[21] Cab 27/479, Cabinet Employment Committee. Conclusions of the Second and Third Meetings, 18 April, 9 June 1932.
[22] Cab 27/237, CP 307, Unemployment Committee. Interim Report, 24 September 1932.
[23] *The Times*, 19 October 1932.

It was irresponsible, they argued further, to embark on such public expenditure as would inevitably reduce the funds available to investors once confidence returned. Keynes's retaliation reflected his growing exasperation with such thinking. He poured scorn on those who believed:

that we can save up our economies against a later day, and that the surplus unemployed men . . . are storing up reserves of energy and enthusiasm which will enable them to work treble time 'when finance permits' . . . Savings are . . . the one thing which will not 'keep'. If they are not used in capital developments pari passu they disappear forever in doles, deficits and business losses.[24]

Superficial examination of the Budget during the world slump might suggest that the authorities were far less deflationary and parsimonious in their approach to the economic malaise than contemporary critics maintained. The Budget balance, conventionally defined, deteriorated by almost £18 million during the fiscal years 1929/30 to 1932/33. According to Middleton, the deficit was actually much worse, amounting to almost £68 million. The situation was disguised by the Treasury's practice of fiscal 'window dressing', under which various categories of expenditure financed by borrowing were excluded from account, whilst other non-recurrent items on the revenue side, which ought properly to have been ignored, were included to preserve the impression of adherence to orthodox financial principles.[25]

Certainly during 1930/31 the government made no serious attempt to reduce government expenditure as a matter of course. On the contrary, the 1930 Unemployment Insurance Act liberalized the benefits scheme and increased the cost to the Exchequer of unemployment benefits from £20.4 million (1929/30) to £57.9 million (1931/32). The government resorted to borrowing from the Treasury and then made little attempt to balance the Insurance Fund or to reduce borrowing.[26] Despite a shrinking revenue base, taxes were increased only marginally so that expenditure growth outpaced the yield of government income. Rather than risk the deflationary consequences of higher taxation or any damage to confidence and sterling, the Treasury disguised the mounting deficit which, when stripped of 'window dressing', amounted, on Middleton's figures, to £45.7 million during 1931/32, compared with the conventional estimate for the period of a small £4 million surplus.

In practice, then, the deficit deteriorated faster than the Treasury was prepared to declare publicly; the pretence of budgetary orthodoxy was retained for the sake of sustaining confidence in the stability of British credit both at home and abroad. But this deterioration in fiscal stance did not

---

[24] *New Statesman and Nation*, 4 February 1933.
[25] Middleton, *Towards the Managed Economy*, 96–7.   [26] See chapter 2.

reflect discretionary action for stabilization purposes. On the contrary, the Treasury, faced with mounting budgetary imbalance, set its face against any substantial increases in capital expenditure rather than contemplate higher taxation. As a result budgetary policy, far from proving reflationary by a progressive if unplanned move towards deficit, became progressively more restrictive. Middleton, adopting a measure of the constant employment budget,[27] has demonstrated the extent of discretionary changes in fiscal policy during the slump; his estimates suggest that budgets in the early thirties were even more deflationary than has hitherto been supposed as the authorities sought to raise the ratio of receipts to GDP. During the trough of the depression, in other words, desperate efforts were made to balance the Budget by severe tightening of revenue and expenditure. The constant employment budget moved into substantial surplus down to 1932/33 as taxation rose and expenditure was cut. The effect of this highly deflationary approach could have been partially offset by an increase of public investment and local authority expenditure, both of which lay outside the conventionally defined Budget, but, if anything, the fetish for economy hardened.

The power of budgetary orthodoxy in severely limiting the scope of alternative economic policy should not therefore be underestimated. It is customary, nevertheless, to stress the beneficial effect which the pursuit of balanced budgets had on business confidence, and upon the capacity of London to attract foreign capital to preserve the stability of sterling down to 1931. Aldcroft has argued, furthermore, that the offsetting nature of different fiscal measures and the time-lag between decision-making and implementation tended to neutralize the aggravating effects of budgetary policy.[28] In addition, extra-budgetary outlays in the form of public semi-public investment and local authority expenditure are frequently alleged to

---

[27] Budget balances as conventionally portrayed are inadequate as a measure of change in fiscal stance since they fail to separate the budget's influences on the economy from the economy's influence on the budget. Middleton has recalculated the budget for the 1930s to account for the influence of variations in economic activity on the budget balance. The resulting 'constant employment budget' represents 'the budget balance that would result (with the same nominal taxes and public spending plans) if private sector demand was just sufficient continuously to maintain activity at a constant rate of unemployment'. The constant employment balance, therefore, is an estimate of what deficits or surpluses would have occurred annually if the economy has remained on its trend path of growth. Middleton, *Towards the Managed Economy*, chapter 7. Alternative measures, adopting a similar approach, can be found in T. Thomas, 'Aggregate Demand, 1918–45' in *The Economic History of Britain*, Vol. 2, ed. Floud and McCloskey, 332–46. Inadequate data and disagreements over the most appropriate measure of fiscal influence leave room for doubt as to the validity of such exercises but as yet the issue remains unresolved. For details of the difficulties involved see S. N. Broadberry, 'Fiscal Policy in Britain During the 1930s' and R. Middleton, 'The Measurement of Fiscal Influence in Britain in the 1930s', *Economic History Review*, 2nd ser., 37 (1984), 103–6.   [28] Aldcroft, *The Inter-War Economy*, 302–14.

have been a stabilizing influence, especially during the years 1929–31, acting as 'a sea-anchor against the drift of national income to lower levels'.[29] But, as we have indicated, fiscal 'window-dressing' disguised the extent to which budgets in the early thirties were draconian in their effect; high unemployment merely intensified orthodoxy in the extreme, giving full rein to a destabilizing budgetary policy probably sufficient to have outweighed any positive influence upon business confidence and certainly the death knell of any expansionary public works programme. Much of the increase in public and local authority capital expenditure during the first two years of the depression, moreover, 'was financed out of additional current revenue and new borrowing was partially offset by simultaneous repayment of debt, while, in addition, expenditure was lowest in those areas with the highest unemployment'.[30]

DEFENDING THE 'STATUS QUO': FISCAL STANCE AND ECONOMIC
RECOVERY, 1933–37

On balance, therefore, it appears that government fiscal policy during 1931/32 was inherently deflationary. This was particularly perverse given the substantial volume of unemployment at the depth of the slump, plus the fact that the achievement of a balanced budget was crucially dependent on the level of economic activity. Keynes appreciated this latter point, claiming in 1933:

You will never balance the Budget through measures which reduce the national income. The Chancellor would simply be chasing his own tail – or cloven hoof! The only chance of balancing the Budget in the long run is to bring things back to normal, and so avoid the enormous Budget charges arising out of unemployment . . . Even if you take the Budget as your test, the criterion of whether the economy would be useful or not is the state of employment . . . I do not believe that measures which truly enrich the country will injure the public credit . . . It is the burden of unemployment and the decline in the national income which are upsetting the Budget. Look after the unemployment, and the Budget will look after itself.[31]

The Treasury was in no mood, however, to relax its fiscal grip, even when economic recovery set in from 1933. The co-existence of low interest rates, a boom in private housebuilding and a rise in the real per capita income of those in work (a significant proportion of which began to be spent upon the consumer durable products of the so-called 'new' industries) initiated a domestic market recovery which the National Government was loath to

[29] International Labour Office, *Public Investment and Full Employment*, Studies and Reports, New Series, 3, 1946, 173.   [30] Middleton, *Towards the Managed Economy*, 138.
[31] *JMK*, Vol. 21, 149–50.

compromise, least of all by indulging in 'unsound investment'. Moreover, though insured unemployment fell rapidly during 1933, reducing the total outlay on unemployment expenditure, the government's contribution to the unemployment benefits system, charged to the Budget as conventionally defined, fell proportionately less. Central government remained responsible for the whole cost of transitional payments to the longer-term unemployed (whose numbers fell away more slowly than did those in the insurance scheme proper) and for any deficit on the Unemployment Insurance Fund beyond its statutory maximum of £115 million.[32] Thus the burden of unemployment charges on the Budget responded only slowly to recovery, as did the yield of taxes on income. Lower interest rates and the near abandonment of Sinking Fund payments eased the situation somewhat but it was the sharp reduction in government expenditure in other directions which fostered a substantial Budget surplus in 1933/34. This permitted some remission of taxation and the restoration of previous expenditure cuts during the following year, but given the authorities' determination to adhere to orthodox finance for the sake of sustaining confidence both at home and in the international financial community, there was little hope of the Budget being used as an instrument of stabilization. Overall 'the direct contribution of fiscal policy to recovery was extremely limited. By 1935 fiscal stance had changed comparatively little since the depression years'.[33]

As Chancellor, Chamberlain remained as wedded to orthodoxy as his predecessors, refusing to countenance deliberately unbalanced budgets. Real prosperity lay in relying upon 'normal' channels to promote trade recovery not in following the whims of the 'new' economics. Some local authority works schemes and some increases in government spending (e.g. on railway electrification) survived the economy drive of the thirties, but the search for a solution to unemployment came increasingly to be sought in the rejuvenation of trade and commerce.'It should be clear by now', the Minister of Labour informed the Cabinet in July 1933:

that no direct intervention by the Government in the employment market, through the provision of public works etc., can do anything to the employment figures comparable to the effect of ordinary trade improvement which flows from the soundness of the Government's general policy . . . The trade improvement in the last two months took over a quarter of a million men off the unemployment registers. This is more than twice the highest number of men that have been put into employment at any time on State-aided public works in this country, despite the enormous expenditure on those works.[34]

[32] For further details see chapter 3.
[33] Middleton, *Towards the Managed Economy*, 139–40.
[34] Cab 24/242, CP 189, Training and Occupation for the Unemployed Next Winter. Memorandum by the Minister of Labour, 21 July 1933.

Phillips at the Treasury was also clear as to the parameters of policy, writing in 1934:

If we can hold out to industry a prospect of stable rising prices, a reasonable stability in exchange, cheap capital and money, a check on the rise in taxation and possibly some reduction, *and a guarantee against revolutionary and dislocating departures in public enterprise* confidence will revive, enterprise will quicken and employment will expand.[35]

Budget deficits, it was conceded, could facilitate a rise in prices, output and employment if they were financed by creating credit, but such improvements could be better achieved by cheap money.

There is no doubt that to the majority of contemporary politicians, civil servants, city financiers and industrialists a policy of deliberately unbalancing the Budget in the hope of expanding employment was a fearful prospect, not least in its potential for encouraging repeated demands for yet further increases in public expenditure. Keynes may have believed that once economic priorities became increasingly dependent upon continuous political decisions the authorities would act intelligently and responsibly; contemporaries feared, perhaps more realistically, that the political pressures towards even greater expenditure would merely intensify. Hubert Henderson, who had defended Lloyd George's investment programme in 1929, argued in subsequent years that subsidized public works would merely replace projects which local authorities would normally have undertaken without grant aid, but which they held back in order to secure a subsidy from public funds.[36]

Ironically, it was just when the authorities were setting their face against any budgetary changes that might upset the prevailing (and possibly fragile) domestic economic recovery, that an intensified campaign was launched in favour of a more positive reflationary policy to ease unemployment. By March 1933, according to Hutchison, quite a large percentage of the country's university economists 'were advocating publicly a policy of Government spending and expansion and suggesting a means by which it should be organised by "deficit finance"'.[37] Not surprisingly, it was Keynes

[35] T172/1821, Gold Standard: Conditions Required for Return to Gold, 1934. Emphasis added.

[36] For evidence of this changed position see H. D. Henderson, 'Do We Want Public Works?', in *The Inter-War Years*, ed. H. Clay, 151–60.

[37] T. W. Hutchison, *Economics and Economic Policy in Britain 1946–1966* (1968), appendix, 289. See the letter signed by Keynes, together with Professors Pigou and Macgregor, Sir Walter Layton, Sir Arthur Salter, and Sir Josiah Stamp, in *The Times*, 17 October 1932, and a similar letter signed by 37 economists in March 1933 calling upon the government to raise demand by borrowing on capital account. See also the arguments of nine Oxford economists in favour of deficit finance as a cure for unemployment in G. D. H. Cole (ed.) *What Everybody Wants to Know about Money* (Oxford, 1933).

who spearheaded the attack on conventional wisdom. He argued his case with greater confidence, convinced by this time of the fundamental importance of investment expenditure to economic prosperity. An important influence in this respect was the emergence in the early thirties of a more precise formulation of the cumulative effect on employment of deficit-financed public works. As members of the Economic Advisory Council, both he and G. D. H. Cole had asked as early as May 1930 for an estimate to be made of the direct and indirect effects on employment of the maximum feasible expansion of exports. Colin Clark, author of a memorandum in reply, calculated that the effect of a rise in exports of £100 million at 1929 prices (an increase of some 13.7 per cent) would lead to a rise in employment of between 385,000 and 450,000. The latter figure was based on the assumption that there had been no change in labour productivity since 1924; the figures, moreover, included an estimate of the effect on employment in transport and wholesale trading, but they did not attempt to capture any possible further repercussions. Clark cautiously warned against:

any crude method of calculation, such as assuming that a further rise in employment owing to the spending in the home market of any given proportion of the earnings of the re-employed workers in the export trades, would lead to assuming an infinite series of beneficial repercussions. The limiting factors are obscure and economic theory cannot state the possibilities with precision.[38]

It was Richard Kahn's pioneering article 'The Relation of Home Investment to Unemployment', published in the *Economic Journal* in June 1931, which strengthened the case for deficit-financed public works by demonstrating the means by which the ratio of secondary to primary employment generated by a once-and-for-all increase in government expenditure could be calculated. The basic idea of the multiplier process had been in circulation before 1931. Kahn's achievement was to present what we would now describe as a dynamic multiplier. He established that the multiple impact of expanded expenditure would be greater than unity but finite, due to leakages in the form of savings, imported goods, unspent profits and high prices. Keynes's attack on the 'crowding out' view of the Treasury had been based in 1929 on the contention that increased government investment would not be entirely at the expense of private investment, but would itself generate an increase in saving sufficient to permit a net increase in investment. It was Kahn, however, who first addressed himself to the question of the quantitative relationship between these two increases, demonstrating that investment could increase saving and by precisely the

[38] BT/70/27, Export Trade in Relation to Unemployment, May 1930.

amount required to finance the additional government expenditure involved.[39] And by insisting that the inflationary impact of public works would be of little concern, given the extent of surplus capacity, Kahn's work provided a contemporary counter-attack to the prevailing conviction that governments should reduce their expenditure and balance their budgets in straitened times.

Kahn's contribution proved to be of strategic importance in the developing debate over how best to tackle involuntary unemployment. Even so its explicit support for raising the demand for labour via public works expenditure merely recast, albeit in a more sophisticated and challenging form, an idea which, in principle at least, had already captured the attention of supposedly more orthodox economists. There was widespread support by the end of the 1920s for the view that unemployment was largely involuntary and that, strict classical teaching apart, there was little opportunity of reducing it by trying to persuade or force workers to accept lower money wages. There was no slavish acceptance, in other words, of the classical postulate that unemployment was either voluntary or frictional or that in the short run the government was powerless to act on its own to influence the demand for labour.

The critical missing link was the concept of aggregate effective demand. Contemporary economists were quite able to accept the principle of the counter-cyclical timing of public works once the inherent difficulties of relying upon labour market adjustments to activate cyclical recovery were acknowledged. In the early thirties there were numerous competing theories as to the role of demand, supply, prices and profitability in perpetuating the slump and what might be the appropriate mix of remedial policies. Economic theorists saw a role for demand stimulation but frequently interpreted it in microeconomic terms, regarding demand as the major influence on the output decisions of the individual firm. Demand, in other words, was perceived as a possible constraint at the micro-level, but in the aggregate it was output which was regarded as the main determinant of demand rather than the other way around. Such theorists 'recognized how a net injection of demand could alleviate a depression through its microeconomic impact, but did not yet interpret macroeconomic fluctuations in terms of an aggregate demand constraint'.[40]

By 1932 Keynes's defence of public works depended far less upon the existence of the 'special circumstances' operating during the period of the

[39] R. F. Kahn, 'The Relation of Home Investment to Unemployment', *Economic Journal*, 41 (1931), 173–98; cf. D. Patinkin, 'Keynes and the Multiplier', *Manchester School*, 3 (1978), 209–23.

[40] M. Bleaney, 'Macroeconomic Policy and the Great Depression Revisited', *Scottish Journal of Political Economy*, 34 (1987), 117.

restored gold standard. Before the thirties he had not formally acknowledged, at least in his published writings, that falling output and employment could be caused directly by a contraction of demand. But thereafter he proved far more sensitive to the evil of thrift in times of economic sluggishness and more willing to concede the importance of the aggregate demand for output as a whole.[41] If an increase in saving because of greater thriftiness was not translated via the capital market into increased investment, he argued, the result could be a depression of the overall level of income, demand and employment. The rate of interest, as a purely monetary phenomenon, could not be relied upon to reconcile saving and investment decisions. Had Keynes continued to believe in the supremacy of monetary policy he would have welcomed the opportunity provided by the abandonment of gold in September 1931 for a more systematic use of interest rate policy, i.e. the policy prescription overshadowed in previous years by the fear of its effects on the level of gold reserves. But although low interest rates followed the demise of the gold standard, Keynes came to believe that they would not, for a variety of reasons, work quickly enough or positively enough to stimulate sufficient investment to generate full employment. Although holding down interest rates to encourage investment was desirable, there were too many other variables at work affecting businessmen's decisions to invest. Monetary policy alone could not be relied upon to produce the required economic stimulant.

Investment and not saving, therefore, was the key to raising output and employment. In an economy with under-utilized capacity, increased investment, Keynes argued, would generate a convergent series of ever diminishing waves of expenditures (the 'multiplier') creating additional incomes and so additional saving.[42] It was commonplace that increased loan expenditure could only be met out of increased saving; but whereas the latter was previously thought to be dependent upon higher rates of interest and the former upon the prevailing level of national income, Keynes argued that in conditions of large-scale unemployment loan expenditure would increase output and demand both directly and indirectly, increasing the national income from which the increased saving would be found. 'Thus', he wrote, 'the contemporary economist, as a result of living in a world where unemployment has become chronic, puts more stress on our power of drawing on resources which were not fully employed and less stress on

---

[41] Kahn's earlier analysis of the relation between investment and employment was an explicitly dynamic one representing the time sequence of successive secondary employments generated by a once-and-for-all increase in public works expenditure. It was not, however, couched in the post-Keynesian context of an equilibrium analysis of national income linked to a theory of effective demand.

[42] See D. Moggridge, 'From the Treatise to The General Theory: An Exercise in Chronology', *History of Political Economy*, 5 (1973), 72–88 and *JMK*, Vol. 23.

the diversion of resources already in use'.[43] If investment was deficient then the level of national income upon which savings depended would be below that required to produce full employment. The state's responsibility was to create more optimistic conditions for the expansion of business enterprise by undertaking new loan-expenditure on a scale sufficient to raise the level of aggregate demand. 'It is impossible', Keynes wrote in September 1933, to increase employment

> without first increasing demand, and . . . there is no conceivable way of putting more purchasing power into use except by increasing loan expenditure . . . We have been suffering . . . from a simple and foolish fallacy. An individual who abstains can enrich himself . . . Most people infer from this that in the same way a community as a whole can enrich itself by abstention . . . But this is impossible . . . There is, and can be, no way of enrichment or of employment except by building houses, electrifying railways, erecting the grid, or whatever the appropriate activity might be.[44]

By the mid-thirties, then, significant changes had taken place in the idea of manipulating fiscal policy to combat unemployment. The initial nineteenth-century view of 'making work' for the able-bodied, itself transformed by the early twenties into a proposal for 'shifting' investment from years of prosperity to years of decline, had developed into an argument for reviving and sustaining employment by measures specifically designed to maintain effective demand.

In the circumstances the campaign for a more radical and interventionist economic policy continued with renewed vigour, even though Britain's recovery from the world slump was earlier and more sustained than that of most other European countries. The reports of the Committee of Economic Information[45] consistently advocated the use of cheap money and public works to counteract economic recession. Although *The Economist* in February 1933 shrank from advocating 'extravagant schemes of an inflationary nature', it publicly repudiated 'the gloomy Calvinism of a Chancellor of the Exchequer who bids us live by faith alone', arguing that 'at a time when idle balances are accumulating in the banks and idle persons waiting in vain for employment' it was a mistake to scrutinize too critically expenditure which promised to create jobs, even if it offered little remunerative return in the immediate future.[46]

---

[43] 'Government Loan Policy and the Rate of Interest', cited in *JMK*, Vol. 21, 539.

[44] J. M. Keynes, 'Two Years Off Gold: How Far Are We From Prosperity Now?', *Daily Mail*, 19 September 1933, reprinted in *JMK*, Vol. 21, 287–8.

[45] Established in July 1931 to complement the work of the Economic Advisory Council by offering advice on the prevailing situation and making suggestions for future development. Its original members were Keynes, Stamp, Citrine, Cole, Lewis, Henderson. See Howson and Winch, *The Economic Advisory Council*.   [46] *The Economist*, 25 February 1933.

Using the Labour Party's Acland travelling fund, Hugh Dalton sent a group of young scholars abroad in the mid thirties to study European financial policy. The results of their endeavours appeared to substantiate Keynes's recommendations for strategic financing. In a reflective comment on the published findings,[47] Dalton noted that 'those who advocate the expansionist doctrine have the better case but . . . their policy, in order to be fully effective, needs to be pushed a good deal further than most of them seem willing to push it'.[48] Keynes's fellow economist James Meade also became convinced that the prevailing volume of unemployment would never be cured by monetary policy alone; consumption and investment had to be raised to appreciably higher levels, the former, he suggested, by a scheme of unemployment benefits paid for from borrowed funds and the latter by a combination of monetary and fiscal policies. 'Because the demand for consumption goods is low', he wrote in 1935:

the profitability of industry is small and there are few profitable opportunities for capital development. This is so in spite of the fact that interest rates are generally low in times of depression; profits are so depressed that low interest rates do not stimulate fresh capital development.[49]

In similar vein Hugh Gaitskell argued for an expansionary investment programme financed by government loan to increase employment, even at the cost of a slight depreciation of sterling; with proper controls, he argued, the pound was unlikely to collapse.[50]

Nor was Lloyd George's fiscal campaign yet finished. Contemptuous of the 'many Micawbers who wait with simpering optimism for something to turn up'[51] he called in 1935 for a deliberate plan to use state credit to foster national economic development. The time had come, he maintained in a lengthy memorandum, for the state to 'further the guarantee of its own credit to ensure sound, economic progress'. The nation, he urged,

must set up machinery which can take in hand the task of surveying our industrial and agricultural possibilities; of planning how best to realise them; and of furnishing such financial assistance on the basis of the national credit as may be needed to carry out the proposed developments and enterprises. In the past, successive Governments have already done this kind of thing sporadically by rule of thumb in isolated cases. We propose that henceforth they shall do it systematically and

---

[47] The results were published in H. Dalton, *Unbalanced Budgets: A Study of the Financial Crisis in Fifteen Countries* (1934).   [48] Quoted in Durbin, *New Jerusalems*, 221.

[49] Durbin, *New Jerusalems*, 196.

[50] H. Gaitskell and C. Catlin (eds.), *New Trends in Socialism* (1935).

[51] Cab 24/254, CP 59(A), Revised Text of Mr. Lloyd George's Memorandum on Unemployment, 12 July 1935, 1.

deliberately, according to well thought out plans, and that a permanent administrative organ shall be set up for the purpose.[52]

This 'New Deal', as he called it, bore many of the general characteristics of the Liberals' 1929 programme. It encouraged action, initially over a two-year period, on land settlement and reclamation, drainage and afforestation, housing and slum clearance, improved docks, canals, railways and bridges, and extended electricity and telephone services, including the electrification of suburban railway lines, the whole to be financed by a Prosperity Loan of £250 million. The labour-intensive schemes were designed to draw upon materials from industries most in need of rejuvenation, particularly those in the depressed areas where the bulk of the long-term unemployed were to be found. The 'administrative organ' charged with reviewing, guiding and planning this major initiative and with directing 'financial resources into the most beneficial channels of investment' was to be a National Development Board, reporting directly to the Prime Minister. He in turn would refer the Board's recommendations to a reconstituted Cabinet composed, as in the First World War, of himself and up to five Ministers without departmental duties. As to finance, it was 'very easy for the State, in the present condition of the money market, to borrow to almost any extent at a very low rate of interest'. Accordingly, development programmes could be carried out 'with the utmost economy if their financing is based upon the credit of the nation'.

Lloyd George's confidence, verging on abrasiveness, stemmed from his conviction that such a bold public works programme would practically solve the unemployment problem as he saw it. It was essential, he declared, to recognize that unemployment was not a static pool. Many people passed through only short periods of unemployment and it was for the benefit of the longer-term unemployed that the proposals were framed. By omitting from the unemployment register some 250,000 workers regarded as unemployable and a further 350,000 who would be eliminated from the labour market through the adoption of a contemporaneous policy to provide training facilities and to raise the school-leaving age to 15, the unemployment problem for which the proposals were designed could be judged to amount, not to a 'constant figure of 2,100,000', but to 1,500,000.

The 'New Deal' assumed that the immediate implementation of the listed public works would provide work for 500,000 workers. Moreover, additional jobs would be created in supporting industries for men currently unemployed from time to time, equivalent to the employment of a further

[52] Cab 24/254, CP 59(A), 12.

500,000 workers. Thereafter the general infusion of confidence and enterprise would provide work for a further 500,000 men in various other trades, equivalent to the number remaining on the unemployment register after all necessary deductions had been made.

Lloyd George could hardly contain himself. Public works expenditure, he claimed in echoes of his 1929 appeal:

> would quicken trade all round. Orders for material and machinery . . . would flow in. There is hardly an industry that would not be benefitted . . . Apart from that, the increase in the purchasing capacity of the unemployed households by the substitution of wages for the dole, and by the increase in the profits of business would increase the volume of trade, and therefore of employment.

Were the government to be bold enough to accept the challenge:

> to embark immediately on a policy of bold schemes supported by adequate finance . . . people would say: 'That means an era of good trade!' and they would forthwith prepare to take full advantage of the coming prosperity by launching out in their own industries . . . More production would be undertaken, more orders placed, and the existing industries of the nation would take on more hands.[53]

Despite the vigour with which it was conducted, neither Lloyd George's passionate appeal for a 'New Deal' nor any other radical programme of fiscal expansion made much headway within government circles in the mid thirties. The Labour Party remained content to indulge itself in discussion of the likely benefits to be derived from nationalization of the banking sector, a vital step in its eyes in the march towards socialism. It retained a dismissive view of the importance of finance, and never came to any clear understanding of the relationship between monetary and real variables. The reduction of unemployment, it conceded, would ease budgetary stringency; but that was no argument for using the Budget as a direct means of boosting employment.

Within the Treasury, officials continued to worry about the impracticability of any large-scale public works programmes, given the length of time they took to bring into operation, and about whether recourse to substantial borrowing would raise the long-term rate of interest, perhaps to the point where public confidence would be so diminished that the authorities would be forced to monetarize the debt, threatening inflation and the stability of the pound. Some senior Treasury officials are known to have discussed during 1935 the need for stimulating capital expenditure in order to sustain the momentum of economic recovery, and to compensate for the permanent decline of industry in the depressed areas. But the outcome was merely a recommendation that the government should

[53] Cab 24/254, CP 59(A), 43, 45.

encourage local authorities to raise loans for public works up to a total of £60 million,[54] representing about half the total sanctioned by the Labour government between June 1929 and June 1930. This hardly supports Hutchison's claim that the Treasury had been 'largely converted to "Keynesian" policies . . . at least a year before the publication of *The General Theory*'.[55] Consider Leith-Ross's warning issued in a Treasury memorandum in 1935. 'The nation', he wrote, had to remember that:

> whenever the policy of Government spending has been tried as a remedy for unemployment it has proved a will o' the wisp. State intervention can do little to stimulate employment; it tends merely to produce a temporary alleviation, followed by a relapse. The Government can help best by preserving the public credit and lowering money rates so as to encourage the active use of capital . . . Grandiose projects of public expenditure will, by undermining confidence and deterring enterprise, create far more unemployment than they cure. Unemployment is like insomnia: worrying will do no good: stimulants will make matters worse: the best prescription is a simple regime and an orderly life.[56]

A KEYNESIAN CONVERSION? REARMAMENT, PUBLIC SPENDING AND THE REDUCTION OF UNEMPLOYMENT, 1935–39

The decision of Treasury officials in 1937 to encourage local authorities to prepare additional public works schemes on a counter-cyclical basis might suggest that the influence which Keynes and other economists exerted on economic thinking in the later thirties was greater than is generally supposed. There is little evidence to support this view. The action in 1937 was modest in scope – the proposed expenditure was for only £50 million over two years – and was motivated more by a desire to prevent unemployment worsening during an anticipated slump than to drive it to substantially lower levels by the deliberate timing of expenditure over the course of the trade cycle.

Treasury thinking had not moved significantly from its 1929–30 position; officials remained alert to the prospective state of the national finances, to the need to sustain the primacy of monetary policy, and to the acknowledged difficulty of ever abandoning works policies once they had been implemented.[57] That said, such attitudes do not appear to square with the government's commitment to substantial rearmament expenditure from 1936 onwards, the more so when, from April 1937, defence spending began increasingly to be met from borrowing rather than from taxation.

---

[54] Howson and Winch, *The Economic Advisory Council*, 130–1.
[55] T. W. Hutchison in *The Economic History Review*, 2nd ser., 31 (1978), 155.
[56] T188/117, The New Deal and British Trade, 1935.
[57] G. C. Peden, 'The "Treasury View" on Public Works'; Peden, "Keynes, the Treasury and Unemployment in the later Nineteen-Thirties', *Oxford Economic Papers*, 32 (1980), 1–18.

Appropriations for defence loans rose from £64.9 million in 1937/38 to £128.1 million in 1938/39, whilst defence spending as a whole increased from £139 million in 1935 to £244 million in 1937 and to £353 million in 1938.[58]

Although the announcement of a substantial defence programme in February 1937 raised the threshold of government capital expenditure to fresh heights, the significance of the shift in fiscal policy on Treasury priorities can be exaggerated. Rather than being fashioned to effect adequate preparations, the rearmament programme down to 1939 was limited and controlled by the overriding desire to preserve national and international economic stability. With deterrence, diplomacy and appease-ment to the fore, defence expenditure was kept under close scrutiny. Its scale was never allowed to threaten industrial performance, government credit or the general balance of trade, principally because the preservation of prosperity was regarded as 'the fourth arm of defence'. Reshaping or distorting civil or export production for the purposes of rearmament threatened to undermine the policies already implemented by the govern-ment to sustain economic prosperity. As a consequence, Treasury commit-ment to rearmament spending was limited, down to the outbreak of war, to what was thought to be required in light of the international situation and with regard to its anticipated effects upon costs, the balance of payments and the sterling exchange rate.[59]

At the outset, the substantial increase in government expenditure threatened to intensify the boom in the more favoured areas of the country by increasing raw material prices and by aggravating existing shortages, particularly in the supply of iron and steel. In the circumstances even Keynes, the keenest advocate of increased public expenditure, called for the retardation of investment in 1937 at the upper turning point of the cycle, not because he regarded the scale of rearmament as sufficiently permanent or large enough in itself to sustain prosperity but because he feared that extra government borrowing could precipitate a slump.

Faced with an abnormally inflated demand and a rigid economic structure, it was necessary in his view to reduce the stimulus to aggregate demand in favour of distributing it in such a way as to avoid temporary congestion, unacceptable levels of inflation and the threat of a rise in the

[58] H. W. Richardson, 'Fiscal Policy in the 1930s' in *The Managed Economy. Essays in British Economic Policy and Performance*, ed. C. H. Feinstein (Oxford, 1983), 68–92.

[59] For further discussion see G. C. Peden, *British Rearmament and the Treasury. 1932–1939* (Edinburgh, 1979); R. Shay, *British Rearmament in the Thirties. Politics and Profits* (Princeton, 1977); R. Parker, 'Economics, Rearmament and Foreign Policy: The United Kingdom before 1939 – A Preliminary Study', *Journal of Contemporary History*, 10 (1975), 637–47; R. Parker, 'British Rearmament, 1936–1939; Treasury, Trade Unions and Skilled Labour', *English Historical Review*, 96 (1981), 306–43.

long-term rate of interest. Reflecting on the likely impact of the Chancellor's decision in March 1937 to borrow £80 million a year for rearmament, Keynes noted that:

> though the new demand will be widely spread (since it will not be limited to the primary employment for armaments, but will also spread to the secondary employments to meet the increased demand of consumers), we cannot safely regard even half of those unemployed insured persons as being available to satisfy home demand. For we have to subtract the unemployables, those seasonably unemployed etc., and those who cannot be readily employed except in producing for export. If we suppose the full rate of Government spending to begin immediately, without any improvement in the export industries or any reduction in other activities, supported by organized overtime, by careful planning and an interval for the planning to take effect, there is a risk of what might fairly be called inflation.[60]

It seemed prudent, therefore, to encourage sound investment but to discourage other postponable capital expenditure lest it should worsen the situation elsewhere. With recorded unemployment at almost 12 per cent, the objective was not to abandon counter-cyclical public works but rather 'to keep our most easily available ammunition in hand for when it is more required'.[61]

Defence spending certainly helped to compensate for the decline in business activity during 1937/38, but it offered no guarantee that the government would be adequately prepared to accelerate capital investment as a whole if and when conditions demanded it. The Ministry of Labour argued that in addition to meeting current and exceptional needs some attention ought to be given to the likely benefit of reserving public works for a future depression.[62] And although the economic circumstances of 1937 put Keynes on the defensive, he remained convinced of the validity of more general schemes of national reconstruction if a prolonged economic recession was to be avoided in the foreseeable future. Revising a proposal which had appeared in the Liberal Yellow Book of 1928, Keynes called in March 1937 for the appointment of a Board of Public Investment to be charged with preparing detailed schemes of civilian investment prior to the decline in economic activity. 'In two years time or less, rearmament loans may be positively helpful in warding off depression', he wrote, 'On the other

---

[60] *The Times*, 11 March 1937.
[61] J. M. Keynes, 'How to Avoid A Slump', *The Times*, 12–14 January 1937. Keynes's views were reflected in a report of the Committee on Economic Information, issued in February 1937, which noted: 'We can no longer anticipate that the stimulus to economic activity generally associated with an increase in investment will make any substantial impression on the remaining volume of unemployment . . . Apart from the special areas the postponement of such investment activity as is not of urgent character would, on balance, prove beneficial to the average level of employment over a period of years.' See Howson and Winch, *The Economic Advisory Council*, 346.
[62] Lowe, *Adjusting to Democracy*, 221–2.

hand, the War Departments may not succeed – they seldom do – in spending up to their time-table.'[63] Unprepared and ill-timed attempts to boost capital spending in an emergency could prove seriously inadequate; what was required was a policy ready for application at the right time and on the right scale. 'The weight both of authority and of public opinion in favour of meeting a recession in employment by organized loan expenditure', Keynes argued further in 1938, 'is so great that this policy is practically certain to be adopted when the time comes'.[64]

On closer inspection, it is clear that the shift in Treasury policy towards substantial loan-financed expenditure in the late thirties did not represent a conversion to 'Keynesianism', at least in the now familiar terms of saving, investment and aggregate demand. Rather, a combination of political, economic and psychological factors associated with the finance and management of rearmament enforced a deliberate but temporary lapse from orthodoxy. 'The unsoundness of the Budget exists only in that part of the Budget which relates to defence expenditure', wrote Phillips in 1936, 'We do not want financial control weakened in respect of the non-defence services; on the contrary we want it to be stricter than ever.'[65] The decision to finance rearmament partly by borrowing created in the official mind a dangerous precedent for later peacetime economic management. Nevertheless, such was the scale of defence spending by April 1939 that the Treasury took its first tentative steps towards actively managing demand via the Budget. It realized that only by achieving full employment could the levels of saving and taxation rise to an amount sufficient to permit greater borrowing without undue loss of confidence. But this was far removed from any formal commitment to the maintenance of a high and stable level of employment. Initially it was the Treasury's intention to balance the Budget in 1942/43, once the rearmament programme was completed.[66]

This is not to deny that the shift in fiscal stance in the three or four years prior to the outbreak of war provided a much-needed boost to employment in the basic trades. At first, defence contracts were allocated to the depressed areas more as a way of relieving pressure on capital and labour resources elsewhere in the economy rather than with the intention of reducing

[63] 'Borrowing for Defence', The Times, 11 March 1937, cited in JMK, Vol. 21, 408.

[64] Cited in 'Keynes versus the Keynesians', in T. Hutchison, The Politics and Philosophy of Economics (1981), 117–18. The Treasury agreed. A committee established to review public capital expenditure reported in August 1937 that although 'it is impossible to anticipate the date or extent of the next depression, it is certain that whenever it occurs the provision of a considerable amount of employment, on work of real importance, which has been postponed on a definite plan, will be of real value'. Howson and Winch, The Economic Advisory Council, 141.

[65] Swann and Turnbull, Records of Interest to Social Scientists, 21.

[66] Middleton, Towards the Managed Economy, 118–20.

interregional unemployment percentages *per se*. Nonetheless, rearmament expenditures during 1935–38 generated in total more than one million jobs, some 81 per cent of the increase in civil employment during the period. Industrially, the chief beneficiaries were coal, iron and steel, and engineering. Certainly, in the absence of rearmament, the 1937 recession would have bitten harder into the gains in output and employment achieved over the previous five years.[67]

The initial impact of rearmament expenditure can, however, be exaggerated, even though ultimately it played a significant part in easing the plight of those industries and regions suffering the greatest concentrations of unemployment. Firms located within the depressed areas were given preference in the allocation of defence contracts, but only after the rearmament boom was already in progress. Regionally, the principal beneficiaries of the spending programme were the south west, Wales, the midlands and, to a lesser extent, central Scotland, the north east and eastern England.[68] In the early stages, there were frequent complaints from the depressed regions that contract allocation did not discriminate sufficiently in their favour and that a more determined effort was required to channel a higher proportion of orders in their direction. The government decided in 1936, however, that the speed of the rearmament programme was not to be sacrificed entirely to the needs of the less prosperous areas and that factories would only be built in those places where there existed an adequate supply of suitably skilled labour.[69]

Even so, the proportion of contracts awarded both to the Special and scheduled areas[70] increased down to 1937. They amounted to approximately 12 per cent of defence spending during the financial year 1935/36; by 1936/37 the proportion had increased to 27 per cent of defence orders placed, and to 31 per cent during the first half of 1937.[71] To the direct impact on employment have to be added the beneficial effects of subcontracts and the induced demand for coal. It is difficult to be precise about the sectoral and regional impact of defence spending, especially in terms of its local multiplier effects. Nevertheless the percentages of registered unemployment in the coal, iron and steel, engineering and shipbuilding industries, all heavily concentrated in the depressed areas, declined from 27.2, 23.5, 13.6 and 44.4 respectively in 1935 to 16.7, 19.5, 7.0 and 21.4

[67] M. Thomas, 'Rearmament and Economic Recovery in the late 1930s', *Economic History Review*, 2nd ser., 36 (1983), 552–79.
[68] Thomas, 'Rearmament and Economic Recovery', 570.
[69] A. Booth, 'The Timing and Content of Government Policies to Assist the Depressed Areas, 1920–1939', Ph.D. Thesis, University of Kent (1975), 247–9.
[70] The difference between the two types of area is explained in chapter 9.
[71] M. Daly, 'Government Policy and the Depressed Areas in the Inter-War Period', D. Phil. Thesis, University of Oxford (1979), 314–15.

in 1938, with further falls recorded during the following year. Within the Special Areas the rate of unemployment in England and Wales fell from 32.7 in 1935 to 27.9 in 1936 and to 21.1 by 1939.[72]

Rearmament, in other words, provided a stimulus to increased expenditure and employment in the areas of chronic unemployment beyond anything that government had achieved or contemplated on their behalf in previous years. And by stimulating the economy as a whole, it revived economic confidence and a belief that the inherent difficulties of such areas could prove more manageable in the foreseeable future. The stimulus to increased government outlays did not transform outright official attitudes to the limitations of fiscal policy, as we have already indicated.[73] Keynes was clearly aware of this, writing in August 1938:

We are at this moment allowing war expenditure for defence to help solve our problem of unemployment as a by-product of such spending, whereas if disarmament had prevailed we might have allowed a serious recession to have developed by now before introducing loan-expenditure on a comparable scale for the productive purposes of peace.[74]

But public works, 'albeit not of the kind advocated by economists',[75] did combat the recession of 1937/38. In doing so they established the presumption that the avoidance of a fiscal stimulus throughout the thirties was a missed opportunity for the economy. Though Treasury thinking remained strictly orthodox to the end, persistent and large-scale unemployment was finally swept away by policies undertaken for other reasons.

POWER TO THE CENTRE? DEFICIT FINANCE, STATE RESPONSIBILITY AND THE LOCAL AUTHORITIES

The challenge which economic radicals posed to the conduct of public policy on behalf of the unemployed raised more fundamental worries within Whitehall than arguments over deficit-financed expenditure alone would suggest. Opposition to the ambitious employment programmes of Keynes and Lloyd George was partly reinforced by profound fears over their likely

---

[72] See chapter 9.
[73] Booth has reminded us that the Treasury remained essentially orthodox so far as budgetary practice was concerned down to the mid-1940s, if not beyond. 'On every occasion at which employment policy was seriously considered by the wartime administration', he writes, 'the Keynesians and the Treasury were on opposite sides.' Moreover, it would be unwise to 'see the [1944] White Paper as a definite statement of Keynes's views on the extent to which governments should depart from the principles of orthodox finance in pursuit of employment policies'. A. Booth, 'The "Keynesian Revolution" in Economic Policy-Making', *Economic History Review*, 2nd ser., 36 (1983), 116.
[74] Cited in Peden, 'Keynes, the Treasury and Unemployment', 6.
[75] Howson and Winch, *The Economic Advisory Council*, 148.

effect on the political and administrative role of the state, particularly in relation to local authorities. When Keynes remarked in the thirties that the solution to economic recession in the short term might require a comprehensive 'socialisation of investment', he implied only that the state should be prepared when necessary to augment private investment sufficiently to help restore full employment.[76] He was concerned less with 'planning' the economy than with seeking ways of managing it better, encouraging the minimum amount of state intervention consistent with the fullest use of the country's resources. There was no presumption here that the state would control the economy through budgetary policy, merely that Budget deficits would be resorted to as a means of pulling the economy out of a slump. However, what worried contemporary politicians (not least within the Labour Party) about the development programmes of Lloyd George and Mosley was their implicit assumption of a powerful central executive, their rejection of the inherent efficacy of market forces in favour of some form of 'managed capitalism', and a suggested timetable of action which smacked of bureaucratic dictatorship.

And behind the Treasury's notorious rejection of large-scale public works expenditure lay the powerful conviction that it would undermine the democratic structure of local government and threaten private property rights. Local authorities between the wars were a far more important source of domestic capital formation in aggregate than was central government. A much expanded public works programme, therefore, would have entailed either a very generous system of grants to the localities or a greater concentration of public investment under direct control. Neither option held much appeal within official circles, and for good reason. There were at local level an inordinate number of separate spending units and an almost complete absence of uniformity of financial circumstances. No serious consideration had ever been given to the planning or execution of long-term local investment. Central responsibility for local government, moreover, was diffused and fragmented, dispersed across a wide range of government departments, none of which had any overall co-ordinating function.[77] In such circumstances, the prospect of overriding the machinery of local government or of contemplating a new series of legal, practical and constitutional arrangements to accommodate an active public works policy was never seriously entertained within Whitehall.

It might be thought that the Ministry of Labour, acknowledged by 1930 to be the unrivalled source of practical and statistical expertise in the area of

---

[76] See R. Skidelsky, 'The Political Meaning of the Keynesian Revolution', in *The End of the Keynesian Era*, ed. R. Skidelsky (1977), 33–40.

[77] Middleton, 'The Treasury and Public Investment', 356–9.

unemployment, could have fostered a more adventurous economic policy. Almost from its inception in December 1916, however, it had succumbed to Treasury control. Instead of developing as a powerful initiator of policy, akin to its Edwardian predecessor the Board of Trade, the Ministry worked within the confines of what was felt to be pragmatic and politically realistic. As a spending department it remained unashamedly self-restrained, unable to develop any positive or independent role because of regular intervention and delay by Treasury officials. Continually denied any political authority, the Ministry failed both to rival the Treasury as a forum for 'alternative' economic advice or to emerge as a 'national authority for unemployment'.

As a consequence unemployment policy became divided among a number of separate Ministries. A great deal more energy was expended upon creating administrative machinery than upon devising new policy. Almost inevitably, emphasis came to be laid upon the *alleviation* of unemployment rather than upon the stimulation of employment. Although it is true that the Ministry of Labour eventually managed to evade the full impact of Treasury control, undertaking a greater share of responsibility for policy in the thirties in the fields of unemployment relief (with the Unemployment Assistance Board) and regional policy (under the Special Areas legislation), it failed at an earlier stage to provide any effective counterattack to the opposition, mounted on practical and administrative grounds, to large-scale programmes of state-sponsored public works.[78]

In any event, the chances of overcoming such opposition were always slight. There was little evidence at the time that Whitehall could have co-ordinated policy to the degree required by any scheme of national reconstruction. The idea of creating an 'economic general staff' to consider problems outside the administrative confines of the existing government departments, along the lines of the Committee of Imperial Defence for example, had been actively discussed during the twenties. Nothing of substance was achieved, however, until MacDonald created the Economic Advisory Council in 1930 to bring experts and Ministers together. But, despite its promise, the Council had no perceptible success in influencing economic policy and ceased to meet after 1932.

It was because of deficiencies in the framework of decision- making that Mosley and Lloyd George argued strongly in the thirties that radical

---

[78]   See R. Lowe, 'Bureaucracy and Innovation in British Welfare Policy, 1870–1945', in *The Emergence of the Welfare State in Britain and Germany 1850–1950*, ed. W. J. Mommsen (1981), 263–95; Peden, 'The Treasury as the Central Department of Government, 1919–1939', *Public Administration*, 61 (1983), 371–85; and R. Lowe, 'Bureaucracy Triumphant or Denied? The Expansion of the British Civil Service, 1919–1939', *Public Administration*, 62 (1984), 291–310.

economic initiatives should be accompanied by a vigorous reorganization of the administrative machinery of government. In his infamous memorandum of January 1930, Mosley sought to transfer the responsibility for road programmes from local to central authority, and to subordinate departmental responsibilities for unemployment policy to a strong executive planning body under the direction of the Prime Minister, free from detailed criticism and obstruction. To tackle the immediate unemployment crisis and to plan for long term economic reconstruction, he wrote:

a far larger and more comprehensive organisation is required than has yet been employed, or is even now contemplated . . . At present it is the business of the Lord Privy Seal to produce Unemployment plans with the assistance of a small staff which was responsible for the conduct of policy under the late Government. It is the business of the other Departmental heads to get on with the normal work of their Departments. They are in no sense mobilised for an attack upon Unemployment as the primary obligation upon them. The whole problem is to secure that mobilisation of the Government machine, and ultimately the resources of the Nation, in a co-ordinated and consistent effort of economic reconstruction.[79]

To promote the necessary mobilization and co-ordination of effort, Mosley suggested that the Prime Minister should be assisted by a committee composed of the heads of the various Departments concerned with unemployment, plus the Unemployment Ministers.

Such elemental proposals for administrative reform were never likely to win political approval. Shaw, Secretary of State for War, described them blandly as 'unsuitable and impracticable', remarking that it 'was out of the question to add to the Prime Minister's burdens the full time job of a super Minister of Employment'.[80] Though the Minister of Health Arthur Greenwood agreed that some changes in 'machinery' were necessary, he thought that 'there should be little difficulty in persuading Sir O. Mosley and his colleagues that this point had been satisfactorily met by the establishment of the Economic Advisory Council'.[81] Large-scale public works proposals had already received scathing criticism from the Treasury on economic and practical grounds; its criticism of Mosley's administrative reforms went deeper. His plan cut

at the very root of the individual responsibility of Ministers, the collective responsibility of the Cabinet and the special responsibility of the Chancellor of the Exchequer. It is no less obvious that, regarded merely as an essay in organisation, it involves such complexity and duplication of machinery as no well ordered business would tolerate except at the expense of chaos and bankruptcy.[82]

[79] Cab 24/209, CP 31, Unemployment Policy. Copy of a letter from Sir Oswald Mosley to the Prime Minister, 23 January 1930.

[80] Cab 27/418, UPC (30), Unemployment Policy Committee. 14 March 1930.

[81] Cab 27/418, UPC (30), 14 March 1930.

[82] T175/42, Sir O. Mosley on Unemployment Policy. Memorandum by Sir F. Leith-Ross, 1 February 1930.

The administrative reforms suggested by other hard-line critics as a means of expediting economic policy fared little better. Keynes's political assumption that the management of the economy could be controlled by a mandarin of elite civil servants largely protected from the pressures of demagogic politics was naive, to say the least. It is not surprising, either, that Lloyd George's parallel assault on administrative arrangements within Whitehall was accorded short shrift. Frustrated by the inadequacies of central co-ordination and by the structure and organization of Cabinet, he pleaded in 1935 for the establishment of a National Development Board to exercise the necessary planning and co-ordinating functions associated with land development and public works, and for the creation of a 'Super Cabinet' capable of settling plans of action with the speed required in a national emergency. By this time, however, Lloyd George, like Mosley, was discredited as a political figure; though he had not embraced extremist politics to the same extent as Mosley he was regarded as a consummate showman, prone to dangerous stunts and ruled more by emotion than by reason. His cavalier approach elicited a swift rebuff. Internal changes of the sort proposed, the government claimed, would divorce policy from administration; far from promoting action they would cause delay and confusion. In particular the functions to be entrusted to the new Development Board would cover

so wide a field and trench on so many departments of Government as to require almost superhuman qualities of wisdom, foresight, judgement, experience and technical acquirements in its members . . . The task of discovering persons competent to undertake [such] functions . . . would . . . be a formidable one.

Even if the right personnel could be found, they would be obliged to submit their plans to the Cabinet, which in turn would have to submit them to Departments. Was it not inevitable

that the Cabinet would attach more weight to the views of Ministers, based on the accumulated knowledge and experience of their Departments, than to those of an external committee out of touch with the actual problems of administration? And, if so, will the Board acquiesce in the rejection of plans on which they may have spent many hours or even weeks of thought? . . . It can . . . hardly be supposed that the Board . . . would consent to remain so muzzled. Yet if it were to be given freedom to express its views it would be in a position to appeal to the public over the heads of the Cabinet, and responsibility would cease to reside in those constitutionally appointed to exercise it.[83]

We need not labour the point. Even the most cursory examination of the official record demonstrates that the administrative objections levelled

---

[83] Cab 24/256, CP 150, Statement by His Majesty's Government on Certain Proposals Submitted to them by Mr. Lloyd George, 14 July 1935, paras 120–2.

against ambitious spending programmes embraced more wide-ranging and subtle considerations than ever would be gathered from the detail of economic or theoretical debate alone. Not that such considerations were mutually exclusive. As Middleton reminds us:

The Keynesian case for public works rested upon a favourable response by the corporate sector to the announcement of a large-scale programme. The Treasury believed that this response was largely determined by this sector's acceptance of, or antipathy towards, the political and administrative implications of pursuing such a policy. There was thus a strong interconnection between the administrative and theoretical constituents of the 'Treasury view'.[84]

APPENDIX

Could Lloyd George have done it? Reflections on the fiscal policy debate of the 1930s

The so-called 'crisis' in Keynesian economics in recent years, stimulated by the intellectual onslaught of the neo-classical monetarist school, has centred around the alleged failure of Keynesian policies to stem inflation and large-scale unemployment. Such has been the willingness to discredit the post-war consensus which favoured deficit-financed 'pump priming', the policy option believed to have received formal government approval in the 1944 Employment Policy White Paper, that historians have embarked upon a renewed and highly critical reappraisal of interwar employment policy. No amount of deft prose can disguise the fact that this re-examination has been nurtured largely by the belief that since Keynesian policies in the post-1945 period have not only failed to live up to their promise but have proved to be the direct precursor of a deep-rooted economic malaise, then the 'Keynesian-type' programmes urged upon the uninitiated between the wars must at least have been misguided and, at worst, positively harmful.

As we have seen already, Lloyd George's confident (some would say extravagant and reckless) claim that his 1929 loan-financed programme of national reconstruction would combat abnormal unemployment in two years aroused bitter controversy; contemporary hostility frequently arose, however, less from reasoned assessment than from the 'certainty' that such brash political stunts were bound to be flawed. At the same time, supporters of a more radical interventionist policy assumed that the effectiveness of such a bold alternative strategy should have been manifestly apparent to anyone prepared to open their mind to the challenge of fresh ideas.

In an effort to cut through the verbosity and dissonance of interwar

[84] Middleton, 'The Treasury and Public Investment', 367.

Table 16. *Effects of the Lloyd George public works programme*

	Actual unemployment	Reduction in unemployment from the programme	Change in GDP from the £100m increase in government spending (£m)
1929	1,503,000	268,000	97.2
1930	2,379,000	300,000	108.3
1931	3,252,000	329,000	119.0
1932	3,400,000	346,000	125.0
1933	3,087,000	359,000	129.7

Source: T. Thomas, 'Aggregate Demand in the United Kingdom 1918–45', in *The Economic History of Britain Since 1700. Volume 2. 1860 to the 1970s,* ed. R. Floud and D. McCloskey (Cambridge, 1981), 337.

debate, recent commentators have applied the cold steel of econometric modelling to test the efficacy of public works schemes similar to those proffered in the late twenties. Thomas, for example, has modelled a variant of Lloyd George's 1929 proposals, postulating the effects of a five-year programme of £100 million annual expenditure. The suggested impact on employment and Gross National Product is given in table 16.

Although these estimates relate to a programme that was never actually proposed, let alone implemented, they have subsequently been interpreted as proof enough that Lloyd George's programme (or one very much like it) would not have solved the unemployment problem. One implication of Thomas's calculations is that unemployment would have been reduced in the first year of the programme not by the 586,000 predicted by the Liberals in 1929 but only by 268,000. The model suggests, in addition, that government spending on national income would have been much smaller than originally anticipated. An expenditure of an extra £100 million a year on public works sustained over the years would have raised employment by almost 360,000 after four years and Gross National Product by £130 million, and that after taking into account the delayed effects of similar spending in earlier years. In Thomas's view, it would have taken an increase of spending of £280 million a year to raise employment by one million.[85]

---

[85]   T. Thomas, 'Aggregate Demand, 1918–45', 337–8. His analysis is derived from his Ph.D. thesis, 'Aspects of U.K. Macro-Economic Policy during the Inter-war Period: A Study in Econometric History', University of Cambridge (1976).

According to Glynn and Howells, the scale of government expenditure required to have provided jobs for the (under-) recorded level of unemployment in 1932 (2.8 million) would have amounted to £537 million, equivalent to a 70 per cent increase in current spending. 'Even before one asks where the funds to meet the deficit might have come from', they write, 'the required amount can already be seen to be the realms of political and economic fantasy'.[86] Viewed from this perspective, the Keynesian prescription of deficit-financed public works implied politically unacceptable and economically implausible increases in government expenditure. Furthermore, they contend, it was a stratagem wholly unsuited to the prevailing regional and structural maladjustment of the economy, unlikely to benefit the nation's most disadvantaged regions and industries.[87] One of the principal difficulties with Glynn and Howells's argument, however, is that they test the anticipated effects of Lloyd George's programme during the depths of the world slump, whereas it had been put forward in 1929 when unemployment was less than half the level of 1932.

Clearly, the expected impact of a deficit-financed public works programme depends upon the presumed value of the expenditure multiplier. Thomas's calculations are based on a multiplier value of 1.5 in the long run (12 years) and of unity in the short-run;[88] Glynn and Howells's estimate of 1.26 is biased upwards and regarded, therefore, as favourable to the Keynesian case. Richard Kahn judged the value of the multiplier to be between 1.5 and 1.75; subsequent calculations in the later thirties put it in the range of 1.5 to 2.0.[89] None of these figures can be regarded as sacrosanct. There is even greater uncertainty as to the size of interwar regional multipliers, but most commentators agree that they would normally be lower than their national counterparts. The standard contention is that because regions are less self-sufficient than is the nation as a whole, an addition to regional income involves a significant import factor which reduces the potential increase in regional income to be expected from an injection of national expenditure.

Doubts as to the feasibility of a 'Keynesian' attack on interwar unemployment do not, however, rest solely upon the estimated multiplier effects of expanded public investment. Although the frightening budgetary implications of the investment programme outlined by Glynn and Howells

---

[86] S. Glynn and P. G. Howells, 'Unemployment in the 1930s: The "Keynesian Solution" Reconsidered', *Australian Economic History Review*, 20 (1980), 42.

[87] Glynn and Howells, 'Unemployment in the 1930s', 31–5.

[88] Thomas's low multiplier value was based on the assumption that there would be notable lags in the speed by which increments of wage income would be spent on consumption goods and in the response of investment to any increase in profits.

[89] Kahn, 'The Relation of Home Investment to Unemployment', 173–98; 'Determination of the Multiplier from National Income Statistics', *Economic Journal*, 48 (1939), 435–48.

can be dismissed as too damaging to the Keynesian case, since the estimated deficit is the one calculated to have been necessary to eradicate registered unemployment in the most depressed interwar year, it is about the effect which rising public indebtedness might have had upon confidence, interest rates and Britain's position in the international financial community that critics have expressed considerable concern. A large public works pro-gramme, writes Middleton,

> would have created an atmosphere in which the combination of massive budget deficits and . . . adverse trade flows not only caused a capital outflow, but a capital flight of gigantic proportions . . . A substantial fiscal stimulus would have required for its success 'the transformation of the British economy into a largely State-controlled, if not planned, economic system'. Such dirigism was possible in Nazi Germany, the tightly controlled markets and insulated economy being a necessary accompaniment to deficit financing . . . For Britain, however, such developments were inconceivable.[90]

The balance of payments, in other words, is seen as a formidable constraint upon any sustained expansion of the interwar domestic economy. Given her precarious external balance in the thirties, critics maintain, it is difficult to conceive how Britain could have accommodated the import stimulation arising from a substantial fiscal stimulus, even with floating exchange rates after 1931. Any enforced rise in prices would only have weakened export competitiveness further, with additional conse-quences for the trade balance. A deficit-financed programme of public works, to put it another way, could only have worked in a more closed, autarkic economy than existed in interwar Britain.[91]

Such pessimistic assessments of the potential effects of Keynesian-type policies have not gone unchallenged. Hatton takes a more optimistic view of the likely upper-bound value of the interwar income multiplier and admits less anxiety about the budgetary implications of a substantial fiscal stimulus, given the likely positive effect of built-in stabilizers, such as tax yields, and the expected reduction in unemployment benefit expenditure following the boost to primary and secondary employment. He calculates that, even on the Glynn and Howells model, such compensatory items could have yielded £102 million and £140 million respectively, and that, when all other endogenous components of the accounts are ignored, 'the determination in the budget . . . would have been little more than half of the figure they use'.[92]

Using Middleton's calculation of the response of the Budget to income

---

[90] Middleton, *Towards the Managed Economy*, 179.
[91] Middleton, *Towards the Managed Economy*, 178.
[92] T. Hatton, 'Unemployment in the 1930s and the "Keynesian Solution": Some Notes of Dissent', *Australian Economic History Review*, 25 (1985), 139.

variations during the fiscal year 1931/32 (i.e. the ratio of the change in the Budget surplus to the change in Gross Domestic Product, in this case 0.44) Hatton has postulated the impact of a £100 million public spending programme in the manner shown in table 17. 'In terms of the number of man-years of employment which could be bought for £1 million of loan-financed deficit', he concludes, 'even the most pessimistic outcome is only slightly worse than the picture painted by Glynn and Howells while the most optimistic is nearly three and a half times better'.[93]

The case against Keynesian 'pump priming' on regional and structural grounds merits closer examination. It is well known that interregional differences in unemployment may either increase or decline as economic activity rises; in other words, the structure of unemployment prevailing at a time when the economy is depressed may not be a fair reflection of what that structure could be at a higher level of activity. Closer examination of interwar unemployment data suggests that the pattern of regional unemployment differentials is attributable not only to the fact that some regions suffered from a disproportionate share of declining industries, but also that all industries in high unemployment areas tended to have unemployment rates above the average for those industries. To a large extent, the imbalances arose from the way in which a given level of aggregate demand impinged upon the various regions.[94] In addition, there are indications that the proportionate rise and fall in employment in booms and slumps between the wars was greater in regions with high unemployment rates than in those with low average rates. The implication, in other words, is that there was a tendency for unemployment rates amongst regions to move closer in booms, suggesting that at higher levels of activity demand could spill over from one region to another.[95]

It is customary, nonetheless, to assume that the effect of a deliberate expansion of demand would have been partially offset by labour immobility and resource 'bottlenecks'. This is to suppose, however, that workers would have baulked at the opportunity of seeking fresh employment elsewhere if real openings existed; but the failure of labour migration to even out differences in interwar unemployment rates was more a *consequence* of the low overall level of labour demand rather than its cause. Conventional wisdom has it, however, that the 'new' industries in the south and the midlands were characterized by such a degree of interdependence, in terms of technology and access to labour and capital resources, that their

[93] Hatton, 'Unemployment in the 1930s', 140.
[94] T. J. Hatton, 'Structural Aspects of Unemployment Between the Wars', in *Research in Economic History*, Vol. 10, ed. P. Uselding (Connecticut, 1986), 55–92.
[95] W. R. Garside and T. J. Hatton, 'Keynesian Policy and British Unemployment in the 1930s', *Economic History Review*, 2nd ser., 38 (1985), 84.

Table 17. *Effects of a £100 million public spending programme*

	Income change	Changes in Budget deficit (£m)	Employment change	
			Using Thomas's employment function	Using Glynn and Howells's productivity of labour (£241.65)
Multiplier				
1.00	100	56	2,765,000	4,138,000
1.25	125	45	3,456,000	5,173,000
1.50	150	34	4,148,000	6,207,000

Source: Adapted from Hatton, 'Unemployment in the 1930s and the "Keynesian Solution"', *Australian Economic History Review,* 25 (1985), 140.

relocation could have occurred only on a major scale, involving a high level of policy activity.

The degree of such interdependence within 'development blocks' is itself questionable; the feedbacks and forward linkages between the 'new' and the 'old' industries appear to have been more pronounced between the wars than is generally conceded, the 'new' industries making significant labour demands upon the staple sectors.[96] Jones's estimated interwar purchase coefficients for the north-east region are high for 'new' sectors such as chemicals, aircraft, electrical engineering and gas, electricity and water. Moreover, in three out of five so-called 'new' industries, disaggregation of their regional multiplier effect shows the impact upon employment to have been greater in the 'old' sectors than in the more diverse industries.[97] To the extent therefore that the 'old' and 'new' industries could together have provided a basis for expanding employment, there may have been some positive advantage between the wars in pressing for a policy of publicly funded investment, linked with a vigorous regional policy, to encourage firms to locate in the more depressed areas.

Just how far the stimulation of aggregate demand would have encouraged local job creation and/or the transference of indigenous labour to other areas remains a contentious issue. The assumption still open to question is that the prevailing distribution of industries across regions and the existence of widely differing rates of regional unemployment disaffirm on *a priori* grounds the potential of deficit-financed works to create jobs for the involuntarily unemployed. 'Unemployment is somewhat widely spread,' wrote Keynes and Henderson in 1929, 'and transference is duly proceeding out of the industries where the curtailment of opportunity looks like lasting. It is the general failure of industry as a whole to show absorptive power which is keeping the aggregate unemployment at so high a figure'.[98] Any perceived difficulty arising from the 'transfer' problem was not in their view a reason

for delay, for holding back, or for timidity, but for pushing on with redoubled efforts. For the longer we delay, the more difficult will the task become and the harder will it be to employ those who have been forced into long-continued habits of unemployment. It is useless to try to tackle the 'transfer problem' seriously until jobs have first been created elsewhere, and employers are crying out for men . . . Then, when men are being clamoured for, will be the time to tackle the transfer problem with both hands.[99]

[96] See G. N. Von Tunzelmann, 'Structural Change and Leading Sectors in British Manufacturing, 1907–68', in *Economics in the Long View*, Vol. 3, ed. C. P. Kindleberger and G. di Tella (1982), 1–49.
[97] M. Jones, 'Regional Unemployment and Policy in the 1930s', Unpublished mimeo, 1981.
[98] 'Can Lloyd George Do It?' in *JMK*, Vol. 9, 109.   [99] *JMK*, Vol. 9, 89–90.

The precise effect of increased investment upon particular regions between the wars could only be gauged if we knew the magnitude of the appropriate regional multipliers, which we do not. Most commentators accept the presumption of low values because of the leakage of regional expenditure in exchange for imported capital goods. And yet by definition such leakages represent autonomous injections into other regions, which, had they occurred between the wars, might well have induced therein, via the multiplier-accelerator process, their own repercussionary effects on incomes and employment.[100]

One cannot claim, however, that a higher overall level of aggregate demand would have eliminated regional unemployment. It may have ameliorated conditions by stimulating greater investment in the depressed areas. But it has to be conceded, that the specificity of demand for labour on the part of expanding industries may have operated against adult men (by far the most important group of the registered unemployed) and in favour of other groups such as women and juveniles, whether unemployed or new to the labour force (see chapter 9).

What of the alleged constraints posed by the balance of payments and the sterling exchange rate? Contrary to popular belief, Keynes was not unaware of the potential external repercussions of deliberately expanding domestic demand for the purpose of reducing unemployment. Writing in 1939 he accepted that:

The proportion of the increased incomes which is spent on imported goods raises a dangerous complication. For both directly and indirectly the Government's loan expenditure will worsen the trade balance. And here . . . there is little or nothing to be hoped from a high rate of interest, which import control and Government priorities cannot do better.[101]

Earlier discussion has revealed how circumspect Keynes was from 1925 in the role he was prepared to assign to public works when protection of gold reserves was of paramount importance. By 1930, however, he argued vigorously for increased national investment for the sake of employment, provided it was coupled with measures designed to protect the balance of payments and confidence in sterling. Such measures included the use of a revenue tariff to help defray expenditure, the introduction of export subsidies, an embargo on overseas issues and the encouragement of countervailing policies by the American and French authorities to help neutralize the potential impact of domestic reflation on the stability of the exchange rate.

But it was the conspicuous absence of international economic co-

---

[100] Garside and Hatton, 'Keynesian Policy and British Unemployment', 85.
[101] *JMK*, Vol. 21, 539.

Table 18. *Effects of a £100 million public spending programme (in 1930)*

Multiplier value	Low (1.25)	Middle (1.5)	High (1.75)
(a) With a fixed exchange rate			
Income Change (£m)	125.0	150.0	175.0
Employment Change (000s)	345.6	414.8	483.9
Change in the budget (£m)	−50.0	−40.0	−30.0
Change in the balance of payments (£m)	−26.3	−31.5	−36.8
(b) With a floating exchange rate			
Income change (£m)	167.0	214.0	269.0
Employment change (000s)	461.8	591.7	743.8
Change in the budget (£m)	−33.2	−14.4	+7.6
Depreciation (%)	5.1	6.5	8.2

Source: Hatton, 'The Outlines of a Keynesian Solution', in *The Road to Full Employment*, ed. S. Glynn and A. Booth (1987), 88.

operation which convinced contemporary politicians that if Britain embarked unilaterally upon an expansion of public works she would soon find herself seriously out of step with the rest of the world. Deficit spending, it was feared, would stimulate imports more than it would exports and would harm not just the balance of trade but also, through its negative impact on confidence, the level of foreign investment and the stability of sterling.[102]

Even those sympathetic to the Keynesian position accept that under a system of fixed exchange rates increased government expenditure would have encountered balance of payments constraints. Hatton's estimates of the likely effects of a fairly modest public works programme under different exchange rate regimes illustrate the point (see table 18).

The implication of section (a) of table 18 is that with exchange rates fixed even a limited pump-priming exercise would have required some degree of tariff protection, to provide a breathing space for domestic expansion to operate without severe dislocation of the international payments system. Nor it seems would such a policy stance have eradicated unemployment, even during the early phases of the world slump. After Britain's departure

---

[102] The critical point here is the assumed capacity of exports to grow relative to the income elasticity of demand for imports. Thomas calculates that every £100 million increase in GNP in the early thirties would have increased imports by £20.8 million. Thomas, 'Aggregate Demand', 338. This estimate is based on the assumption that prices would not be materially affected by an expansion of output, given the prevailing elasticity of supply of factors of production.

from gold in 1932, however, there was a strong tendency for the exchange rate to appreciate. Once lower exchange rates became not only feasible but an object of policy, it is possible, following Hatton, to suggest potential beneficial effects of a combined policy of public spending and devaluation, not only on jobs but also on the Budget and the balance of payments, as illustrated in section (b) of table 18.

It is tempting to regard such counterfactual reasoning as fanciful nonsense. After all, critics contend, Britain would never have contemplated any measure of unilateral devaluation in the thirties. The world was autarkic and riddled with trade barriers. Moreover, there was little freedom of manoeuvre with regard to fiscal policy, given the predilection for balanced budgets and the fear that expanded government borrowing would wreck confidence and foster inflation, rather than stimulate output and employment.

Such fundamental criticisms have served only to sharpen the Keynesian counterattack. Expansionist programmes of public spending may well have been subject to practical and political limitations, Keynesians argue, but that does not necessarily mean that an alternative strategy aimed at raising aggregate investment and demand could *never* have worked. It may not have cured unemployment within the time-span of a single programme, nor would it necessarily have held out much immediate hope for, say, the elderly long-term unemployed in the depressed regions. But given substantial evidence of the beneficial effects on industry and employment of the rearmament programme of the late thirties, Keynesian sympathizers refuse to reject out of hand the potential beneficial effects of spending programmes. 'With the benefit of hindsight', writes Hatton, 'one might suggest that projects which came on stream at almost any time from the early 1920s until rearmament would have been a welcome addition to demand'.[103]

Would increased aggregate demand have proved self-defeating by encouraging inflation? Keynes certainly anticipated that a progressive anti-unemployment policy would lead to price rises; but, he contended, it was only by raising the severely depressed level of prevailing prices that one could provide firms with the means by which to expand output and jobs. He had always opposed policies likely to produce severe fluctuations in the price level; what Keynes sought was the restoration of the world price level to its previous 'normal' state. Any potentially damaging effects, he believed, would be eased by the existence of large pools of underused resources. It is thus possible to suggest a bridge between the internal and external dimensions of the Keynesian paradigm: Keynes basing his domestically orientated programmes of the 1920s upon the premise of rising export

---

[103] Hatton, 'The Outlines of a Keynesian Solution', 91.

competitiveness under the stimulus of increasing world prices, and in the 1930s, with that expectation gone, upon the need to persuade the USA to take a lead in restructuring world trade and finance to bolster programmes of domestic economic recovery.[104]

In the end, the principal difficulty in coming to terms with the array of assertion and counter-assertion surrounding fiscal policy and interwar unemployment is that questions are being asked and answers are being offered about policy options which were never officially regarded at the time as being politically acceptable. Nor can the issue be judged merely in terms of the technical restraints on public finance and the balance of payments. An additional indictment of the Keynesian prescription, levelled then and now, was its slavish regard for rationality and self-discipline and its belief in the ability of government to exercise demand management free from the competing claims of democratic pressure groups. Political expediency and the stranglehold of vested interests, however, wreak havoc with neat analytical counterfactual models.

From this perspective it is a simple matter to undermine the nonconformist economists of the interwar period as at best muddled purists and at worst harbingers of economic ruin. But therein lies a dangerous presupposition, namely that the official policies pursued on behalf of the unemployed between the wars were and are defensible, even if at the time they were patently ineffective, simply because they did not challenge the political and administrative status quo. It cannot be denied that to have followed the expansionist path would have been to challenge the very fundamentals of economic orthodoxy and to have demanded a courageous reappraisal of political priorities without any certainty of success, least of all within the time-span favoured by electioneering politicians. But it is one thing to postulate that the existence of such constraints damaged the likelihood of alternative policies ever being implemented and quite another to claim that such policies would have remained flawed even if the authorities had had the courage themselves to challenge the foundations of their existing policies. This is equivalent to arguing that modern day monetarist ideas are sacrosanct, ruling out of court any other economic viewpoint incapable of being accommodated within the confines of prevailing dogma.

Few can deny the unequal battle waged during the interwar period between orthodoxy and the 'new economics'. Those who stress that Keynesianism could not have worked because officials would never have contemplated trying it will always find a hearing. But surely it is pressing the critical case against Keynesianism too far to suggest that alternative policies aimed at stimulating demand for the sake of employment were

---

[104] Booth and Pack, *Employment, Capital and Economic Policy*, 183.

fundamentally misguided. The argument still to be engaged is whether Keynes spent much of his private and public life in vain, attempting to find a way out of the morass of chronic unemployment by means which 'sensible' minds should now view with healthy scepticism. It will never be satisfactorily resolved, however, until protagonists at each extreme begin to consider the limitations of their own reasoning. Although Keynesians stress the primacy of government intervention as a means of avoiding long-drawn-out recessions, it does not follow that demand-management policies could have been devised between the wars in a manner sufficient to have ensured that the economy always stayed close to full employment. Given the precariousness of investment, it is probable that Keynes himself would, in time, have had to concede the enormous difficulties involved in 'fine-tuning' the economy. Likewise, a successful attack on interwar unemployment would most probably have required a policy mix beyond the confines of monetary and fiscal policy alone, involving perhaps the deliberate encouragement of industries with a high export and technological potential and measures designed to influence the scale and direction of private investment.

There is room for conjecture, therefore, as to how far Keynes's emphasis upon raising aggregate demand within the economy was entirely misplaced, even if we accept the audacity of some of the claims made on its behalf. Econometric and counterfactual analyses have heightened the extremity of argument and assumption in a vain effort to have the last word. It is still not too late to urge caution in accepting unreservedly the view that Keynesian pump priming would have been of very limited value. In a recent discussion of the possible effects of a public works programme in the 1930s, Aldcroft estimates that the variant of Lloyd George's programme devised by Keynes and Henderson would have reduced unemployment by 359,000 after five years. This he rejects dismissively as 'very small beer indeed'.[105] Yet this figure represented at least 20 per cent of those out of work at the time. And it is worth recalling Matthews's judgement that: 'Throughout the whole of the interwar period after 1920 there was clearly Keynesian demand deficiency. Certain bottlenecks were encountered in the late 1930s . . . but not to such an extent as to invalidate the proposition that a substantial increase in output could have been brought about by a general increase in demand.'[106] Moreover, as I have argued elsewhere:

The very low level of net capital accumulation between the wars and the dominance of replacement investment in gross domestic capital formation suggest that the prevailing deficiency of investment demand could well have benefitted from positive

[105] D. H. Aldcroft, *Full Employment: The Elusive Goal* (Sussex, 1984), 40.
[106] Matthews, 'Why has Britain had Full Employment since the War?', 555–69.

stimuli. Far more empirical research needs to be conducted, therefore, into assessing the extent to which an early and possibly sustained programme of selective investment financed by the state and aimed at raising the level of effective demand, could have provided in the short to medium term a more successful attack on the problem of interwar unemployment than did the policies actually pursued by either major political party.[107]

[107] Garside and Hatton, 'Keynesian Policy and British Unemployment', 88.

14 ✳ *Conclusion*

Unemployment remained a matter of prime concern between the wars because it was no longer a minority issue of 'surplus labour' affecting the sub-stratum of the industrial workforce; it emerged instead as a major blemish on the economic and moral face of society, an endemic disease of the industrial heartlands of the country but one obstinately immune to the supposed curative powers of market forces. Yet however serious the problem, the reduction of unemployment in the immediate term never became the overriding determinant of economic policy, primarily because of the lingering belief within government that orthodox responses in other spheres of activity would lay a path towards fuller employment with less long-term damage to the health and stability of the economy. One lesson which successive administrations learned in earnest between the wars, however, was that it was much easier to treat the symptoms of persistent unemployment than it was to overcome its causes. Neither major political party ever had much faith in its ability to solve the problem and in consequence fashioned responses which were characteristically ameliorative, pragmatic and gradualist.

Driven by an intense desire to restore Britain's economic, financial and trading pre-eminence, governments in the 1920s worked assiduously to forestall inflation, sustain sound budgetary practice and protect the value of the currency, even if the concomitant policies of deflation, retrenchment and minimum intervention in the workings of the free-market system afforded little opportunity for the adoption of a deliberate anti-unemployment strategy. The preference within official circles for regulatory devices such as control of the money supply, balanced budgets and the restoration and maintenance of the gold standard coincided with prevailing neo-classical teaching and with the declared priorities and prejudices of majority financial and industrial opinion.

For much of the first post-war decade, unemployment was seen as a short-term cyclical phenomenon for which only temporary palliatives were required. National insurance thus became the dominant first-line defence, even though the sheer scale and persistence of unemployment necessitated within a very short time a series of devices to preserve the facade of a self-financing system and to safeguard vulnerable claimants from the stigma of the Poor Law. In addition, small-scale public works, mainly locally financed, preserved the image of an active policy as governments doggedly urged the need for cost reductions in the depressed export industries as the ultimate means of improving industrial and trading competitiveness and employment. Any policy which compromised this objective was summarily rejected; make-work programmes on any larger scale, for example, threatened to raise taxes, harm public credit and hinder necessary wage reductions by maintaining an 'artificial' demand for labour.

Enforced cuts in money wages held a particular attraction in the earliest years until the General Strike demonstrated the danger, politically and socially, of regarding workers' living standards as the expendable item during periods of economic depression. Thereafter, industrial rationalization was championed as a unique long-term remedy for unemployment, despite its more immediate threat to jobs. Fears of upsetting the cost-reduction process in the export trades meanwhile precluded any discriminatory assistance being offered to particular regions or industries. Unemployed workers after all could be redistributed to vacancies at home or abroad, given sufficient encouragement and a will to co-operate. For the greater part of the twenties, therefore, cautious pragmatism, combined with a firm belief in the beneficial effects on trade and employment of stable exchanges and provident spending, convinced most of the financial, academic and industrial community, and the majority of electorate, that Ministers were exploiting as responsibly as they could the range of viable options open to them.

The Labour Party had no difficulty in accepting the policy agenda of the post-war period, given its covert desire to seek political respectability through moderation, persuasion and compromise. During its brief periods in office, it chose to tackle unemployment by strictly conventional means, encouraging local public works, sponsoring industrial reorganization, limiting public expenditure, and above all, protecting the rights of the legitimately unemployed to cash benefits, even though the latter two objectives put policy on a collision course down to 1931 as rising expenditure on unemployment relief made increasing demands on the national Exchequer.

Although the world slump shattered two dominant symbols of economic orthodoxy, the gold standard and free trade, it did not effect any radical transformation in the principal objectives of public policy. The changes that did occur certainly contrasted sharply with the priorities of the previous decade. Budgetary and financial pressures in the early thirties hastened the revamping of the unemployment benefits system, whilst the forced abandonment of gold released the economy from the grip of high interest rates. Further deterioration in the condition of the basic export trades, moreover, transformed the search for industrial efficiency, characteristic of the rationalization movement of the later twenties, into the deliberate sustenance of price and profit levels along reactive defensive lines, whilst the adoption of protection fostered a degree of economic nationalism in the field of world trade.

In fairness, this reorientation of policy provided some safeguards against any more rapid deterioration in the labour market and in the condition of the national finances which, had they occurred, may well have occasioned even more reactionary responses. But it fell short of any deliberate plan to reflate the domestic economy for the sake of reducing unemployment. The official determination to sustain confidence at home and abroad through budgetary restraint and minimum intervention in the economy remained paramount and pervaded most branches of economic policy. The decision to ease the burden of relief expenditure by means-testing unemployment benefits and the introduction in 1934 of legislation to co-ordinate and expand voluntary welfare activity amongst the unemployed in the more depressed areas, primarily as a way of raising morale and diffusing social discontent, allowed the National Government to appear sensitive to the unemployment problem without prejudicing the 'natural' forces of recovery. Each initiative worked, however, to contain rather than improve the situation and to stem demands for increased financial and administrative involvement by the state, posing little threat in other words to the basic tenets of conventional economic policy. Likewise, rehabilitation of the private sector against a background of stable and preferably low exchange rates and an accommodating monetary policy promised to safeguard domestic confidence, ruling out the need for deliberate budget deficits or interventionist policy. At the same time industrial diplomacy worked to attach trade and industry pressure groups to the existing parliamentary process and to forestall the need for overt manipulation of industrial decisions.

The preponderant bias in government towards safeguarding financial stability at home and abroad was evident even in the midst of radical departures in policy. Despite the rise of protectionist sentiment within industry and the Conservative Party in the 1920s the proximate cause of the abandonment of free trade in 1932 was the fear of inflation and excessive currency depreciation following the enforced abandonment of gold. Tariffs were introduced knowing that they could exacerbate domestic unemployment in the short term. Efforts were subsequently made to extract from protection and enhanced imperial preference some trading advantage for depressed export industries but with only meagre results. Even the Ottawa agreements, which locked Britain into an archaic trading pattern, were seen more as a means of protecting sterling by helping to prevent financial defaults overseas than as a lasting source of trade revival. In all, governments of each major political persuasion remained wedded to a nineteenth-century attitude towards Britain's role in the world and towards the priorities which the state should adopt in its relentless battle to defend the status quo.

Neither the organized trade union movement nor the employers did much to rescue unemployment policy from the dead hand of conventional orthodoxy. Each retained a deep sense of economic self-interest and suspicion of co-operation with the state. Governments, it must be said, were not particularly concerned to incorporate either side of industry into the decision-making process. For much of the interwar period therefore, Ministers, trade unionists and employers talked past each other. The National Confederation of Employers' Organizations, representing employers in the staple export trades, argued repeatedly for reduced social expenditure, especially on unemployment relief, lower wage costs and taxation, and freedom to seek a private enterprise solution to economic depression. Industry would seek its own economic salvation, untrammelled by any overriding obligation to reorganize, alter working hours, reduce competition or shoulder its share of the burden of unemployment.

The TUC on the other hand demanded active government support for measures to ease the financial hardships of the unemployed and to raise employment opportunities. But it remained ambiguous on other fronts, particularly with regard to monetary and fiscal policy. It opposed deflationary policy in the 1920s but supported a balanced budget in 1931; it failed to add its considerable weight to objections to the return of gold yet advocated devaluation; it accepted minimalist state involvement in industry whilst voicing belief in socialism as the only lasting cure for unemployment; it advocated counter-cyclical public works before 1924 but gave way to a lukewarm attitude to their effectiveness in the 1930s. Above all, it remained determined to protect the living standards of the employed, who represented the majority of the industrial workforce, and thereby encouraged those who were enjoying or anticipating rising real wages to look towards economic orthodoxy to sustain their relatively privileged position *vis-à-vis* the unemployed.

The TUC's campaign in 1933 for the 'right to work' and not merely the 'right to maintenance', incorporating the first explicit endorsement of deficit-financed public works, suggested that the majority of its members had become converted to an unorthodox expansionary policy on behalf of the unemployed. However, no such policy prescription appeared in any other resolution or TUC statement during the remainder of the decade. Congress disregarded a blueprint for macroeconomic management circulated by the International Federation of Trade Unions in the 1930s. It was more inclined towards remedies for structural unemployment – 'reorganizing industry under capitalism' – and was fearful of any extension of state influence in the management of industrial and economic affairs, not least in the area of free collective bargaining. Support for Keynesian-type policies within the TUC was compromised in other words by a more determined search for the restoration of capitalism via 'collective *laissez-faire*'.[1]

Had both sides of industry pressed the government to formulate a more purposeful attack upon unemployment, it is by no means certain, of course, that any more immediate response would have ensued. As we have implied thus far, the predilection of governments to adopt *ad hoc*, piecemeal policies in the face of mass unemployment appeared to officials to be both consistent and adequate in relation to the problem as they saw it, and left little scope for any serious consideration to be given to less orthodox strategies. This tendency was reinforced by the innate conservatism of the Civil Service. The expectation fostered at the end of the First World War that the reorganization and expansion of the bureaucracy of the Civil Service would enable specialist Ministries to play a creative role in the evolution of economic and social policy was only partly fulfilled. This is understandable up to a point. Civil servants were not expected to adopt an aggressive role in the determination of policy; they tended, on the whole, to react constitutionally to the political environment in which they worked. Nonetheless, the extent to which their advice became markedly consistent, even ossified, between the wars hints at a degree of bureaucratic insensitivity to the range of alternative measures that may have provided a more appropriate and effective response to large-scale unemployment. The defence of bureaucratic order and the constant search for compromise became synonymous with 'good' government, to the detriment of policy.

The Ministry of Labour frequently challenged received orthodoxy on pragmatic grounds, particularly the presumptions held elsewhere in government about the negative influence of unemployment insurance on wages, labour mobility and the incentive to work, the ineffectiveness of counter-cyclical public works, the inappropriateness of diversifying the industrial structure of the depressed areas and the efficacy of a 'free market' remedy for unemployment, in contrast to one based upon active government intervention. Yet it rarely challenged political decisions. The Ministry

[1] B. Malament, 'British Labor and Roosevelt's New Deal. The Response of the Left and the Unions', *Journal of British Studies*, 17 (1978).

lacked any effective counterweight to the Treasury and had to work within an administrative structure which divided responsibility between itself and the Board of Trade. As such, employment policy was consigned to a departmental limbo which prevented officials from surveying rival policies coherently and providing the kind of administrative response which might readily be translated into effective political action. The range of advice available on a regular basis from experts outside of government expanded with the creation of the Economic Advisory Council in 1930, but even this initiative did not live up to the claims made on its behalf. Although the Council provided a forum in which economists and others could make definite policy recommendations, there was marked lack of consensus amongst its members on fundamental matters of economic analysis. The airing of such theoretical disagreements may have increased Treasury awareness of the principal issues at stake, but neither the Council nor its successor, the Committee on Economic Information, exercised any significant influence on the policies actually pursued by government.[2]

The official tendency to tread a cautious path in the face of mass unemployment did not, of course, go unchallenged. Contemporary critics who doubted the capacity of the liberal market order to promote or sustain economic prosperity were keen enough to challenge complacency. Did the orthodox requirement of seeking a balanced budget by cutting government expenditure worsen rather than improve economic conditions? Had the search for and the defence of a gold parity harmed industry and jobs? Did low wages and cuts in unemployment benefits perpetuate a low level of demand through underconsumption? Would reflationary budget deficits lead to faster economic recovery and much reduced unemployment? Questions such as these posed such a threat to conventional thinking, however, that Ministers frequently took refuge in the comfortable belief that there were natural impulses to recovery that had yet to work their way through the national and international economic order, precluding therefore the need for innovative action.

Not surprisingly, the sharp contrast that existed during the interwar period between the essentially fragmented response by governments to the need to create new jobs, supposedly nurtured by political expediency, faltering will-power and intellectual flabbiness, and the emergence of radical pleas by Keynes, Henderson, Lloyd George and Mosley for a more positive and planned interventionist programme centred around government-financed schemes of national reconstruction, creates a distinct impression of a major 'missed opportunity' in economic policy. It was Labour's misfortune to be in power at the time unemployment soared and

---

[2] Lowe, *Adjusting to Democracy*; Howson and Winch, *The Economic Advisory Council*.

when the shortcomings of official policy seemed so transparently clear. Much of the reflective criticism of interwar unemployment policy has therefore focussed on MacDonald's second administration. One widely accepted view is that the failings of the Labour Party arose from its commitment to a form of 'Utopian socialism' which prevented it from coming to terms with economic reality, encouraging it to search mistakenly for a total solution to the problem of poverty instead of trying more practically to meet the immediate crisis of unemployment.[3]

Labour's socialist rhetoric certainly posed a major dilemma. If unemployment was seen as an inevitable product of capitalism then it could only be overcome, not by managing the system, but by replacing it. The party was obliged, however, to institute progressive reform in a depressed market economy and was forced to compromise its long-term socialist commitment in favour of policies that could be implemented within the given political and economic framework. In the event, it attempted neither to overthrow capitalism nor to correct its worst defects. Unemployment came to be viewed, therefore, as an unfortunate but inevitable setback to be endured in the short term, tempered by as much partial relief as could be mustered within the confines of high politics. Efforts to promote more radical policies as a cure for unemployment were continually hamstrung. They either offended principled critics within the party because they appeared to be bolstering the capitalist system or, if they were based on sound socialist principles, involved such extravagant expenditure or demands to nationalize industry and the banking system as to bring the party into direct conflict with the establishment, threatening Labour's image as a respectable alternative government.[4]

It is tempting to argue more generally that until Keynes provided a convincing elucidation of the theoretical model by which effective policies could be formulated for the solution of chronic unemployment, neither Labour nor Tory governments could have been expected to adopt alternative policies which at the time of their most vigorous exposition lacked sufficient intellectual rigour to challenge the ruling canons of classical economic theory. To some extent the shortcomings of the more radical proposals pressed upon Ministers between the wars add weight to such an argument. It is quite clear, for example, that although there was within the labour movement of the early twenties an intuitive grasp of the necessity to maintain or expand the level of consumption in order to increase employment, neither the TUC nor the Labour Party actually embraced the idea of deficit-financed 'pump priming' for the sake of creating work, nor did

[3] Skidelsky, *Politicians and the Slump.*
[4] Cf. R. Lyman, 'The British Labour Party: The Conflict between Socialist Ideals and Practical Politics between the Wars', *Journal of British Studies*, 5 (1965), 140–52.

either body fully appreciate the financial implications of any expanded programme of public works. Although the Independent Labour Party supported schemes of public works it was more preoccupied with promoting social justice than with defending unorthodox budgets. Underconsumptionists such as Hobson supported public works but insisted that they be accompanied by measures of progressive taxation directed towards the redistribution of wealth in favour of the wage-earning classes. The emphasis, in other words, was upon income as the determinant of saving and investment, precluding any systematic use of monetary or fiscal controls to stimulate investment.

The support given in the twenties to the more limited device of altering the timing of existing levels of capital expenditure over the course of the trade cycle was not accompanied by any systematic analysis of the proportion of public to total demand and its likely effect on employment. Furthermore, in the absence of regular detailed data as to the composition of the unemployed, their duration of unemployment and their life-cycle of employment and unemployment, there could be no guarantee that those individuals most in need of a job would necessarily be those with the ability or the opportunity to gain employment from any work created during a period of depression.

The radical programmes in support of national schemes of public works were by no means free of ambiguity, vagueness or inconsistency. Although the Liberal proposals of 1929 are noteworthy for their early if somewhat rudimentary exposition of a dynamic policy, implicitly recognizing the role of the multiplier, of expectations and of the accelerator, they were attacked as unrealistic because they were not presented in any finite terms, envisaging no upper limits to the process of cumulative expansion. The Liberals' repeated claim that public works expenditure would pay for itself from savings on the Unemployment Fund and from increased Exchequer income ignored the fact that income and commodity tax receipts would be subject to a time-lag following any rise in effective purchasing power. Lloyd George, moreover, assumed in 1929 that the Liberal plans could be implemented whilst retaining both the gold standard and free trade.

Neither the Labour Party's heady plans for national reconstruction nor Mosley's strident demand that public works be accorded utmost priority as a means of home-market recovery was matched by any ready (let alone convincing) analysis of their financial implications or their likely cumulative impact on demand and employment. Likewise, Lloyd George's enunciation of the effects on jobs of his 1935 plan of national development was based upon such an involved analysis of the 'real' components of demand and supply in the labour market that the government dismissed his estimates as mere 'hopeful prophecies'.

It is customary, nevertheless, in support of the view that inadequate economic theory was a major stumbling block to the adoption of large-scale interventionist policies in aid of employment, to point to the extent to which Keynes frequently changed his mind as to the appropriate roles, methods and goals of monetary and fiscal policy, to how dependent he was upon Kahn's pioneering analysis of the primary and secondary employment effects of increased investment which only became available in 1931, and to how it was not until March 1933 that Keynes made his first full statement of deficit-finance, distinguishing between capital and current accounts.

There are good reasons, however, for not dwelling unduly on the absence of a coherent body of economic analysis in support of deficit-financed public works as an excuse for the shortcomings of government policy. It is clear that within the economics profession there was growing support for policies designed to expand home investment, demand and employment long before Keynes provided the full weight of his theoretical analysis. Keynes himself maintained that practically every leading economist by 1929 supported the need for an expansionist programme involving an easier monetary policy and large-scale government expenditure. It might still be argued, of course, that it was not the absence of proto-Keynesian ideas that was important so much as the speed by and the extent to which they developed an authority sufficiently persuasive to secure the sympathetic support of policy makers. Much is made in this context of the alleged conversion of the Treasury and the Bank of England to 'Keynesian-type' policies at least a year before the publication of the General Theory, following upon a supposedly more enlightened climate of economic reasoning than had been apparent in the twenties.

But this is to miss the point. The absence for most of the interwar period of any precise or comprehensive analysis of the dynamic effects of expanded government expenditure should not imply that such a policy would have gained earlier acceptance had the progressive elucidation of the concept of the multiplier or the considerable support for a positive programme of 'pump priming', evident within informed circles by 1933, occurred much earlier. The influences determining the official response to interventionist remedies on behalf of the unemployed have to be sought outside of the imperfections of economic knowledge. After all, Keynes had an instinctive grasp of policy priorities long before the General Theory provided the theoretical foundations to support many of his proposals. It was the imperfections and injustices of the *laissez-faire* system and not the blatant inadequacies of economic theory that spurred Keynes to action.

It was not, therefore, the clash between the 'conservatives' and the 'radicals' that was so crucially important between the wars. It was the distinct absence within the political establishment of any real dissent from an economic orthodoxy which powerfully influenced the essential objectives of government policy. Added to this was a predisposition on the part of every party in power to give undue prominence to the bearers of that orthodoxy, especially in the City, thus helping to reinforce the powerful influence they wielded within the Establishment.

In the period down to 1931 especially politicians remained trapped in a body of thought which gave particular prominence to Britain's unique entanglement in the world economy. From this followed an entrenched belief in economic internationalism as the foundation of nineteenth-century economic success and the justification for opposing any policies for the relief of unemployment which put the pursuit of national self-determination above the maintenance of a healthy international economy. This helps to explain why the efforts to remedy structural unemployment in the late 1920s placed so much emphasis upon reduced capacity and rationalization, lower unit costs and the reduction or redeployment of the labour force as a way of expanding exports. Politicians were unaware of or unwilling to accept any policy trade-offs. Labour's decisive links with nineteenth-century Liberalism made acceptance of the gold standard, free trade and the finance-capitalism of the City of London easy to equate with socialism. But by the same token it put the party at odds with those such as Keynes who insisted in the late twenties and early thirties that to avoid cumulative deflation in conditions of international disequilibrium the ties between national and international economics had to be severed.[5]

Although some of the constraints on the evolution of a more positive unemployment policy eased somewhat after 1931 with the abandonment of the gold standard, the reduction of interest rates and the break with free trade, neither the doctrine of minimum government interference nor the innate hostility towards unorthodox economic policy was seriously challenged. The rise of the 'radical alternative' had almost the opposite effect to that desired by its eminent exponents. It served only to strengthen orthodoxy within government, primarily because of the explicit challenge which deficit-financed programmes of public works posed to sound money, to minimum state interference in the fields of industry and domestic investment, and to the balance of power between central and local government. The implications for public sector debt, with all the concomitant pressure it was believed an unbalanced budget would have on London's international financial standing, merely reinforced the author-

[5] R. Skidelsky, '1929–1931 Revisited', *Bulletin of the Society for the Study of Labour History*, 21 (1970), 6–7; Skidelsky, 'The Reception of the Keynesian Revolution', in *Essays on John Maynard Keynes*, ed. M. Keynes, 89–106.

ities' desire to secure stability and to maintain confidence by alternative and safer means.

From the National Government's point of view it was preferable in the 1930s to retain political and financial credibility by isolating and containing unemployment with a flexible system of unemployment relief, with discriminatory and limited action in favour of particularly depressed areas and with microeconomic measures to support prices and profits in industry than it was to tread the suspect path of deficit finance with all the attendant risks of inflation, balance of payments crises and increased state control. Expansionist and interventionist policies threatened to weaken the restorative influence of the slump in purging the system of 'unsound' investment and unproductive practices. Acutely conscious of the interests which supported it politically and financially, the National Government vigorously pursued orthodox policies in order to retain confidence and to avoid the further economic crisis it felt was forever imminent.

There was never much pressure from the unemployed themselves for any more radical approach. If anything, the depression blunted rather than sharpened the edge of social discontent. The TUC proved reluctant to mobilize working-class support for a reflationary economic policy and neither it nor the Labour Party was willing to support protest organizations such as the National Unemployed Workers' Movement, fearing its Communist taint. Insecurity made the unemployed themselves fearful and dependent. With their confidence and hope already eroded, only a minority retained any burning desire for militant protest; to many of the unemployed, their condition appeared less as a remedial injustice than as misfortune to be stoically endured.

Although economic policy in the 1930s was more nationally orientated than in the previous decade, it was essentially supportive and discretionary, designed to minimize the need for immoderate action in the spheres of monetary, fiscal and industrial activity. Ministers were thereby able to portray themselves as the guardians of the national interest, prepared to act only at the time and to the extent dictated by circumstances, but never out of panic or under duress. Such a pragmatic, *ad hoc* approach was symptomatic less of a blatant denial of responsibility than of a deep-seated desire not to disturb capitalism's struggle for stability and survival. A consistent and deliberate absence of action along radical lines, in other words, was itself a purposeful policy.[6]

Keynes may have attributed the failure of governments to deal with the unemployment problem to 'muddle' and to blunders 'in the control of a delicate machine, the workings of which we do not understand'. But this

---

[6] Miller, 'The Unemployment Policy of the National Government', 454.

underestimates the fallacy of believing that ideas alone are powerful enough to determine the course of events. Economic policies involved political and moral choices in contexts very different from those posed by the academic community.[7] To understand more fully the limited response of British governments to the desperate need for jobs between the wars, it is not illogicality, ignorance, opportunism or obscurantism (be it of the Treasury or other departments) that we should recall with relish, so much as the powerful influence which custom, convention and entrenched institutional opinion had upon the formulation of economic policy at the time. The key to understanding the gap between opportunity and reality lies not in the observed robustness of economic science as it was called into service, nor in the inherent characteristics of political parties – whether Utopian or gradualist – but rather in the strength and influence of a political and economic orthodoxy inside and outside of Whitehall which elevated within official circles the acceptance of particular policy goals which were essentially incompatible with the effective reduction of mass unemployment.

[7] D. Winch, *Economics and Policy. A Historical Study* (1969), 20.

Bibliography

PUBLIC RECORDS AT THE PUBLIC RECORD OFFICE, LONDON

Apart from the guides and handbooks available at the PRO, useful additional information regarding interwar official papers can be obtained from B. Swann and M. Turnbull (eds.), *Records of Interest to Social Scientists, 1919–39*, 3 vols. (1971–8).

Board of Trade (BT 56, 70)
Cabinet (Cab 23, 24, 25, 27, 37, 58)
Colonial Office (CO 57, 323)
Ministry of Labour (Lab 2, 4, 8)
Prime Minister's Office (Prem 1)
Treasury (T1, 160, 161, 170, 172, 175, 188, 208)

THESES

Bamberg, J. H. 'The Government, the Banks and the Lancashire Cotton Industry, 1918–39', Ph.D. Thesis, University of Cambridge (1984).
Booth, A. 'The Timing and Content of Government Policies to Assist the Depressed Areas, 1920–1939', Ph.D. Thesis, University of Kent (1975).
Daly, M. 'Government Policy and the Depressed Areas in the Inter-War Period', D. Phil. Thesis, University of Oxford (1979).
Deacon, A. 'Genuinely Seeking Work? A Study of Unemployment Insurance in Britain, 1920–1931', Ph.D. Thesis, University of London (1979).
Dintenfass, M. 'The TUC, the FBI and British Economic Policy Between the Wars', M. Phil. Thesis, University of Warwick (1980).
Heim, C. 'Uneven Development in Interwar Britain', Ph.D. Thesis, Yale University (1982).
Janeway, W. H. 'The Economic Policy of the Second Labour Government, 1929–31', Ph.D. Thesis, University of Cambridge (1971).
Pitfield, D. 'Labour Migration and the Regional Problem in Britain, 1920–1939', Ph.D. Thesis, University of Stirling (1973).
Roberts, J. 'Economic Aspects of the Unemployment Policy of the Government, 1929–31', Ph. D. Thesis, University of London (1977).
Rodgers, T. 'Work and Welfare: The National Confederation of Employers' Organisations and the Unemployment Problem', Ph.D. Thesis, University of Edinburgh (1981).

Shaw, S. 'The Attitude of the TUC towards Unemployment in the Inter-War Period', Ph.D. Thesis, University of Kent (1979).
Thomas, T. 'Aspects of U.K. Macro-Economic Policy during the Inter-War Period: A Study in Econometric History', Ph.D. Thesis, University of Cambridge (1976).

PUBLISHED SOURCES

The place of publication is London unless otherwise stated.

OFFICIAL PUBLICATIONS

Command papers
1909. Royal Commission on the Poor Laws. Minority Report. Cd. 4499.
1913. Board of Trade. First Report of the Proceedings of Trade under Part II of the National Insurance Act 1911. Cd. 6965.
1917. Final Report of the Departmental Committee on Juvenile Education in Relation to Employment After The War. Cd. 8512.
1917–18. Report of Committee Appointed to Consider the Measures to be Taken for Settling Within the Empire Ex-Servicemen Who May Desire to Emigrate after the War. Cd. 8672.
1918. Final Report of the Committee on Commercial and Industrial Policy After The War. Cd. 9035.
1918. Committee on Currency and Foreign Exchanges after the War. First Interim Report. Cd. 9182.
1918. Civil War Workers Committee. Second Interim Report. Cd. 9192.
1919. Final Report of the Committee of Inquiry into the Scheme of Out-of-Work Donation. (The Aberconway Inquiry). Cmd. 305.
1923. Ministry of Labour. Report on the Administration of Section 18 of the Unemployment Insurance Act, 1920. Special Schemes of Unemployment Insurance by Industries. Cmd. 1613.
1925. Committee on the Currency and Bank of England Note Issues. Report. Cmd. 2392.
1926. Inter-Departmental Committee Appointed to Consider the Effect on Migration of Schemes of Social Insurance. Report. Cmd. 2608.
1927. Report of the Ministry of Labour for the Year 1926. Cmd. 2856.
1928. Report of the Ministry of Labour for the Year 1927. Cmd. 3090.
1928. Industrial Transference Board. Report. Cmd. 3156.
1929. Final Report of the Committee on Industry and Trade. Cmd. 3282.
1929. Memorandum on the Shortage, Surplus and Redistribution of Juvenile Labour During the Years 1928 to 1933. Based on the views of Local Juvenile Employment Committees. Cmd. 3327.
1929. Memoranda on Certain Proposals Relating to Unemployment. Cmd. 3331.
1929. Report of the Committee on Procedure and Evidence for the Determination of Claims for Unemployment Insurance Benefit. (The Morris Committee). Cmd. 3415.
1930. Report of the Ministry of Labour for the Year 1929. Cmd. 3579.
1930. National Advisory Council for Juvenile Employment (England and Wales). Third Report. Provision of Courses of Instruction for Unemployed Boys and Girls. Cmd. 3638.

1930–31. First Report of the Royal Commission on Unemployment Insurance. Cmd. 3872.

1930–31. Report of the Committee on Finance and Industry. Cmd. 3897.

1930–31. Report of the (May) Committee on National Expenditure. Cmd. 3920.

1932. Royal Commission on Unemployment Insurance. Final Report. Cmd. 4185.

1933. Report to the Minister of Labour by the Commissioners appointed to Administer Transitional Payments in the County of Durham. Cmd. 4339.

1933. Final Report of the Unemployment Grants Committee. Cmd. 4354.

1934. Report to the Secretary of State for Dominion Affairs of the Inter-Departmental Committee on Migration Policy. Cmd. 4689.

1934. Reports of Investigations into Industrial Conditions in certain Depressed Areas of (i) West Cumberland and Haltwhistle, (ii) Durham and Tyneside, (iii) South Wales and Monmouthshire, (iv) Scotland. Cmd. 4728.

1935. Ministry of Labour. Report for the Year 1934. Cmd. 4861.

1936. Third Report of the Commissioners for the Special Areas (England and Wales). Cmd. 5303.

1936. Absorption of the Unemployed Into Industry. Discussions between the Minister of Labour and Representatives of Certain Industries. Cmd. 5317.

1937. Statement Relating to the Special Areas. Including a Memorandum on the Financial Resolution to be Proposed. Cmd. 5386.

1937. Ministry of Labour. Report for the Year 1936. Cmd. 5431.

1938. Unemployment Assistance Board. Report for the Year 1937. Cmd. 5752.

1939–40. Royal Commission on the Distribution of the Industrial Population. (Barlow Report.) Cmd. 6153.

Other official publications

Ministry of Labour. *Memorandum on the Proposal to Use Unemployment Benefit in aid of (A) Wages on Relief Work, or (B) Wages in Industry,* 1923.

Balfour Committee. *Factors in Industrial and Commercial Efficiency,* 1927.

Board of Education Consultative Committee. *Report on the Education of the Adolescent,* 1927.

Ministry of Labour. *Memorandum on the Transfer of Juveniles from Distressed Mining Areas to Employment in Other districts,* 1928.

Coal Mines Reorganisation Commission. *Colliery Amalgamations,* 1931.

Ministry of Labour. *Memorandum on the Shortage, Surplus and Redistribution of Juvenile Labour in England and Wales During the Years 1930–38,* 1931.

Royal Commission on Unemployment Insurance. Minutes of Evidence. 1931.

Appendices of the Minutes of Evidence taken before the Royal Commission on Unemployment Insurance. Part III: *Report of a Special Investigation in Eight Industrial Areas into the Subsequent History of Persons with Disallowed Claims to Unemployment Benefit,* 1931.

Committee on Finance and Industry. Minutes of Evidence. Vol. II, 1931.

An Industrial Survey of Merseyside. Made for the Board of Trade by the University of Liverpool, 1932.

An Industrial Survey of South West Scotland. Made for the Board of Trade by the University of Glasgow, 1932.

An Industrial Survey of the Lancashire Area, excluding Merseyside. Made for the Board of Trade by the University of Manchester, 1932.

An Industrial Survey of the North-East Coast Area. Made for the Board of Trade by Armstrong College, 1932.

An Industrial Survey of South Wales, Made for the Board of Trade by University College of
    South Wales and Monmouthshire, 1932.
Ministry of Labour. National Advisory Council for Juvenile Employment (Scotland).
    Fifth Report. Supply of, Demand for and Redistribution of Juvenile Labour in Scotland
    During the Years 1932–40, 1933.
Unemployment Insurance Statutory Commission. *Financial Report*, 1934.
Ministry of Labour. *Report on Juvenile Employment for the Year 1933*, 1934.
Royal Commission on the Distribution of the Industrial Population. Minutes of
    Evidence, 1937–39.
Ministry of Labour Gazette, 1921–39.
Ministry of Labour. *Annual Reports*, 1933–38.
Unemployment Assistance Board. *Annual Reports*, 1936–39.

NEWSPAPERS AND PERIODICALS

Daily Herald
The Economist
The Evening Standard
The Nation
Nation and Athenaeum
New Statesman and Nation
The Times
The Times Educational Supplement

CONTEMPORARY SOURCES

Books and articles
Allen, G. C. 'Labour Transference and the Unemployment Problem', *Economic
    Journal*, 40 (1930), 242–8.
Astor, J., W. Layton, A. L. Bowley and S. Rowntree. *Is Unemployment Inevitable?*
    (1924).
    Unemployment Insurance in Great Britain. A Critical Examination (1925).
Bakke, E. *Insurance or Dole? The Adjustment of Unemployment Insurance to Economic
    and Social Facts in Great Britain* (Yale, 1935).
    The Unemployed Man (New Haven, 1933).
Baumann, A. 'An Attack [on rationalisation]', *Business*, March 1928.
Beveridge, W. H. *Unemployment: A Problem of Industry* (1909).
    'Unemployment Insurance in the War and After', in *War Insurance*, Sir N. Hill *et
    al.* (1927), 229–50.
    'An Analysis of Unemployment', *Economica*, 3 (1936), 357–86.
    'An Analysis of Unemployment II', *Economica*, 4 (1937), 1–17.
    'An Analysis of Unemployment III', *Economica*, 4 (1937), 168–83.
    Full Employment in a Free Society (1944).
Bevin, E. *My Plan for 2,000,000 Workless* (1933).
Bourker, B. *Lancashire Under the Hammer* (1928).
Bowley, A. L. 'The Regularisation of the Demand for Labour by the Advancement or
    Retardation of Public Works', in *The Regularisation of Industry*, National
    Movement Towards a Christian Order of Industry and Commerce (Cambridge,
    1924), 34–41.

Brailsford, H. N., J. A. Hobson, A. C. Jones and E. F. Wise. *The Living Wage: A Report to the ILP* (1926).

British Association. *Britain in Depression* (1935).

Cannan, E. 'The Problem of Unemployment', *Economic Journal*, 40 (1930), 45–55.

Clark, C. 'Determination of the Multiplier from National Income Statistics', *Economic Journal*, 48 (1938), 435–48.

Clay, H. 'Unemployment and Wage Rates', *Economic Journal*, 38 (1928), 1–15.
The Post-War Unemployment Problem (1929).

Cole, G. D. H. (ed.). *What Everybody Wants to Know About Money* (Oxford, 1933).
'Wages and Employment', in *Unemployment Problems in 1931*, International Labour Office, Studies and Reports, Series C, No. 16 (Geneva, 1931), 255–80.

Dalton, H. *Unbalanced Budgets: A Study of the Financial Crisis in Fifteen Countries* (1934).

Daniel, G. H. 'Some Factors Affecting the Movement of Labour', *Oxford Economic Papers*, 3 (1940), 144–79.

Daniels, G. W. and H. Campion. 'The Cotton Industry Trade', in *Britain in Depression*, British Association (1935).

Daniels, G. W. and J. Jewkes. 'The Post-War Depression in the Lancashire Cotton Industry', *Journal of the Royal Statistical Society*, 91 (1928), 153–92.

Davison, R. *The Unemployed. Old Policies and New* (1929).

Dawson, W. H. 'Empire Settlement and Unemployment', *Contemporary Review*, 127 (1925), 576–83.

Dennison, S. *The Location of Industry and the Depressed Areas* (1939).

Francis, E. V. *Britain's Economic Strategy* (1939).

Gaitskell, H. and C. Catlin (eds.) *New Trends in Socialism* (1935).

Gibson, R. S. 'The Incentive to Work As Affected by Unemployment Insurance and Poor Law Respectively', *Manchester School*, 1 (1930), 21–7.

Gilson, M. *Unemployment Insurance in Great Britain* (1931).

Gregory, T. E. 'Rationalisation and Technological Unemployment', *Economic Journal*, 40 (1930), 551–67.

Hawtrey, R. G. 'Public Expenditure and the Demand for Labour', *Economica*, 5 (1925), 38–48.

Henderson, H. D. 'Will Unemployment Increase?' *The Nation*, 4 April 1925.

Hilton, J. 'Statistics of Unemployment Derived from the Working of the Unemployment Insurance Acts', *Journal of the Royal Statistical Society*, 86 (1923), 154–93.

Hobson, J. A. *Rationalization and Unemployment* (1930).
'The State as an Organ of Rationalization', *Political Quarterly*, 2 (1931), 30–45.

Jewkes, J. and A. Winterbottom. *An Industrial Survey of Cumberland and Furness: A Study of the Social Implications of Economic Dislocation* (Manchester, 1933).

Kahn, R. F. 'The Relation of Home Investment to Unemployment', *Economic Journal*, 41 (1931), 173–98.
'Public Works and Inflation', *Journal of the American Statistical Association*, 28 (1933), 168–73.
'Determination of the Multiplier from National Income Statistics', *Economic Journal*, 48 (1939), 435–48.

Kaldor, N. 'Wage Subsidies as a Remedy for Unemployment', *Journal of Political Economy*, 44 (1936), 721–42.

Keynes, J. M. 'Free Trade', *The Nation*, 1 December 1923.

A Tract for Monetary Reform (1923).

'Does Unemployment Need a Drastic Remedy?' *Nation and Athenaeum*, 24 May 1924.

'Foreign Investment and National Advantage', *Nation and Athenaeum*, 9 August 1924.

The Economic Consequences of Mr. Churchill (1925).

'The First Fruits of the Gold Standard', *Nation and Athenaeum*, 26 June 1926.

'Unemployment and Treasury Policy', *Nation and Athenaeum*, 4 August 1928.

'The Question of High Wages', *Political Quarterly*, 1 (1930), 110–24.

'Economic Notes on Free Trade', *New Statesman and Nation*, 28 March 1931.

'Some Consequences of the Economy Report', *New Statesman and Nation*, 15 August 1931.

'An Economic Analysis of Unemployment', in *Unemployment as a World Problem*, ed. Q. Wright (Chicago, 1931), 1–42.

'Two Years Off Gold: How Far Are We From Prosperity Now?' *Daily Mail*, 19 September 1933.

'How to Avoid a Slump', *The Times*, 12–14 January 1937.

'Borrowing for Defence', *The Times*, 11 March 1937.

'Crisis Finance', *The Times*, 17 April 1939.

'Relative Movement of Real Wages and Output', *Economic Journal*, 49 (1939), 34–51.

Keynes, J. M. and H. D. Henderson, *Can Lloyd George Do It? The Pledge Examined* (1929).

Llewellyn-Smith, H. *New Survey of London Life and Labour* (1932).

Lloyd George, D. 'The Statesman's Task', *Nation and Athenaeum*, 12 April 1924.

Makower, H., J. Marschak and H. W. Robinson. 'Studies in the Mobility of Labour: Analysis for Great Britain, Part I', *Oxford Economic Papers*, 2 (1939), 70–97.

Maurette, F. 'Is Unemployment Insurance a Cause of Permanent Unemployment?' *International Labour Review*, 24 (1931), 663–84.

Mond, Sir Alfred. *The Remedy for Unemployment. Get the Workers Back to Work* (1925).

'Amalgamation – Rationalization – Imperial Arrangement. The Latest Phase in Industry', *System*, October 1927, 161–3.

Mosley, O. *Revolution by Reason* (1925).

Owen, A. D. K. 'Social Consequences of Industrial Transference', *Sociological Review*, 29 (1937), 331–54.

Pigou, A. *Unemployment* (1913).

'Wage Policy and Unemployment', *Economic Journal*, 37 (1927), 355–68.

The Theory of Unemployment (1933).

Pilgrim Trust, *Men Without Work* (Cambridge, 1938).

Robbins, L. *The Great Depression* (1934).

Robertson, D. H. *A Study of Industrial Fluctuations* (1915).

Banking Policy and the Price Level (1925).

Rueff, J. 'Les Variations du Chômage en Angleterre', *Revue Politique et Parlementaire*, 125 (1925).

Seager, Sir W. 'British Industry Must Nationalise or Rationalise', *Business*, May 1932.

Seymour, J. B. *The British Employment Exchange* (1928).

Singer, H. W. 'Regional Labour Markets and the Process of Unemployment', *Review of Economic Statistics*, 7 (1939), 42–58.

Tawney, R. H. *The Possible Cost of Raising the School-Leaving Age* (1927).

'Unemployment and the School-Leaving Age', *New Statesman*, 18 November 1933.

Juvenile Employment and Education (Oxford, 1934).

Thomas, B. 'The Movement of Labour into South-East England, 1920–32', *Economica*, 1 (1934), 220–41.

'The Influx of Labour into London and the South-East, 1920–36', *Economica*, 4 (1937), 323–6.

'The Influx of Labour into the Midlands, 1920–37', *Economica*, 5 (1938), 410–34.

Urwick, L. 'Rationalisation', *British Management Review*, 3 (1938).

Wilson, E. 'Unemployment Insurance and the Stability of Wages in Great Britain', *International Labour Review*, 30 (1934), 767–96.

Witmer, H. 'Some Effects of the English Unemployment Insurance Acts on the Number of Unemployed Relieved under the Poor Law', *Quarterly Journal of Economics*, 45 (1931), 262–88.

Other contemporary publications

Labour Party. *The Prevention of Unemployment After the War*. 1917.

Safeguarding of Industries Bill. Manifesto by the Parliamentary Committee of the Trades Union Congress and the Labour Party Executive. 1921.

Unemployment: A Labour Policy. Being the Report of the Special Committee on Unemployment Appointed by the Parliamentary Committee of the Trades Union Congress and the Labour Party Executive. 1921.

British Labour and Unemployment. Resolutions to be Discussed at the Special Conference of the Trades Union Congress and the Labour Party. January 1921.

National Confederation of Employers' Organisations. *Unemployment Insurance*. 31 January 1924.

Trades Union Congress. *Annual Report*. 1925.

Unemployment Insurance in Great Britain. A Critical Examination by the Authors of 'The Third Winter of Unemployment'. 1925.

On the Dole or Off? What to do with Britain's Workless Workers. Report on the Prevention of Unemployment by a Joint Committee representing the General Council of the Trades Union Congress, the National Executive of the Labour Party, and the Executive of the Parliementary Labour Party. 1926.

Conference of Northern Poor Law Unions and Other Local Authorities. *Distress Due to Unemployment. Deputation of the Minister of Labour*. 27 October 1927.

Liberal Party. *Britain's Industrial Future. Being the Report of the Liberal Industrial Inquiry*. 1928.

International Association for Social Progress (British Section). *Report on 'The Raising of the School Age and its Relation to Employment and Unemployment'*. 1928.

We Can Conquer Unemployment. Mr. Lloyd George's Pledge. 1929.

Conference on Industrial Reorganisation and Industrial Relations. *Interim Report on Unemployment*. 1929.

How to Tackle Unemployment. The Liberal Plans as Laid Before the Government and the Nation. 1930.

Trades Union Congress, *Annual Report*. 1930.

Federation of British Industries. *The Passing of Free Trade*. 1931.

National Confederation of Employers' Organizations. *The Industrial Situation*. 1931.

Labour Party. *Annual Conference Report*. 1933.
Engineering and Allied Employers' National Federation. *Unemployment. Its Realities and Problems*. 1933.
Trades Union Congress. *Annual Reports*. 1930, 1934.
Unemployment Among Young Persons. Report Submitted to the Nineteenth Session of the International Labour Conference. 1935.
Joint Committee of Cotton Trade Organisations. *Report by the Executive on Remedial Measures Applicable to Present Position of the Lancashire Cotton Industry*.
Parliamentary Debates. Fifth Series. 1935.

SECONDARY SOURCES: BOOKS AND ARTICLES

Abbott, G. C. 'A Re-Examination of the 1929 Colonial Development Act', *Economic History Review*, 2nd ser., 24 (1971), 68–81.
Abel, D. *A History of British Tariffs, 1923–1942* (1945).
Aldcroft, D. H. 'Economic Progress in Britain in the 1920s', *Scottish Journal of Political Economy*, 13 (1966), 297–316.
    'Economic Growth in the Inter-War Years: A Reassessment', *Economic History Review*, 2nd ser., 20 (1967), 311–26.
    The Inter-War Economy: Britain, 1919–1939 (1970).
    Full Employment: The Elusive Goal (Sussex, 1984).
Allen, G. C. 'The Growth of Industry on Trading Estates, 1920–39, with special reference to Slough Trading Estate', *Oxford Economic Papers*, 3 (1951), 272–300.
Barker, R. *Education and Politics, 1900–51* (Oxford, 1972).
Beenstock, M. 'Real Wages and Unemployment in the 1930s: A Reply', *National Institute Economic Review*, 119 (1987), 76–8.
Beenstock, M., F. Capie and B. Griffiths. 'Economic Recovery in the United Kingdom in the 1930s'. Bank of England Panel of Academic Consultants, Panel Paper No. 23, 1984.
Beenstock, M. and P. Warburton. 'Wages and Unemployment in Inter-War Britain', *Explorations in Economic History*, 23 (1986), 153–72.
Benjamin, D. K. and L. A. Kochin. 'Searching for an Explanation of Unemployment in Interwar Britain', *Journal of Political Economy*, 87 (1979), 441–78.
    'Unemployment and Unemployment Benefits in Twentieth-Century Britain: A Reply to Our Critics', *Journal of Political Economy*, 90 (1982), 410–36.
Blank, S. *Industry and Government in Britain. The Federation of British Industries in Politics, 1945–65* (Saxon House, 1973).
Bleaney, M. 'Macroeconomic Policy and the Great Depression Revisited', *Scottish Journal of Political Economy*, 34 (1987) 105–19.
Booth, A. 'An Administrative Experiment in Unemployment Policy in the Thirties', *Public Administration*, 56 (1978), 139–57.
    'The "Keynesian Revolution" in Economic Policy-Making', *Economic History Review*, 2nd ser., 36 (1983), 103–23.
    'Britain in the 1930s: A Managed Economy?' *Economic History Review*, 2nd ser., 40 (1987), 499–522.
Booth, A. and S. Glynn, 'Unemployment in the Interwar Period: A Multiple Problem', *Journal of Contemporary History*, 10 (1975), 611–36.
Booth, A. and M. Pack. *Employment, Capital and Economic Policy. Great Britain, 1918–1939* (Oxford, 1985).

Boyce, R. W. *British Capitalism at the Crossroads, 1919–1932* (Cambridge, 1987).

Bretherton, R. F., F. A. Burchardt and R. S. G. Rutherford. *Public Investment and the Trade Cycle in Great Britain* (Oxford, 1941).

Briggs, E. and A. Deacon. 'The Creation of the Unemployment Assistance Board', *Policy and Politics*, 2 (1973), 43–62.

Broadberry, S. 'Unemployment in Interwar Britain: A Disequilibrium Approach', *Oxford Economic Papers*, 35 (1983), 463–85.

'Fiscal Policy in Britain During the 1930s', *Economic History Review*, 2nd ser., 37 (1984), 95–102.

The British Economy Between the Wars. A Macroeconomic Survey (Oxford, 1986).

Brown, A. J. *A Framework of Regional Economics* (Cambridge, 1972).

Brown, K. D. *Labour and Unemployment, 1900–1914* (1971).

Burns, E. *British Unemployment Programs, 1920–1938* (Washington, 1941).

Buxton, N. K. 'The Role of the New Industries in Britain during the 1930s: A Reinterpretation', *Business History Review*, 49 (1975), 205–22.

'Efficiency and Organization in Scotland's Iron and Steel Industry during the Interwar Period', *Economic History Review*, 2nd ser., 29 (1976), 107–24.

The Economic Development of the British Coal Industry (1978).

Buxton, N. K. and D. H. Aldcroft (eds.). *British Industry Between the Wars* (1979).

Capie, F. 'The British Tariff and Industrial Protection in the 1930s', *Economic History Review*, 2nd ser., 31 (1978), 399–409.

'The Pressure for Tariff Protection in Britain, 1917–31', *Journal of European Economic History*, 9 (1980), 431–47.

Depression and Protectionism: Britain Between the Wars (1983).

'Unemployment and Real Wages', in *The Road to Full Employment*, ed. S. Glynn and A. Booth (1987), 57–69.

Carnegie UK Trust. *Disinherited Youth* (Edinburgh, 1943).

Casson, M. *Economics of Unemployment. An Historical Perspective* (1983).

Catterall, R. 'Attitudes to and the Impact of British Monetary Policy in the 1920s', *International Review of the History of Banking*, 12 (1976), 29–53.

Clay, H. (ed.). *The Inter-War Years and Other Papers* (Oxford, 1955).

Clay, Sir Henry. *Lord Norman* (1957).

Clegg, H. A. *A History of British Trade Unions since 1889.* Vol. 2. *1911–1933* (Oxford, 1985).

Collard, D. A., N. H. Dimsdale, C. L. Gilbert, D. R. Helm, M. Scott and A. K. Sen. *Economic Theory and Hicksian Themes* (Oxford, 1984).

Collins, M. 'Unemployment in Interwar Britain: Still Searching for an Explanation', *Journal of Political Economy*, 90 (1982), 369–79.

Constantine, S. *The Making of British Colonial Development Policy, 1914–1940* (1984).

Crafts, N. F. R. *British Economic Growth during the Industrial Revolution* (Oxford, 1985).

'Long-Term Unemployment, Excess Demand and the Wage Equation in Britain, 1925–1939', Centre for Economic Policy Research, Discussion Paper No. 147, December 1986.

'Long-term Unemployment in Britain', *Economic History Review*, 2nd ser., 40 (1987), 418–32.

Davenport-Hines, R. P. T. *Dudley Docker. The Life and Times of a Trade Warrior* (Cambridge, 1984).

Deacon, A. *In Search of the Scrounger: The Administration of Unemployment Insurance in Britain, 1920–31* (1976).

'Concession and Coercion: The Politics of Unemployment Insurance in the Twenties', in *Essays in Labour History, 1918–1939*, ed. A. Briggs and J. Saville (1977), 9–35.

Dean, D. W. 'Difficulties of a Labour Education Policy: The Failure of the Trevelyan Bill, 1929–31', *British Journal of Educational Studies*, 17 (1969), 286–300.

Dimsdale, N. H. 'British Monetary Policy and the Exchange Rate, 1920–38', in *The Money Supply and the Exchange Rate*, ed. W. A. Eltis and P. Sinclair (Oxford, 1981), 306–49.

'Employment and Real Wages in the Inter-War Period', *National Institute Economic Review*, 110 (1984), 94–103.

Dowie, J. A. 'Growth in the Inter-War Period: Some More Arithmetic', *Economic History Review*, 2nd ser., 21 (1968), 93–112.

'1919–20 is in Need of Attention', *Economic History Review*, 2nd ser., 28 (1975), 429–50.

Drummond, I. M. *British Economic Policy and the Empire, 1919–1939* (1972).

Imperial Economic Policy, 1917–1939 (1974).

Durbin, E. *New Jerusalems. The Labour Party and the Economics of Democratic Socialism* (1985).

Eichengreen, B. 'The Macroeconomic Effects of the British General Tariff of 1932', Mimeograph 1979.

Sterling and the Tariff, 1929–32 (Princeton, 1981).

'Keynes and Protection', *Journal of Economic History*, 44 (1984), 363–73.

'Unemployment in Interwar Britain: New Evidence from London', *Journal of Interdisciplinary History*, 17 (1986), 335–58.

'Unemployment in Interwar Britain: Dole or Doldrums?' *Oxford Economic Papers*, 39 (1987), 597–623.

Eichengreen, B. and T. J. Hatton. 'Interwar Unemployment in International Perspective: An Overview' in *Interwar Unemployment in International Perspective*, ed. B. Eichengreen and T. J. Hatton (Dordrecht, 1988), 1–59.

Eichengreen, B. and J. Sachs. 'Exchange Rates and Economic Recovery in the 1930s', *Journal of Economic History*, 45 (1985), 925–46.

Elbaum, B. and W. Lazonick. 'The Decline of the British Economy: An Institutional Perspective', *Journal of Economic History*, 44 (1984), 567–83.

The Decline of the British Economy (Oxford, 1986).

Eltis, W. A. and P. Sinclair. *The Money Supply and the Exchange Rate* (Oxford, 1981).

Feinstein, C. H. *National Income, Expenditure and Output of the United Kingdom, 1855–1965* (Cambridge, 1972).

Foreman-Peck, J. 'The British Tariff and Industrial Protection in the 1930s. An Alternative Model', *Economic History Review*, 2nd ser., 34 (1981), 132–39.

'Seedcorn or Chaff? New Firm Formation and the Performance of the Interwar Economy', *Economic History Review*, 2nd ser., 38 (1985), 402–22.

Frielander, D. and R. J. Roshier. 'A Study of Internal Migration in England and Wales. Part I: Geographical Patterns of Internal Migration, 1851–1951', *Population Studies*, 19 (1966), 239–79.

Garside, W. R. 'Juvenile Unemployment Statistics Between the Wars: A Commentary and Guide to Sources', *Bulletin of the Society for the Study of Labour History*, 33 (1976), 38–46.

'Juvenile Unemployment and Public Policy between the Wars', *Economic History*

Review, 2nd ser., 30 (1977), 322–39.

'Management and Men: Aspects of British Industrial Relations in the Inter-War Period', in *Essays in British Business History*, ed. B. Supple (Oxford, 1977), 244–67.

The Measurement of Unemployment. Methods and Sources in Great Britain 1850–1979 (Oxford, 1980).

'Unemployment and the School-Leaving Age in Inter-War Britain', *International Review of Social History*, 26 (1981), 159–70.

'The Real Wage Debate and British Interwar Unemployment', in *The Road to Full Employment*, ed. S. Glynn and A. Booth (1987), 70–81.

Garside, W. R. and T. J. Hatton. 'Keynesian Policy and British Unemployment in the 1930s', *Economic History Review*, 2nd ser., 38 (1985), 83–8.

Gilbert, B. *The Evolution of National Insurance in Great Britain* (1966).

British Social Policy, 1914–1939 (1970).

Glynn, S. and A. Booth (eds.). *The Road to Full Employment* (1987).

Glynn, S. and P. G. Howells. 'Unemployment in the 1930s: The "Keynesian Solution" Reconsidered', *Australian Economic History Review*, 20 (1980), 28–45.

Gupta, P. *Imperialism and the British Labour Movement, 1914–1964* (1975).

Hancock, K. 'The Reduction of Unemployment as Problem of Public Policy', *Economic History Review*, 2nd ser., 15 (1962), 328–43.

Hancock, W. K. *Survey of British Commonwealth Affairs. Vol. 2. Problems of Economic Policy, 1918–1939* (Oxford, 1940).

Hannah, L. *The Rise of the Corporate Economy* (1976).

Hannington, W. *Ten Lean Years: An Investigation of the Record of the National Government in the Field of Unemployment* (1940).

Harris, J. *Unemployment and Politics. A Study in English Social Policy, 1886–1914* (Oxford, 1972).

William Beveridge. A Biography (Oxford, 1977).

Hatton, T. J. 'Unemployment in Britain Between the World Wars: A Role for the Dole?' Essex Discussion Paper, No. 139, 1980.

'Unemployment Benefits and the Macroeconomics of the Interwar Labour Market: A Further Analysis', *Oxford Economic Papers*, 35 (1983), 486–505.

'The Analysis of Unemployment in Interwar Britain: A Survey of Research', Centre for Economic Policy Research, Discussion Paper No. 66, June 1985.

'The British Labor Market in the 1920s: A Test of the Search – Turnover Approach', *Explorations in Economic History*, 22 (1985), 257–70.

'Unemployment in the 1930s and the "Keynesian Solution": Some Notes of Dissent', *Australian Economic History Review*, 25 (1985), 129–47.

'Structural Aspects of Unemployment Between the Wars', in *Research in Economic History*, Vol. 10, ed. P. Uselding (Connecticut, 1986), 55–92.

'The Outlines of a Keynesian Solution', in *The Road to Full Employment*, ed. S. Glynn and A. Booth (1987), 82–94.

Heim, C. 'Industrial Organization and Regional Development in Inter-War Britain', *Journal of Economic History*, 43 (1983), 931–52.

'Limits to Intervention: The Bank of England and Industrial Diversification in the Depressed Areas', *Economic History Review*, 2nd ser., 37 (1984), 533–50.

'Structural Transformation and the Demand for New Labor in Advanced Economies: Interwar Britain', *Journal of Economic History*, 44 (1984), 585–95.

Henderson, H. D. 'Do We Want Public Works?', in *The Inter-War Years and Other*

Papers, ed. H. Clay (Oxford, 1955), 151–60.

Holland, R. F. 'The Federation of British Industries and the International Economy, 1929–1939', *Economic History Review*, 2nd ser., 24 (1981), 287–300.

Britain and the Commonwealth Alliance, 1918–1935 (1981).

Howson, S. '"A Dear Money Man"?: Keynes on Monetary Policy, 1920', *Economic Journal*, 83 (1973), 456–64.

'The Managed Floating Pound, 1932–39', *The Banker*, 126 (1976), 249–55.

'The Management of Sterling, 1932–1939', *Journal of Economic History*, 40 (1980), 53–60.

Sterling's Managed Float: The Operations of the Exchange Equalisation Account, 1932–39 (Princeton, 1980).

'Slump and Unemployment', in *The Economic History of Britain Since 1700*. Vol. 2. *1860 to the 1970s*, ed. R. Floud and D. McCloskey (Cambridge, 1981), 265–85.

Howson, S. and D. Winch. *The Economic Advisory Council, 1930–1939* (Cambridge, 1977).

Hume, L. J. 'The Gold Standard and Deflation: Issues and Attitudes in the 1920s', *Economica*, 30 (1963), 225–42.

Hutchinson, Sir Hubert. *Tariff Making and Industrial Reconstruction* (1965).

Hutchison, T. W. *Economics and Economic Policy in Britain, 1946–1966* (1968).

On Revolutions and Progress in Economic Knowledge (Cambridge, 1978).

The Politics and Philosophy of Economics (1981).

International Labour Office, *Public Investment and Full Employment*, Studies and Reports, New Series, 3, 1946.

Irish, M. 'Unemployment in Interwar Britain. A Note', University of Bristol, Mimeo, February 1980.

Johnson, H. G. 'Keynes and British Economics', in *Essays on John Maynard Keynes*, ed. M. Keynes (Cambridge, 1979), 108–22.

Jones, M. E. F. 'The Regional Impact of an Overvalued Pound in the 1920s', *Economic History Review*, 2nd ser., 38 (1985), 393–401.

'Regional Employment Multipliers, Regional Policy and Structural Change in Interwar Britain', *Explorations in Economic History*, 22 (1985), 417–39.

Kaldor, N. 'Keynesian Economics after Fifty Years', in *Keynes and the Modern World*, ed. D. Worswick and J. Trevithick (Cambridge, 1983), 1–48.

Keynes, M. *Essays on John Maynard Keynes* (Cambridge, 1979).

The Collected Writings of John Maynard Keynes, ed. D. E. Moggridge for the Royal Economic Society.

Vol. 9: *Essays in Persuasion* (1972).

Vol. 19: *Activities 1922–1929: The Return to Gold and Industrial Policy* (2 Vols. 1981).

Vol. 20: *Activities 1929–1931: Rethinking Employment and Unemployment Policies* (1981).

Vol. 21: *Activities 1931–1939: World Crises and Policies in Britain and America* (1982).

Vol. 23: *Activities 1940–1943. External War Finance* (1979).

Kindleberger, C. P. and G. di Tella. *Economics in the Long View. Vol. 3* (1982).

Kirby, M. W. 'The Control of Competition in the British Coal-Mining Industry in the Thirties', *Economic History Review*, 2nd ser., 26 (1973), 273–84.

'Government Intervention in Industrial Organization: Coal Mining in the Nineteen Thirties', *Business History*, 15 (1973), 160–73.

'The Lancashire Cotton Industry in the Inter-War Years: A Study in Organizational Change', *Business History*, 16 (1974), 145–59.

The British Coalmining Industry, 1870–1946 (1977).

Lazonick, W. 'The Cotton Industry' in *The Decline of the British Economy*, ed. B. Elbaum and W. Lazonick (Oxford, 1986), 18–50.

Lee, C. 'Regional Structural Change in the Long-Run: Great Britain, 1841–1971', in *Region and Industrialization: Studies on the Role of the Region in the Economic History of the Last Two Centuries*, ed. S. Pollard (Gottingen, 1980), 254–75.

'Regional Growth and Structural Change in Victorian Britain', *Economic History Review*, 2nd ser., 34 (1981), 438–52.

Loebl, H. *Government Factories and the Origins of British Regional Policy, 1934–1948* (1988).

Lonie, A. and H. Begg. 'Comment: Further Evidence of the Quest for an Effective Regional Policy, 1934–37', *Regional Studies*, 13 (1979), 497–500.

Lowe, R. 'The Erosion of State Intervention in Britain, 1917–24', *Economic History Review*, 2nd ser., 31 (1978), 270–86.

'Bureaucracy and Innovation in British Welfare Policy, 1870–1945', in *The Emergence of the Welfare State in Britain and Germany, 1850–1950*, ed. W. J. Mommsen (1981), 263–95.

'Welfare Legislation and the Unions during and after the First World War', *Historical Journal*, 25 (1982), 437–41.

'Hours of Labour: Negotiating Industrial Legislation in Britain, 1919–39', *Economic History Review*, 2nd ser., 35 (1982), 254–71.

'Bureaucracy Triumphant or Denied? The Expansion of the British Civil Service, 1919–1939', *Public Administration*, 62 (1984), 291–310.

Adjusting to Democracy. The Role of the Ministry of Labour in British Politics, 1916–1939 (Oxford, 1986).

Lowe, R. and R. Roberts. 'Sir Horace Wilson, 1900–1935: The Making of a Mandarin', *Historical Journal*, 30 (1987), 641–62.

Lyman, R. *The First Labour Government. 1924* (1957).

'The British Labour Party: The Conflict between Socialist Ideals and Practical Politics between the Wars', *Journal of British Studies*, 5 (1965), 140–52.

Lynes, T. 'Unemployment Assistance Tribunals in the 1930s', in *Justice, Discretion and Poverty*, ed. M. Adler and A. Bradley (1975), 5–31.

'The Making of the Unemployment Assistance Scale', Supplementary Benefits Commission, SBA Paper No. 6, *Low Incomes* (HMSO, 1977).

McDonald, G. 'Insight Into Industrial Politics: The Federation of British Industries' Papers, 1925', *Business Archives*, 38 (1973), 29–37.

Malament, B. 'British Labor and Roosevelt's New Deal. The Response of the Left and the Unions', *Journal of British Studies*, 17 (1978), 136–67.

Marrison, A. J. 'Businessmen, Industries and Tariff Reform in Great Britain, 1903–1930', *Business History*, 25 (1983), 148–78.

Marquand, D. *Ramsay MacDonald* (1977).

Matthews, R. C. O. 'Why Has Britain Had Full Employment Since the War?' *Economic Journal*, 78 (1968), 555–69.

Matthews, R. C. O., C. H. Feinstein and J. C. Odling-Smee. *British Economic Growth 1856–1973* (Oxford, 1982).

Maynard, G. W. 'Keynes and Unemployment Today', *Three Banks Review*, 120 (1978), 3–20.

Metcalf, D., S. J. Nickell and N. Floros. 'Still Searching for an Explanation of

Unemployment in Interwar Britain', *Journal of Political Economy*, 90 (1982), 386–99.

Middlemass, K. and J. Barnes. *Baldwin. A Biography* (1969).

Middleton, R. 'The Treasury in the 1930s: Political and Administrative Constraints to Acceptance of the "New" Economics', *Oxford Economic Papers*, 34 (1982), 48–77.

'The Treasury and Public Investment: A Perspective on Interwar Economic Management', *Public Administration*, 61 (1983), 351–70.

'The Measurement of Fiscal Influence in Britain in the 1930s', *Economic History Review*, 2nd ser., 37 (1984), 103–6.

Towards the Managed Economy (1985).

'Treasury Policy on Unemployment', in *The Road to Full Employment*, ed. S. Glynn and A. Booth (1987), 109–24.

Miller, F. 'National Assistance or Unemployment Assistance? The British Cabinet and Relief Policy, 1932–33', *Journal of Contemporary History*, 9 (1974), 163–84.

'The Unemployment Policy of the National Government, 1931–36', *Historical Journal*, 19 (1976), 453–76.

'The British Unemployment Assistance Crisis of 1935', *Journal of Contemporary History*, 14 (1979), 329–51.

Millett, J. D. *The Unemployment Assistance Board* (1940).

Moggridge, D. 'The 1931 Financial Crisis – A New View', *The Banker*, 120 (1970), 832–9.

'Bank of England Foreign Exchange Operations, 1924–1931', *International Review of the History of Banking*, 5 (1972), 1–23.

British Monetary Policy, 1924–1931. The Norman Conquest of $4.86 (Cambridge, 1972).

'From Treatise to the General Theory: An Exercise in Chronology', *History of Political Economy*, 5 (1973), 72–88.

Moggridge, D. and S. Howson. 'Keynes on Monetary Policy, 1910–1946', *Oxford Economic Papers*, 26 (1974), 226–47.

Newhall, A. and J. Symons. 'Wages and Employment Between the Wars', Centre for Labour Economics, London School of Economics Discussion Paper No. 257, October 1986.

Ormerod, P. A. and G. D. N. Worswick. 'Unemployment in Interwar Britain', *Journal of Political Economy*, 90 (1982), 400–9.

Palmer, S. and G. Williams. *Chartered and Unchartered Waters* (1982).

Parker, R. 'Economics, Rearmament and Foreign Policy: The United Kingdom before 1939 – A Preliminary Study', *Journal of Contemporary History*, 10 (1975), 637–47.

'British Rearmament, 1936–1939: Treasury, Trade Unions and Skilled Labour', *English Historical Review*, 96 (1981), 306–43.

Parkinson, J. R. 'Shipbuilding', in *British Industry Between the Wars*, ed. N. K. Buxton and D. H. Aldcroft (1979), 79–102.

Parkinson, M. *The Labour Party and the Organization of Secondary Education 1918–65* (1970).

Parsons, D. W. *The Political Economy of British Regional Policy* (1985).

Patinkin, D. 'Keynes and the Multiplier', *Manchester School*, 3 (1978), 209–23.

'The Development of Keynes' Policy Thinking', in *Anticipations of the General*

Theory? ed. D. Patinkin (Oxford, 1983), 200–14.

Peden, G. C. *British Rearmament and the Treasury, 1932–1939* (Edinburgh, 1979).
'Keynes, the Treasury and Unemployment in the later Nineteen-Thirties', *Oxford Economic Papers*, 32 (1980), 1–18.
'The Treasury as the Central Department of Government, 1919–1939', *Public Administration*, 61 (1983), 371–85.
'The "Treasury View" on Public Works and Employment in the Interwar Period', *Economic History Review*, 2nd ser., 37 (1984), 167–81.

Plant, G. F. *Overseas Settlement. Migration from the United Kingdom to the Dominions* (Oxford, 1951).

Pollard, S. 'Trade Union Reactions to the Economic Crisis', *Journal of Contemporary History*, 4 (1969), 101–15.
Region and Industrialization: Studies in the Role of the Region in the Economic History of the Last Two Centuries (Gottingen, 1980).

Porter, J. H. 'The Commercial Banks and the Financial Problems of the English Cotton Industry, 1919–1939', *International Review of the History of Banking*, 9 (1974), 1–16.
'Cotton and Wool Textiles', in *British Industry Between the Wars*, ed. N. K. Buxton and D. H. Aldcroft (1979), 25–47.

Reddaway, W. 'Was \$4.86 Inevitable in 1925?' *Lloyds Bank Review*, 96 (April 1970), 15–28.

Redmond, J. 'An Indication of the Effective Exchange Rate of the Pound in the Nineteen-Thirties', *Economic History Review*, 2nd ser., 33 (1980), 83–91.
'The Sterling Overvaluation in 1925: A Multilateral Approach', *Economic History Review*, 2nd ser., 37 (1984), 520–32.

Richardson, H. W. 'New Industries Between the Wars', *Oxford Economic Papers*, 13 (1961), 360–84.
'Over-Commitment in Britain Before 1930', *Oxford Economic Papers*, 17 (1965), 237–62.
'Fiscal Policy in the 1930s', in *The Managed Economy. Essays in British Economic Policy and Performance since 1929*, ed. C. H. Feinstein (Oxford, 1983), 68–92.

Roberts, R. 'The Administrative Origins of Industrial Diplomacy' in *Businessmen and Politics*, ed. J. Turner (1984), 93–104.

Rodgers, T. 'Sir Allan Smith, the Industrial Group and the Politics of Unemployment, 1919–1934', *Business History*, 28 (1986), 100–23.

Rooth, T. 'Limits of Leverage: The Anglo-Danish Trade Agreement of 1933', *Economic History Review*, 2nd ser., 37 (1984), 211–28.
'Trade and Trade Bargaining: Anglo-Scandinavian Economic Relations in the 1930s', *Scandinavian Economic History Review*, 34 (1986), 54–71.

Rowland, B. M. (ed.). *Balance of Power or Hegemony?* (New York, 1976).

Sadler, B. 'Unemployment and Unemployment Benefits in Twentieth Century Britain: A Lesson of the Thirties', in *Out of Work: Perspectives of Mass Unemployment*, Dept. of Economics, University of Warwick (1984), 18–30.

Saul, S. B. 'The Export Economy, 1870–1914', *Yorkshire Bulletin of Economic and Social Research*, 17 (1965), 5–18.

Sayers, R. S. *The Bank of England, 1891–1944.* (Cambridge, 1976).

Schultz. J. A. 'Finding Homes Fit for Heroes: The Great War and Empire Settlement', *Canadian Journal of History*, 18 (1983), 99–110.

Shay, R. *British Rearmament in the Thirties. Politics and Profits* (Princeton, 1977).

Sheldrake, J. and S. Vickerstaff. *The History of Industrial Training in Britain* (1987).

Simon, B. *The Politics of Educational Reform, 1920–1940* (1974).
Skidelsky, R. *Politicians and the Slump. The Labour Government of 1929–1931.* (1970).
'1929–1931 Revisited', *Bulletin of the Society for the Study of Labour History*, 21 (1970), 6–7.
'Retreat from Leadership: The Evolution of British Economic Foreign Policy, 1870–1939' in *Balance of Power or Hegemony?* ed. B. M. Rowland (New York, 1976), 149–89.
'The Political Meaning of the Keynesian Revolution', in *The End of the Keynesian Era*, ed. R. Skidelsky (1977), 33–40.
'The Reception of the Keynesian Revolution', in *Essays on John Maynard Keynes*, ed. M. Keynes (1979), 89–106.
Oswald Mosley (1981).
'Keynes and the Treasury View: The Case for and against an Active Unemployment Policy', in *The Emergence of the Welfare State in Britain and Germany*, ed. W. Mommsen (1981), 167–87.
Slaven, A. 'British Shipbuilders: Market Trends and Order-Book Patterns Between the Wars', *Journal of Transport History*, 3 (1982), 37–61.
'Self-Liquidation: The National Shipbuilders' Security Ltd. and the Rationalization of British Shipbuilding in the 1930s' in *Chartered and Unchartered Waters*, ed. S. Palmer and G. Williams (1982), 125–47.
Snyder, R. K. *The Tariff Problem in Great Britain, 1918–1923* (Stanford, 1944).
Swann, B. and M. Turnbull, *Records of Interest to Social Scientists: Employment and Unemployment* (1978).
Tawney, R. H. 'The Abolition of Economic Controls, 1918–1921', *Economic History Review*, 2nd ser., 13 (1943), 1–30.
Thirlwall, A. P. 'Keynesian Employment Theory is not Defunct', *Three Banks Review*, 131 (1981), 14–29.
Thomas, M. 'Rearmament and Economic Recovery in the late 1930s', *Economic History Review*, 2nd ser., 36 (1983), 552–79.
'Labour Market Structure and the Nature of Unemployment in Interwar Britain', in *Interwar Unemployment in International Perspective*, ed. B. Eichengreen and T. J. Hatton (Dordrecht, 1988), 97–148.
Thomas, T. 'Aggregate Demand, 1918–45', in *The Economic History of Britain Since 1700. Vol. 2. 1860 to the 1970s*, ed. R. Floud and D. McCloskey (Cambridge, 1981), 332–46.
Thomas, W. A. *The Finance of British Industry, 1918–1976* (1978).
Tolliday, S. 'Tariffs and Steel, 1916–1934: The Politics of Industrial Decline', in *Businessmen and Politics*, ed. J. Turner (1984), 50–75.
'Steel and Rationalization Policies, 1918–1950', in *The Decline of the British Economy*, ed. B. Elbaum and W. Lazonick (Oxford, 1986), 82–108.
Business, Banking and Politics. The Case of British Steel, 1918–1939 (Harvard, 1987).
Tomlinson, J. 'Women as "Anomalies": The Anomalies Regulations of 1931, Their Background and Implications', *Public Administration*, 62 (1984), 423–37.
Turner, J. *Businessmen and Politics* (1984).
University of Warwick. Dept of Economics. *Out of Work: Perspectives of Mass Unemployment* (Warwick, 1984).
Von Tunzelmann, G. N. 'Structural Change and Leading Sectors in British Manufacturing, 1907–68', in *Economics in the Long View*, Vol. 3, ed. C. P.

Kindleberger and G. di Tella (1982), 1–49.

Webster, C. 'Health, Welfare and Unemployment During the Depression', *Past and Present*, 109 (1985), 204–30.

Whiteside, N., 'Welfare Insurance and Casual Labour: A Study of Administrative Intervention in Industrial Employment, 1906–26', *Economic History Review*, 2nd ser., 32 (1979), 507–22.

'Welfare Legislation and the Unions during the First World War', *Historical Journal*, 23 (1980), 857–74.

'Industrial Labour and Welfare Legislation after the First World War: A Reply', *Historical Journal*, 25 (1982), 443–46.

'Social Welfare and Industrial Relations, 1914–1939' in *A History of British Industrial Relations. Vol. 2. 1914–1939*, ed. C. Wrigley (1987), 211–42.

Whiting, R. C. 'The Labour Party, Capitalism and the National Debt, 1918–24', in *Politics and Social Change in Modern Britain*, ed. P. J. Waller (1987), 140–60.

Winch, D. *Economics and Policy. A Historical Study* (1969).

Worswick, D. and J. Trevithick. *Keynes and the Modern World* (Cambridge, 1973).

Wright, J. F. 'Britain's Inter-War Experience', in *The Money Supply and the Exchange Rate*, ed. W. A. Eltis and P. Sinclair (Oxford, 1981), 282–305.

'Real Wage Resistance: Eighty Years of the British Cost of Living', in *Economic Theory and Hicksian Themes*, ed. D. A. Collard, N. H. Dimsdale, C. L. Gilbert, D. R. Helm, M. Scott and A. K. Sen (Oxford, 1984), 152–67.

Index